Media & Minorities

THE SPECTRUM SERIES

Race and Ethnicity in National and Global Politics

Series Editors
Paula D. McClain
Duke University

Joseph Stewart Jr.
Clemson University

The sociopolitical dynamics of race and ethnicity are apparent everywhere. In the United States, racial politics underlie everything from representation to affirmative action to welfare policymaking. Early in the twenty-first century, Anglos in America will become only a plurality, as Latino and Asian American populations continue to grow. Issues of racial/ethnic conflict and cooperation are prominent across the globe. Diversity, identity, and cultural plurality are watchwords of empowerment as well as of injustice.

This new series offers textbook supplements, readers, and core texts addressing various aspects of race and ethnicity in politics, broadly defined. Meant to be useful in a wide range of courses in all kinds of academic programs, these books will be multidisciplinary as well as multiracial/ethnic in their appeal.

TITLES IN THE SERIES

Muted Voices: Latinos and the 2000 Election edited by Rodolfo O. de la Garza and Louis DeSipio

Latino Politics in America: Community, Culture, and Interests by John A. Garcia

The Navajo Political Experience, Revised Edition by David E. Wilkins

Asian American Politics: Law, Participation, and Policy edited by Don T. Nakanishi and James S. Lai

American Indian Politics and the American Political System by David E. Wilkins

Media & Minorities: The Politics of Race in News and Entertainment by Stephanie Greco Larson

Media & Minorities

*The Politics of Race in News
and Entertainment*

Stephanie Greco Larson

ROWMAN & LITTLEFIELD PUBLISHERS, INC.
Lanham • Boulder • New York • Toronto • Oxford

ROWMAN & LITTLEFIELD PUBLISHERS, INC.

Published in the United States of America
by Rowman & Littlefield Publishers, Inc.
A wholly owned subsidiary of The Rowman & Littlefield Publishing Group, Inc.
4501 Forbes Boulevard, Suite 200, Lanham, Maryland 20706
www.rowmanlittlefield.com

P.O. Box 317, Oxford OX2 9RU, UK

British Library Cataloguing in Publication Information Available

Library of Congress Cataloging-in-Publication Data

Larson, Stephanie Greco, 1960–
    Media & minorities : the politics of race in news and entertainment / Stephanie Greco Larson.
       p.   cm. — (Spectrum series, race and ethnicity in national and global politics)
    Includes bibliographical references and index.
    ISBN 0-8476-9452-6 (cloth : alk. paper)—ISBN 0-8476-9453-4 (pbk. : alk. paper)
    1. Minorities in motion pictures.   2. Minorities on television.   3. Minorities in mass media.   I. Title.   II. Series.
    PN1995.9.M56L37   2006
    302.23'089—dc22   2005003589

Printed in the United States of America

♾ ™ The paper used in this publication meets the minimum requirements of American National Standard for Information Sciences—Permanence of Paper for Printed Library Materials, ANSI/NISO Z39.48-1992.

For Diana Greco and the late Cora Brooks

Contents

Figures and Tables

Acknowledgments

When it comes to research, I'm claustrophobic. I'd rather be lost in a crowd or a vast empty space than confined to a small place, even if it is a familiar one. So, although I was trained as a quantitative political scientist who was expected to publish in the *American Political Science Review*, I've taken a different path. I study and teach media and politics—defining both broadly. This means I end up spending a lot of time outside of my discipline and on the front part of the learning curve. It's an exhilarating ride.

This book is my attempt to pull together research on race, politics, and media from across the academy. I have ventured into American studies, communications, cultural studies, history, journalism, media studies, political science, sociology, and all of the ethnic/racial studies areas. Although I respect all the theories, methods, and terminologies of these fields, I have found some more useful than others for introducing these topics to an undergraduate audience. The omissions and emphases here are likely to disappoint some readers, but my intention was not to oversimplify, misrepresent, or minimize the importance of any field or subfield or the contributions of its scholars.

In terms of race, I focus on the four major racial-minority groups in the United States—African Americans, Native Americans, Hispanics, and Asian Americans. When naming these groups, I have tried to retain the terminology of the authors whose work I am citing. I treat the terms "African American" and "black" and "Native American" and "Indian" as interchangeable. I apologize to any readers who do not and are offended by any of these terms. Similarly, my use of the word "minorities" is not meant to connote "lesser than." Throughout the book, I have tried hard to retain a multiracial focus and not to privilege a white/black dichotomy. However, the unequal amount of research on the four groups has compromised balance in the chapter sizes (particularly in part III).

In each chapter, I try to describe both mainstream and alternative media. By mainstream media, I primarily refer to national and local television news, newspapers, major newsmagazines, films, and commercial television entertainment. I have briefly referred to radio, documentaries, cable television, advertising, and the Internet. I have excluded music entirely. This does not reflect any judgment regarding the importance of these communications. I simply needed to limit the scope of the book to make the project more manageable and to work in the areas I best comprehend.

I do not know if I would have written this book if I worked anywhere but Dickinson College. The institution's commitment to crossing borders and interdisciplinarity helped me take the risk of stepping into academic worlds outside of political communications. The college put its money where its mouth was by providing me with support and time to find, wrestle with, and integrate the vast and rich literatures that were necessary to address this topic and its multiple audiences.

This support took many forms. The first was their providing a wonderful, encouraging, problem-solving administrative assistant, Vickie Kuhn. The second was the many faces of the Library and Information Technology. They provided me with excellent facilities, helpful personnel, and generous policies that allowed me to get my hands on books and journals both old and dusty and hot off the press. Third, opportunities were provided by the financial support of Dickinson College's Research and Development (R&D) Committee.

In May and June of 2000, the R&D Committee funded a Summer Study Group on Film Studies, which helped familiarize me with the techniques, language, and literature of film studies. Learning from Mara Donaldson, Beverly Eddy, David Kranz, and Nancy Mellerski gave me the confidence to tackle part I of this book. The R&D Committee also funded the sabbatical (fall 1997) during which I wrote the book proposal. It also gave me a one-course reassigned time one semester allowing me to get started. Dickinson also funded trips to conferences so that I could vet early versions of chapters 2, 5, 14, 16, 17, and 19. These included the Journalism Education Association (Sydney, Australia, November 2003), the Western Political Science Association (Denver, Colorado, March 2003), the Southern Political Science Association (Savannah, Georgia, November 2002), the Southwestern Political Science Association (New Orleans, Louisiana, March 2002), the Southwestern Political Science Association (Fort Worth, Texas, March 2001), and the Southwestern Political Science Association (Galveston, Texas, March 2000). Finally, my sabbatical during the 2003–2004 academic year allowed me finish the manuscript away from the usual distractions (and near some more appealing ones) in Brisbane, Australia, and Brevard County, Florida. Thanks to the help of Bill Tow, I was a visiting scholar at the School of Journalism and Communications at the beautiful University of Queensland.

I would like to thank the following friends for commenting on various chapters: Lydia Andrade, Mark Byrnes, Amy Farrell, David Hernandez, Pat Hurley, Vickie Kuhn, Steve Rockwell, and Leslie Winston. I am also indebted to the patient people at Rowman & Littlefield: Jen Kelland, Renee Legatt,

April Leo, and especially Jennifer Knerr. Once again, I have Joe Stewart to thank profusely for my survival as an author, a political scientist, an AP table leader, and a sober Bourbon Street casualty.

I want to express appreciation to friends who provided me with emotional support and help as I struggled to write this book and to overcome the health disasters that too often kept me from writing it. They are Cathy Anderson, Lydia Andrade, Marcelo Borges, Brian Demarco, Mara Donaldson, the Eisenhauers, Amy Farrell, Susan Feldman, Sam Fisher, Matthew Heddinger, Ann Hill, Bill Hudson, Patty Johnson, Jamie Juarez, Vickie Kuhn, Christopher Lemelin, Andrea Lieber, Nancy Maveety, Harry and Pat Pohlman, Doug Preston, John and Jane Ransom, David and Steve Rockwell, Gisela Roethke, Allen Rossman, Cindy Samet, Dan Schubert, Sharon Stockton, Julie Winterich, and Viki Zavales. David Srokose (my treasure) deserves a special thanks for his generous and cheerful help at the end of this project, allowing me to enjoy a birth week in the face of a pressing deadline. Finally, I dedicate the book to my inspiring mother, Diana Greco, and her mother, Cora Brooks.

Some of my earliest fond memories include playing school with my grandmother when I was too young to join my older sister, Connie, in the first grade. After Grandma Brooks got her cup of coffee and "her eyes opened," she would ring a bell, indicating it was time to get started on our "reading, writing, and 'rithmetic." I do not remember any arithmetic. I do recall learning how to sound out words and put them in interesting patterns, using mysterious punctuation marks. It was an exciting challenge. It continues to be.

1

"Reality" Television: American
Myths and Racial Ideology

~~~~~~

"No cultural representation can offer access to the 'truth' about what is being represented, but what such representations do provide is an indication about how power relations are organized in a society, at certain historical moments."[1]

"YOU'RE FIRED!" BECAME THE CATCHPHRASE IN THE SPRING OF 2004 AS THE first season of *The Apprentice* captured public and media attention. The four-time Emmy-nominated NBC reality show brought sixteen ambitious business people together to compete for a position in Donald Trump's empire. Each week the participants were divided into two teams and given a sales, advertising, or negotiating task. At the end of each show, Trump eliminated one member from the less successful team.

NBC Universal's coordinated promotion contributed to the program's success and created a buzz that extended to other networks, print media, and the metaphorical watercooler.[2] The show received a popular time slot and aggressive advertising, and episodes aired more than once a week (on both NBC and CNBC). After being fired, contestants appeared on talk shows and soft news shows (like *Today* and *Larry King Live*). An entire *Dateline NBC* episode looked "Behind the Apprentice." The two-hour grand finale included a live reunion of the losing contestants and Trump's selection of the winner.

The advertising and network promotions may explain why viewers knew about the show and tuned into it initially but not why they kept watching. For it to become such a cultural phenomenon, *The Apprentice* had to appeal to large numbers of people. As with other popular reality television shows, audiences were invited to enjoy the blend of routine and drama, of unpredictability and familiarity, as well as the battle between appealing and annoying personalities. Viewers watched attractive young people compete, cooperate, emote, and reveal to the viewers their analysis of the game (and each other) as it unfolded. The casting made it easy to root for some competitors and against others. The editing made the weeks of work and cohabitation dramatic and thematic. The individual alliances and adversaries, the romantic possibilities, and the initial girls-versus-boys organization of teams became the show's story lines and guided media discussion. The talk centered on personalities and gender: Did Amy and Nick get together? Why did the women's team beat the men's so consistently? Did the women use their sexuality unfairly? Why did the women self-destruct on the mixed gender teams?

This attention to what the show might have told us about gender (particularly gender and the workplace) distracted us from what it said about race. Like most television programs and movies, *The Apprentice* was not explicitly about race. Yet, like other media, it contained (and reinforced) racial messages that are part of the dominant American ideology. Media (entertainment, news, and their hybrids) represent reality in a way that promotes certain meanings and interpretations of how the world works and why. These representations are selected and constructed in ways that consistently promote the status quo—the current beliefs, structures, and inequalities. This includes the racial hierarchy.

MEDIA DISCOURSE AND THE RACIAL STATUS QUO

The racial status quo is one of inequality with whites at the top of the hierarchy. Racial minorities are underrepresented in government, education, and corporations; they are overrepresented among the poor and in prison populations. The nation has a long history of legal and extralegal racial oppression; yet, this is inconsistent with American values of equality and fairness. Most Americans abhor the idea that political, social, and economic structures might be racist.[3] This is not the story they want to hear; it is not the one white people believe. So, mainstream media (the major television networks, newspapers, magazines, and motion pictures) do not tell it. Nevertheless, the stories told by the mass media help justify a system in which some groups (such as racial minorities) are subordinate to others by using narratives that reconcile the fact of racial inequality with belief in justice and equality. Ideologies that guide these stories make the status quo seem natural, inevitable, and right.[4] These discourses provide explanations for why things are the way they are. They deny the extent and the systemic causes of racial inequality.

American values and familiar narratives such as the "American Dream" make up one of the dominant discourses. This narrative holds that America is a "land of opportunity" where the circumstances of birth do not determine people's status in life, so anyone who works hard enough can go from "rags to riches."[5] Rather than being threatened by the existence of racial inequality, this narrative (which is so central to American identity) is used to understand racial inequality.[6] It focuses attention on the faults of individuals rather than the problems shared by groups and determined by social, economic, and political structures. The individualist perspective prevents people from seeing themselves as members of collective groups with different opportunities and access to power.[7]

The "assimilation narrative" says that once legal impediments to equality were lifted, racial minorities could "pull themselves up by their bootstraps" like other immigrants had.[8] Failure to do so was interpreted as the result of individuals' own inadequacies or attitudes. This simplistic explanation for failure reassures those who have succeeded and want to believe in the justness of the system. The media provide examples of racial-minority success stories in entertainment and news to show that minorities can enjoy the American Dream. If individuals from a minority group are shown overcoming adversity, the audience assumes that they all can, that is, as long as they are the "right kind" of individuals.[9]

Attention to the "wrong kind" of racial minorities also serves to justify the status quo. Due to continued racial segregation, the media are the primary forum through which whites come to "know" nonwhites; therefore, individual minorities in the media come to symbolize these groups for white audiences. Stereotypes use negative attributes of members of racial-minority groups to stigmatize the entire group.[10] These negative stereotypes help legitimate racism and the racial status quo by exacerbating white anxieties and fears.[11] In these ways, the popular media deny that racism exists and provide other explanations for the economic, criminal, and cultural problems racism creates.[12]

This book illustrates the different ways in which the media help maintain the racial status quo, including ignoring racial minorities and their problems, stereotyping racial minorities, and explaining and justifying racial inequality in a way that forestalls major reforms. *The Apprentice* demonstrates many of these.

IDEOLOGY ON *THE APPRENTICE*

The Apprentice is a good example of how entertainment media convey the dominant ideology about race. Four of the sixteen competitors were racial minorities. Omarosa and Kwame were clearly identifiable as African Americans. Neither the show nor the official website made clear that Katrina was a Cuban American.[13] Tammy's biography identified her as an Asian American from Seattle, but the show made no on-air references to this; nor was attention paid to her ethnicity in other ways. Although we can interpret Tammy's dismissal for disloyalty (when other women had been fired for being "too loyal") as reinforcing racial stereotypes of Asian Americans, the coverage of these two characters says more about invisibility and the denial of racial diversity than it does about stereotyping. Any influence race might have had on them or their experiences during the competition was overshadowed by their characterization as oversexualized and catty females.

Omarosa became the focus of most of the overt racial discussions. She talked about herself, her firing, and how the other contestants treated her in racial terms during and after the show. The most extended dialog about race and the show occurred in response to Omarosa's claim that Ereka used the "N word." This accusation was widely covered on the news, as was Trump's statement that a thorough review of the tapes found no evidence of this. Ereka denied the allegation and took a lie detector test on the *Howard Stern* radio show to prove it. This controversy helped solidify Omarosa's role as the antagonist on the show. Presented as embodying the "bad black" stereotype, she became the character the audience was invited to dislike (and most of them seemed to accept the invitation).

Consistent with this stereotype, Omarosa appeared to be a combative, lazy, self-pitying complainer who did not work well with others. Trump fired her because he thought she made too many excuses, was rude and abrasive, and had a chip on her shoulder. Yet, she remained on the show longer than her talents seen on screen seemed to justify. This served to extend the drama on the show, but it also invited criticism that she was getting "special treatment" because of her race.

Not only did these racial stereotypes seem to influence the casting of Omarosa and the way the show was edited and advertised, but their embodiment in a reality-show character helped to reinforce them. The "real" Omarosa can be seen as "evidence" of why racial inequality persists in America. This evidence is reassuring to white audiences because it says the problem is with "them" (blacks), not with "us" (whites) or the sociopolitical system.

Kwame fit the "good black" stereotype, which also supports the status quo. Soft-spoken, dignified, nonthreatening, and cooperative, he was shown as fitting comfortably in the "white world" with a Harvard MBA, his inability to communicate with hip-hop producer Russell Simmons (on episode 6), and his deferential approach to Trump and the white players.

By focusing a lot of attention on Kwame's friendship with Troy (the only competitor with a drawl), the show fit him into the "white man's sidekick" stereotype. Their relationship illustrated that "race doesn't really matter" because on a personal level, "we can all get along." It also reinforced the racial hierarchy of whites as leaders and blacks as followers. Although Troy got fired before Kwame did, he was still shown as the leader of the pair. It was Troy's idea in episode 4 that Kwame sign basketballs to increase merchandise sales at Planet Hollywood (a strategy that used racial stereotypes to deceive consumers). Kwame eagerly went along with this and other suggestions from the guy he called his "main man." Even on tasks when Kwame was officially the leader, Troy seemed to call the shots. In episode 12, Trump's decision came down to Troy and Kwame after Troy decided to go head-to-head with Kwame instead of Bill. In the boardroom, Troy said that Kwame was a "steady Eddie" but had never shone. Trump agreed that in three opportunities as project leader, Kwame never exhibited leadership. Yet, Trump fired Troy instead of Kwame, thereby inviting viewers to use a "reverse discrimination" explanation for the black man's success.

The fact that the competition came down to two men, one black and one white, conveyed another system-supportive message (messages that justify the status quo—its institutions, processes, and inequalities). It said that *The Apprentice* and all it represented (big business, competition, capitalism, American values) was fair and provided equal opportunity regardless of race. In fact, it did this explicitly when Kwame looked into the camera and said, "My grandfather signed his name with an 'X.' If this isn't the American dream, what is?"[14] The show makes this comforting and attractive idea more real. Kwame's example serves to refute the fact that there are a multitude of others for whom the dream does not come true. These people do not seem real: they are nameless and faceless; Kwame is not. Of course, viewers need only look at Omarosa to understand why some minorities fail to realize the American Dream.

Because of the all-or-nothing nature of the competition, Kwame's second-place finish put him in the same position as the fourteen other people who lost.[15] What did his loss to Bill in the final episode say about race? The simple answer might be that a "good black" is inferior to a "good white." But that sounds like old-fashioned racism and out of step with what a modern American audience wants to believe. A more convincing explanation needs to concern something within Kwame's control.

In episode 13, Kwame and Bill chose teams from the final six contestants, which they would lead in the final competition. Omarosa was not the last one selected; Kwame picked her before he selected Heidi (the Jewish New Yorker Omarosa said lacked class).[16] The final episode showed Omarosa bringing the same deficiencies shown earlier to this last task. She did not do her job, she blamed someone else for her mistakes, she was rude to an employee, she was late and irresponsible, and she lied to Kwame. Trump chastised Kwame for selecting Omarosa and for failing to fire her when she screwed up (something that Trump had failed to do in more than one boardroom). These decisions became the justification for Trump's choice of Bill as his apprentice.

Ultimately, the qualities that made Kwame the "good black" and helped him stay in the game for so long ended up getting him fired. He was deferential when he needed to be a leader. He was calm and cool when he should have gotten angry. He stuck with the rules of the game when he should have thought outside of the box and fired Omarosa (an option he was unaware he had). His kindness was weakness. His loyalty was a character flaw. The lesson that the white audience got was that "good blacks" are brought down and held back by "bad blacks" because "they" stick together in a world that "we" know is color-blind. The implication is that "they" are at fault for any remaining racial inequality, not "us" or the system.

The Apprentice in its first season looked like the rest of America's mainstream popular culture. It presented race in America as white and black, overlooking the greater range of racial diversity. It created characters that fit dominant racial stereotypes through its contestant selection and video editing. In a variety of ways, it used dominant ideologies to defend and justify the race/sex/class status quo. It did this without most viewers even noticing because the ideologies are so familiar that they seem like common sense. The media help create this common sense through the continued use of racial discourses.

STRUCTURE OF THE BOOK

This book examines the American media's racial discourses and shows how the dominant ones help maintain inequality. It analyzes the ideological content of the mainstream media that generally reinforces the racial status quo in which blacks, Native Americans, Hispanics, and Asian Americans are subordinate to whites.

Most of the information in this book is drawn from the scholarly literature on race, media, and politics from a variety of academic disciplines and approaches.[17] Some of the studies used are empirical (using data to test hypotheses); others are theoretical. The methodologies used to describe the media messages include both quantitative and qualitative approaches. Part IV includes original research that analyzes newspaper coverage.

Throughout, the book examines alternative media that challenge the mainstream media and its racial discourse. Mainstream media differ from alternative media in their intended audience, resources, goals, and content. Produced by industries that sell their products to mass audiences for direct payments or advertising, the mainstream media present shows, films, and papers that are intended to make a large profit. To do this, they must cater to mass audiences. Therefore, their content promotes mainstream ideas. Because they operate and thrive within a capitalist economic framework, it is in their self-interest to maintain the system and promote the status quo by presenting a "reality supportive of existing social and economic class power."[18]

Alternative media appeal to narrower audiences and have goals that supercede profits. Alternative media include independent films, minority newspapers, and websites offering oppositional messages that challenge the dominant discourse. They provide comfort to their audiences, as well as information and alternative interpretations. Alternative news media aim to encourage debate, to monitor the mainstream press, and to increase the visibility of certain groups.[19] These media not only represent ideas found in groups excluded from mainstream, but they provide a place where ideas are developed, communities are built, and people are empowered.[20] These media "offer a place for counteracting the effects of hegemony, by constructing alternative narratives which contain different heroes and different plots."[21]

The term "parallel spheres" is used to indicate the places where groups without access to the mainstream press create alternative communication networks.[22] Alternative media and the debates they foster in parallel spheres respond to what is going on in the mainstream press, providing counterpoints and criticisms. Sometimes ideas and rhetoric in the alternative media find their way into the mainstream.[23] While this is relatively rare and sometimes co-optive rather than influential, it shows a potential for diversifying mainstream news.[24]

The book is organized into four parts that move from subjects not generally understood to be political to those that are. I argue that all of these media representations are political. Part I (chapters 2–6) addresses entertainment; part II (chapters 7–11) discusses news about the general minority public; part III (chapters 12–14) examines coverage of racial rights movements; and part IV (chapters 15–19) looks at coverage of nonwhite candidates and politicians. Chapter 20 concludes by pointing to similarities between groups and media and addressing some remaining questions.

This book deals with entertainment first, even though entertainment is not typically thought of as political. Yet, as *The Apprentice* example illustrates, entertainment does serious ideological work by avoiding or hiding social issues and problems.[25] Movies and television programs have consequences for how viewers understand real life, even when they know that the stories are made up. By excluding minorities, the entertainment media fail to tell stories that draw attention and emotion (like empathy or anger) to problems with the racial status quo. By including minorities but treating them as undifferentiated members of a unified group (such as Americans or women), the entertainment media deny both racial discrimination and diversity. By using racial stereotypes, films and television categorize people of color according to assumptions held by white people. These categories provide explanations for why "those people" are "like that."[26] While all groups have stereotypes, those of less powerful groups are stronger and more numerous and have a greater impact on how others perceive people in the group.[27] By focusing on individuals rather than social groups, entertainment media remind viewers that problems are because of "bad" individuals, not flawed social structures.[28]

Part I explores these issue by looking at racial minorities and entertainment television and movies. Chapter 2 begins with an explanation of how entertainment is political and can disempower and subjugate minorities. The efforts of minorities to fight these images and create alternative ones are discussed as forms of political action. The next four chapters look separately at films and television entertainment that include blacks (chapter 3), Native Americans (chapter 4), Hispanics (chapter 5), and Asian Americans (chapter 6). Each of these chapters is organized into sections on exclusion, selective exclusion, stereotypes, system-supportive messages, challenges to main-stream media representations, and alternative media.

Dominant values are not just embedded in entertainment; they are also found in journalism. People think of news as "true" and as "how things are," rather than as a collection of stories put together to promote certain ideas. Yet, the news has narrative structures that include "characters" who are drawn in ways that rely on popular understandings and misunderstandings.[29] Even though the news is "factual," it is presented as a morality tale. Political communications scholars Dan Nimmo and James Coombs call television news "real-fiction" because the segments contain narrative structures and characters and promote certain lessons.[30] These legitimize existing institutions and power relations and promote nationalism, capitalism, minimal government, and individualism.[31] Even when news reports something that has gone wrong, it still does so in a way that promotes the status quo by blaming individuals for the problems, by characterizing these problems as exceptions that have been detected and solved, and by concluding that major social changes are unnecessary, too risky, or impossible to accomplish.[32]

Part II looks at news coverage of the four groups when they are not acting as political activists or governmental actors. It describes how the day-to-day, as well as the crisis, coverage of racial-minority masses selectively excludes them, stereotypes them, and restricts their place in society through its themes and emphasis. Once again, resistance to this coverage and efforts to create alternative news through black and ethnic presses are examined. Chapter 7 introduces research on news coverage of minorities and discusses the consequences and causes of this coverage. It also includes an explanation for why increasing the number of minority reporters has not solved the problems. Chapter 8 looks specifically at news about blacks. Chapter 9 does the same for Native Americans, chapter 10 for Hispanics, and chapter 11 for Asian Americans.

Not only can the racial status quo be criticized in alternative media, but it can be challenged on the streets. When racial-minority groups and their allies organize in social movements to protest the status quo, they try to use the mainstream media to accomplish their goals. They offer alternative discourses that challenge the status quo and use or redefine values to promote policy change.[33] The press does not typically carry these messages in the form that the protest movements desire. Yet, adjustments to the dominant ideology sometimes result during periods of social upheaval when the media contain "mixed messages" (some progressive and some regressive).[34] These complex and contradictory narratives in popular culture can provide hope to audiences.[35]

Nevertheless, it is important to realize that cultural values are more static than changing and that the media are more often obstacles to than facilitators of fundamental change. Typically, the news media neutralize criticisms of the dominant ideology by incorporating some of them, overwhelming them with system-supportive messages, and demeaning or refuting challenges. When the dominant ideology shifts, it tends to do so incrementally as elites adjust to challenges from below and within their ranks. Thus, favorable coverage of social movements seems to follow a breakdown in the elite consensus rather than to create it.

Part III looks at media coverage of racial social movements that challenged the racial hierarchy in the 1950s to the 1970s. Chapter 12 reviews literature on media and social movements generally to explain why and how the media usually work against social movements. Chapter 13 looks at coverage of the civil rights movement (and its aftermath) and challenges the conventional wisdom that the media was consistently its champion. Chapter 14 examines how the media covered the three other racial-minority groups' movements.

Ultimately, it is the politicians who change policy. They use the media to get elected and promote their agendas. Therefore, it is important to look at coverage of candidates and politicians of color when considering media, race, and politics. Part IV discusses the most explicit political news coverage of racial minorities. Chapter 15 reviews the literature on how the media cover candidates and politicians generally. Chapter 16 looks at studies that access how various black candidates and politicians have been covered over time. The rest of part IV relies on case studies of newspaper coverage. Chapter 17 analyzes coverage of two Native American candidates and their white competitors, as well as one year's worth of news about Native American state legislators. Chapter 18 looks at coverage of Mexican American, Puerto Rican, and Cuban American candidates and politicians. Chapter 19 does the same for a Chinese American, a Korean American, and a Japanese American. These chapters illustrate that exclusion and stereotyping become less prevalent when the media cover political insiders of color than when they cover the public and social movements. This finding might do more to illustrate than to refute the system-supportive nature of the mainstream media. After all, like Kwame, major party candidates and politicians tend to play by the rules rather than to challenge the system fundamentally.

I

Racial Minorities in Films and Television Entertainment

Broken Arrow appears courtesy of The Kpobal Collection/20th Century Fox.

2

Racial Politics in Fictional Media:
Films and Television

∧∧∧∧∧∧∧∧∧∧∧∧∧∧∧∧∧∧∧∧∧∧∧∧∧∧∧∧∧∧∧∧∧∧∧∧∧

AMERICANS SPEND MORE TIME USING MEDIA FOR ENTERTAINMENT THAN FOR news. Yet, entertainment is also a source of knowledge about the world. Therefore, its content is an important influence on how people think about race. Even when entertainment messages do not have explicit or intentional political agendas, they show power relationships. Entertainment media permeate, reproduce, and influence culture and should not be ignored as apolitical or irrelevant. The politics of race in films is not confined to those about politicians and government.[1]

Part II describes the images of racial minorities and themes in film and television entertainment that usually reinforce the racial status quo. It also describes the efforts of interest groups, activists, and people inside of the entertainment industry to challenge and change these representations. You will see how mainstream entertainment media can be a tool for racial oppression and how alternative entertainment can be used as a weapon against it.

The chapters in this part of the book organize coverage of each racial group into five sections, which this chapter introduces. The first section, exclusion and selective exclusion, discusses the prevalence of racial-minority characters and where they appear. One place might be in a certain genre (such as Westerns or comedies). Another place is in supporting roles. The second section deals with stereotyping and looks at the reoccurring roles that racial minorities have played that confine viewers' sense of the "natural" characteristics of that race. As you will see, many of these stereotypes show racial minorities as inferior and dangerous to whites. The third part looks at dominant themes and messages in films and television programs that support the status quo. Of particular interest are the story resolutions because they tell the audience how ultimately to judge characters' actions. Typically, minority characters who behave in ways that support the racial hierarchy are rewarded. Those who challenge their "place" are punished. The fourth section provides examples of how the racial-minority groups have tried to stop representations they find offensive. The fifth section looks at how racial minorities have created their own representations in independent films, which can raise political consciousness and stimulate activism.

THE POLITICS OF REPRESENTATION

The media are the primary sources of information about the world outside of our immediate surroundings. It helps make sense of the things we do not experience and the people we do not know.[2] Entertainment media, as well as news, teach us about society by repeatedly showing us certain types of people in certain types of roles. These patterns encourage us to see others and ourselves in certain ways. We learn who and what to value and who and what to dismiss. This seeing influences how we treat each other. Scholars refer to this as the "politics of representation."[3]

The media do not create these representations out of thin air; they are a part of a cultural discourse that reinforces a racial hierarchy found in society. This hierarchy privileges whites. A discourse is the "collective discussion or interplay of meanings and ideas circulating around a particular subject."[4] Dominant discourses reflect the values of the culture in which they are produced. These discourses are repetitive; in other words, they tell the same stories again and again. The values held by the majority in a culture are the "dominant values" and are those most often embedded in media messages. The way the majority gets its values is complex. The media are only part of the answer, and they tend to reinforce values more than they change them. The values television and film reinforce are those that promote some people's interests and obstruct other people's. Since members of the dominant groups own the media, their self-interest lies in telling stories that justify and reinforce the status quo rather than in critiquing it.

This argument—that entertainment promotes a particular point of view that reinforces the status quo—does not assume that these messages are necessarily *self-consciously* embedded in stories. Ideas about how society works and should work (our ideology) tend to exist on an unconscious level. The politics of representation does not result from a conspiracy between producers/writers and politicians. There is no meeting in which these people plan how they are going to tell system-supportive stories in films in order to safeguard their power and wealth. Although Hollywood and Washington worked together to produce war propaganda and although congressional hearings during the Red Scare of the 1950s resulted in self-censorship and blacklisting, most movies are produced without government involvement.[5] Instead, the producers and writers are telling stories that make sense to them from the position they occupy in society and that they assume will appeal to people who have the money to invest in the production and consumption of films.[6]

Both of these factors push films that promote the values and interests of mid-
dle- to upper-class white men.[7] The desire to maximize profits prevents the
production of films with alternative points of view or those with mostly minority actors.[8]

> Films implement ways of looking at class, gender, and race differences. Film-
> makers can make us see these differences, but they can also hide them from our
> sight by creating pleasing fictions. This way of seeing carries the individual and
> social biases of the filmmakers but also the biases and standpoints of the culture
> of people for which the films are produced, the culture to which the films belong.[9]

Entertainment does not just tell stories; it tells particular stories in a way
that privileges some people and points of view over others. This privileging
can be seen in a variety of ways, for instance, by creating a hierarchy of characters in stories, making some more important than others. The important
ones get to speak and make things happen, and the viewer sees the action
from their points of view.[10] Traditional storytelling includes conflicts that
contrast "good" and "bad." These conflicts get resolved in ways that promote
"social peace" and acceptance of the world more or less as it is, rather than
changing it.[11] Stories normalize behavior by habitually showing certain ways
that people relate to each other. When racial-minority groups' actions and
relations to others are shown on film, they are presented or seen not as political acts and decisions but as something "natural." Producer and viewers of
these images might not even see this because their roles and the stories told
in films seem so common or "normal."

HOW ENTERTAINMENT REINFORCES SUBORDINATION

By excluding racial minorities or presenting them in stereotypical and limited
ways, the dominant culture subordinates and justifies this subordination of
racial-minority groups.[12] Negative images of racial minorities become part
of the collective consciousness that indicts racial-minority groups as being
"responsible for their own conditions."[13] The particular negative images used
in television and films were not created there; they are historically constituted. In other words, they come from a long legacy of social inequality and
oppression, and their retelling strengthens these beliefs in white supremacy.[14]
Essentially, "Media excluding, dehumanization, and discrimination are part
of the cultural domination inherent in unequal power relations, and a key
feature of the historical process by which people of color have been and continue to be subordinated."[15]

Exclusion and Selective Exclusion

Television and films without racial diversity promote an inaccurate picture
of American society. They deprive minority viewers of role models and ignore

the contributions of people of color. They also marginalize racial minorities through their omission. "Marginalized" literally means to be "pushed to the margin." In this context, we can think of it as telling whites, "these people are not important," or telling people who are not white, "you are not important." Exclusion also masks social problems. It says that the problems of people of color are theirs alone and not worthy of widespread attention. This masks significant issues of social inequality relevant to all members of a society.

Through "selective exclusion" racial minorities are included in film in a way that constrains or misrepresents them. One type of selective exclusion is the ignoring of national and ethnic variations within a race, for instance, by using one group to represent all the others (having Japanese American actors and characters represent all Asian Americans) or by homogenizing subgroups into a "generic" Indian, Hispanic, or Asian American.[16] Chinese Americans might be treated as no different from Korean Americans, or the customs and attributes of different Indian tribes might be combined. Omitting differences is not only inaccurate, since the cultures, languages, histories, and dominant physical attributes among these group vary, but it conveys the impression that the only "important" thing about minorities is the fact that they are racially "marked"; in other words, that they lack "whiteness."[17]

Selective exclusion can also occur when people of color are included in films and television without any of their cultural distinctiveness. This is like coloring in a *Charlie's Angels* coloring book using a brown crayon and saying that you now have a representation of black people. The failure to present people of color as culturally unique human beings is a form of exclusion.[18] For the representation to be realistic, it needs to consider the "historical and material situation of that minority and its very real differences from the dominant society."[19]

Stereotypes

Stereotyping is another means of subordinating racial minorities in the dominant discourse. Racial stereotypes in films and on television are often drawn from literature. They are limiting because they suggest that certain characteristics are "natural" in certain groups and universal (found in all members of that group). Usually, these characteristics are unappealing, but even the more "sympathetic" qualities suggest inferiority to whites.[20] Negative stereotypes serve the status quo because if a group is inherently inferior to whites then it is "nobody's fault" that the individuals comprising it are in subordinate positions (maids, cooks, janitors).

Racial stereotypes serve to justify white control and authority.[21] Without whites' having to claim superiority explicitly, stereotypes work subtly to maintain domination and disenfranchise minorities.[22] It is easy to conclude that people who are "inherently inferior" will end up in a subordinate position in a fair society. It follows then to think that if the fault is in individuals and not the social structures, then there is no need to reform the system. This is how racial stereotypes are system supportive, regardless of their specific content.

Stereotypes in entertainment have political consequences and should not be dismissed as "just fiction." Asian American studies professor Darrell Y. Hamamoto considers the term "stereotype" inadequate for conveying the symbolic power and control that these images provide for the dominant society. He, like other scholars, prefers to call them "controlling images."[23] He reminds us that media distortions become part of how people think about racial inequality and serve to justify status inequalities. This is particularly true of film images of racial minorities because "any negative behavior by any member of the oppressed community is instantly generalized as typical, as pointing to a perpetual backsliding toward some presumed negative essence. Representations thus become allegorical."

In addition to speaking to the dominant culture, these images are seen by members of racial-minority groups. Just as stereotypes reinforce beliefs about their own superiority for whites, they can lead nonwhites to view themselves as inferior.[24] Negative images of minorities can undermine self-esteem and a sense of ethnic pride.[25] "Internalized oppression" is the term used to describe people's belief in negative stereotypes about themselves.[26] People who have internalized oppression accept the blame for their disadvantaged social position and are unlikely to fight the system. Speaking as a female member of one such group, Jessica Hagedorn says that "we have learned to settle for less—to accept the fact that we are either decorative, invisible, or one dimensional."[27]

System-Supportive Themes

Although movie themes might not be deliberately or consciously constructed to serve dominant groups, they usually do. Television entertainment and films tell stories that promote certain values and ideas in ways that are not obvious to viewers caught up in the unfolding stories and involving audiovisual experience.

Genres and narratives promote certain narratives.[28] Entertainment genres (such as Westerns, horror movies) are predictable to audiences because they share familiar elements or conventions. These conventions "place the audience on a predetermined path, even if they themselves feel they have freely chosen a route through the text."[29] These paths reinforce the dominant ideology, showing certain values and characters as superior to others. For example, romantic comedies promote heterosexual coupling. Content is regulated in genres and precludes a political challenge to the dominant ideology.

Narratives make sense of experiences by putting events into a sequence that tells a story about what happens and why. They identify certain people, behaviors, and values as wrong and right, as important and unimportant, and provide a moral. Films work out problems by focusing on individual characters who overcome obstacles. They invite audiences to relate to and share the point of view of certain characters. Who those characters are, what they do and say, and what happens to them in the story all convey the dominant ideology of the film.[30]

Formula films dominate Hollywood, and formulas do not typically mix well with explicitly political themes.[31] Hollywood films are not in the business of advocating social change.[32] Instead, they make us laugh, cry, or scream based on the exploits of individuals in specific situations. Nevertheless, they celebrate whiteness and deny and obscure white privilege and the systems that maintain it by promoting "sincere fictions," such as the idea that whites are natural and noble leaders and that minorities loyally want to follow, serve, and love them.[33]

Explicitly political films either celebrate historical moments, leaders, or institutions or show us how much better off we are now than in the "bad old days." Whether the hero in a film is a real government leader (Abraham Lincoln in *Abe Lincoln in Illinois*, 1940; Colonel Robert Gould Shaw in *Glory*, 1990; John Quincy Adams in *Amistad*, 1997) or a fictional common man pushed into leadership (*One Flew Over the Cuckoo's Nest*, 1975; *Stargate*, 1994; or *The Matrix*, 1999), he is a white man. "The messianic white self is the redeemer of the weak, the great leader who saves blacks from slavery or oppression, rescues people of color from poverty and disease, or leads Indians in battle for their dignity and survival."[34]

System-supportive messages that celebrate American values also have implications for racial attitudes. Hollywood makes and distributes films domestically and abroad. These films promote America ideals and myths. These include ideas like "justice for all," "all men are created equal," the "land of opportunity," "home of the free and the brave," and the "melting pot." The contradictions between these myths and reality, especially for racial minorities, are ignored or reconciled in the stories we tell ourselves. For instance, they are reconciled by using the "ideology of individualism," which places the blame for failure and the credit for success with individuals rather than society.

Media routinely support the dominant ideology without government incentive. Nevertheless, such incentives are sometimes provided. From 1932 to 1968, the Production Code Administration (PCA), or Hays Office, gave the government a mechanism to influence the content of movies in order to promote certain values. The PCA approval process influenced how widely a film could be distributed. National interests and the dominant cultural values of the time were inherent in the guidelines and decision making. "Its role was not simply to control matters of decency. More and more it played a political role."[35]

For years, the PCA's antimiscegenation rule promoted a racist ideology by making sure that films did not show interracial couples. For blacks and whites, the rule was strictly enforced; it was applied inconsistently to white–Latina/Latino relationships.³⁶ The PCA also limited the distribution of more progressive shows about Mexican Americans (*Salt of the Earth*, 1954, and *The Lawless*, 1950).³⁷ *The Lawless* suggested that social problems were due to racism and were widespread. As a result, white censors claimed that the film was a communist threat and censored it.³⁸

FIGHTING BACK: HOW ENTERTAINMENT CHALLENGES SUBORDINATION

Entertainment can challenge subordination of racial minorities in two ways. First, negative images and messages in entertainment can politicize minorities and galvanize them to protest their representation. Second, more realistic and positive representations can challenge notions of inferiority and systems of inequality.

Protesting Entertainment Media Messages

Negative images can act as catalysts for political organization and activism. The prevalent stereotypes and restrictive themes can motivate racial minorities to form and join groups that fight these images. They try to educate and galvanize the public into pressuring media companies to change. The goal is to increase minority employment in the entertainment industries, to provide more realistic roles to minority actors, and to alter the stories that are told so that they confront, rather than ignore or justify, white privilege.

By protesting at the studios or movie theaters, leading boycotts of films, and releasing critical reports, racial-minority groups draw attention to offensive content. They can be effective by having the content or casting of films or television shows altered, or they can have films that are not changed get limited or no distribution. If the films are released, these groups can promote negative news coverage to discourage viewers from watching them.

Even if shows or films are released and watched, protests can help members of the racial minority groups. It can sensitize viewers to the dangerous messages in the films and help them resist incorporating these messages into their own thinking. Protesting media representations also contributes "to the ongoing goal of community empowerment and the development of a collective political consciousness, organizational capacity, and an effective, accountable leadership."³⁹

Creating Alternative Images and Messages

We can also fight negative images and messages in entertainment by providing alternatives. In the hands of members of the racial-minority group, films can challenge the status quo and empower minority writers, producers, actors, and viewers. These efforts begin outside of Hollywood and the television industry in independent films and production houses that provide a place to create messages different in style and content from the those of the dominant discourse. Although the lower budgets result in smaller distribution of these films, they also provide more freedom to address new themes, offer alternative points of view, and experiment stylistically.[40]

It might seem that when independent films draw mainstream audiences, they can inspire more progressive messages in Hollywood films trying to appeal to these audiences. However, these adjustments are likely to be incremental and not really radical.[41] When outsider communications are co-opted by the mainstream, their messages tend to be neutralized and domesticated. This is one way in which the dominant ideology is maintained.[42] The dominant culture can appropriate the contributions of racial minorities without fully understanding or respecting them.[43]

CONCLUSION

The next five chapters will illustrate many similarities in the ways that four different racial-minority groups have been excluded and stereotyped in entertainment media providing system-supportive messages. Each group has also tried to create better representations and block destructive ones.

Hispanics, blacks, Native Americans, and Asian Americans have all been excluded or selectively excluded in film and television. White actors have played characters of each of these races. The intraracial distinctions within all four racial groups have been erased in their generic treatment. Each group has been segregated into certain, distinct types of films and television shows. For example, historically, Asians rarely performed in musical variety shows, whereas blacks were common there. Blacks have infrequently appeared in Westerns, a genre that segregated both Hispanics and Native Americans.

All four groups are shown as "naturally" inferior to whites through stereotypes that ridicule, subordinate, and demonize them. The Latino buffoon, the frivolous Latina, the black coon, the Asian American nerd, and the drunken, foolish Indian were created to be laughed at. Characters like black Toms, mammies, and Uncle Remeses, Asian American houseboys and China dolls, and Native American Tontos reassure whites that racial minorities are there to serve and defer to them. Each group has demonizing stereotypes that show them as a threat to whites who are characterized as justified in fighting (or even exterminating) them. These include Hispanic banditos and gang members; savage Indian warriors; dragon ladies and Asian evil geniuses; and black bucks, pimps, and whores.

Similar system-supportive themes resonate in the movies and television shows that include different racial minorities. These themes maintain myths about American values and history. They deny racism by confining it to history rather than looking at its contemporary manifestations. Films show Japanese American internment and Native American genocide as "past mistakes" that need to be understood in the context of the times. Entertainment celebrates the American Dream, arguing that it is color-blind, that failure to achieve is the fault of certain individuals. It shows that success simply requires that Asian Americans stop being foreigners, that blacks "act white," and that Hispanics go back to the barrio. As for Indians, the "good" ones can share in the dream by serving whites; since the "bad" ones got in the way, they could be eradicated.

System-supportive themes show that to the extent that there is racial inequality, it is because of minorities. Racial problems are blamed on flawed Hispanic families, domineering black matriarchs, sexually out-of-control black men, Asian Americans who have mysterious "foreign" ways, and Indians who prefer nature, the reservation, and the bottle to pulling themselves up by their boot straps. The blame for problems that are not the minorities' own fault, say films and television shows, rests with a few "crazy white people" who can be stopped by "good whites" (great white fathers, buddies, and saviors) who carry the burden well of protecting and "civilizing" racial minorities.

3

African Americans in Film and Television Entertainment

〜〜〜〜〜〜〜〜〜〜〜〜〜〜〜〜〜〜〜〜〜〜〜〜〜〜〜〜〜〜

DESPITE SOCIAL CHANGES OVER THE PAST FEW DECADES, MEDIA IMAGES HAVE continued to represent blacks as inferior to whites. This is done in a variety of ways on television and in films. While African Americans were once excluded from film screens and most television shows, they are now widely visible. However, they continue to play narrowly construed and stereotypical roles. They are represented as subservient to whites, hypersexual, and incomplete. This chapter looks at these stereotypes and the themes that deny institutional racism prevalent in entertainment that includes African Americans. Finally, it looks at how blacks have organized to fight these images and messages. This has involved challenging mainstream entertainment directly and providing alternative representations through black independent films.

EXCLUSION OF BLACKS IN ENTERTAINMENT MEDIA

African Americans have appeared in films and television more often than other racial-minority groups, beginning with silent films[1] and early-1950s television.[2] The first white-produced film to include a black actor was *Uncle Tom's Cabin* in 1914.[3] Although the number of movies with blacks in them did increase in number after World War II,[4] African Americans were largely excluded from movies about the wars.[5] Their representation in films increased from the 1950s to the 1970s, then decreased substantially in the early 1980s (going up again later in that decade).[6] According to the Stage Actor's Guild, African Americans were cast in 13.2 percent of theatrical film roles in 2001,[7] which is slightly more than their percentage in the population (12.3 percent).

In 1952, only an estimated 0.4 percent of television performances were by blacks. By the end of the 1950s, even fewer black actors were getting jobs on television. In the 1960s, larger numbers of blacks appeared on television, but these appearances were brief; only one-fifth of them were on screen for more than three minutes. For years, television avoided racially political themes to avoid offending white Southerners. It also presented a world without overt racial segregation during the time of segregation. Shows that addressed the deplorable conditions in the inner cities (*East Side/West Side*, 1963–1964) or black anger (*The Outcasts*, 1968–1969) were short-lived.

Even in the 1970s, when more blacks were on television, they were relegated to supporting roles.[8] Many of the shows in which they played major roles were short-lived. In the fall of 1970, nineteen prime-time network shows cast blacks in major roles, but most of those programs were canceled that year. Issue-oriented themes in television entertainment during the 1970s were also fleeting, replaced by escapist programming.[9]

Little improved in the early 1980s.[10] In the late 1980s and the 1990s, the number of black characters increased, largely due to the counterprogramming of cable networks (FOX, UPN, and WB). In 1990, eight shows featured black lead characters. In 1997, the number rose again to twenty-one.[11] A study of racial representation on prime-time television shows from 1999 found that blacks played 18 percent of speaking roles. Yet, not as many of them played leading roles as whites (37 percent versus 57 percent). Almost half of the black characters appeared on WB or UPN—networks with fewer viewers than ABC, CBS, and NBC.[12]

Including Black Characters while Excluding Black Actors

The 1903 film version of *Uncle Tom's Cabin* included the first black character in a motion picture, but it did not include the first black actor. A white actor in blackface played the role of Tom.[13] The term "blackface" refers to white's literally blackening their faces with burnt cork in order to portray blacks. The blackface tradition was inherited from the stage where it had existed since before the Civil War, when blacks were not allowed to appear there.[14] Whites dressed as blacks in blackface minstrelsy where they would sing and dance burlesques. Their songs romanticized slavery by having men in blackface sing nostalgically about plantation life.[15]

The blackface convention was transferred from the stage to early films, where it persisted into the late 1920s.[16] Black faces were rendered grotesquely for comic effects.[17] Once sound was introduced, the practice generally died off in dramatic films that sought realism. At the same time, blackface minstrelsy gained popularity in musicals like *The Jazz Singer* (1927).[18] Musicals excluded black actors and used blackface to present a vision of slavery that treated the Civil War as if it were a disruption in a world of interracial harmony.[19] Blackface was still used in some prominent films in the 1930s and 1940s. Popular stars of the day who wore blackface included the Marx Brothers (*A Day at the Races*, 1937), Mickey Rooney and Judy Garland (*Babes in Arms*, 1939),

Fred Astaire (*Swing Time*, 1939), Bing Crosby (*Holiday Inn*, 1942), and Doris Day (*I'll See You in My Dreams*, 1951).

Blackface did not translate well to television, where there were no minstrel shows and where songs were sung in blackface on variety shows only occasionally (*Colgate Comedy Hour*, 1950–1955).[20] Although white actors played the black parts on the *Amos 'n Andy* radio show, black actors were cast for these roles when the show debuted on television in 1951. These black actors had to be coached to act stereotypically and speak with heavy dialects like the whites who had mocked them on radio.[21]

Blackface was not the only technique whites used to play African Americans in the movies. Whites were also cast in mixed-race roles forsaking the make up. This occurred in films such as *Show Boat* (1929, 1936, 1951), *Pinky* (1949), and *Imitation of Life* (1959). This casting served to enhance the white audiences' identification with the characters and to sidestep interracial sexual contact when scripts called for a mulatto character to kiss a white character. Interestingly, when mulatto characters were played by white actresses, they had a much better chance of finding happiness than if a black woman or women of mixed race played the part.[22]

SELECTIVE EXCLUSION OF BLACKS IN ENTERTAINMENT MEDIA

Blacks have experienced "selective exclusion" by being relegated to certain genres, roles, and stories. Blacks were virtually absent from romance and family drama on televisions. For years, they were largely excluded from Westerns, detectives series, and shows set in the South, such as *The Andy Griffith Show* and *Mayberry RFD*, both popular in the 1960s. Blacks were most prevalent on musical variety shows and in comedies.[23] They still appear in comedies more frequently than dramas.[24] Selective exclusion is also at work when blacks are presented in limited types of roles. For example, they more frequently costar in detective films, a genre in which the main character is an outsider and alone.[25]

Black communities and characters with black cultural identities are missing in film and television. One example of this is the post–*Color Purple* (1985) films of Whoopi Goldberg.[26] *Sister Act* (1992) exemplifies how "filmmakers assume that their black character does not need cultural references (other than occasional jokes about race) or a semblance of a black community to anchor her."[27] Goldberg also plays the only black character in *Boys on the Side* (1994). In it she nurses a white friend and jokes away racial issues conveying the message that "love conquers all."[28]

> While they (Goldberg's characters) looked black, everything about them seemed expressed in a white cultural context; and, in the long run, characters were nei-

ther black nor white but a tan blend. Even so, tan, like black, was often kept in the background.[29]

Not only do black characters lack a cultural identity, but they often lack the background, family, and unique characterization that would make them more developed and understandable. Black characters are usually shown in the context of their relationships with whites rather than with each other. Take, for example, Hoke, the chauffeur played by Morgan Freeman in *Driving Miss Daisy* (1989): "left undramatized is his other life and world, his relationships and his perspective when away from Daisy's house, Daisy's car, Daisy's life."[30]

Blacks played sidekicks to white males in the 1980 detective films and to white women in the 1990s. In these films, black characters are denied romantic and sexual involvements, see less action than their white male counterparts, and operate in a white middle-class community. Racial issues are sidestepped by having the black character appear "raceless" (able to be played just as easily by a white actor) or made "different" by virtue of his class or place of origin. In the popular *Beverly Hills Cop* (1984, 1987) series, Eddie Murphy's character, Axel Foley, is taken out of Detroit and cut off from the black community.[31] He has no black friends, girlfriend, or family.[32] This is true of most of the black partners (but not the white ones) in 1980s interracial buddy films.[33]

Even films about the civil rights movement, which try to indict racism, undermine that message by putting whites at the center of the film and using their points of view to tell the stories. For example, *The Long Walk Home* (1990), set in Montgomery, Alabama, during the bus boycott of 1955, is told as the story of "a White woman's political transformation."[34] *Mississippi Burning* (1988) is a simplistic film that fictionalizes the FBI's investigation into the murders of three real-life civil rights workers.[35] The film does not tell the story of black experiences under segregation because it is preoccupied with "good whites" battling "bad whites."[36] History is distorted through its storytelling, characterization, and visual framing. It puts black activism in the background and makes the FBI the crusaders for racial justice, when in reality the agency worked against the civil rights movement more than it did for it.[37] *Ghosts of Mississippi* (1996) also focuses on a white lawyer and defendant rather than the slain civil rights leader, Medgar Evers, whose murder the trial was about.

Another form of selective exclusion is the sidestepping of racial issues. Interracial romances are avoided sometimes by desexualizing the black male characters. For example, the couplings of black men and white women in detective films in the 1990s keep their relationships platonic (*The Pelican Brief*, 1993) or interrupt and block opportunities for romance between characters (*Kiss the Girls*, 1997, and *The Bone Collector*, 1999).[38] A movie that did involve an interracial love affair between the main characters, *The Body-*

guard (1992), sidestepped the issue by ignoring it. There was no discussion of the characters' different races, the obstacles their union might have faced, or evidence of differences between them.[39]

STEREOTYPES OF BLACKS IN ENTERTAINMENT MEDIA

The inclusion of blacks in films and television is not necessarily good news because they tend to fit into certain negative stereotypes, showing them as subservient, hypersexualized, dangerous, or incomplete. There are numerous examples of these stereotypes in the descriptions that follow.

Black Subservient Stereotypes: Mammies, Toms, and Coons

Until 1961, blacks in television sitcoms were portrayed in the subservient roles derived from the minstrel shows.[40] Therefore, domestics, butlers, chauffeurs, and handymen were common servant roles for blacks. Although the major comedies of the time, *The Beulah Show* (1950–1953) and *Amos 'n Andy* (1951–1953), did not include explicit references to race or segregation,[41] they illustrate three of the most resilient subservient roles for black characters: mammies, Toms, and coons.

Mammies

The traditional mammy was a slave or servant who worked for a white family. She was an unattractive, large, desexualized woman who lived to serve. *The Beulah Show*'s main character embodied the mammy stereotype. She was beloved, long suffering, and faithful and derived her identity from serving white people. She was "a portly, conscientious, and lovable stereotype of the black domestic. She might berate her black friends, but around her boss, 'Mr. Harry,' and his wife, 'Miss Alice,' Beulah was always respectful."[42] While she was one of the earliest mammies on television, she was certainly not the only one.

Television's black mammies remained on television long after the 1950s were over. The "loud-but-lovable" Aunt Esther on the 1970s *Sanford and Son* (1972–1977),[43] Louise Jefferson (*The Jeffersons*, 1975–1985), and Nell Carter's various roles in the 1980s (including *Gimme a Break*, 1981) are all examples of this stereotype.[44] The soap opera *All My Children* (1970–present) included a mammy who worked for the rich white Wallingford family. She "was constantly shown in her cook's uniform, providing food, counsel, and an occasional wagged finger in reprimand."[45]

Film mammies are typically played by dark-skinned actresses. They include "big, fat, and cantankerous" outspoken characters, such as in *Coon Town Suffragettes* (1914), and the "sweet, jolly, and good-tempered" version often played in the 1930s by Louise Beavers (including *Imitation of Life*, 1934).[46] Probably the most familiar rendering of the outspoken mammy is Hattie McDaniel's in *Gone with the Wind* (1939), for which she won an Academy Award. They have appeared for decades in films such as *Song of the South* (1946), *The Member of the Wedding* (1952), *A Raisin in the Sun* (1961), *Hurry Sundown* (1967), *Clara's Heart* (1988), and, more recently, *Passion Fish* (1992).[47] Jannette Dates differentiates between film mammies who are "domineering, strong-willed, and bossy" and those who are "kind, generous, caring, and sincere" (she calls these "Aunt Jemimas").[48] Both ultimately maintain white authority.

Toms

Donald Bogle describes the Tom stereotype as "socially acceptable Good Negro characters"; though they are "chased, harassed, hounded, flogged, enslaved, and insulted, they keep the faith, never turn against their white massas, and remain hearty, submissive, stoic, generous, selfless, and oh-so-very kind."[49] The stereotype got its name from a character in *Uncle Tom's Cabin* (1903, 1914, 1927). Film versions of the book by Harriet Beecher Stowe presented the story of the obedient slave who is good and faithfully goes from a kind slave owner to an evil one. He ends up being beaten to death for his Christian beliefs.[50]

Other Tom characters appeared in early films (*Confederate Spy*, 1910, and *For Massa's Sake*, 1911). "Uncle Billy" (played by Bojangles Robinson), who appeared in numerous films with Shirley Temple, also fits the stereotype. He happily serves this little girl. He shows her how to tap dance and entertains her when she asks him to. He also risks his safety for hers when he saves her from the Yankees in *The Littlest Rebel* (1935).[51]

Sidney Poitier's success and acceptability to white audiences in the 1950s can be attributed to the fact that he played Tom characters. "He never made a move against the dominant white culture. Instead he nourished it."[52] Poitier brought dignity and intelligence to subservient roles in movies such as *No Way Out* (1950). He sacrifices his freedom for a white in *The Defiant Ones* (1958) and sacrifices his life for another white in *The Edge of the City* (1957).[53] In other films, Poitier's characters help white nuns, white school children, and a white blind woman.[54] A more recent "tamed black man" is the character of Roger Murtaugh played by Danny Glover in the *Lethal Weapon* series (1987, 1989, 1992, 1998). Murtaugh follows his white partner's lead, shows more fear than he, and is less active, more domesticated, and often the butt of humiliating scenes and jokes.[55]

Starting with Amos Jones on *Amos 'n Andy*, Toms have also been common on television.[56] A recent television Tom was Dr. Greg on the *Ally McBeal* (1997–2002) show. His character is "rendered sexless and impotent by the stereotypical White fear of Black male sexuality."[57] Although Chef on

South Park (1997–present) has been described as an Uncle Tom character for his moralizing to the white children on the cartoon, he is provided with more of a sexual identity than most Tom characters.[58]

Coons

The coon stereotype exists for comic relief and as a result demeans blacks by ridiculing them. Coons come in three varieties: pickaninny, Uncle Remus, and the pure coon.[59] The pickaninny is a buffoonish child, a "harmless, little screwball creation whose eyes popped, whose hair stood on end with the least excitement, and whose antics were pleasant and diverting"[60] This characterization has a long history in film. His first appearance was in Thomas Edison's experimental film, *Ten Pickaninnies* (1904). The best example of this stereotype in film is the 1920s *Our Gang* comedy series in which the antics of Farina, Stymie, and Buckwheat demonstrate the foolishness and simple-mindedness of the pickaninny character.[61] Television descendants of these characters are Arnold on *Diff'rent Strokes* (1978–1986), Webster on *Webster* (1983–1987), and Eddie Murphy's *Saturday Night Live* (1975–present) parody of Buckwheat.[62]

The Uncle Remus version of the coon is "harmless and congenial[;] he is a first cousin to the tom, yet he distinguishes himself by his quaint, naïve, and comic philosophizing."[63] Two films with Uncle Remus characters are *The Green Pastures* (1936), an all-black film visualizing bible stories, and *Song of the South*, Disney's partially animated film set in the Old South. In it, the character after whom this category is named sings and tells stories to white children.[64]

Donald Bogle considers the pure coon "the most blatantly degrading of all black stereotypes."[65] He is a "lazy, no-account, good-for-nothing, forever-in-hot-water, natural-born comedian," like Stepin Fetchit, who created a "lazy man with a soul."[66] The 1930s and 1940s were full of comedies where coon characters mugged in a typically degrading fashion. Years later, a "new-style coon: a coon with a double consciousness" appeared in the form of the black sheriff in *Blazing Saddles* (1974) and Richard Pryor's characters in *Silver Streak* (1976) and *Which Way Is Up?* (1977).[67] More recent examples include the wide-eyed, jive-talking minor characters and roles played by Martin Lawrence and Chris Tucker and Orlando Jones's performance in *Evolution* (2001).

On television, another *Amos 'n Andy* character, George "Kingfish" Stevens, was presented as "the stereotypical scheming 'coon' character, whose chicanery left his pals distrustful and the audience laughing."[68] Television coons were "rascalish, loud, pushy, and conniving."[69] The "assimilated hybrid minstrelsy" of television sitcoms of the 1972–1983 period was full of coon images: George Jefferson (*The Jeffersons*), J. J. Evans (*Good Times*, 1974–1979), and Grady Wilson (*Sanford and Son*).[70] The popularity of Jimmie Walker's mugging, strutting, and uttering "Dy-no-mite!" as J. J. Evans transformed

Good Times from a story about a family surviving in the projects to a show-case for buffoonery.[71] More recently, Will Smith's early characterization of the Fresh Prince (*The Fresh Prince of Bel Air*, 1990–1996) was described as coonish clowning.[72] Some of *Martin*'s (1992–1997) foolishness also fits the stereotype.

Subservient Stereotypes and the Status Quo

All the mammies, Toms, and Uncle Remuses work for whites. Although they vary in competence and outspokenness, none seriously criticizes or tries to change the system. Uncle Remuses, Toms, and mammies are the more competent helpmates, but the pickaninnies and pure coons amuse whites with their harmless havoc. Each reinforces the status quo. "Remus's mirth, like tom's contentment and the coon's antics, has always been used to indicate the black man's satisfaction with the system and his place in it."[73] Emblematized in *Gone with the Wind*, mammies demonstrate that, before or after emancipation, the role of black women is to serve, nurture, rescue, and love white women.[74]

Mammies, Toms, and coons are stereotypes that desexualize blacks. In these characterizations, black men are "rendered romantically unappealing to white women, thereby constituting no rivalry to white male prowess."[75] Even the black male detectives on prime time in the late 1980s were "neutered."[76] *Designing Women* (1986–1993) provided a good example of the desexualizing of subservient, male, black characters. "Always there with assistance or sympathy, Anthony operated around them like an ebony eunuch."[77] Sexless subservient black roles have been used for more than just comic relief.

> For the mass white audience, Sydney Poitier was a black man who had met their standards. His characters were tame; never did they act impulsively, nor were they threats to the system. They were amenable and pliant. And finally they were non-funky, almost sexless and sterile. In short, they were the perfect dream for white liberals anxious to have a colored man in for lunch or dinner.[78]

Black Sexual Stereotypes: Black Bucks, Pimps, and Whores

Alternatives to these desexed images are those of blacks who are "oversexed." Neither version usually allows black characters romantic love stories (a common feature of plots involving white characters).[79] Not only was interracial romance and sexual contact generally unseen on television and movies, but blacks kissing each other did not occur until 1967, when Bill Cosby Jr. and Janet MacLachlan kissed on *I Spy* (1965–1968). Even after that, it continued to be rare.[80] Both the hypersexualized and the desexualized images of blacks are more about power and privilege than about sex.

The stereotype of a hypersexualized black male dehumanizes black men, helping to justify their subordination. Associations can be made between being a sexual threat and a threat to the political status quo. "In the movies, most black men politically militant or merely politically motivated are simplified by the scenarists into unreasonable, animalistic brutes."[81] An analysis of cartoons in *Hustler* magazine from the late 1970s to the mid-1980s illustrated how black males were dehumanized as sexual predators. Drawings exaggerated their muscles, lips, and penises, while making their heads small and ape-like.[82]

The Birth of a Nation (1915) included the hypersexualized and dangerous stereotype of black men that Donald Bogles calls the "brutal black buck."[83] He describes bucks as "oversexed and savage, violent and frenzied as they lust for white flesh."[84] Movies with the black brute stereotype include *The Emperor Jones* (1933), *Carmen Jones* (1954), *Porgy and Bess* (1959), the Jim Brown movies of the late 1960s, *Rocky III* (1982), *The Color Purple*, *New Jack City* (1991), *What's Love Got to Do with It* (1993), and *Training Day* (2000).[85]

Due to television restrictions on sexual content in the 1960s, early television versions of the black buck were muted and allowed for some positive (albeit brief) examples of black male empowerment. For example, Otis Young of *The Outcasts* has the militancy and rage of the buck without the uncontrolled sexual treat. He "was the first modern black hero to lash out at white society when he felt it to be oppressive and unjust."[86] Even the "big and black and menacing" Mr. T. (B.A. Bad Attitude Barracus) on *The A-Team* (1983–1987) is one of the good guys and not presented as a sexual threat.[87]

The frequent characterization of black women as sexually promiscuous has been used to subjugate them, providing an excuse for their sexual mistreatment by white men.[88] The first black whore appeared in film in 1929 (*Hallelujah*). Many more followed, especially in the urban action films of the 1970s[89] and the new ghetto aesthetic films of the 1990s.[90] Oversexed black women appear on television in parodies by Flip Wilson and in sitcoms;[91] they appear as prostitutes in dramas like *L.A. Law* (1986–1994).[92] Although directed by blacks, films like *New Jack City* and *Boyz n the Hood* (1991) still present women as bitches and whores[93] or sexual victims.[94] Ally McBeal's black roommate, Renee Radick, provides a recent version of a female black buck (or Jezebel). This character goes quickly from being "all business" (as a lawyer who usually loses her cases) to a "sexualized other" who tempts and threatens men.[95]

Black Stereotypes of Incompleteness: Mulattoes, Man-Children, and Matriarchs

Mulatto characters are presented as exotic but tragically flawed. Some of the fair-skinned "tragic mulattos" are introduced sympathetically but are ultimately ruined by their passing for white. Often, these films show the masquerading African American pulled back to the black community by a dark-skinned mammy figure.[96] Examples of movies including this stereotypical character are *Imitation of Life* (1934), *Lost Boundaries* (1949), *Pinky* (1949), *Kings Go Forth* (1958), *The Cotton Club* (1984), and *Angel Heart* (1987).[97]

Blacks also tend to be childlike in film and television. Sharing the screen with tiny Shirley Temple are her black adult playmates who exhibit a "constitutional infantilism" that they will not outgrow.[98] In the all-black play *The Green Pastures*, which was a movie (1936) and a television show (1957 and 1959), "All the characters were essentially Sambos—uncomplicated children whose mischief would be handled by the inexorable acting out of the New Testament story."[99] Richard Pryor plays the role of a man-child in *The Toy* (1983) when he is hired to be a playmate for a spoiled, rich, white child. Black characters also appear childlike when they are given limited mental or verbal capacities (*The Hand That Rocks the Cradle*, 1992, or *The Green Mile*, 1999).[100] These simple characters sometimes have magic or divine powers that are used to help white people.[101]

The matriarch stereotype portrays black women as domineering, driving away or emasculating men with their aggressiveness.[102] This historical stereotype is frequently found on television.[103] It began there with Sapphire, a "shrewish woman continually browbeating" Kingfish on *Amos 'n Andy*.[104] The stereotype got even more use in 1970s sitcoms like *That's My Mama* (1974–1975), in which a thirty-year-old man lives at home with his controlling mother.[105] This image is also found in films (like *Jungle Fever*, 1991). The creation of matriarchs invites audiences to blame the victimization of black men on black women rather than on white institutions or individuals.[106]

The stereotypes of the mulattoes, man-children, and matriarchs reveal blacks as being seriously flawed. Either they hurt themselves or others in the black community, or they exist for whites. They reify the racial hierarchy that places blacks below whites.

SYSTEM-SUPPORTIVE THEMES AND MESSAGES

The reoccurring themes in black film and television reinforce the status quo in two major ways. One attempts to justify inequality, and the other denies it. The first approach blames blacks and celebrates whites. Movies characterize blacks as inferior to whites, thereby justifying their unequal status in society. These films show dangerous, immoral, or mentally deficient black characters as emblematic of their race. The failings of these characters are presented as indicative of inherent weaknesses in blacks that are "facts of life"; they are "no one's fault," and therefore, there is nothing to reform. Or, black, rather than white, characters might utter racist or system-supportive dialog.

The second way that themes reinforce the status quo is to deny racial inequality by focusing on individuals and ignoring social structures. In this way, films can tell viewers that race does not matter. Some of these films present a rosy picture of racial relations where blacks and whites live equally and cooperatively together. Others present racial inequality as a thing of the past. Both of these approaches tell white viewers "there is no need to blame yourself or your government for the status of blacks" because it is due either to problems with the race as a whole or with individuals.

Blaming Blacks and Celebrating Whites

A movie can be system supportive by blaming blacks and celebrating whites in three major ways. First, it can show blacks as inferior, thereby justifying their oppression and white privilege. This can be seen in films about the white man's burden. Second, it can show that blacks are prejudiced too. Focusing on black prejudice diverts attention from systems of inequality and individualizes blame. Third, it can put system-supportive statements in the mouths of black characters, indicating that they endorse the status quo.

The White Man's Burden

The white man's burden theme treats whites as the noble champions and protectors of blacks, who cannot do for themselves because of their own deficiencies. This theme is present in literature of the nineteenth century as part of the justification for European imperialism, the idea at the time being that if whites were a superior race (more moral, intelligent, and civilized) then it was justifiable to colonize Africa and Asia. In fact, it was the "responsible" thing to do. The character of Tarzan from the movies (1950s) and television (1960s) embodies this theme, showing how a white man saves the "primitive" Africans.[107]

A Shirley Temple movie showing the (little) white girl's burden illustrates white superiority in the movies even more starkly. In *Kid 'n Africa* (1931), Temple "plays a missionary in Africa trying to civilize the 'cannibal' tots, played by anonymous black kids."[108] The idea that blacks are uncivilized and need to be tamed is not confined to Africa. The theme song "Welcome to the Jungle" is used in the urban high school drama *Lean on Me* (1989).[109] Inner-city schools have been the site of white man's burden dramas on television for decades. *Room 222* (1969–1974), *Welcome Back, Kotter* (1975–1979), *The White Shadow* (1978–1981), and *Boston Public* (2000–2004) all feature white "savior" teachers. Since *Room 222* and *Boston Public* also include black teachers,[110] they challenge the assumption that blacks are inherently inferior. However, these shows continue to avoid laying blame on social institutions for the status of blacks by showing the success of the individual black teachers.

Historical films often conform to the white man's burden theme. In *Mississippi Burning*, blacks are confined to the background and shown as unable to act during a period of fervent social activism among blacks. They are submissive, dull-witted, and frightened. Two white FBI agents are the heroes of the story, solving the civil rights workers' murders.[111] Another historical movie set during the Birmingham bus boycotts (*The Long Walk Home*, 1998) gives credit to white women for the boycott's success. Black people are shown as suffering, not as heroic or creatively solving problems.[112] The movie *Amistad* glorifies the role and intentions of John Quincy Adams and celebrates the Supreme Court.

Another reoccurring version of the white man's burden theme on television occurs in shows in which white families adopt black children (*Diff'rent Strokes* and *Webster*). "The racial condescension in this scenario was obvious. . . . Predictably, U.S. television has never scheduled a series where a loving black couple 'rescued' a white child by adopting him."[113]

Black Prejudice

Some films and television shows deny sociopolitical racism while acknowledging prejudice. Not only do they focus on the attitudes and actions of individuals, rather than on the policies of institutions, but the prejudiced characters are often blacks. One of the first stories to tackle racism on television was a *Ben Casey* (1961–1966) episode during the 1963–1964 season about an antiwhite, black doctor.[114]

The issue of black bigotry toward whites was revisited in the social-issue comedy series of the 1970s. The bigoted attitudes expressed by Archie Bunker on *All in the Family* (1971–1979) and those of George Jefferson on *The Jeffersons* are seen as balancing each other. Yet, while Jefferson was a joke (mocked by his own maid), Bunker remained in charge. Many white viewers saw Bunker as "telling it like it is" and speaking for them, rather than as a buffoon.[115]

Black characters are also used to voice antiblack attitudes and racial slurs. The Academy Award–winning *Guess Who's Coming to Dinner* (1967) puts a liberal white patriarch struggling with the marriage of his daughter to a black doctor at the center of the story. His black maid has the most racist dialog in the film. She accuses the doctor, played by Sidney Poitier, of "gettin' above hisself" and calls him a "smooth-talking, smartass nigger, just out for all you can get." Both she and the doctor's father call him "boy" and oppose the marriage that the white father ultimately endorses.[116]

Black Support of the Status Quo

Black characters can be used to support the system by having them speak explicitly for the status quo. The comedy *Benson* (1979–1986) features a black butler who goes on to become an administrative assistant to a daffy governor. In it, the main character "fit the pattern that scripted African American male characters as innocuous true-believers in the system, who supported, defended, and nurtured mainstream, middle-class American values, interests, concerns, and even faults."[117]

The black character in *Imitation of Life* (1959) voices a religious rationale for black oppression. Slavery is endorsed by Mammy in *Gone with the Wind*, forgiven by slave Rau-Ru in *Band of Angels* (1957), and sentimentalized by Uncle Remus in *Song of the South*. In a denial of gender and racial power relations of the time, *Jefferson in Paris* (1994) shows a teenage, black slave girl seducing Thomas Jefferson. Humor can also be used to minimize the horror of the past. On *Gimme a Break*, Nell Carter's character gets a laugh for saying that her grandmother "immigrated to this country on a slave ship."[118]

The idea that it is the responsibility of middle-class blacks, not of the government or of white taxpayers, to help poor blacks offers whites a comforting explanation for inequality.[119] *The Fresh Prince of Bel Air* also absolves whites of any responsibility for inner-city blacks. Films like *Claudine* (1974) and *Car Wash* (1975) explicitly promote conservative social policies that reject government assistance and the systemic reasons behind inequality.[120]

Denying Inequality

The system-supportive message that institutional racism does not exist is asserted in a variety of ways. First, racial injustice can be denied entirely by omitting racial diversity or failing to acknowledge that race makes a difference. The system is absolved by the idea that if blacks and whites get to know each other, the problems of prejudice will disappear.[121] This message underlies the "Huck Finn fixation." Second, blacks who are hardworking and stay within the system can serve as evidence of a successful, color-blind society. Third, racial injustice can be acknowledged as a thing of the past or as due to the actions of bad (or mentally ill) individuals who can be brought to justice by good people in a nonracist system. All of these messages work together to deny inequality and support the status quo.

The Huck Finn Fixation

The Huck Finn fixation articulates a fantasy of interracial male bonding that "wipes away any fears about tensions between black and white."[122] As the name implies, it draws on the lessons learned from the relationship between Huck Finn and the slave, Jim, in the Mark Twain novel. While the efforts of Huck to free Jim are consistent with the white man's burden, their friendship and adventures together illustrate the reassuring idea that blacks can be nonthreatening friends and helpmates to whites. In fact, they can morally and physically save and redeem whites. Since blacks are the supporting players in these interracial relationships,[123] they reassure whites that interracial friendships enhance rather than reduce white power.

In addition to being the subordinate member of the duo, black characters are often sacrificed for the white ones. *The Defiant Ones* shows the journey of a black and a white convict who were initially handcuffed together. The characters progress from fighting each other to cooperating in order to survive. Along the way, they build a friendship that demonstrates how below the surface (skin color), we are all the same. Yet, the black character is the one who gives up his chance at freedom to save the white character. This message is also found on television in the Philco Television Playhouse drama *A Man Is Ten Feet Tall* (1955) in which the black character loses his life saving his white friend.[124]

Sidney Poitier was not the only black actor to be gain popularity in these buddy roles. Bill Cosby was the first black actor to star in a dramatic television series[125] by playing a black "second banana" on *I Spy*.[126] Richard Pryor's films, such as *Silver Streak* (1976), combine humor and adventure, showing how racial differences can be reconciled on a personal, rather than political, level.[127] The same message is found in *Brian's Song* (1971) and *48 Hours* (1982), which show initially hostile adversaries cooperating and bonding.[128] Some more recent buddy films that continue to present the black as a sidekick, rather than as a leader or an equal, are *Rocky III and IV* (1982, 1985), *Heart Condition* (1990), *Rising Sun* (1993), and *Men in Black* (1997).[129]

Buddy films proliferated in the 1980s and 1990s with interracial teams bonding.[130] Examples include *Nighthawks* (1982), *48 Hours*, *Trading Places* (1983), *White Nights* (1985), *Running Scared* (1986), *Lethal Weapon 1, 2, and 3*, *Another 48 Hours* (1990), and *White Men Can't Jump* (1992).[131] These movies are popular with both black and white audiences. They appeal to black audiences because the black characters are active and successful and have appealing characteristics (i.e., they are funny, physically attractive, and clever). During moments in these films, black characters get to challenge authority and show up the white character. Whites find the films appealing because of the positive representations of the white characters, who ultimately have the upper hand. They also enjoy the message that racial tensions can be resolved interpersonally without systemic reforms. These stories have hegemonically supportive plots that do not ultimately disrupt white authority.[132] They show how success is based on merit and ability rather than influenced by class or racial privilege, as well as how racial integration is dependent upon blacks assimilating. They also argue that essential elements of the status quo (capitalism, consumer culture, and America's criminal justice system) should be, and can be, preserved with the help of "good blacks."[133]

The Assimiliationist Theme

The assimilationist theme used in television and film storytelling reassures white audiences that America is color-blind. It says that the system works by rewarding hard-working, law-abiding blacks, just as it does by rewarding hard-working, law-abiding whites. On one hand, we can think of these images of black achievement in films and television entertainment as progressive. They contradict the assumption behind the white man's burden theme that blacks are inherently inferior. On the other hand, they still privilege white culture by presenting a certain picture of what acceptable and successful blacks should be like.

The classic assimilationist television show, *Julia* (1968–1971), portrays a black nurse, who is a war widow, as a good mother, friend, employee, and neighbor. The show was criticized for being unrealistic and lacking any racial-political content. Julia and her son live in a "white world" without black friends, topical discussions, or trappings of black culture. Diahann Carroll's Julia is "a 'white Negro,' the overly good, overly integrated fantasy production of white writers."[134] Julia is not the only black character on television to be characterized as whitewashed. "Black sitcoms are not 'Black' in that they exhibit an African American worldview or a Black philosophy of life. Rather they are Black because the performers are Black."[135]

The Cosby Show (1984–1992) was a popular television comedy starring Bill Cosby Jr. as the father of a large loving family. He plays a doctor married to a lawyer. The family is financially well off, living in a large, well-furnished, beautiful house. Some critics claimed that it was a sugarcoated assimilationist story similar to *Julia*.[136] Yet, the characters on *The Cosby Show* do not lack racial distinctiveness. Unlike Julia's home, theirs includes African American art,[137] an "End Apartheid" banner, discussions about Martin Luther King Jr.,[138] and visits from black friends, performing artists, and extended family.[139] Yet, the show conveys the impression that racism does not get in the way of achieving the American Dream. While some viewers thought the family acted "too white" to be authentic,[140] many more characterized the family as an example of what "real" blacks would be like if they tried. Systematic audience studies indicated that "white TV viewers felt racism was a sin of the past; *The Cosby Show*, accordingly, represented a new 'freedom of opportunity' apparently enjoyed by black people. If Cliff and Clair can make it, then so can all blacks."[141] Of course, the Huxtables did not really "make it"; they are idealized images.[142]

See No (Current Systemic) Evil

Historical dramas serve to reassure modern audiences that racism is a thing of the past. *To Kill A Mockingbird* (1962) came out during the early civil rights movement, but it dealt with bigotry during the Depression. Its story about a heroic white lawyer fighting (unsuccessfully) for an innocent black defendant conveys the idea that the current system is more just.

Roots (1977) is a twelve-hour, multigenerational miniseries based on Alex Haley's book about his family's history. It drew a larger television audience than any program had before.[143] Like other historical dramas of the time (such as *The Prime of Miss Jane Pittman*, 1974), it shows how black people had suffered and triumphed. *Roots* was seen as socially progressive because blacks are sympathetically rendered and because Haley's story was embraced as a representative American experience.[144] However, the story is conservative in many ways. Psychologist Melvin Moore argues,

> Their triumphs are depicted as triumphs of the will, the will to survive, not the will to change the system, the source of most of their suffering. In fact, the system is never challenged, or even questioned. Evil becomes the act of individual white folks, to be overcome through the belief that solutions are found within the American system and the American way.[145]

In addition to failing to indict the system, the show allows white viewers to feel better about themselves. Because the acts of prejudice shown in *Roots* are so extreme, white viewers can judge their own feelings as mild in comparison. The show highlights the extreme racism of the past, making contemporary problems seem small.[146]

> Black viewers who might have expected an indictment of the American system were disappointed in *Roots* and *Roots: The Next Generation*. Instead, they encountered evil individuals who personally subjugated blacks. The economic and moral system which produced and tolerated such brutal citizens was never adequately presented. If anything, with the middle-class prosperity seen ultimately in Alex Haley's personal affluence, the system was applauded.[147]

PROTESTING NEGATIVE IMAGES AND MESSAGES

African Americans have been active in protesting negative images and themes. Through organizations like the National Association for the Advancement of Colored People (NAACP) and black media professional organizations, they have lobbied for improved representation and against entertainment they find racially insensitive. Their targets have been both media organizations and the government. These efforts have met with some success but have also resulted in backlash.

Confronting the Industry

Organized black protests of material considered offensive has a long history. The NAACP picketed the premier of *The Birth of a Nation* in 1915 and demonstrated outside of other theaters showing the film. In fact, riots followed in some cities. The protest seems to have had an impact, since the film was banned in five states and nineteen cities.[148] The premiere of *Song of the South* was also picketed when the NAACP and the National Negro Congress called for a national boycott of the film.[149]

In addition to street activism, organizations have tried to improve coverage of blacks by appealing directly to the media producers. This was the case in 1942 when an agreement was reached between the NAACP and Hollywood studios to abandon pejorative racial roles and increase the number of black employees.[150] Organizations have had some success in meeting with network officials (as early as the 1950s) to voice their concerns over certain shows. Complaints successfully gutted *Tennessee Johnson* and *We've Come a Long, Long Way*.[151] More recently, they had comedian Andrew Dice Clay banned from *Saturday Night Live* due to his racist and sexist jokes.[152]

Another approach has been to issue and publicize reports on the status of blacks in the media to shame organizations into improving. For example, the Coordinating Council for Negro Performers issued a report on television in 1954 criticizing blacks' progress in the entertainment industry. The NAACP, the Congress on Racial Equality (CORE), the Writers Guild of America West, various entertainers' unions, and the New York chapter of the National Academy of Television Arts demanded more employment of blacks in the entertainment industry in 1963.[153] Since 2000, the NAACP has made fighting diversity problems on television a priority. It has presented awards to film and television representatives for positive treatment of blacks, provided a million-dollar budget to a media-diversity task force, and negotiated agreements with networks to increase minority employment after threatening a boycott.[154]

Seeking Government Help

Efforts to improve black representation on television and films have also focused on the government. The NAACP sought a federal court injunction to keep CBS from televising *Amos 'n Andy*. In a lawsuit against the network, they enumerated the objectionable content of the show.[155] The association also sought a ban on showing *The Birth of a Nation*[156] and tried to get state legislatures to outlaw films containing racial slander.[157] In addition to trying to stop shows, the NAACP successfully pressured the Office of War Information and the Department of the Army to make the war propaganda film *The Negro Soldier* (1944).[158]

Rep. Adam Clayton Powell Jr. (D-NY) held congressional hearings in 1962 on the topic in the entertainment industry. He invited black performers to voice complaints. The Congressional Black Caucus also heard testimony about racism in broadcasting in 1972. The caucus was able to keep CBS from airing *Mr. Dugan*, a sitcom about a black congressman they found offensive. Rather than offend the black congressmen, the production company took a loss of $750,000 when the show was scrapped.[159] This outcome probably would not have been possible if the show's creator, Norman Lear, had not asked for the group's input.[160]

In the 1970s, various groups tried to use the Federal Communications

Commission (FCC) to increase minority representation on television. Petitions were filed with the FCC to block renewal of television station licenses on the grounds of racial discrimination in programming.[161] Although some of these efforts were successful, the FCC did not generally rule in favor of citizens' groups.[162] In fact, black lobbying groups eventually saw the FCC's equal employment opportunity policies as too weak to be a useful tool. Other commissions have also investigated these issues. The New York State Civil Rights Commission looked into racial employment discrimination in film and video trade unions in 1970 and the U.S. Civil Rights Commission issued reports in the late 1970s about minority stereotyping.[163]

Limited Success

Despite some victories, efforts to alter black representations on film and television have met with much resistance. Black groups have not been able to transform and initiate programming dramatically, in part because they do not have institutionalized relationships with the network standards and practices department.[164] They have also paid a price for getting some shows stopped. For example, after the NAACP helped to force *Amos 'n Andy* off of television in 1953, fifteen years went by before another black family was featured in a comedy.[165]

Activists on the other side of the issue have also curtailed success. Opposition to progressive images of blacks on television has come from government officials and white citizen groups. In a 1952 newspaper editorial, Georgia governor Herman Talmadge threatened to lead a boycott against network television. He claimed that programming showing whites and blacks dancing together threatened his state's policies of segregation. There are examples of scripts being changed because of corporate concerns about Southerners potentially boycotting products they saw advertised during shows they found racially offensive.[166]

Beulah Land (1980), a six-hour miniseries set during the Civil War, illustrates the amount of effort required and the limited effect of organizing against a proposed television program considered racially offensive. Black actors and activists found the script offensive, claiming it showed "the image of the slave as ignorant, oversexed, sloven, dependent on the whim of his master, and filled with love for that master and that master's land."[167] Seen as particularly disturbing were scenes of slaves who perpetuated their own mistreatment, breastfed a white baby, danced after one of them was beaten by the master, and rejected freedom.

After the program's black actors failed to get the script changed, the following efforts were made to prevent the show from airing: An activist group (the Media Forum) was created. A meeting was held with the chairman of the FCC. Members of the Hollywood chapter of the NAACP met with a representative of Columbia Pictures. A position paper against the film was distributed to the press, political leaders, and the network. Actors in the production spoke out against the show. More groups joined the protest and created the Coalition against the Airing of *Beulah Land*. Celebrity members of the coalition held a public speaking tour and appeared on local television shows. A full-page advertisement appealing to the producers and the network and signed by sixty-six people ran in the *Daily Variety*. The president of the NAACP sent telegrams to the producers and network. A meeting was held between the coalition and representatives of NBC and Columbia Pictures. Black political leaders wrote to network executives. Network television critics published their concerns. Coalition members demonstrated, handed out leaflets, ran an ad (listing thirty-six supporting organizations), and issued a second position paper to convince affiliates not to air the show in their local markets. The coalition got petitions signed and sent them to NBC and Columbia Pictures. It held a town hall meeting. There was an attempt to boycott the show's sponsors after *Beulah Land* was aired.

The protest lasted nine months, and as a result, the miniseries was postponed, edited, and defended in the press. Despite all these efforts, it was eventually aired nationwide. Only two local affiliates (WBAL in Baltimore, Maryland, and WLBT in Jackson, Mississippi) did not show it. Despite bad reviews, the show did well in the ratings. It was also rebroadcast on NBC in 1983 and numerous times on cable television. It was sold to overseas markets, where it was shown with the scenes that had been cut out.

CREATING ALTERNATIVE IMAGES AND MESSAGES

Independent black filmmaking began in the early 1910s, reaching its first heyday in the 1920s with the Harlem Renaissance.[168] Independent films "put on the screen Black lives and concerns that derive from the complexity of Black communities . . . [and] provide alternative ways of knowing Black people that differ from the fixed stereotypes of Blacks in Hollywood."[169] Some of these films were explicitly political, emphasizing black pride and consciousness, and others presented middle-class blacks free from racial misery.[170] Whether overtly or not, independent films challenge the racial status quo through social and political statements and images.[171]

An early example of a black political film is *Birth of a Race* (1915), an Afrocentric counterpoint to *The Birth of a Nation* created by the major director/writer/producer of black films of the time, Oscar Michaeux. Michaeux was known for films about middle-class black families.[172] His films showed both the hope and dangers of assimilation.[173] He addressed topics such as migration and the urban ghetto (*The Homesteader*, 1919), lynching (*Within Our Gates* and *The Brute*, both 1920), racism and anti-Semitism (*The Gunsaulus Mystery*, 1921), and the terrorist tactics of the Ku Klux Klan (*The Symbol of the Unconquered*, 1920).[174] With the Great Depression, the advent of sound films, and Hollywood's efforts to capture the black audience, black independent filmmaking receded for decades.[175]

"Blaxploitation" films of the early 1970s, such as *Sweet, Sweetback's Baaadassss Song* (1971) and *Shaft* (1971), featured black male leads violently fighting white characters and the system ("the Man"). They attracted large, young, black audiences, who found the strong and angry drug dealers and pimps appealing. Yet, these same characters (usually pimps and drug dealers) have been criticized as another version of the black savage stereotype.[176] Some black activists saw the films as too simplistic, negative, exploitive, violent, and sexist. The films have been criticized for being too political and for not being political enough.[177] Those who see the films as not political enough argue that the revolutionary spirit of the times was transposed from politics to criminality or crime fighting (as in the case of *Shaft*). Blacks are shown working for the system or caught by it, rather than substantially challenging it.[178]

A new wave of black independent filmmakers emerged out of Los Angeles in the 1970s, inspired by the success of the black exploitation films but unhappy with their ideology. They sought to replace the false images of African American history and culture.[179] These filmmakers saw film as "a means of political struggle, continuing and extending the racial struggles of the 1960s. They wrote a declaration of independence [from Hollywood], proposed an alternative curriculum for the UCLA film school, and held off-campus study groups to discuss film politics and techniques."[180] Some of the tenets of that declaration were

"Accountability to the community takes precedence over training for an industry that maligns and exploits, trivializes and invisibilizes Black people" and "to reconstruct cultural memory, not slavishly imitate White models."[181]

Bush Mama (1975), *Killer of Sheep* (1977), and *Passing Through* (1977) typify the West Coast black independent films of the time, which focused on black inner-city communities and characters whose identities were shaped by socioeconomic forces.[182] That "realness" was a core feature of these black independent films is illustrated in *Bush Mama*, which begins with shots of its own camera crew being accosted by the Los Angeles police. It then tells the story of a woman on welfare who kills a policeman rapist.[183] These movies have not been as popularly received or as widely distributed as the Hollywood versions of the genre.[184]

Probably the best-known black director is Spike Lee. Scholars disagree over whether his films are cultural resistance.[185] Thomas Cripps claims,

More than any other figure in African American filmmaking, Lee has calculatedly linked himself with the history of black independent filmmaking, has self-consciously reached for a black audience, and used a rhetoric (of both filmmaking and marketing) that has rendered his work accessible to crossover audiences without compromising the inner values of this work.[186]

Mark A. Reid argues, however, that Lee's feature films lack a re-vision of black experience and are not technically independent films because they are studio distributed.[187] Lee's celebration of patriarchy through silencing, stereotyping, and objectifying women has also been criticized as repeating oppressive messages from mainstream cinema.[188] Lee's *Malcolm X* (1992) also elicited controversy over the depoliticizing of the subject matter in order to appeal to a large audience.[189] Nevertheless, young blacks became more knowledgeable, racially conscious, and concerned about race relations after seeing the film.[190] Lee's *Do the Right Thing* (1989) confronts racism and advocates for fighting the powers that be, while ultimately critiquing violence as a solution.[191]

John Singleton became the first black nominated for an Academy Award for best director for his popular urban rite of passage film, *Boyz n the Hood*.[192] On one hand, the film was criticized for its treatment of women[193] and its focus on black-on-black violence, characteristics that might mitigate its systemic critique.[194] On the other hand, it indicted Ronald Reagan, the police, and the media, while advocating black men and their role and responsibilities within the black community.[195] These are not messages frequently found in mainstream cinema.

Black women directors have offered alternative visions. Many black independent films have been criticized as male dominated and heterosexist.[196] *Losing Ground* (1982) was the first feature-length film to be directed by an African American woman and the first independent black film to have a black professional woman as the protagonist.[197] In another black feminist film, *Daughters of the Dust* (1991), black history is interpreted through generations of women's stories.[198] The film was innovative in its perspective, visual style, and nonlinear narrative.[199]

CONCLUSION

The racial status quo is promoted in films and television shows that stereotype blacks and ignore racial inequality or justify it, for instance by showing whites as "naturally" superior and therefore worthy of their power. The Huck Finn fixation shows blacks as complicit in this relationship and as enjoying their support of white leaders. The racial status quo is also promoted by stories that sugar-coat reality by showing racial harmony and cooperation. When stories do show racial discrimination, it is confined to the past and has been "fixed" by whites. The prejudice that remains is characterized as balanced (because some blacks are bigots, too) and relatively benign, not something that requires government reforms.

Black organizations, inside and outside of the entertainment industry, have been fighting to improve programming. There have been some successes and some failures regarding stopping productions and limiting the audience for others. Independent black films have provided alternative entertainment to audiences since the early 1900s. Some of these films provide explicit counterpoints to offensive mainstream movies, and others share new perspectives on the black experience. Some of these perspectives have been criticized for being sexist and violent.

4

Native Americans in Film and Television Entertainment

CLICHED IMAGES OF NATIVE AMERICANS IN FILM AND TELEVISION HAVE DEEP roots in American culture.[1] The problem is not so much that the stories told in the entertainment media have excluded Native Americans, but that their inclusion misrepresents them, their history, and their treatment by whites. One critic argues that the commercial movies about Native Americans are objectively racist on all levels.[2] A continuing fascination with Indians, yet a resistance to representing them and their history with whites accurately, is evident in the frequent, yet superficial, retellings of James Fenimore Cooper's *The Last of the Mohicans*, in which the novel's main theme about the destruction of Native Americans is lost to the romanticizing of a white man's quest.[3] Their selective exclusion and stereotyping and the political themes found in movies including Indians demonstrate the entertainment media's use of Native Americans to promote the dominant ideology.

EXCLUSION AND SELECTIVE EXCLUSION OF NATIVE AMERICANS IN ENTERTAINMENT MEDIA

More than 2,000 Hollywood films have depicted Native Americans.[4] In fact, some of the earliest film images were of Indians. These include a Sioux ghost dance recorded by Thomas Edison in 1894 and *Buffalo Bill's Wild West* show recorded in 1898. Since 1909, there have been thirteen English film versions of *The Last of the Mohicans*.[5] Native Americans' film images are limited to certain genres, geographies, and historical periods. Therefore, as Westerns receded in popularity, Native Americans became less visible in films.[6] The Stage Actors' Guild reported that only 0.37 percent of acting roles in 2001 went to Native Americans.[7]

Westerns were common television fare in the late 1950s and early 1960s.

Gunsmoke (1955–1975), *Wagon Train* (1957–1965), and *Bonanza* (1959–1973) lack major or even secondary Indian characters. The shows are about white people, and Native Americans are usually merely nameless foils or threats or are excluded. *Cheyenne* (1957–1963), *Law of the Plainsman* (1959–1963), and *The Lone Ranger* (1949–1957) do feature continuing Indian characters in roles supportive of whites. During one season, a Cheyenne chief is the central character in *Brave Eagle* (1955–1956); he is presented as sympathetic and doomed.[8]

The first major modern-day Indian character appeared on television in the title role for *Hawk* (1966). Burt Reynolds played the half-Iroquois New York City policeman in this short-lived drama. The second major Indian character, a Navajo deputy sheriff in New Mexico, appeared in *Nakia* (1974–1975). Both shows lasted only three months. After fifteen years of virtual invisibility on television, two major Native American characters were included in the Alaska comedy *Northern Exposure* (1990–1995). *Lakota Woman: Siege at Wounded Knee* (1994) included a large Indian cast (90 percent of the roles) and crew (40 percent).[9] The title character of *Walker, Texas Ranger* (1993–2001) was part Native American.[10] Despite these examples, little progress has been made over time. A report on diversity in television reported that Native Americans were invisible in 2001.[11]

When not excluded, Native Americans appear in certain kinds of films and roles that are not affirming, and an amalgamated Hollywood Indian masks tribal and individual differences.[12] Even *Northern Exposure* "dilutes native identity to one generic form."[13] It creates anonymous tribes with Tlingit cultural identifiers and the Athabaskan's geographic locations. Cultural studies scholar Annette Taylor argues that this is "akin to fabricating a Canadian town in Mexico or identifying New Yorkers as the majority population of Louisiana: It is ridiculous."[14]

The Western genre draws on the historical period of frontier expansion (mid- to late 1800s) and is set in the Great Plains or the Southwest.[15] Because the images of Indians are so limited in time and so devoid of contemporary attention, Native Americans appear to the modern audience to be visually extinct. It is as if they have "vanished somewhat mysteriously, along with the bison and the open prairie."[16] Even sympathetic films like *The Vanishing American* (1925) treat them as "emblematic of the past, rather than as viable participants in the world of the present."[17]

Even when tribes are identified by name, selective exclusion goes on. Some tribes are absent from films while others get most of the attention. By the late 1990s, there were around six hundred films about Apaches, probably because their history made them better bad guys since they had aggressively resisted white intrusions.[18] Westerns also tend to exclude Indian women or present them as minor unnamed characters.[19]

Tribes are often inaccurately rendered.[20] For example, *A Man Called Horse* (1970) identifies the tribe as Lakotas but gives them other tribes' hairstyles, tipi designs, and rituals.[21] Although there have been some improvements in the use of authentic costumes and customs, there has been little progress in representing the "subjective American Indian experience."[22]

Indians become "generic" in most films and television that ignore tribal culture, history, and differences.[23] Oneida actor/comedian Charlie Hill calls this "a weird sort of Indian stew."[24] This "stew" haphazardly combines different tribes' dress, religious rituals, speech, and physical stature to create a hybrid Hollywood Indian who "exists nowhere but within the fertile imaginations of its movie actors, producers, and directors."[25] In this way, films reflect whites' views of Indians.[26]

The frequent casting of white actors (or Latinos, blacks, or even Japanese) to play Indian lead parts goes beyond the denial of tribal uniqueness.[27] In the 1950s, white actors darkened their skin to "play Indian" in films. Burt Lancaster appeared scantly clad in *Apache* (1954).[28] Thirty years later, Raquel Welch played a Sioux in *The Legend of Walks Far Woman* (1984).[29] Chicano A. Martinez starred in *Powwow Highway* (1989). Since the Hollywood Indian comes from the white imagination, white impersonations of them are considered "more believable" by whites.[30] *Smoke Signals* (1998) screenplay writer Sherman Alexie argues that it is essential to cast Indians as Indians because their "performances are not the result of years of training and study on how to 'act' like an Indian. They are the result of years of living as an Indian, of years of 'being' Indian."[31]

Also excluded are Indian voices and points of view.[32] Indians in films are often literally seen and not heard.[33] The wooden Indian, silent and suffering, silent and stupid, or silent and scary, and the yelling hordes in Western stampedes fail to articulate a Native American point of view.[34] Even during the 1960s, when television was dominated by Westerns, Indians served only as "foils or backdrops to the stories of how the West was won."[35] Westerns put white characters in the foreground and Indians in the background.[36] Films supposedly sympathetic to Indians (*Soldier Blue*, 1970; *Little Big Man*, 1970; and *Dances with Wolves*, 1990) still use white main characters to tell the stories.[37] Some scholars believe that even when Native Americans are literally in a film, they may be symbolically absent from the story because they serve as surrogates for other alienated groups (such as hippie white youth in *Little Big Man*).[38]

STEREOTYPES OF NATIVE AMERICANS IN ENTERTAINMENT MEDIA

In *The White Man's Indian*, historian Robert F. Berkhofter Jr. examines the history of Indian imagery created by whites from Columbus to the late 1970s. He argues that these representations reveal much about white people's values, fears, and sense of self because Indians were seen as alien and the antithesis of whites. Despite witnessing differences between Native individuals and tribes, whites have continued to talk about and consider them as one "separate and single other."[39] They have been described and judged according to their differences from whites. "That Indians lacked certain or all aspects of white civilization could be viewed as bad or good depending upon the observer's feelings about his own society and the use to which he wanted to put the image."[40] As a result, three major conceptions of Indians have dominated white representations of them. They are the "good Indian," the "bad Indian," and the "degraded Indian."[41]

The good Indian is friendly, courteous, hospitable, attractive, strong, modest, calm, dignified, brave, tender, and appreciative of nature. The bad Indian is lecherous, vane, promiscuous, brutal, cruel, cannibalistic, dirty, lazy, dishonest, and superstitious. The degraded Indian has succumbed to white influence and lost his "Indianness" without being able to assimilate. He carries the vices of both societies. He is degenerate, poor, often drunken, and beyond redemption.[42]

The notion of a noble savage encompasses both the "good" and "bad" Indian and has a long history in literature, film, and television. Early settlers evoked this idea in letters they wrote about the primitive, yet admirable, qualities of Native Americans.[43] They felt ambivalent about Indians whom they saw as both helpful and mysterious.[44] Some of the more recent Westerns draw on this contradictory stereotype, which combines the good and bad elements of the stereotypes to make points about the mixed blessing of modernity or the flawed rationale behind the Vietnam War.[45] Rather than tackle the complexity of individual Indians being both noble and savage, much television and film tends to represent some Indians as "good" (the noble ones) and others as "bad" (the savage ones). While *Dances with Wolves* tries to handle the complexities of individual Native characters, it also uses the good/bad dichotomy when the Wise Elder accepts "the inevitability of white domination, whereas younger hotheads protest."[46]

The movie *Broken Arrow* (1950), a story about the signing of a treaty between the American government and the Apache in 1870, is a good example of the contrast drawn between "good" and "bad" Indians. Chief Cochise is shown as cooperative with the U.S. government liaison and Geronimo is shown as a troublemaker who refuses to sign a peace agreement. Scholar Frank Manchel describes how this dualistic representation of the two Indian leaders misrepresents Geronimo's position and exaggerates the conflict between the two leaders.[47]

Good Indian Stereotypes: Helpers and Victims

What makes the good Indian good is his or her alliance with whites.[48] Good Indians have something to offer whites, which may or may not be accepted,[49] such as knowledge, assistance, material goods, or compliance. Good Indians include those who accommodate white aggression.[50] They are romanticized, but powerless, and come in different versions: the "cooperative helper," the "child of nature," and the "stoic victim."

> They are physically strong, but structurally impotent. Constantly, they represent a dying culture, even when not dying themselves, as they are loved by more powerful White women, or serve as the sidekick for more powerful White men. They evoke admiration and pity, but they are not a threat.[51]

The good Indian as helper held a prominent place on early television in the form of the *Lone Ranger*'s Tonto, a stereotypically good (generic) Indian with the "pinto pony, broken English dialect, fringed buckskin attire, and secondary status relative to the White hero."[52] In Western films, the good Indians cooperate with the government and white settlers. Apache Chief Cochise is the good Indian in *Broken Arrow* when he signs a treaty with the U.S. government.[53] In *Tell Them Willie Boy Is Here* (1969), the good Indian tries to teach whites the meaning of love.[54]

Women can also be good Indians when they take the form of "Indian princesses" who are attracted and devoted to white men. While these films might sound socially progressive in their flirtation with interracial coupling, they ultimately keep the couple apart in a way that is both sexist and racist. Essentially, these women represent "the virgin land that will be possessed by the White man."[55] The movies tend to sacrifice the Indian princesses (*Broken Arrow*; *The Man Who Loved Cat Dancing*, 1973; and *A Man Called Horse*). The death of the Indian princess shows that men are worth more than women; her desire and sacrifice shows that white men are more desirable than Indian men.[56]

The animated *Pocahontas* (1995) celebrates a self-sacrificing helper, child of nature, and teacher of white men.[57] Like many films, *Pocahontas* revises white–Native American history, rendering it more mutually cooperative than it actually was. The film makes it seem like the Indians are on equal footing with the settlers and avoids dealing with the history of white conquest. Probably not coincidentally, Pocahontas is shown as the wisest Indian in the film and the most similar to the settlers.[58] As anthropologist S. Elizabeth Bird points out,

> No one could deny that Pocahontas bears little relationship to history. The voluptuous, dark-skinned beauty and her blond, square-jawed suitor, both appearing to be in their twenties, are a far cry from the (probably) twelve-year-old Pocahontas and (probably) forty-two-year-old Captain John Smith. It seems fairly certain that whatever happened between them did not include falling in love.[59]

Like Pocahantas, the good Indian knows much about nature.[60] This assumption has its roots in the European romantic's view of the noble savage as "living in unspoiled wilderness, spiritually pure, uncorrupted by civilization and one with nature."[61] Indians have come to symbolize "New Age spiritual values . . . wise, mystic shaman and guardians of environment."[62] The 1992 film version of *The Last of the Mohicans* emphasized Indians' harmony with nature.[63]

One specific version of the good Indian who has knowledge of nature is the "wise elder." He is a desexualized, peace-loving man portrayed as isolated from other Indians and helpful to whites who seek spiritual redemption and truth. He can be found in *One Flew over the Cuckoo's Nest, Dances with Wolves, Free Willy* (1993), and *Legends of the Fall* (1994), as well as in television episodes of *Walker, Texas Ranger* and *Touched by an Angel* (1994–2003).[64] Two prominent examples in television advertising from the 1970s include the Mazola Margarine corn maiden and the Indian who silently shed a tear when people littered in the "Keep America Beautiful" public service commercial.[65] Examples from *Star Trek: The Next Generation* (1987–1994) include a "space-age shaman of a futuristic Taos Pueblo space colony" who was a "New Age mentor."[66] Marilyn, the silent sidekick in *Northern Exposure*, often fits the role of the "wise saintly chief."[67]

The good Indian is also a stoic victim, "honorable and brave, yet [the target] of racism."[68] *Cheyenne Autumn* (1964) shows the dignity of the beaten Cheyenne as they walk hundreds of miles to return to their homeland.[69] The "doomed Indian" is one version of the stoic victim. He "knows his time is past, but accepts it with honorable resignation."[70] Revisionist Westerns, such as *Little Big Man*, lead the audience to side with the Indians by showing the murder of peaceful Indian women and having the main character identify with the Indians.[71] Yet, this main character is played by Dustin Hoffman, showing that the best good Indian is a white person.

Bad Indian Stereotypes: Sadistic Warriors

Bad Indians get in the way of white people and their interests. They are portrayed as "evil, sadistic, blood thirsty, 'Redskins,' warriors in war paint and feathers, ready to ravish white women and massacre white folk trying to carve homes for themselves on the frontier."[72] This savage representation of exaggerated and oversimplified brutality reflects white fears and some envy for qualities essentialized as "Indian."

Warriors were shown as bad Indians in that they did not fight fairly and instead committed inhuman act of violence.[73] "Especially in Western films, the bloodthirsty, war-crazed Indian has been Hollywood's stock in trade," typically including an Indian raid to establish extreme cruelty.[74] This savagery was often so horrendous that it was not shown or described; instead, the reactions of the main white characters would convey its hideousness (much like a low-budget horror film).[75] Music that accompanied Indians on screen also invoked "a sense of threat and suspense."[76] Although Westerns showed whites shooting Indians, they left the most extreme brutality (like mutilation and torture) to Indians.[77]

This Indian-as-warrior image is at odds with the farming and fishing cultures of most tribes. Focusing on the Indian as warrior allows movies to use action, high death counts, and white victories to appeal to a mainstream audience.[78] It also serves to justify explicitly racist dialog, punishments for violating racial sexual segregation, and story lines that demonstrate the evil consequences of having any Indian blood.[79] The warrior images make it seem acceptable for a film to celebrate Indian deaths and grieve white ones.[80] Recent films, such as *Predator* (1987) and *Indian in the Cupboard* (1995), continue to naturalize the warrior instincts of Indians.[81] While the warrior image emphasizes how violent Indians are, it also manages to show them as incompetent[82] or as mentally inferior to whites.[83] Since films show Indians outnumbering whites and still being defeated,[84] they become ideal "emblems of the downtrodden, the impoverished, and the vanquished."[85]

Degraded Indian Stereotypes

Degraded Indian stereotypes show Indians as weak, unsuccessful, mentally deficient, or chemically dependent. Portrayed as inherently inferior to whites, they are infantilized, shown as children "incapable of taking on adult responsibilities—especially governing themselves."[86] They might also appear naive and gullible[87] and as used for white gain like the drugged out Seminoles in *Adaptation* (2002).

Inferiority can also be demonstrated by showing whites as more masterful than Indians. The portrayal of Indian languages in film and television (as simple grunts, sounds, and one-syllable words)[88] equates Indians with animals.[89] In a reversal of historical fact, whites are shown teaching Indians how to grow corn in *Apache*.[90] Drunken Indians characterize Indians in general as weak and beyond help (*Tell Them Willie Boy Is Here*).[91]

Some of the images of intellectual inferiority are meant to be funny. They trivialize and mock Native Americans, making them look like buffoons.[92] This comic image appears in Western spoofs like the Marx Brothers' *Go West!* (1940) and Abbott and Costello's *Ride 'Em Cowboy* (1942).[93] "This Indian was simple and simple-minded, a comedic foil usually speaking in a dialect that can only be described as 'baby' English."[94] The name Tonto (from the *Lone Ranger* television series) literally means "fool, dunce, or dolt" in Spanish.[95] The drunken Indians are also sometimes played for laughs.[96]

SYSTEM-SUPPORTIVE THEMES AND MESSAGES

Since the reality of the United States' history of genocide against indigenous people is difficult to accept in a modern context, films and entertainment television that include Native Americans serve to deny, justify, or forgive the atrocities committed against them. Mythologizing history can do all three. Denial comes from excluding certain facts or distorting them so that the injustices are hidden. Justifications can also come from using the theories of the time that propelled the actions, portraying Indians as villains who deserved what they got. Forgiving comes from admitting the wrongs and claiming that they were historical exceptions, the fault of specific bad or crazy whites, and denying that Indians are still victimized.

Westerns reached their peak popularity in the 1950s, but they never disappeared. It can be argued that the genre was seriously altered during the 1960s and 1970s because the Vietnam War shed doubt on the morality of expansionism.[97] Some scholars refer to Westerns produced during this time as revisionist Westerns (in contrast with traditional ones).[98] Others posit the emergence during this period of "sympathetic Westerns," beginning with *Broken Arrow* in which Jimmy Stewart's character goes from Indian fighter to Indian friend and spouse.[99] Another school of thought holds that there have always been more and less progressive representations of Native Americans' history with whites.[100] Roberta E. Pearson's analysis of silent films about the Battle of Little Big Horn (also known as Custer's Last Stand) illustrates that they "reflected and refracted the complex and contradictory position and representation of Native Americans within contemporary U.S. society and culture."[101]

While there are some variations in Westerns, it is important to remember that the basic conception of Indians has persisted more than it has changed, regardless of the intellectual or political climate,[102] because the dominant racial ideology has remained the same. The narratives have been adjusted to hide, explain, or forgive it.

Distorting History and Justifying It

For whites, Western expansion was part of the American Dream, which included a new beginning, individualism, and open spaces of opportunity.[103] Both government policy and popular mythology asserted that it was the white man's manifest destiny to move westward and to conquer the wilderness and whatever got in the way.[104] The literature of the mid-1800s followed government policies that defined Indians as a problem that obstructed this expansion.[105] Long after the expansion occurred, film and television continued to justify this history in Westerns.[106]

Westerns tell stories from white people's points of view. These viewpoints do not acknowledge that Indians were fighting to survive, while whites were fighting for material acquisitions.[107] Fights are individualized and decontexualized in Westerns by putting a white character at the center of the narrative for audiences to identify with and showing Indians as inhuman aggressors. This allows any violence against Native Americans to be seen as understandable self-defense.

One way to justify military action against Indians in Westerns was to "prominently feature white women and children who are jeopardized by an Indian presence, their jeopardy automatically justifying the military actions of the Cavalry."[108] A "captivity narrative," which tells the story of Indians stealing white women or children, promoted fear of Indian males by coupling sexuality with aggression. Although rapes of white women by Native Americans were rare, news reports and fictional accounts of it were common in the mid-1800s. Captivity stories were common in the literature of the time and later repeated often in films.[109]

The changes and omissions in *Broken Arrow* nicely illustrate how a film text can be based upon a historical event but told in a way that sidesteps government culpability. In this film, a Euro-American perspective is used to tell a story about the negotiation of a U.S.-Apache treaty. The story ignores the failure of the government to honor previously recognized territorial rights.[110] The film's treatment of the Chiricahua Apache culture minimizes the importance of land to their lives; it ignores the diseases, devastation, and disruption brought by Euro-Americans to Native American society; and it legitimates the treaty signed between Cochise and the U.S. government. Its characterization of the relationship between Cochise and Jeffords (the government official) grossly distorts the experiences of both men, misrepresents their motives for peace, and callously ignores the consequences of their tragic treaty.[111]

Distorting History to Forgive It

Revisionist Westerns relegate racism to history by admitting that something bad happened long ago. These stories acknowledge some of what was done against Indians during Western expansion and provide sympathetic representations of Native Americans. By acknowledging this, the white audience gets to feel absolved of guilt for what their predecessors did.

Early attempts to rethink the Western genre (*The Searchers*, 1956, and *Cheyenne Autumn*) include showing the white violence against Indians and a reason for Indian rage.[112] In later films, like *Tell Them Willie Boy Is Here* (1969), killing Indians is presented as morally wrong.[113] *Little Big Man* treats Indians as "amiable and moral—and victimized—characters for whom the audience has great empathy." It shows the virtues of the Cheyenne and conveys "regret for the destruction of a culture in the name of progress."[114]

Little Big Man demythologizes westward expansion and gives Indians the high ground. The moral center of the film is Chief Old Lodge Skins (a wise elder), even though the main character (Jack) is white. Jack lives and empathizes with the Cheyenne and criticizes American imperialism.[115] The film indicts white culture as "artificial, deceitful, fraudulent, greedy, and intolerant."[116] This box-office hit was especially popular with a youth audience critical of American foreign policy at the time.[117] Having white characters side with the Indians gave modern white audiences someone to identify with. Being able to identify with open-minded Jack instead of the racist white authorities eased the audience's white guilt. This technique was also used in *Dances with Wolves*.[118]

Placing the blame for atrocities in the hands of a few bad or crazy white people, rather than portraying the problem as systemic, can also soften guilt. This is done in *Little Big Man* by making General Custer appear crazy.[119] Putting blame on certain bad Indians can also do the trick. So can spreading the blame around.

Whites are absolved in narratives that universalize prejudice and cruelty across races. This tells the audience that both sides were to blame. For instance, both the Indians and the whites sing the derogatory song "Savages! Savages!" thereby stereotyping each other in *Pocahontas*.[120] Movies like *Dances with Wolves*, *Little Big Man*, and *Broken Arrow* include scenes in which the white protagonists are forced to experience the violence of whites, to witness white violence toward Indians, and to witness Indian violence toward whites.[121] These illustrate how both groups are victims and villains. While better than Westerns that demonize Indians and romanticize whites as the good guys, these films do not acknowledge a policy of genocide and continue to center around heroic whites.

While the captivity narrative is used in some Westerns to justify killing Indians (because they were "naturally" sexual brutes), it is also used to help audiences forgive the past. It does this by romanticizing the captivity for both parties. Rather than raping and killing captured white women, Indian men fall in love with them. Their attraction to white women indicates their desire for white culture and its superiority to their own. The Indian man's ultimate loss or relinquishing of the white woman (*Follow the River* 1995) demonstrates Indians' inevitable vulnerability, powerlessness, and forgiveness. Reconciliation of the couple at the end (amid a decimated Indian village, as in *Stolen Women, Captured Heart* 1997) shows that "love conquers all."[122] It also makes the fate of these individuals more important than that of the collective.

Stories that feature good Indians helping whites "explain to whites their right to be here and help deal with lingering guilt about the displacement of native inhabitants."[123] Pocahontas and Squanto stories tell us that white conquest was inevitable. Television's *Dr. Quinn, Medicine Woman* (1993–1998), a program set in a post–Civil War Cheyenne village, tries to lead viewers "to see the destruction of Indian culture as both inevitable and as somehow accidental."[124] The show uses good Indians to explicitly forgive and absolve "progressive" audiences of historical "mistakes."[125]

Protesting Negative Images and Messages

Prominent Native Americans joined Latinos in protesting film stereotypes as far back as the early 1900s.[126] They sent a delegation to talk to President

Robert Taft about their representation in films.[127] In 1949, the Association on American Indian Affairs interest group created film committees to monitor and counsel Hollywood on Indian's film representation.[128] Despite these examples, Native Americans have generally lagged behind other ethnic groups in lobbying Hollywood.[129] Only in the last few decades have Indian activists and interest groups had some impact on film content.[130]

In one of their successes, Native Americans challenged misrepresentations in a made-for-television adaptation of the novel *Dark Wind* (1992). One of their objections was the casting. Not only did a non-Native (Lou Diamond Phillips) receive the central role of a Navajo policeman, but Native American casting ignored physical tribal differences. Specifically, a six-foot Indian (Gary Farmer) was cast to play a member of a tribe of diminutive stature (Hopi). Both the Navajo and Hopi tribal governments considered the story line offensive on spiritual grounds. Both tribes lodged complaints, and as a result, the film was not released in America.[131]

More activist attention has been paid to changing the names and images used in advertising and sports than to film and television representations.[132] Many campaigns against the use of Indian mascots have succeeded.[133]

> Sports mascots simply provide a convenient and highly visible example of the deeper issue, but because of this visibility, they can act as a catalyst for collective action among Native Americans and a tool that can be used to attempt to educate and sensitize people.[134]

Other protests have been launched against product names and advertising. Crazy Horse's grandnephew, Big Crow, tried to stop the naming of a beer after the Sioux leader. He claimed that it insulted Crazy Horse's legacy and insensitively ignored the problem of alcoholism among Native Americans. A federal judge ruled on behalf of the Hornell Brewing Company on the grounds of free speech.[135] Native Americans advocacy groups were more successful at getting Budweiser to stop advertising its product in Great Britain by using images of a beer-guzzling Indian.[136]

CREATING ALTERNATIVE IMAGES AND MESSAGES

Scholar Ted Jojola argues that for groundbreaking progress to occur, a Native director or producer needs to "[break] into the ranks of Hollywood, hopefully to challenge the conventional credos of the industry from within."[137] Native Americans have made some efforts to create their own entertainment images and fight mainstream stereotypes, but most of this has been from outside the Hollywood film system in independent films.

Native Americans have only recently begun writing, directing, and producing films. The Indian Actor's Workshop started in the early 1960s, and the

American Indian Registry for the Performing Arts was organized in the 1980s, but neither made much progress in getting Native American actors into films, much less in gaining control of films. In fact, casting non-Indians to play Native parts spiked in the 1980s. Finally, in 1992 the Native American Producer's Alliance was born.[138] The alliance created a "Producer's Statement" articulating a commitment to "quality and culturally appropriate productions involving Native Americans."[139]

Seasons of Grandmothers (1980) was an early effort at creating a film with a tribal point of view. It tells the intergenerational story of families of the Nez Perce tribe. Another film, *Return of the Country* (1985), presents a comic reversal of Native-white relations.[140] The docu-drama, *The Trial of Standing Bear* (1989), used a Standing Rock Sioux cinematographer and a Creek-Seminole assistant director.[141]

Powwow Highway was based on a novel by Indian rights activist Huron David Seals.[142] Although the movie was criticized because a Chicano played the lead role, Native Americans played many of the other major characters.[143] The film brought Native Americans into a contemporary setting rather than using the romantic nostalgia of historical films.[144] The film saw a limited release by Warner Brothers[145] and had low viewership.[146] An important advancement for Native Americans on television was the widely viewed HBO film *Grand Avenue* (1996), which focuses on urban Indian life. It was coproduced and written by Pomo/Miwok Greg Sarris.[147]

Not until 1998 did an Indian direct a major motion picture. Arapaho Chris Eyre directed and coproduced *Smoke Signals* with Sherman Alexie, a Spokane who wrote the screenplay. Religion professor Mara Donaldson argues that *Smoke Signals* is about the Native characters' redemption, showing how they transcend "the apocalyptic history of their tribe" and find "reconciliation with their past."[148] According to its screenplay author, *Smoke Signals* demonstrates the beauty of the reservation and breaks stereotypes by showing "the kind of powerful Indian I've known all my life."[149] Like most independent films, it had a limited release.[150]

These are examples of the type of films needed to tell new stories about Native Americans. Yet, they are a small contribution to a long history of Native Americans in film that is dominated by the images of "savages on the warpath." Communications scholar Ward Churchill argues,

> Only a completely false creation could be used to explain in "positive terms" what has actually happened here in centuries past. Only a literal blocking of modern realities can be used to rationalize present circumstances. Only a concerted effort to debunk Hollywood's mythology can alter the situation for the better.[151]

CONCLUSION

The image of Native Americans in film and television entertainment is a narrowly defined one. They are mostly found in Westerns that show them in one historical period and place. Even though the Western is a genre in decline, the traditional John Wayne versions are still shown on television and available in the rental stores. With little to counterbalance it, the representation of Native Americans in these Westerns is still dominant in mainstream entertainment.

The notion that Indians are noble savages is promoted through various representations of "good" and "bad" Indians. The good Indian stereotypes include the cooperative helper, child of nature, wise elder, Indian princess, and stoic victim. The bad Indian is a savage killer whose murder is justified by his actions. The remaining Indian characters tend to be powerless fools and drunks. Native American characters are provided with power either because they are "one with nature" or because they are "beasts." Both images draw on a "physical versus mental" dichotomy, positioning Indians as inferior to whites. Native Americans have only begun to protest these representations successfully and to produce more realistic and complex ones.

5

Hispanics in Film and Television Entertainment

~~~~~~

HISPANICS ARE PRESENTED IN TELEVISION ENTERTAINMENT AND FILMS IN LIM-
ited ways that simultaneously reinforces their inferior status while denying
that it exists. This is done through exclusion, stereotyping, and the system-
supportive stories that are told about them. Hispanics are underrepresented
in entertainment. When they appear, they tend to be criminalized, sexualized, or demeaned. Film messages say that their best path to success is assimilation, but that it is a perilous road. The Hispanic press and Hispanic social
groups and filmmakers have challenged these representations and imagined
new ones.

EXCLUSION AND SELECTIVE EXCLUSION OF
HISPANICS IN ENTERTAINMENT MEDIA

Relative to their numbers in the population, Hispanics have been drastically
underrepresented in television entertainment,[1] and little progress has been
made in the number of television roles they play. During the 1950s, when
Cuban American Desi Arnez Jr. starred in the early *I Love Lucy* (1951–1957)
sitcom, 3 percent of the characters on television were Hispanic. By the mid-
1990s, this percentage had dropped to 1 percent.[2] By the fall of 1999, 2.9 percent of prime-time characters were Hispanic. Since the number of Hispanics
in the United States has increased to almost 12 percent according to the 2000
census, their underrepresentation has worsened over time.[3] When film roles
are included, their percentage representation improves slightly. The Screen
Actors Guild reported that Hispanics held 4.8 percent of film and television
roles in 2001.[4] Not until the late 1980s did a television show focus on a Hispanic family.[5] This show, *A.K.A. Pablo* (1984), was short-lived. Others that

followed lasted a little longer. They include: *Resurrection Boulevard* (2000–2002), *American Family* (2000–2004), and *The George Lopez Show* (2000–).

In addition to being scarce, Hispanics are also selectively excluded from television and film in four major ways. First, they appear primarily in specific genres. For instance, Mexican Americans appear in Westerns that take place in the Southwest;[6] Puerto Ricans appear in crime films set in cities. Second, Hispanics with different national heritages are treated as interchangeable. For example, Jennifer López played the title character of Mexican American *Selena* (1997) despite being of Puerto Rican descent. The different histories, cultures, and experiences of Mexican Americans, Cuban Americans, and Puerto Ricans are not recognized in the narratives or characters. Instead, they are treated as indistinguishable. Third, white actors play Hispanic characters, resulting in misrepresentation and limited opportunities for Hispanic actors. The lead Puerto Rican roles in the award-winning *West Side Story* (1961) were played by white actors Natalie Wood and George Chakiris.[7] Recent examples include Italian American Marissa Tomei starring in *The Perez Family* (1995) and another Italian American, Nicholas Tortorro, playing a Hispanic on *NYPD Blue* (1999).[8] Fourth, Hispanic cultural identifiers are avoided in films that include Hispanic characters and actors. Actors of Hispanic descent play white characters in order to get lead roles that are otherwise unavailable to them.[9] For example, Anthony Quinn played the title role in *Zorba, The Greek* (1964) and Jennifer López played an Italian American in *Out of Sight* (1998). Some roles played by Hispanics were written with whites in mind. Therefore, they lack the sociopolitical contexts that would make them authentic representations. Scholar Carlos Cortés argues that the flawed characters from what he calls "the Golden Age of Hispanic film" (1945–1970) were actually preferable to the current images that lack any cultural uniqueness.[10] "Give me those strong, intelligent Chicana prostitutes anytime over the current carload of Hispanic Barbie-doll characters."[11] Linda Williams explains,

> Although one might think that the natural opposition to stereotype would be to individualize the kind of characters who have so often been stereotyped in the past, in fact, this very effort often ends by adopting the representational forms of the dominant Anglo culture—forms which implicitly negate any real differences between the Anglo and the Chicano experience.[12]

STEREOTYPES OF HISPANICS IN ENTERTAINMENT MEDIA

Particular stereotypes dominate the representations of Hispanics in film and television entertainment. These stereotypes sexualize both women and men. Villainous representations of Hispanic men include sexually threatening males, criminals, gang members, drug dealers, and illegal aliens. More than whites, blacks, or Asian Americans, Hispanic characters are portrayed negatively on prime-time television.[13] Aggressiveness also forms part of one sexualized female Hispanic stereotype (the spitfire), but passivity and frivolity dominate the other two. Both men and women are also presented as clowns, victims, and simpletons.

Males: Violent Villains

Hispanics are predominantly stereotyped as violent criminals. This stereotype has a long history in literature and news coverage, predating film. Characterizations of Hispanics' cruel criminality were part of the propaganda during Texas's war for independence.[14] The Mexican "bandit" stereotype, or "the greaser," dates back to silent movies and early Westerns.[15] Charles Ramírez Berg calls this basic Hollywood stereotype "el bandido" and describes him as "treacherous, shifty, and dishonest."[16] He notes that the bandido is emotional, irrational, violent, and neither very smart nor ultimately successful. One version of the Hispanic villain is the "violent-tempered but ultimately ineffective Puerto Rican man."[17]

The Hispanic villain image did not fall out of favor when Westerns did; it was simply transferred to the gang member or drug dealer in urban-violence films.[18] Other contemporary versions of the bandido include foreign drug runners, rebels, and dictators.[19] Clara E. Rodríguez argues that this historical association between Latinos and violence in film has grown in recent times with the extremely violent images presented in contemporary films like *Carlito's Way* (1993), *The Specialist* (1994), *American Me* (1992), *Mi Vida Loca* (1993), *El Mariachi* (1992), and *The Mambo Kings* (1992).[20] These images not only extend across time and various film genres but are also found on television. One study found that the "occupation" of criminal was the most common for Hispanics on a television series.[21]

Puerto Ricans are primarily portrayed as juvenile delinquents and criminals.[22] Statements like "All spics are good with a knife" (*The Young Savages*, 1961) essentialize the ethnicity as violent. These stereotypes are used in stories to justify actions taken against Hispanic characters by whites. For example, *Falling Down* (1993) stars Michael Douglas as a frazzled white man in Los Angeles who fights back. In one scene, he targets two Hispanic thugs.[23] This scene conveys the message that because violence is part of Hispanics' criminal "nature," violence against them is desirable and just.[24]

Films show that whites and Hispanics live in two different worlds. They define the "appropriate place" for Hispanic characters as the streets or prison.[25] Numerous, often nameless, criminal characters are found in television crime dramas, especially those set in Miami, New York, and Los Angeles. "*West Side Story* depicts a fight for urban space" in which Puerto Ricans threaten "white spaces."[26] In this fight, Puerto Rican gang members are shown as violent, primitive, and foreign. The white "Jets" gang members and a white policeman use racist language to talk about them.[27]

Males: Buffoons, Simpletons, and Lovers

The buffoon and simpleton stereotypes demean Hispanics by presenting them as having limited intellectual capacity. The Hispanic buffoon is a character to laugh at often because he speaks English so badly.[28] Buffoons are usually "second bananas," rarely at the center of a film.[29] Exceptions include the low-budget films of the comedy team Cheech and Chong. Films like *Up in Smoke* (1978) and *Cheech and Chong's Next Movie* (1980) put these clueless stoners at the center of the comedies. The buffoon's broken English earned laughs for "Jose Jimenez" on *The Ed Sullivan Show* (1948–1971) and for Ricky Ricardo on *I Love Lucy*, and it was still used as a source of humor in roles played by Paul Rodriquez and George Lopez.

The simpleton's inferiority is not always represented for comic relief. He is a mental defective or a "poor, ineffective, Puerto Rican 'loser'" in need of saving or demeaning.[30] This stereotype includes "brutish farmworkers" who are not very intelligent[31] and seemingly semiretarded (like the teenager in the *Blackboard Jungle*, 1955).[32] These characters are often overly emotional and ridiculed for their shortcomings.

Characteristics of the "Latin lover" are his "suavity and sensuality, tenderness, and sexual danger."[33] Latin lovers are typically presented as lighter-skinned members of the upper class and are more likely to be European than South or Latin American.[34] The Latin lover stereotype has some positive attributes (sexual prowess and good looks) and some negative ones (hypersexuality and irresponsibility).[35] The romantic Latin lover faded in the early 1930s and was eventually transformed into a gigolo,[36] although he has been resurrected to some extent by Spaniard Antonio Banderas (as in *Never Talk to Strangers*, 1995).[37]

The sexualized and villainous stereotypes are sometimes combined to show Hispanic men as sexual predators. Andy Garcia's character in *8 Million Ways to Die* (1986) and Al Pacino's in *Scar Face* (1983) are gangster/drug runner versions of this deviant stereotype.[38]

> Dark Latino men often provided interracial sexual threats to Anglo women, with Anglo men (usually Anglo cowboys) asserting their superiority by riding to the rescue of their racially-sexually threatened damsels and whipping the bumbling Mexican villains.[39]

Females: Sexual and Pitiful

While Latinas are less likely to be characterized as violent than their male counterparts, they are even more likely to be sexualized. The sexual images of Hispanic women vary in their explicitness and their narrative purpose. They tend to fall into two types: innocent-yet-desirable and hot-and-aggressive.[40] There, stereotypes also demean Latinas by treating them as pitiful or ridiculous.

Chicanas had a central presence in the film depictions of Hispanics in the 1930–1945 period identified by Carlos E. Cortés as the period of "Sexuality and Frivolity."[41] The roles played by major Mexican and Mexican American actresses of the time (Carmen Miranda, Dolores Del Río, and Lupe Vélez) demonstrate three different types of sexual images: frivolous, sensual but restrained, and lusty. All three were to be thought of as exotic entertainment for men, but they delivered on the promise of their sexuality differently.

Carmen Miranda usually played the sexy and frivolous roles, which provide a colorful exaggeration of Hispanic culture. She would be seen "dancing the samba with a bizarre headdress, belting out a hotly rhythmed Latin song, or speaking heavily accented lines."[42] These characters are in the background of stories about white characters in an exotic setting (such as *Nancy Goes to Rio*, 1950). The more desexualized version of this stereotype appears as exotic and frivolous but is campy rather than titillating.[43]

Dolores Del Río appeared during the 1920s and 1930s in film roles that demonstrated the second stereotype of restrained sensuality.[44] Del Rio eventually stopped making American films because of the narrowness of these roles and chose to star in cinema produced in Mexico.[45] Her appeal was in her aloofness, reserve, and opaqueness.[46] Such characters' desirability comes from their being "unknowable." This gives mystery to "the dark lady," but it also keeps the characters undeveloped. "She is mysterious, virginal, inscrutable, aristocratic—and alluring precisely because of these characteristics."[47]

Lupe Vélez's roles exemplified the third female stereotype, the "Mexican spitfire" or the "halfbreed harlot."[48] This character is hot-tempered and explosive.[49] Vélez appeared in seven films with the words "Mexican spitfire" in their titles (including *Mexican Spitfire's Baby*, 1941, and *Mexican Spitfire Out West*, 1940). Spitfires are lusty, hot-tempered, sexual, and a slave to their passions. They are sometimes prostitutes who "like the work."[50] The spitfires in contemporary films are "easy, supersexed, or violent and vulgar Latinas who fume and fornicate, without substance, and without much intelligence."[51] Although the spitfire can sometimes exhibit positive attributes (such as spunkiness, smarts, and action), she tends to have been "put in her place" by the end of the film.[52] For example, in *West Side Story*, both the spitfire and the alluring innocent meet with sad story resolutions.[53] *Six Days, Seven Nights* (1998) includes a recent version of this stereotype.[54]

The sexual stereotype and the victim stereotype are combined to punish Latina sexuality, especially when it goes outside the bounds of racial segregation. Hispanic women paired with white men tend to suffer negative consequences, typically by dying or watching their husbands die.[55] This is most often the case when the women are dark skinned.[56] Film victimization is not reserved for the spunky Hispanic women who fall in love with white men. It is also a common fate for characters identified by scholars as the "long suffering Fat Mama" and the "Poor Pean."[57]

SYSTEM-SUPPORTIVE THEMES AND MESSAGES

By using stereotypes to tell certain types of stories, movies and television entertainment can promote the idea that the political/social system works and does not need to be reformed. These include blaming Hispanics for the problems they have and by showing that good things happen to those who assimilate or do not make trouble for whites. Since this message is sometimes accompanied by the message that it is impossible for them to assimilate, it presents a double bind for Hispanics. They are doomed if they do not assimilate, but assimilating in not really an option for them.

Films reward passive traits in racial minorities (like cooperation and loyalty) and punish aggressive ones (like ambition and competitiveness). Hispanics are instructed not to rock the boat by threatening the dominant order.[58] Both victim and villain stereotypes locate problems' causes and solutions with individuals. Essentially, they show that there are "good" and "bad" Hispanics. The bad ones are personally flawed, come from bad families, or are deficient *because* they are Hispanic.[59]

Blaming dysfunctional families for Latino violence is a common theme in social-problem films like *The Young Savages*[60] and, more recently, *American Me*.[61] Poor Hispanic mothers are both pitied for being abandoned and blamed for being overprotective and smothering. They provide an explanation for why their sons are weak or Anglo-hating, which absolves discriminatory institutions.[62] The movies promote the conclusion that social institutions are not responsible for racial inequality and the ways in which Hispanics rebel against it. Therefore, Hispanic criminals (so common in films) are "social misfits and personally-inadequate victims."[63]

Whereas the crime narrative individualizes problems, the assimilation narrative individualizes solutions.[64] It celebrates the American Dream by showing that material success results from assimilation. Films tell Hispanics to give up "who you are for what you want to become."[65] Yet, these films also tend to include mixed messages about the desirability and efficacy of doing this. They show how Hispanic characters are doomed even when they do try to conform to white culture. The narratives show that the compromises assimilation requires cost characters too much, perhaps even their lives. This was the message in *La Bamba* (1987), a film about musician Ritchie Valens's transformation into a middle-class American rock star, whose life was cut short by a plane crash.[66] *Selena* (1997) depicts a female singer's initial success as dependent upon her staying close to her Spanish roots. Her fame among white audiences ends just as it gets started with her death at the hands of another Hispanic woman.

Some films provide a solution to the dilemma by showing upwardly mobile racial minorities who "go home" (to the barrio) after they learn that abandoning their culture is too high a price to pay for success.[67] The message here is that Hispanics can be "good Americans" by staying where they are (as individuals and a group).[68] Since such characters make this choice themselves, it does not represent discrimination or segregation imposed on them by an unfair social structure. This keeps the message system supportive. Urban missionary films that show whites attempting to save resistant Hispanics tend to characterize these youths as both violent and as victims.[69]

West Side Story celebrates assimilation and yet shows how it is ultimately an unworkable solution. It does this by asking the audience to root for Maria and Tony, an appealing romantic couple, but dooming their relationship. The film contains mixed messages. On one hand, Puerto Rican characters sing "America," which compliments the mainland United States and denigrates Puerto Rico. On the other, it ends with interracial hostility and segregation. The film denies that a racist society and racial inequality prevent (Puerto Rican) Maria and (Italian American) Tony from ending up together. It does this by having a Puerto Rican kill Tony at the end of the film.[70] This popular film seems to say that loving America and a white American is not enough to earn Maria a happy ending. In fact, we are led to believe that none of these bad things would have happened if Maria had "stayed in her place." Ultimately, *West Side Story* reinforces racism in the existing social structure rather than providing an assimilation alternative or celebrating racial and ethnic diversity.[71]

Film messages warning Hispanics not to rock the boat are not limited to sexual or romantic relations. They can also be more explicitly about politics. *Badge 373* (1973) depicts radicals for Puerto Rican independence as aligned with heroin dealers. "*Badge 373* criminalized the Puerto Rican independence movement. It made it appear that no law-abiding, rational Puerto Rican supported independence for Puerto Rico, only a small criminal fringe element."[72] The film was released in the same year that the U.S. government declared its position on Puerto Rican independence in opposition to the international community. The UN General Assembly approved a resolution affirming "the inalienable right to independence and self-determination for the Puerto Rican people."[73]

PROTESTING NEGATIVE IMAGES AND MESSAGES

Opposition to the criminal bandit image of Mexican Americans has a long history. In 1911, *La Crónica*, a weekly newspaper in Texas, aggressively attacked the treatment of Mexican Americans and Native Americans in movies. Additional support for this campaign came from other newspapers and from prominent Native Americans who lodged protests with the Bureau of Indian Affairs. For decades, native Texan Mexican newspapers continued to speak out against the stereotypes common in the Anglo popular culture of the time.[74] In the 1930s, criticism in Spanish-language newspapers nationwide and abroad convinced some Hispanic actors to refuse demeaning roles.[75]

In addition to concern voiced by Spanish newspapers, political organizations formed to fight discrimination in the media. These included some of the first Puerto Rican migrants after World War I.[76] The release of *Badge 373* "signaled the beginning of modern Puerto Rican protest against media stereotyping."[77] The Puerto Rican Action Coalition condemned the movie as racist because it "denigrated the Puerto Rican community" and "vividly expresses the lack of respect for the dignity of the Puerto Rican people."[78] Although demonstrations at the corporate headquarters and public outcry did not convince Paramount to stop distribution of the movie, the film was withdrawn from New York theaters after demonstrations and a bomb explosion at one film showing.[79]

In 1979, a group of community college students in Los Angeles formed the Gang Exploitation Film Committee to protest the negative images of Chicanas/os in the gang films prevalent in the late 1970s. They picketed and called for a boycott of *Boulevard Nights* (1979). This group was joined by other Chicano organizations (such as the Chicano Cinema Coalition and the actor's guild Nosotros). Their protest seems to have convinced Universal to drop some of the other gang films it had planned to produce.[80]

In 1980, efforts by the Committee against *Fort Apache* diminished the profitability of the film *Fort Apache, the Bronx* (1981). A statement by the committee illustrates how negative film images were a catalyst for political action: "It was a fighting movement which engaged the enemy on a number of fronts, added to the historical legacy of past battles, and advanced the starting point for the next struggles against media racism and for freedom."[81] In the 1990s, Latinos for Positive Images called for a boycott of *The Perez Family.*[82]

CREATING ALTERNATIVE IMAGES AND MESSAGES

The Chicano Film Culture (or Chicano Cinema) creates alternative images and messages to those found in Hollywood films. It began in the late 1960s as part of the Chicano political movement. It was "by, for, about" Chicanos with cultural politics at its core.[83] The goal was to counter the stereotypes in the mainstream media with "oppositional forms of knowledge about Chicanos," which "interjected onto the social/cultural imagination Chicano countervisions of history, identity, social reality, resistance politics."[84] The Chicano Cinema began by documenting social protests (marches, strikes, creation of a national political party, and protests) and later infused themes of resistance to oppression into more dramatic formats.[85] For example, while the film *Después del Terremoto* (1979) focuses on interpersonal relationships, the main character's boyfriend explicitly criticizes dictator Anastasio Somoza and the U.S. support for his regime.[86]

One of the first Chicano films was *I Am Joaquin* (1969), a visual representation of a poem by Rodolfo "Corky" Gonzales, the founder of Crusade for Justice (a Denver, Colorado, civil rights organization). The film reinterprets the history of Chicanos and ends with an image of political activism (marchers with the Farmworkers Union flag).

> The film, as well as the poem, was a call for revolutionary struggle. The film's combative, confrontational, and polemical style stems from the fact that its intended spectators were Chicana and Chicano audiences; it aimed to instruct them on their history and also to urge them to revolutionary action.[87]

The films of the Chicano Cinema celebrated a different cultural identity than the one denigrated through mainstream institutions.[88] They presented a collective rather than an individualistic vision, promoted identity politics over assimilation, and defined citizenship as cultural rather than national.[89] Although racial politics dominated their early films, critiques of sexism and classism were also present in many Chicana/o films.[90] The filmmakers had explicitly political intentions. They argued that "picking up the camera was equivalent to 'picking up the gun' in defense of civil and human rights in the United States."[91] In the words of Lillian Jiménz, the mother of the National Latino Film and Video Festival at El Museo del Barrio,

> These films and videotapes are our testament to survival. They forced us to look at ourselves, to step outside of our condition and objectify our reality, to deconstruct and then visually reconstruct it with a new vision and power extracted from that painful process. They allowed us to reflect on ourselves—the films were our passageway into ourselves.[92]

Hispanic filmmakers have begun to address more mainstream audiences and create commercial films as well as independent ones.[93] Some critics think that the need to make a profit compromises the political bite of films too much for them to be considered Chicano or Latino Cinema.[94] They criticize commercial films produced by Hispanics for not indicting systemic racial inequality or celebrating Chicano identity and culture. Others point to the impact Hispanic involvement in production has had on increasing the variation in Hollywood film images of Hispanics.[95]

Hispanic Americans have also been able to create alternative television entertainment programming through the use of Spanish-language networks, including Univisión, Galavisión, and Telemundo. These shows constitute a "second television world" for Spanish speakers. Although much of the programming is imported or dubbed U.S. commercial products, some shows have been created by Hispanics for Hispanics. These shows promote Hispanic family values and moral lessons and challenge some of the stereotypes on the major networks.[96]

CONCLUSION

This chapter illustrates how exclusion, selective exclusion, stereotypes, and system-supportive themes continue to work against Hispanic pride and empowerment. While Hispanics actively resist these messages and create new ones in Chicano and Latino films, negative stereotypes have not disappeared. They continue to demean, ridicule, and oversimplify Hispanics and to blame them for their status in society. When biographies of dead Hispanic singers tell stories of failed assimilation in *La Bamba* and *Selena*,[97] the sad endings are blamed on "bad luck" and "bad Hispanics."

6

Asian Americans in Film and Television Entertainment

~~~~~~

LIKE THE OTHER RACIAL-MINORITY GROUPS, ASIAN AMERICANS HAVE BEEN EX-
cluded from film and television roles. Those they have been given promote
stereotypes. These include inscrutable evil foreigners, China dolls, dragon
ladies, desexed sidekicks, criminals, nerds, and mystics. The themes that ac-
company Asian Americans in entertainment convey mixed messages. On one
hand, they criticize prejudice. On the other, they show that since white heroes fight injustice, the system needs no reform. These shows applaud assimilation but fail to show that Asian Americans can join the melting pot. Like
other racial-minority groups, Asian Americans have protested these representations and produced new, more complex ones.

EXCLUSION AND SELECTIVE EXCLUSION OF ASIAN AMERICANS IN ENTERTAINMENT MEDIA

Asian Americans, especially those of certain national origins (such as Filipinos, Vietnamese, and Cambodians), appear infrequently in American films
and television entertainment. Asian Americans also rarely play the leads[1] or
appear in musical variety shows or product endorsement ads.[2] Even in shows
that were set in Hawaii, where Asian Americans are the majority (*Big
Hawaii*, 1977; *Hawaii Five-O*, 1968–1980; *Magnum, PI*, 1980–1988), whites
are the main characters.[3] Similarly, television shows set in Asian countries
(*M*A*S*H*, 1972–1983; *Shogun*, 1980) are about white people and lack major
Asian characters.

One show that did star a Japanese American character was the short-lived
detective drama *Ohara* (1987–1988).[4] Another rare exception, the comedy
All-American Girl (1994–1995), was the first prime-time television show to

center around an Asian American family.[5] The show, starring Korean American comedian Margaret Cho, ran briefly.

White actors have played Asian American characters in movies.[6] Famous white actors such as Mary Pickford, Katherine Hepburn, Shirley MacLaine, Jerry Lewis, Peter Sellers, and Joel Grey have all "applied 'yellow face' to star in films."[7] Whites actors play Asian or Asian American roles in movies such as *Broken Blossoms* (1919),[8] *Love Is a Many Splendored Thing* (1937), and *The Good Earth* (1937).[9] White actors play the lead in a number of Charlie Chan films.[10] As recently as 1990, a white actress played the Vietnamese lead in the play *Miss Saigon*.[11] The use of heavy, yellow cream, exaggerated accents, and heavy wigs results in an inauthentic representation.[12]

Actors of Asian descent are excluded from lead roles on television, too. Despite working with the creators of *Kung Fu* (1972–1975), Bruce Lee did not get the role of Kwai Chang Caine in the television show[13] because he looked "too Asian."[14] Instead, the role went to white actor David Carradine, and the character was said to be half American and half Chinese. This casting decision influenced the story lines, making it easier for the writers to portray him as heroic.[15]

Asian American characters are even rarer than Asian American actors. Vietnamese villagers, Japanese soldiers, and Chinese communists are more common than Asian American characters. The appearance of Asian Americans in films and television during the late 1970s and the 1980s increased due to the prevalence of stories about the Vietnamese war.[16] Yet, it remained small. Even in the late 1990s, only 1.3 percent of the characters on television were Asian American, despite their comprising 3.6 percent in the population.[17] Only 2.5 percent of Stage Actor Guild contracts in 2001 went to Asians/Pacific Islanders.[18] On prime-time television in fall 1999, 0.8 percent of the characters on sitcoms and 1.9 percent of those in dramas were Asian American.[19]

When Asian Americans appear in films and television entertainment, they lack distinctive national origins. For example, *All-American Girl* blends aspects of different Asian cultures rather than appreciating that Americans of Korean, Chinese, and Japanese descent are not interchangable.[20] This lack of appreciation of the diversity within the Asian American community extends to how actors are selected. For example, in *The Children of An Lac* (1980), Filipino children portray Vietnamese orphans.[21]

STEREOTYPES OF ASIAN AMERICANS IN ENTERTAINMENT MEDIA

Asian Americans play certain stock characters in movies and television. These are unfavorable stereotypes that should be familiar to viewers. The dominant image is one of inscrutable and dangerous foreigners often possessing mystical or physical powers. This image can apply to either sex. Asian

American men are more often desexualized (helpmates, nerds, victims), while Asian American women are sexualized in two ways: as the passive China doll or fragile exotic, or as the seductive and manipulative dragon lady. Other Asian American stereotypes include nerds and mystics.

Inscrutable and Dangerous Foreigners

Because so many of the movies with Asian American actors are about Asians and not Asian Americans, they are looked at as foreigners. Since most of these stories about Asians show them as enemies or threats to the United States, they are presented as dangerous. Historically, this perception of a "yellow peril" has resulted in fear of Asia, Asians, and Asian Americans.

The source of the threat portrayed in entertainment has changed over time, responding to geopolitical events and international relations. For example, images of Vietnamese became more common and more negative during and after the Vietnam War. Vietnamese were portrayed as "crafty, devious, guerrilla warfare perpetrators of violence"[22] or as victims and prostitutes.[23]

In the 1920s, the most feared Asian country was China. Therefore, films of that time created nefarious Chinese characters. "From the evil Foo Chung, who tries to lure the hero of *Shane* (1921) into a life of crime to Wu Fang, who in *Ransom* (1928) prepares to torture the heroine when she fails to deliver a secret formula, a parade of evil Orientals graced the silent screen."[24] The Chinese Dr. Fu Manchu continued this stereotype of the diabolical movie villain in the 1930s in film and the 1950s on television.[25]

Since the Japanese were a greater threat during World War II, fictional Chinese villains diminished. Anticommunist sentiments in the late 1950s and 1960s helped fuel a resurgence of images of evil Chinese (such as those in *The Manchurian Candidate*, 1962).[26] When the Chinese threat receded again, the Fu Manchu character was reworked into a comic figure. Peter Sellers mocked him in *The Fiendish Plot of Dr. Fu Manchu* (1980),[27] as did Jerry Lewis did in *Hardly Working* (1981).[28]

World War II–era movies commonly presented Japanese soldiers as brutal and inhuman. The racism inherent in the film representation of this war enemy is evident when these images are contrasted with those of Anglo Germans and Italians. The German public in these films is represented as "respectable but misguided people under the influence of the Nazi regime"; the Japanese are shown "strafing Red Cross ships, bayoneting children, and delighting in applying torture techniques presumably handed down from centuries of malevolent practice."[29] Film historian Ralph R. Donald's analysis of feature-length Hollywood war films produced between 1941 and 1946 reveals an "antagonism, revulsion, and racial hatred for the Japanese that remains unmatched in filmed war propaganda either before or since."[30] Japanese were commonly referred to as monkeys or rats.[31]

Although Japanese were treated more sympathetically in the late-1950s and 1960s, negative images were revived in films in the 1980s (like *Gung Ho*, 1986), when the Japanese became a major economic competitor to the United States.[32] This demonizing of Japanese has implications for the portrayal of Japanese Americans.

Despite a long history in the United States, Japanese Americans are still presented on television as foreigners by focusing on recent immigrants and limited language skills. The frequent use of broken English is a "social marker that aurally reaffirms their status as aliens forever consigned to the margins of dominant society."[33] In addition to appearing non-American, Asian Americans can also look un-American because of the associations made in films and entertainment television between them and foreign Asian enemies. Even when presented as Asian American, villains are greedy, opportunistic hustlers, predators, and criminals.

Female Asian American Stereotypes: China Dolls and Dragon Ladies

Films include more Asian American women than Asian American men, although they tend to play minor roles.[34] Asian American women typically fit into two different stereotypes in film and television. While both are exotic and sexualized,[35] one is deferential and the other is aggressive. One is docile and submissive and the other diabolical.[36] "These two seemingly contradictory stereotypes were mobilized to posit the Asian woman's passive welcoming of the American male on the one hand and to reinforce the sexual perversity and moral depravity of Asians in general."[37] Both are sexually available either as prostitutes, like Suzie Wong; as "cute, giggling, dancing sex machines with hearts of gold"[38] and as sexual provocateurs, like Anna May Wong in her roles in the 1920s and 1930s;[39] or as victims (like those in the "China Girl" episode of *How the West Was Won*, 1978–1979).[40] Others, like the Hawaiian hula dancer, hold a sexual allure that is romanticized and exotic.[41]

The "China doll" (also called the "geisha girl" or "lotus blossom") presents Asian women as "exotic, subservient, compliant, industrious, eager to please."[42] A reoccurring image of Asian or Asian American women ready to please white men is the nameless prostitute.[43] Not all China dolls are explicitly sexualized, but all are deferential. For example, one of the first central television roles for a Japanese American was Mrs. Livingston, the dedicated housekeeper and surrogate mother in *The Courtship of Eddie's Father* (1969–1972).[44] Almost fifteen years later, another television war bride (Korean Soon-Lee in *AfterMASH*, 1983–1984) appeared as Klinger's wife; she was "the ideal companion or wife to white Americans who prefer 'traditional' women untainted by such quaint notions as gender equality."[45] These characters clearly present no ideological threat to the dominant order since they are passive and either desire or need white men's protection and attention.

The "dragon lady" represents Asian women as "inherently scheming, untrustworthy, and back-stabbing."[46] The most famous Asian American actress today, Lucy Liu, has played numerous mysterious, domineering, and seductive dragon lady roles, such as the sadomasochistic in *Payback* (1999), the cruel villain in *Kill Bill* (2003), and the cold manipulative lawyer (turned judge) on *Ally McBeal*. Tracey Owens Patton argues that the role of Ling Woo on *Ally McBeal* is particularly damaging because it is the only long-running image of Asian American women on television for years and because the stereotyping of Woo as a dragon lady is so extreme. Her entrances are accompanied by the music from *The Wizard of Oz* (1925) that signaled the wicked witch. She uses sexual tricks and secrets to manipulate men. In one segment of the show, she turns into an alien (showing how "foreign" she is).[47]

Although dragon ladies may seem assertive, white males usually neutralize their power by the end of the show. From *The Forbidden City* (1918) to *Flash Gordon* (1980), Chinese women have exhibited an uncontrollable attraction to white men that renders them vulnerable.[48] In "All or Nothing," an episode of *Wiseguy* (1987–1990), Tzu, a female Chinese American activist, is transformed from a woman who pickets a garment factory, saying that she "battles the evils of 'the system,' whatever form it may take," into "a kinky Asian female sex pot." A leading scholar of Asian Americans and media, Darrell Hamamoto writes, "Tzu might indeed be politically committed, the implied narrator seems to say, but deep down, all Yellow Women truly desire is to have sexual relations with White Man."[49]

The two stereotypes can coexist in a show, film, and even a character. Over a twenty-five-year period, only two Asian American characters appeared on the soap opera *All My Children*: a China doll, An Lee, a dutiful au pair;[50] and a desexualized dragon lady, a Chinese restaurant owner who pushed her son into medical school and away from his white girlfriend. Both characters had limited story lines and short tenure on the show. This female duality also appears in Jackie Chan's films, like *Rush Hour* (1998) and *Rush Hour 2* (2001), in which stereotypes of Asian women "are deployed for comic effects."[51] Trudy, from *The Single Guy* (1995–1997), "manages to evoke the tropes of the geisha girl and the dragon lady simultaneously."[52]

Male Asian American Stereotypes: Asexual Helpers

Another stereotype for Asian American men is the subservient, asexual servant. A good example of their infantilization into "pre-pubescent grown men" is Hop Sing of *Bonanza*.[53] Hop Sing is the Chinese bachelor houseboy who cleans and cooks for the Cartwright men. He is one of television's many Asian bachelor domestics. They appear in *Bachelor Father* (1957–1962), *Have Gun—Will Travel* (1957–1963), *Valentine's Day* (1964–1965), and *Falcon Crest* (1981–1990). These houseboys, butlers, and valets are underdeveloped and asexual characters who seem to exist only to serve whites.

The media image of the asexual Asian men is so widespread that the character of Mr. Sulu from *Star Trek* (1966–1969) was parodied as an "intergalactic eunuch and glorified houseboy" on *In Living Color* (1990–1994). *The Green Hornet* (1966–1967) brings the right-hand man out of the household and on to the streets as Bruce Lee's Kato helps the Green Hornet fight crime.[54] The stereotype also carries over into films, sometimes with an odd twist. *The Manchurian Candidate's* houseboy may be a communist agent. Kato, the manservant in *The Pink Panther* series (1970s and 1980s), routinely brawls with his boss.

Other Asian American Stereotypes: Nerds, Mystics, and Victims

Asian American women and men fit the stereotypes of mystics, nerds, and victims. It is important to realize about each of these representations that it "otherizes" Asian Americans by making them look like they do not fit into modern American society. These images also tend to be one-dimensional, reducing the person to a single characteristic.

The nerd image turns the stereotype of the "model minority" into a joke. Nerds are academic overachievers without social skills (such as the classmate on *Pearl*, 1996–1997)[55] or scholarship winners without romantic attachments (An Lee on *All My Children*).[56] Actor Gedde Watanabe played the "dingy, madcap Asian," first as a foreign exchange student in *Sixteen Candles* (1984) and then in the sitcom *Gung Ho* (1986–1997). Laughing at these characters diffused the competitive threat that whites felt at that time from high-achieving Asian Americans. White viewers were invited to continue to feel superior to these ridiculous characters. Laughter was only one of the techniques used to combat academic or economic success. Films also showed whites fighting back with racial slurs (such as the ones used against the Korean grocer in *Falling Down*, 1993) and physical violence (as in an episode of *Law & Order*, 1990–present, about a Chinese American honor student).[57]

Although the image of the mystic seems to imbue Asian Americans with power, their wisdom and tools are usually only potent when learned and used by whites. A reoccurring narrative has an isolated Asian master tutor a white male in martial arts or mysticism (*The Karate Kid*, 1984). Many of these stories end with the student ultimately using these skills to save his teacher. This story line leaves the white character in a superior position.[58]

Minor characters who hold "Eastern secrets" are also shown as dangerous. The Asian herbalist (*Alice*, 1990), pawnshop owner (*Gremlins*, 1984), and opium dealer (*McCabe and Mrs. Miller*, 1971) provide elixirs, creatures, and drugs that plague white characters.[59] The lesson here is that whites are better off staying away from mysterious Asians. The title of a 1949 show, *Mysteries of Chinatown*, has a double meaning.[60] It indicates both that the program is about solving crimes and that Asian American victims and criminals are mysterious.

Interracial romance films include rapes and abuse of Asian American women by Asian American men. These stories both demonize and victimize Asian Americans, while establishing white male superiority to both Asian American women and men.[61] In the urban crime television dramas of the late 1980s and 1990s (*The Commish*, 1991–1995; *Gideon Oliver*, 1989; *Mac-Gyver*, 1985–1992; *Shannon's Deal*, 1990–1991), Asian American victims are saved or avenged by white characters, or they are criminals who are caught or killed by them. These shows contain clear messages of white superiority and that "the only way to become accepted by white society is for Asians to become passive, dependent, and respectful—that is, to know their place."[62]

SYSTEM-SUPPORTIVE THEMES AND MESSAGES

Entertainment media's representation of Asian Americans contains mixed messages. On one hand, explicit dialog and story resolutions state that racial prejudice is wrong. On the other hand, only white good guys can fix it, which involves criticizing and correcting specific acts of prejudice rather than re-forming social structures. Not only does this narrative disempower Asian American characters, but it portrays racial injustice as an exception that can be remedied on a individual level. Other system-supportive messages celebrate assimilation (for those who fit certain categories) and romanticize historical injustice, thereby minimizing its harmfulness.

The powerful and white Cartwright men on *Bonanza* exemplify the mixed message about racial prejudice. This is particularly evident in an episode that deals extensively with Hop Sing and his extended family. In "The Fear Merchants," thugs who work for an anti-Chinese, nativist mayoral candidate assault Hip Sing, and his cousin is unjustly accused of murder. After the Cartwrights voice progressive ideals, people tell the truth, the innocent man is set free, and the racist loses the campaign. This resolution shows that "the system works." The racial inequality within the Cartwrights' home remains unacknowledged, and the racism common at the time is presented as a "failed exception."

> Although this episode of *Bonanza* explicitly repudiates racism, it nevertheless dramatizes a central fact of Asian American life: so long as the Asian American remains subordinated and infantilized, he is tolerated by the dominant society. Once he becomes a direct economic competitor, however, the Asian American is liable to be targeted for racist hate and persecution.[63]

Hamamoto calls the propensity for white males in authority to guard and protect minorities "the Great White Father syndrome." He contends that the myth is so compelling that "never has there been a single instance in the television Western where discrimination or racism has been condoned by going unpunished by the authorities."[64] This paternalism is not limited to

Westerns. Harry Owens of the *Harry Owens and His Royal Hawaiians* (1994) show on early Los Angeles television is another example of the great white father. He is "depicted as preserving, maintaining, and promoting" the islands. In one show, he talks about the money he raised for lepers on Molokai by recording one of their songs.[65]

Women's studies professor Laura Hyun-Yi Kang suggests that it might seem as though a new spirited, proud, resourceful image of Asian American women appears in the films *The Year of the Dragon* (1985), *Come See the Paradise* (1990), and *Thousand Pieces of Gold* (1991). Yet, she sees these films' protagonists as reinforcing some of the same negative messages. In all three movies, a sexual relationship with a white man actualizes the Asian American woman's character and provides her with redemption, opportunity, or security. In each of these films, the women choose white men over Asian men and are alienated from their ethnic communities. These movies are really about white men "saving" Asian American women from "the silent, alien margins."[66]

White men also save Asian American women from ineffective, disempowered, or cruel Asian American men. The *Year of the Dragon* is a vivid example of this type of savior role. It depicts "one-cop crusade to clean up the hopelessly corrupt and crime-ridden Chinese community."[67] The cop is a white Vietnam War veteran who, with the help of a Chinese American woman journalist, fights corruption in New York's Chinatown. They are not equals in this fight. He possesses the knowledge and brawn; she provides the racial legitimacy for his fight. He kills the evil leader of the Chinese underworld; she gets raped by a street gang the leader controls.[68]

White men fighting Asian American men to save Asian American women is just one version of how Asian Americans are dichotomized into "good" (to be saved and possibly romanced) and "bad" (to be beaten, arrested, or killed). "Good" Chinese Americans and "bad" Chinese Americans are clearly delineated in *Lethal Weapon 4* (1998). Mel Gibson and Danny Glover's cop team of Riggs and Murtaugh fight a sadistic Chinese leader, Wah Sing Ku (played by Jet Li), to save assimilating Chinese. Although Ku demonstrates masterful martial artistry, he is "ultimately exterminated as though he was not human."[69]

History is rewritten in film and television entertainment to make it more compatible with what Americans want to believe about their nation and each other. Westerns promote a pluralist ideal of successful assimilation.[70] Television story lines claim that Asian immigrants are "on par with . . . European immigrants";[71] yet, reoccurring stereotypes send a different message—that Asian Americans are "foreigners who cannot be assimilated."[72] War films show that the injustices suffered by Asians and Asian Americans during World War II and the Vietnamese War were exceptions and are things of the past. *Farewell to Manzanar* (1976) promotes the idea that "the forced relocation and imprisonment of Japanese Americans can be viewed in retrospect as simply a historical accident that attended the general hysteria of life during wartime."[73] Television entertainment promotes the "revisionist post–Vietnam War mythology" that the United States was "victimized by its own good intentions, which were squandered on a less than worthy race of people."[74]

PROTESTING NEGATIVE IMAGES AND MESSAGES

Individuals, formal groups, and coalitions of groups have long protested against the distorted coverage of Asians and Asian Americans in the media. Chinese diplomat Wu Tingfang's 1914 book, *America through the Spectacles of an Oriental Diplomat*, considered the topic.[75] Groups like Media Action Network for Asian Americans fight negative portrayals of Asians in the media in general. They collect data and issue reports on the problem.[76] Japanese Americans protested the film *Rising Sun*.[77] A coalition of Chinese American groups tried to stop the distribution of *Year of the Dragon* by filing a libel suit against the company that released it.[78] Protest against the casting of a white woman as the Vietnamese lead in *Miss Saigon* was only a precursor to the more dramatic protests of the play in 1991.[79]

When Lambda Legal Defense and Education Fund, a national organization that promotes gay rights, intended to show *Miss Saigon* at a fund-raising event, members of the Asian Lesbians of the East Coast and the Gay Asian and Pacific Islander Men of New York formed a coalition and organized two demonstrations. Due to racial slurs, representations of Vietnamese pimps and prostitutes, and themes in the play, these groups viewed *Miss Saigon* as racist and sexist and as undermining relations between Asians and Westerners.[80] They claimed,

> At stake in *Miss Saigon* is how those who control the means of representation and reproduction choose to define people of color and non-Western cultures, and to what ends. *Miss Saigon* rewrites the Vietnam War, pulling a sentimental love story from the carnage of carpet bombing, My Lai, and Agent Orange like a rabbit from a hat.[81]

After failing to convince Lambda to cancel the event, a multiracial group of activists, interested citizens, and artists (including the Asian Pacific Alliance for Creative Equality and Audre Lorde, a lesbian feminist poet) lent its support to the coalition's efforts. This resulted in two demonstrations that received national press coverage. Two protestors who had acquired tickets also briefly disrupted the play.[82]

CREATING ALTERNATIVE IMAGES AND MESSAGES

Both independent films and recent commercial films authored by Asian Americans have offered improved images. Beginning in the 1970s, independent Asian Pacific American films and videos came out of media arts organizations that believed that the media could effect social and cultural change and in the importance of replacing mainstream media stereotypes with more positive and authentic images.[83] The Asian Pacific American media arts movement has begun to create films that

> seek redress from white supremacy. They perform the important tasks of correcting histories, voicing common but seldom represented experiences, engaging audiences used to being spoken about but never addressed, and actively constructing a politics of resistance to racism.[84]

Wayne Wang's low-budget *Chan Is Missing* (1982) was the first American movie directed by a Chinese American and made with an all Asian American cast.[85] It creates a diverse picture of Asian Americans, highlighting "the disparity between Hollywood images of Chinese Americans and their lived experiences."[86] Its exploration of identity issues among new and assimilated Chinese Americans in San Francisco appealed to Asian Americans and white art house audiences.[87]

Many important independent Asian American films produced in the 1990s address particular issues and audiences. Unlike Hollywood films, they acknowledge diversity within Asian Americans. *Sally's Beauty Spot* (1990) identifies Asian American struggles with black politics. In *Two Lies* (1989), "a Chinese American teenager reflects on her mother's pending operation to enlarge her eyes." It highlights issues of self-image and assimilation pressures.[88] In *From Hollywood to Hanoi* (1993), media images and contrasting narratives of the Vietnam War tell the filmmaker's story about growing up a Vietnamese American. A number of films (*Great Girl*, 1994; *Looking for Wendy*, 1998; and *Searching for Go-Hyang*, 1998) tell the stories of Korean American adoptees.[89]

Commercial films have also been created by and about Asian Americans. *The Joy Luck Club* (1993), a big-budget movie adapted from a popular novel by Amy Tan about four Chinese mothers and their Chinese American daughters, was directed by a Chinese American man, cowritten and coproduced by Chinese American women, and starred Asian Americans.[90] Esther Ghymn contends, "By listening to the characters share their experiences in their own voices, the audience is persuaded to be more sympathetic."[91] Others were more critical of the film for its characterization of passive Asian American daughters and for focusing too much on suffering.[92] Helen Wan, an Asian American New York attorney, writes that "when *Joy Luck Club* came out, I heard so many ridiculous comments: 'Do you really cook soup of your own blood when your parents get sick?' Answer: 'Um . . . no.'"[93]

The martial arts experts offer images of power and skill, but also of exoticism. Before he made his first American film, *Enter the Dragon* (1973), Bruce Lee was famous overseas for his martial arts films produced in Hong Kong. Lee's martial arts films provided him with prominent, positive roles in which he demonstrated expertise, power, and bravery. His son, Brandon Lee, played a similar role in *The Crow* (1994). More recently, Jackie Chan has mixed stunts, fights, and humor in films such as *Dragon Lord* (1982), the *Police Story* series (1984 to 1996), and the *Rush Hour* series (1998–2003).[94] On one hand, these films provide images of power, expertise, intelligence, and agency for Asian American stars. On the other hand, they present a narrowly defined role for Asian Americans to excel in. That role also has much in common with stereotypical mysterious and inscrutable attributes.

Although both Lee's and Chan's characters challenge timid and deferential Asian male stereotypes, they do it very differently. Lee's films are more political, using violence to fight colonialism and assert Chinese pride and power. Chan's characters are more likely to be reluctant, middle-class heroes. "Chan has paradoxically presented his films as transnational as well as individualistic, multicultural as well as apolitical, and chronological as well as ahistorical."[95] Not surprisingly, the Chan films have been more lucrative and appealing to white audiences.

CONCLUSION

Asian Americans are underrepresented in film and television. Images of Asian Americans with power that is narrowly constructed (as in martial arts) or used for evil reinforce the idea that Asian Americans are foreign and bad. Mainstream films and television shows have yet to show Asian Americans fighting racism that is configured as ongoing and historically accurate, rather than an exception "taken care of" by whites. Asian American women are also drawn to fit white male fantasies and expectations. Like other racial-minority groups, Asian Americans have fought back and created new, more diverse, complex, and empowering representations. The most commercially successful, like Jackie Chan's films, "make fun of the powerful and identify with the status quo."[96]

II

News Coverage of Racial-Minority Mass Publics

Monica Lozano (left), publisher and chief executive officer of La Opinión, *a Spanish-language newspaper, holds a news conference to announce their new advertising campaign, March 1, 2004, Los Angeles. Courtesy of AP/Wide World Photos.*

7

Representations of Racial-Minority Mass Publics in the News

~~~~~~

EXCLUSION, STEREOTYPING, AND THEMES THAT MASK RACISM AND CELEBRATE a dominant ideology are found in the news as well as entertainment communication. News stories need not concern issues, campaigns, or government activities to be politically important. All news that includes minorities conveys messages to readers and viewers that help them develop, reinforce, or challenge assumptions about race.

Part II of this book deals with the presentation of racial-minority mass publics in nongovernmental news, defined here as news about members of the mass public not engaged in explicitly political activities (such as campaigns, social movements, or governing). This chapter first describes ways that the news represents racial minorities, why, and how this coverage has political implications. The next four chapters look at news coverage of each of the four racial-minority groups, using the same organizational structure found in part I. This structure draws attention again to how minorities are excluded and stereotyped and to the dominant themes conveyed in mainstream media. It also considers alternatives produced by members of the minority groups.

The news media use a variety of techniques to shape news. First, they control what is included and how prominently it is covered. Events are given significance when they are covered early in a television broadcast or published on the front page. Second, reporters choose whom to interview and which quotations to use. They rely extensively on government sources to explain and defend the status quo. Third, since all information about an event cannot be included in a story, and since events usually involve some ambiguity, reporters have a lot of latitude to interpret what is really going on. Fourth, evaluative words and statements are used to slant a story in a particular way.[1] Fifth, reporters "frame" stories with headlines or interpretative introductions that point to what the events mean.[2]

Like films and entertainment television, minorities are typically under-represented in the news relative to their numerical representation in the public. They are also selectively excluded from certain types of news stories and from certain roles in those stories. News story selection, visuals, and terminology convey racial stereotypes similar to those found in television entertainment and film. System-supportive themes in the news include those celebrating assimilation and those that emphasize the need to control or monitor racial minorities. Just as minorities have produced independent films to represent alternative images of them, racial minorities have created newspapers and radio and television broadcasts to redress the biases in mainstream news.

RACIAL-MINORITY EXCLUSION AND SELECTIVE EXCLUSION FROM MAINSTREAM NEWS

Minority exclusion from American newspapers has a long history. Although occasionally mentioned in early American newspapers, racial minorities were not the subjects of news stories. This exclusion reinforced their low status and "signified exclusion from American society, because the function of news is to reflect social reality."[3]

In his analysis of forty hours' worth of programming from twenty-eight local news stations across the country, Christopher Campbell found that hard news stories ignored minority issues, communities, and individuals. He also found that minority individuals were rarely used as news sources to interpret events or issues. The exception was in sports stories.[4] Both sports and entertainment are considered "soft news" rather than "hard news."

Although the inclusion of nonwhites in news coverage has increased over time, racial minorities continue to appear in certain types of stories more than others. Hard news that treats racial minorities as the main subject focuses on their threat to the social structure and their opposition to whites. Thus, racial minorities often appear in crime stories. This suggests or reinforces the idea that minorities are dangerous to whites. Even when acting within the law, racial minorities have been treated as threatening and suspect in American society and the media's coverage of it. For example, the presence of Native Americans was seen as thwarting Western expansion. Chinese laborers in the late 1800s were perceived as threatening whites' employment opportunities, as have Mexican immigrants been more recently. When hard news includes racial issues, coverage emphasizes confrontation and uses an us-versus-them frame, with the assumed "us" being "white."[5]

> These [news] images display America's status and power hierarchy; they also may serve to reinforce it. At the most general level the color pattern of the news conveys a sense that America is essentially a society of White people with minori-

ties—the very word rings pejoratively—as adjunct members who mainly cause trouble or need help.[6]

When racial minorities are the focus of soft news, the emphasis is on how novel and colorful their festivals, celebrations, rituals, and clothing are.[7] Although these images can show a group's pride in its cultural traditions, the repeated images of special occasion coverage[8] ultimately trivialize minorities by demonstrating how "different" they are.

> The general lack of coverage of minority issues and minority communities by local television news contributes to a sense of "otherness" about nonwhite Americans; their existence is not ignored as it was 25 years ago, but the lack of perspective, of depth, can dictate news coverage that continues to advance a dangerous perception of minority life.[9]

STEREOTYPES OF RACIAL MINORITIES IN MAINSTREAM NEWS COVERAGE

Stereotypes are widely held beliefs about the attributes of members of groups.[10] While they were once crude and explicit, they are now subtler. "They can be found now in what stories are selected, the prevalence of minorities in certain types of stories, or in the way a sentence or headline is phrased."[11] Stereotypes ignore individual differences by creating a generic image of a group that is applied to all of its members. Common negative stereotypes of nonwhites hold that they are violent, lazy, and sexually promiscuous.[12] Many of the mainstream news representations of minorities are similar to those found in entertainment. "The practices, traditions, and forms of journalism, rather than challenging the stereotypes in popular culture, have repeated and reinforced them. By doing so, the press has given these images the weight of factuality."[13]

In one way, stereotypes found in the news are harder to resist because the news is seen as real, whereas movies can be dismissed as make believe. In addition to influencing impressions of a racial group by whites, stereotypes can lead members of groups to conform to these typically negative expectations about themselves. Even positive stereotypes can hurt by making it harder on those who do not fit the stereotype. For example, if the stereotype is that all Asians are good at math, what do we make of one who is not? What will he or she make of himself or herself?

Newsworthiness criteria used by journalists help explain why positive stereotypes are less prevalent than negative ones. One of the criteria is that news be familiar to the viewers. Because a racist history generates stereotypes, familiar stories are more likely to be negative. The criteria of conflict and violence also draw reporters to stereotypes that demonize groups. The desire for novel news pushes them toward stories that ridicule minorities.[14]

SYSTEM-SUPPORTIVE THEMES IN RACIAL-MINORITY NEWS COVERAGE

News about racial minorities is paradoxical in that it tells white audiences both "they are just like you" and "they are different from you."[15] This means that minorities are seen as just like the white majority in that the system works as long as they work hard, play by the rules, and assimilate. Yet, they are different in that so often they will not (or cannot) do these things. The two messages allow the news to celebrate American values and justify inequality at the same time.

The news dichotomizes minorities into two types, "good" and "bad." The first type shows middle- and upper-middle-class minorities who have succeeded.[16] These individuals illustrate the American Dream through their ability to "pick themselves up by their bootstraps" and go "from rags to riches" through hard work and persistence.[17] These individuals serve to promote the idea that discrimination is a thing of the past and that we now live in a fair and open society that allows everyone to prosper. The achievers also promote assimilation by showing that "those who escape their designated place are not a threat to society because they manifest the same values and ambitions as the dominant culture and overcome the deficits of their home communities."[18]

The other group includes poor people who are protesters, criminals, and victims.[19] While sometimes explicitly characterized as "bad," they might better be thought of as "problem people" who are either creating problems for others or plagued by their own difficulties.[20] Stories that show minorities as threats to social and political institutions and in conflict with whites also lack clear explanations and historical context. This superficial and action-based news coverage can make their actions appear pathological, self-defeating, irrational, and due to inherent character flaws. Therefore, control of these problem minorities is presented as a good thing because it preserves the social structures enjoyed by whites and the "good" minorities who emulate them.

The prevalent (and exaggerated) image of whites in positions of authority and as guardians of order found on television further racialize the idea of social order.[21] The news emphasizes conflict between minorities and whites in a way that minimizes the legitimacy of minorities' concerns and how they express them. Conflict resolution tends to be demonstrated by reassuring white audiences that police and the courts have succeeded in keeping nonwhites "in their place."[22] Coverage of minorities as problems is also system supportive when providing an explanation for the persistence of racial inequality that blames minorities (rather than whites or mainstream institutions).

REASONS FOR DISTORTED NEWS COVERAGE OF RACIAL MINORITIES

News is not a mirror of society or the events that occur; nor can it be. Many factors lead to biased coverage of racial minorities in news coverage. First, news is a business that sells its audience to advertisers. The larger the audience, the more revenue television commercials and newspaper advertising generate. Therefore, news is in the business of trying to appeal to the mainstream (white, middle-class American) audience. Advertisers are also drawn toward certain demographics. They want to get the attention of people with the money to buy their products. Because of economic inequality and assumptions made by advertisers, minorities are considered "bad demographics" and as less desirable targets than whites.[23]

As the media companies become bigger and acquire and merge with other companies, more individuals have a financial stake in the media's bottom line. Economic pressures grow. The financial pressures "necessarily predispose news organizations to give favorable coverage to their own interests and those of corporate America," which also results in less favorable coverage of political and economic reforms.[24] Advertisers influence news content by discouraging certain stories and encouraging news tailored to certain lucrative audiences.[25]

> In attempting to reach widespread, anonymous audiences, news draws on the most broadly held common social values and assumptions, in other words the prevailing consensus, in establishing common ground for communication with its audiences.[26]

News shows and papers try to draw an audience by presenting information that fits newsworthiness criteria, which make it more interesting to the assumed audiences. Since audiences are assumed to be primarily white, mainstream news talks to and about the concerns of white people.[27] It also reinforces themes that resonate with the assumptions and interests of white audiences. Newsworthiness criteria of conflict and familiarity also invite repetitive, negative stereotyping of minorities.

Limited time and resources push coverage toward the easy stories, those that are simple to get and tell. The resulting news coverage becomes repetitive and oversimplified, with minorities playing the same roles (or no role). It also becomes less likely that people who do not speak English or who live in remote or dangerous areas of the country will be covered.[28]

The goals of objectivity, independence, and fairness, which guide journalists, actually put in place rules and procedures that preclude them from being met. These professional practices "create conditions that systematically favor the reporting of narrow, official perspectives."[29] In practice, the goals of fairness and balance are achieved through defining issues as two sided. This limits complex issues and gives attention to the most familiar and predictable positions of "legitimate groups" (i.e., the two major parties). The norm of neutrality also results in reporters transmitting official positions without evaluating them.[30] Reporters rely on official sources, such as government officials and business spokespeople, who are seen as credible, important, and accessible. Most of these officials are white.[31] "For the most part, the news reports on those at or near the top of the hierarchies and on those, particularly at the bottom, who threaten them, to an audience, most of whom are located in the vast middle range between top and bottom."[32] Coverage of this small number of people in positions of authority promotes American values of individualism, capitalism, and nationalism.[33]

Finally, deliberate choices made by members of news organizations determine what is news. These individuals are gatekeepers who "translate the complex and multi-voiced reality of our times into another, symbolic realm of simpler images and fewer voices."[34] They determine what is important using their own priorities and values.[35] Since the gatekeepers are typically white, they can lack familiarity with, sensitivity to, or knowledge of other groups' issues and perspectives.[36] What they cover, and how they cover it, privileges certain sources, stories, and interpretations.

In 1999, racial minorities made up only 12 percent of the newspaper workforce and 20 percent of broadcasting; 42 percent of the nation's newspapers had no minority employees.[37] The small percentage of news personnel of color is well documented and has not improved drastically over time, despite corporate policies to increase diversity.[38] Since diversifying news organizations has become a goal, some people are optimistic about the future of the news. They believe that as organizations diversify their news personnel, the coverage of race will improve.

Equal employment opportunities are important issues, and there is ample evidence that minority reporters are underrepresented relative to their percentage of the population.[39] Yet, the connection between the race of the reporter and the nature of the reporting is not as clear as it might seem.

LIMITED EFFECTIVENESS OF DIVERSIFYING NEWS PERSONNEL

Do reporters of color bring diverse perspectives to their jobs that change the nature of news coverage? There is some circumstantial evidence that they might. For example, 15 percent of the *Seattle Times*'s news staff is Asian American,[40] and that paper has extensive coverage of Asian Americans.[41] Similarly, scholar Peter Skerry believes that the more sympathetic coverage of Mexican Americans in Los Angeles than San Antonio is due to the higher percentage of Mexican American reporters there.[42]

At the same time, more evidence indicates that the presence of minority journalists is not a panacea for news problems. First of all, journalists are all trained to do their jobs in a particular way.[43] This training and professional socialization minimizes the distinctiveness of any individual's contribution. Furthermore, to succeed and advance in predominately white organizations, minority journalists must conform to norms and perspectives.[44] In addition, the news organization hierarchy minimizes the impact individual journalists can have on news content.[45] Not only are most journalists assigned stories rather than being free to set their own agendas, but they also work with others to create these pieces. Editors and producers have the authority to change or kill their stories.

Minority reporters also might not diversify coverage much because they are not representative of the diversity in the racial-minority communities, nor would they claim to be. Minority reporters tend to be college educated and middle class.[46] Thus, their familiarity with new immigrants, non-English speakers, and the lower class may be similar to that of white middle-class journalists.

Some journalists of color claim it is unfair to expect them to "represent their race" through their reporting. They resist pressure to do so. Being assigned to race stories can be seen as a form of discrimination or tokenism instead of an opportunity. Being "ghettoized into reporting on race" can be undesirable for an ambitious reporter's career path.[47]

Even a reporter trying to bring racial consciousness to his or her reporting will find this difficult due to the pressure on all reporters to demonstrate objectivity. This is particularly difficult for minority reporters who are expected to prove themselves. "To pass an objectivity litmus test, black journalists, then, must show they can freely criticize or even sully the character of other blacks in order to win the acceptance and trust of white editors."[48] There are rewards for "criticizing your own," as demonstrated by the awards given to black reporters covering black pathology.[49] For all these reasons, we cannot assume that problematic exclusion and stereotyping will disappear with the increase of racial diversity in the newsroom.

POLITICAL IMPACT OF NEWS COVERAGE OF RACIAL MINORITIES

The political impact of news about racial minorities can come from coverage influencing the attitudes and behaviors of politicians, the white public majority, or racial-minority groups. News is used to "help justify official policies of social control of racial and other minorities."[50] Politicians use news as an indicator of public opinion, leading them to certain decisions or justifications.[51] For example, editorials and people-on-the street comments might deter them from making progressive reforms. They also use news stories as evidence to support their positions in policy debates.[52] The media can also influence public opinion through cultivation, agenda setting, priming, and framing. Although media could conceivably push the public toward more liberal racial policies, the nature of the coverage tends to lead to attitudes that maintain the racial status quo.

Cultivation Effects

The media influence the public's attitudes and actions because of its pervasiveness. When messages on a topic are consistent over time and across media, they can be hard to resist. When television entertainment, television news (local and national), movies, and newspapers all portray members of a racial group in the same way, that portrait becomes our "commonsense" understanding. This is the idea behind "cultivation theory."

Cultivation theory contends that heavy viewers of television perceive the "real world" based upon the "television world."[53] Research consistently demonstrates this effect; people who watch crime shows think there is more crime than there is; people who watch soap operas exaggerate divorce rates. Cultivation effects are strongest when the audience has little exposure to a reality with which to compare televisions coverage.[54] This means that whites who have few interactions with people of color will find the media stereotypes particularly credible, and the power for media images to shape their attitudes will be great.[55] This is one of the reasons why negative coverage of racial minorities is more influential in shaping white attitudes towards nonwhites than news about whites is in shaping minorities' attitudes toward them.

Another reason is that "it is minority status that makes every minority person a representative of his race."[56] Thus, people are more likely to think that Jennifer Lopez tells them more about Puerto Ricans from New York than Britney Spears tells them about white people from Louisiana. By covering some problems that are generalized to entire groups, the media have generated impatience among whites toward the disadvantaged and recent immigrants.[57] Although viewers may selectively perceive and actively resist the racial messages in the news, most white viewers tend not to question negative news about blacks.[58] Instead, media cultivate in them a distrust toward racial minorities.

Agenda Setting and Priming Effects

News coverage sets the agenda for the American public by covering certain issues and events and ignoring others. The public perceives issues that get extensive coverage in the news as more important than issues that are ignored.[59] To the extent that minorities are excluded from the news and their voices are not heard, their issues and arguments are not part of the public debate.

Priming goes beyond agenda setting to influence how readers and viewers attribute responsibility for problems highlighted in the news. How the news assesses responsibility influences what or whom people perceive as the cause of a problem. The initial studies on priming looked at how covering certain issues more than others leads the public to use the more accessible information to evaluate the president.[60]

Priming can also affect how racial minorities are evaluated. Stories about racial minorities that focus on the individuals and their problems, rather than on social and institutional structures, prime audiences to hold the individuals responsible for their difficulties. As a result, these frames discourage progressive political solutions.[61] One study showed how stereotyping primes certain attitudes toward members of the group stereotyped, even when they do not appear in the story. Specifically, it found that when subjects were exposed to negative racial stereotypes of a fictitious black man, they were more likely to blame Rodney King for his police beating.[62]

Framing Effects

Framing is how the news story emphasizes certain values, themes, or interpretations. A story is framed through the various elements used to tell the story and give meaning to events. These include the headline, quotes, the use, order, or exclusion of arguments and information, photo selection, and word choice. More often than not, the news audience will evaluate a situation or issue in a way consistent with the framing.[63] The way that racial minorities and racial issues are framed will influence how readers and viewers of the news evaluate them and the public policies that deal with minorities.[64] The frames used provide cues to the viewers or readers that lead them to use certain values to evaluate situations.

> Frames categorize events, connect present events with those of the past, indicate causal relationships and create oppositions. They facilitate familiarity; the news is expressed as the known. Frames enable journalists to identify the particular significance of complex events; they also may contain within them moral judgments and suggested remedies.[65]

Various studies have documented the impact that frames have on their audience. For example, when a political march or rally was framed as about free speech, rather than about a disruption of public order, readers were more tolerant of it.[66] When affirmative action was called "reverse discrimination," whites used their economic self-interest to evaluate the issue rather than other considerations.[67]

Political scientist Paul M. Kellstedt conducted one of the most extensive studies of the impact of framing on racial attitudes. He examined thousands of news stories about racial issues appearing in the *New York Times* and *Newsweek* between 1950 and 1994. He categorized the stories by whether they emphasized "individualism" (the idea that people need to succeed on their own) or "equalitiarianism" (the equal worth of all people). The changes in the media's use of the frames over time was tracked with national public opinion polls in a sophisticated statistical analysis. The results showed that when the news used individualism to frame race issues, public opinion was more conservative toward these issues than when stories were framed using equalitarianism.[68] He also found that news coverage that emphasized states rights led audiences to express conservative racial-policy preferences.[69]

Framing effects are not contingent on the communication's being heavy-handed or argumentative. Framing can occur when certain sources are used more prominently than others. One study revealed that when a story about Domino's Pizza's failure to deliver to high-crime, black neighborhoods was given a "crime frame," readers were more likely to support the company's redlining policy than they were when a "race frame" was used. Both articles contained the same facts, were written as news stories, and contained both sides of the dispute. The race frame included a photograph of a black family and a quotation from a resident who said the policy was unfair, and it put the racial argument first; the crime frame quoted a Dominos spokeswoman who said safety was the top priority, showed a picture of a delivery person, and put the safety-concerns argument first.[70]

Framing also works to influence public opinion by activating certain stereotypes that are in the minds of the readers/viewers so that they will be brought to bear on an issue. Stereotypes are part of people's long-term memories, but they might not be used to evaluate a political issue unless they are "cued."[71] The media framing can cue these stereotypes. A study on media-framing effects on attitudes about immigration policy indicated that when the issue was discussed as a material issue (in terms of economics, practicality, and self-interest), rather than an ethical issue (in terms of rights, morals, and principles), racial stereotypes of Mexican Americans were triggered. These stereotypes were then used to justify an opposition to immigration.[72]

How news coverage impacts racial-policy attitudes has been most extensively researched in the areas of welfare policy and crime. This research uses content analysis of news as one part of methodologically sophisticated and complex analyses.

Consequences for Welfare Attitudes and Policy

Polls indicate that the public wants less government spending on welfare. Political scientist Martin Gilens demonstrates in his book *Why Americans Hate Welfare* that this is due in large part to racialized news coverage of poverty and welfare. Newspaper and television news puts a black face on poverty and welfare (even though more whites are actually on welfare). This racial imbalance is particularly true in negative stories about welfare and in stories about the least popular forms of welfare (such as food stamps rather than disability). The news images of blacks on welfare promote a stereotype of blacks as lazy. As a result, viewers see the images and conclude that welfare is a government handout that lazy black people "choose" to take rather than work. The public believes the government should help the "deserving poor," but the racial stereotype of laziness activated by the coverage undermines the assumption that welfare goes to the "deserving." Thus, the public opposes welfare spending. Of course, this stereotype was not created by the news; it is also prevalent in other media and social attitudes. However, the news maintains, reinforces, and "activates" the stereotype in a way that has policy implications.[73]

The association of poverty with blackness was originally made in the media during the late 1960s and early 1970s in the prevalent coverage of the War on Poverty and urban riots. The more messages there were connecting race and poverty, the more polls showed the two associated in the public's minds. As a result, ironically, "the public came to associate race and welfare most closely as blacks became *more* equal in economic terms."[74]

Experiments are also useful for demonstrating the impact of news on radicalizing welfare attitudes. In one experiment, subjects shown news featuring black welfare recipients were harsher in their evaluations of welfare than subjects who saw news showing white welfare recipients. When the stories were explicitly critical of welfare, the difference was even more pronounced.[75]

Consequences for Criminal Justice Attitudes and Policies

Racialized crime coverage triggers people's fears, and their "willingness to hold black people responsible for crime" increases.[76] Whites have become so used to seeing blacks in stories about crime that they assume blacks to be the perpetrators of crimes covered on television even when those stories lack photographs or descriptions of the suspect.[77] "Instead of extinguishing irrational white fear of blacks, the news media more often fuels it (by emphasizing black-on-white crime), causing further polarization along racial lines."[78]

Empirical research consistently shows that exposure to crime coverage negatively influences attitudes toward blacks. White subjects shown crime stories that included a black suspect developed more negative attitudes toward African Americans in general.[79] Coverage also influences attitudes about what the government should do about crime. Both experiments and surveys illustrate that after whites observe local crime news in which a black suspect is shown or the viewer assumes an unshown suspect to be black (a common occurrence), the white viewer is more likely to support punitive criminal justice procedures.[80]

Coverage of crime that prominently displays black men makes them convenient and convincing scapegoats for other people's crimes. White killers use racial stereotypes to try to avoid blame. By making such accusations, they reinforce the stereotype. One prominent example was in 1994 when a white South Carolina woman, Susan Smith, killed her two children and blamed it on a fictitious black man.[81] These accusations got ample coverage on local and national news.

Impact on Racial Minorities

Racial minorities are not immune to cultivation, agenda setting, priming, and framing. However, they can resist media messages when their experiences contradict the news representations. When news is presented in a way that is fundamentally at odds with a group's own sense of reality, the news can lose legitimacy. For example, black viewers have become very skeptical of crime news; studies show that seeing black suspects on television actually leads them "to lower their support for punitive criminal justice policies and [to] reduce their willingness to accept negative characterizations of their group."[82]

Minority groups who see images of themselves that do not resonate with their experiences can resist the communication. Focus groups found that black viewers in Los Angeles belittled and rejected news coverage that portrayed rioters as thugs.[83] Korean Americans in Los Angeles[84] and Chicago[85] also disbelieved the media representations of the Los Angeles conflict. Both groups explained the tensions between their communities in terms of cultural differences rather than racial ones.[86]

At the same time, negative images of racial groups can also undermine political coalition building between them. For example, if blacks believe the stereotypes about Hispanics that they see on the news, and if Hispanics believe the stereotypes about blacks that they see on the news, they are less likely to see a common interest and join together to fight for it. News that shows interethnic conflict can increase distrust and hatred between minority groups.[87] It can even lead to hate crimes by inflaming frustrations and rage.[88]

Coverage can also result in internalized oppression, just as entertainment can. When members of an oppressed group come to believe negative stereotypes about themselves, they think of their status as deserved and blame themselves for their oppression. Members of the Hispanic American community blame their "poor self-concept and lack of cultural pride" on the media's negative portrayals.[89] As earlier chapters demonstrate, this is one of the reasons why groups boycott films and fight in other ways to change media presentations. They believe that it is hard to raise minority children to have high self-esteem when they are bombarded with negative images in the media.[90] One solution is to create alternative news that is more positive in its representation of and more relevant to the minority audience.

COVERAGE OF RACIAL MINORITIES IN THE PARALLEL PRESS

Alternative sources of information created and used by minorities are part of the parallel press.[91] Minority-run newspapers, radio, pamphlets, and Internet sites are communication systems that provide a voice for views and speakers typically excluded from the mainstream mass media. Via these parallel communication channels, groups outside of the majority challenge the dominant ideology and seek empowerment.[92] "Political outsiders . . . construct their own communication infrastructures, rituals, and media, in an attempt to build community, and to influence mainstream social discourse."[93]

The first newspapers created by racial minorities in the United States came out of crises and oppression.[94] Since then they have informed, entertained, and even politicized their audiences, building and nurturing these communities. Immigrants still turn to ethnic media for help adjusting to their new country. "Ethnic media can play a leadership role in the ethnic community. Like all media, ethnic media can protect their groups' interests as well as promote cultural values."[95] There are hundreds of ethnic newspapers across the country. New York City alone contributes almost two hundred. Some of these are foreign-language newspapers that serve large audiences. The Chinese-language *World Journal* has an estimated circulation of 360,000 and Spanish-language *La Opinión*'s is 125,000.[96]

CONCLUSION

Racial minorities are excluded, selectively included, and stereotyped in news coverage. The messages in the coverage defend and support the status quo and the structures of power that maintain it by focusing on individuals rather than on the system. The news praises minority individuals who assimilate and succeed and blames those who do not. It emphasizes conflict between whites and others and legitimates the white majority by showing it in positions of power and force. Through the parallel press, racial minorities contradict these dominant messages and provide information and interpretations that challenge them.

There are a variety of reasons, both ideological and organizational, that the media represent racial minorities in these negative ways. Diversifying the newsroom is unlikely to resolve the problems in large part because of journalistic norms and procedures and because of the socialization and self-interest of minority reporters.

This news coverage of minorities has important political consequences. The news shapes public opinion towards minorities and issues by cultivating certain assumptions, setting agendas, priming the audience, and framing stories. Extensive research demonstrates that news coverage that puts a black face on poverty has resulted in opposition to welfare spending and reinforces the stereotype of blacks as lazy. Crime coverage also exacerbates negative evaluations of racial minorities.

The next four chapters discuss how news about each of the four racial-minority groups furthers exclusion, stereotyping, and system-supportive themes. Many of the stories are similar, as conflict and criminality dominate each group's coverage. However, variations between and within the groups' representations are also revealed. The parallel press includes a wide range of political messages reflecting the diversity within racial groups that the mass media tends to homogenize.

8

African American Mass
Publics in the News

〰〰〰〰〰〰〰〰〰〰〰〰〰〰〰〰〰〰〰

TODAY, AFRICAN AMERICANS RECEIVE FAR MORE ATTENTION IN THE NEWS THAN other racial minorities do. Yet, they remain underrepresented in certain types of stories and roles both nationally and locally. The predominance of crime, poverty, and urban unrest stories featuring blacks reinforces certain stereotypes and undermines racial progress. As an alternative, the black press has provided empowering representations of blacks and political advocacy for civil rights.

EXCLUSION AND SELECTIVE EXCLUSION OF
BLACKS FROM THE MAINSTREAM NEWS

Prior to the civil rights movement in the 1960s, coverage of African Americans was rare in the national news press.[1] After an increase in stories about race in newspapers and newsmagazines after 1963, there was a decrease in the early to mid-1970s.[2] More recent studies have found that this exclusion was rectified in the 1980s when blacks' prevalence in the news became equivalent to their proportion in the population.[3] An analysis of 1997 national network news found that 10 to 14 percent of the stories included blacks (depending upon the network). However, blacks are still selectively excluded. They appear infrequently in news photographs, certain types of stories, and authoritative roles.

Studies of photographs in the *New York Times* and *Newsweek* in the late 1990s revealed that over 50 percent of blacks shown were athletes.[4] In fact, images of athletes (and entertainers) made up a greater proportion of pictures of blacks than they had thirty years earlier.[5] Blacks are also virtually absent from pictures in newsmagazines and newspapers illustrating health stories.[6] An analysis of news photographs in the *Washington Post* found three times more news photos of whites than blacks. Half of the pictures of whites showed them as successful compared to only 31 percent of those of blacks.[7]

Coverage of blacks is also unequally distributed across different types of stories and topics. Blacks are commonly represented in crime and sports stories but not in economic, foreign, and political news.[8] When the *New Orleans Time-Picayune* looked at its own coverage in a 1993 newspaper series on racism, it found virtually no coverage of blacks on the society pages. In fact, 96 percent of the photographs in the society section were of whites.[9]

Since blacks appear mostly in crime and sports stories, it is not surprising that they are most likely to appear in the roles of athletes, entertainers, and criminals (or those accused of law breaking).[10] The tendency to focus on these roles helps explain the extensive coverage of O. J. Simpson, since he fit into all three groups.[11] In most of the stories in which they appear, blacks are not the central focus.[12] Even in predominantly black cities, news coverage puts whites in the dominant roles in stories.[13]

When blacks are in the news, the stories are usually about race. Blacks tend not to be used as experts in news stories unless the story is about race or urban problems. White experts outnumber blacks ninety-four to fifteen in "nonblack" issue stories.[14] A documentary about racial issues will include many blacks, but a documentary on another subject will not. For example, an eight-hour documentary on the Vietnam War produced in the early 1980s showed few black soldiers, despite their extensive service in the war.[15]

STEREOTYPES OF BLACKS IN THE MAINSTREAM NEWS

Although clearly not as badly as in the early part of the 1900s, when blacks were routinely referred to as "coons," "fiends," and "hamfats," reoccurring stereotypical images of blacks continue even in major newspapers.[16] While the "overly bigoted myths of blacks are not stated explicitly, through implicit visual imagery old stereotypes of blacks as dirty, lazy and dependent, and myths of blacks' inferiority are subtly suggested."[17] The violent or oversexed black brute is found in crime coverage. The stereotype of the poor, lazy, and stupid black is part of welfare coverage.

Black Stereotypes in Crime Coverage

The association of blacks with crime is evident in all levels and forms of media coverage and has been for a long time. In fact, stories about slave crimes and rebellions were repeated in colonial newspapers more than any other type of story.[18] There has been a long preoccupation with black men as sexual threats to white women. For example, the *Atlanta Evening News* facilitated the 1906 race riots in that city by calling for lynchings after the rape of a white woman.[19] This continues to influence news story selection and framing.[20]

Today, blacks and crime are featured in local news and national news; prominent in newspapers, television, and magazines; and emphasized in photographs and word choice. For example, terminology equates blacks with animals; consider the connotations of the "black brute" stereotype.[21] This crime coverage "rarely considers the political, social, historical, educational, or economic roots of crime, and therefore constructs individual episodes of violence as stories with no history, entirely void of perspective."[22]

Although local television news is generally drawn to violence and crime, coverage treats blacks and whites differently.[23] Of those who are arrested, blacks are more likely than whites to appear on the news unnamed, with a mug shot, wearing jail clothes, restrained, and in physical custody of the police.[24] Reporters and anchors are also more likely to comment negatively upon them.[25] Ultimately, the crime problem is presented as a "black problem,"[26] while black crime victims are largely ignored.[27]

Criminal justice professor Dennis M. Rome provides examples of how the extent of crime and the nature of its perpetrators are characterized differently by race. He points out that the news of a white investment banker's rape in New York City's Central Park allegedly by a gang of minority teens made headlines across the country for days. Yet, other New York City rapes (and murders) of black and Hispanic women committed on the same day were ignored. He compares the tone of the Central Park rape's coverage to that of the coverage of the gang rape of a retarded girl by white suburban teenagers in New Jersey a few weeks later. Not only was there more coverage of the Central Park assault, but the accused were described with different adjectives. The black assailants were "vicious, sadistic terrorists"; the whites were "honor students," "sweet and obedient," and acting out of character. The tone of the coverage also treated the blacks' crime as "typical" and the whites' as "unusual."[28]

Studies comparing the amount of crime coverage to actual crime statistics have revealed racial distortions. One study of Chicago television news found that black victims were underrepresented, white victims were overrepresented, and black perpetrators were overrepresented, compared to the city's crime statistics.[29] Studies of local Los Angeles television news found that blacks were overrepresented as perpetrators of crimes overall, and of violent crimes and homicides specifically.[30] Blacks made up 44 percent of the felons shown on the evening news, whereas they only made up 25 percent of those arrested for felonies.[31]

Although black criminality is sensationalized most extensively on television news,[32] black crime is also prevalent in newspapers,[33] newspaper photos,[34] and television's "reality" programs.[35] American mainstream newspapers have historically covered black crimes that were both real and imagined, automatically treating blacks accused of a crime as guilty.[36]

The assumption of black male guilt has not disappeared. It helps explain why white criminals fabricate stories about black assailants to cover up their own guilt.[37] In one well-publicized example, Charles Stuart, a white man who murdered his pregnant wife in Boston, claimed that a black man had done it and even went so far as to identify an innocent black man in a police lineup. Because of the cultural stereotypes held by journalists and the white audience, "the Stuart saga was a story the media was conditioned to run—and readers were conditioned to believe."[38]

Racial stereotypes also underlie the coverage of drug crimes. A study of national television news reports in the 1980s found that white cocaine addicts were treated much differently than black crack addicts. The whites were "offenders" in need of rehabilitation; the blacks were "delinquents" who should be imprisoned.[39] In addition, the number of black drug dealers and buyers has been exaggerated in the news.[40]

Black Stereotypes in Los Angeles Riot/Rebellion Coverage

One particular aspect of the black criminal stereotype is the national evening news's focus on "urban America nearly out of control."[41] The news characterized the response in Los Angeles to the Rodney King verdict as senseless black criminality, rather than as a purposeful uprising.[42] This privileged one interpretation of the event, the one consistent with other criminal representations of blacks. Coverage of the Los Angeles disturbances of 1992 in newspapers focused on the law and government, reactions, and the aftermath far more than it did on the causes. Only 7 percent of the extensive coverage in major newspapers discussed possible causes of the disturbance. The format of the coverage and reporters' comments blamed the events on individuals and not the system.[43]

> A persistent but not so subtle othering process was in gear: there was no motive or reason for the violence; the hoodlums were simply inactive people with enough idle time on their hands to entertain themselves by creating a disturbance. With this kind of officially concerted verbal discourse on television, fifty years of Los Angeles social, political, and economic history—indeed, the very notion of causality or context in any form—simply vanished.[44]

While the role of blacks in perpetrating violence was exaggerated, their opportunities to explain what was going on were not. The media chose to interview helicopter pilots who observed the events from the sky rather than the people on the street.[45] They also tended to ignore black victimization during the riot/rebellion.[46]

As is typical of the aftermath of race riots, news coverage of the L.A. riot/rebellion stimulated some discussion of urban issues.[47] It also resulted in some media self-criticism. Black reporters for the *Los Angeles Times* complained that the newspaper excluded minorities and that they had not been allowed to report on police mistreatment of black men prior to the King incident.[48] Carol Bradley Shirley, assistant editor of the Westside section of the *Los Angeles Times*, admitted, "South Central Los Angeles has long been the kind of place that holds little interest for the powerful. It has been neglected for decades, not only by the government, but by the press."[49] This helps explain the anger that people on the street showed toward reporters covering the event.[50]

Black Stereotypes in Poverty Stories

The public closely associates blacks with poverty because of what they see on the news.[51] When television news looks at poverty in America, it looks at urban blacks, ignoring the fact that more whites are poor and more whites are on welfare.[52] Poverty stories tend to focus on the poor as victims or the poor as threatening. The threatening image is most prevalent on local news.[53] The idea that racial discrimination might be a cause of poverty gets little coverage; instead, poverty is presented as an individual problem with individual solutions.[54]

Of the pictures of poor people appearing in poverty-related stories in the three major newsmagazines (*Time, Newsweek,* and *U.S. News and World Report*) between 1950 and 1992, 53 percent were of blacks. Only 29 percent of the poor during this time were black. This overrepresentation has been greatest since 1967, coinciding with an increase in the public's negativity toward government antipoverty policies (see figure 8.1).[55] The trend toward associating blacks with poverty continues. Blacks were still represented in 45 percent of the photographs of the poor in the same magazines between 1993

Figure 8.1   Racial Composition of the Poor, News Media Portrayal versus Reality

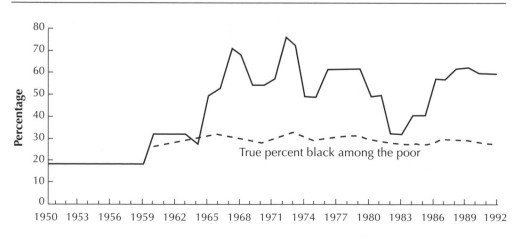

Source: Martin Gilens, *Why Americans Hate Welfare: Race, Media, and the Politics of Antipoverty Policy* (Chicago: University of Chicago Press, 1999), p. 114. Reprinted with permission.

and 1998.[56] Furthermore, negative poverty stories (such as about welfare fraud) were more likely to include pictures of blacks, whereas sympathetic poverty stories (such as those about old-age assistance) were accompanied by pictures of whites.[57] Black welfare recipients are often photographed with large numbers of children, reinforcing the "welfare queen" stereotype of poor black women.[58]

SYSTEM-SUPPORTIVE THEMES ABOUT BLACKS IN THE MAINSTREAM NEWS

These negative images of blacks—dysfunctional, poor, lazy, and criminal—contrast with the assimilationist images of successful blacks in popular culture. After watching "bad blacks" on the news, viewers can watch television sitcoms featuring "good blacks" who have succeeded in the fictional world.[59] Yet, both of these representations applaud American values such as individualism[60] and encourage "enlightened racism,"[61] the attitude among whites that racism is no longer a problem and America has achieved equality of opportunity because there are successful African Americans (like Bill Cosby or the fictional characters he portrays).[62]

Celebrating Black Success Stories to Deny Institutional Racism

Television news also contains black success stories that highlight exceptional cases against a backdrop of coverage of black pathology.[63] This coverage promotes and reinforces the idea that most black people are a problem, but the few who succeed "prove" that this is not the system's fault. Emphasizing achievement resonates with the individualism so central to our national identity and helps to justify a hands-off policy toward racial equality.[64]

News coverage of Martin Luther King Jr.'s birthday celebrates his having had a dream rather than acknowledging the enduring impediments to achieving it. More often than not, the stories celebrate ways the dream has been achieved.[65] "In its coverage of King Day, local television journalism constructed a world in which The American Dream lives."[66]

The presence of a black television anchorperson may contribute to this idea that racism is a thing of the past.[67] "Viewing local news featuring a Black anchor can symbolically affirm for White viewers that they are themselves without racial animus."[68] It also provides viewers with a successful contrast to the negative image of blacks in the news. This contrast conveys the impression that the system is fair and color-blind and that it rewards minorities who work hard and punishes those who do not.

The ABC News feature "Person of the Week" inherently individualized success. When choosing black winners, it also denied institutional oppression. Of the people selected for this accolade, 13 percent were black, and their stories celebrated their overcoming adversity and succeeding, despite humble beginnings. Blacks were more likely than whites to be selected for having overcome victimization.[69] The media apply the Horatio Alger narrative to black people, like Oprah Winfrey, who overcome poverty, abuse, and broken homes to become successful. By showing that they are included in the great American "rags-to-riches" narrative, they paint a picture of a race-neutral society and celebrate "cultural icons of racial harmony and opportunity."[70] This narrative was used in O. J. Simpson's prearrest media biography: "poor ghetto child with nothing but a mother's love and the will to succeed makes it big."[71] After the murders, the story was framed as O. J.'s "return to the ghetto."[72]

Urban Pathology Stories Used to Justify Black Oppression

A CBS News special report titled *The Vanishing Family: Crisis in Black America*, which aired in January 1985, was critiqued for its use of negative images that connected blacks with laziness and criticized the effectiveness of welfare. The message was that "the problem in the black community is not racism or unemployment but the corruption of values, the absence of moral authority, and the lack of individual motivation."[73] The authority figures (the reporter, social workers, police, and psychologist) and the personal stories in the documentary were used to convey this message explicitly. This is just one example of the "urban pathology" story, which is still common on the news.

The stereotypes of blacks as poor and violent contribute to this theme. The idea here is that blacks occupy problem areas and are the cause of these problems. "Ideologically, representations of underclass failure still appeal and contribute to the notion of the black poor as menacing and threatening."[74]

Pictures of blacks appear in bad news stories about crime, AIDS, welfare, and deteriorating cities even when the stories do not talk about race. In this way, aesthetic cues send the message that blacks are problems and reinforce negative stereotypes.[75] Rather than cover the economic reasons for the "black underclass," the media focuses on "mores, living habits and social patterns, such as promiscuity, drug addiction, and crime."[76] This implies that the problem is within the character of black Americans rather than the social structure. The image "distorts the economic and social diversity among African Americans, signaling the homogeneity of the out-group while underlining the salience of Black-White group differences."[77]

Stories Emphasizing Conflict between Blacks and White That Undermine Reform

Conflict between blacks and whites is also a common feature of media coverage, as is evident in racial-issue coverage and crime coverage. This coverage makes it harder for audiences to imagine racial reconciliation. It promotes a fatalism that justifies the status quo. In other words, it says nothing can be done to resolve differences, so why bother trying. It also normalizes the idea that blacks and whites are inherently different, which, in conjunction with images of black inferiority, justifies inequality.

This adversarial framing can be seen in coverage of affirmative action. Rather than reflect the whites' ambivalence and the reality of the programs themselves (for example, how much they have helped white women), the media turned the story into a black-white battle.[78] White and black construction workers, firemen, and police became visual symbols of this conflict on television news. White union leaders and black civil rights leaders were quoted in opposition in newspapers and newsmagazines.[79] "The dominant framing of affirmative action emphasized high-intensity, angry opposition among whites, confronted by obstinate, self-interested support among blacks. Bolstering the misleading depictions of public opinion were the mirror images in sentiments expressed by identifiably black and white sources."[80] This coverage encouraged audiences to evaluate affirmative action using material and self-interested considerations, rather than the program's goals and ethical considerations.[81] It also encourages the reverse-discrimination argument that overlooks ways in which white advantages remain despite affirmative action.[82]

Coverage of the Los Angeles riots/rebellion also reduced the complex events to a binary racial story. Economic and class-based aspects of the event, as well as Latino and white participation in the looting, were generally overlooked (even when caught on camera).[83] Some news eventually provided a multiracial interpretation for the disturbances[84] once it was revealed that Korean Americans sustained about half of the material losses[85] and that one-third of those arrested and killed were Latinos.[86] Even when conflict between racial-minority groups was discussed, it was interpreted "through the lens of black/white relationships,"[87] undermining the likelihood that members of different racial-minority groups will see their commonality and promoting the idea that the "black problem" is unsolvable.

The O. J. Simpson story provides another example of how media emphasis on black-white conflict makes race harder to talk about constructively. Coverage of the public's reaction to the trial emphasized disagreement between blacks and whites. By ignoring the mixed feelings among blacks toward the case, the news oversimplified their positions, while ignoring the context that predisposed many blacks toward suspecting a police setup. By using an Anglocentric focus (one that uses whites as the norm and compares other groups to them), the news largely ignored the fact that blacks were more open-minded than whites on the question of Simpson's guilt. One critic asked, "If the phenomenon of African Americans being more likely to think Simpson is innocent was worth explaining, why didn't the media do stories trying to explain why whites were so overwhelmingly certain of his guilt?"[88]

The focus on the racial makeup of Simpson's jury also framed the story as a black-white conflict. The notion that Simpson got off because of black jurists was promoted in the news.[89] Yet, the fact that the jury was not entirely black and the decision to acquit was unanimous was ignored. Even posttrial interviews in which jurists said that the deliberations had not been divided by race failed to alter this story line.

THE BLACK PARALLEL PRESS

The parallel black press emerged as a result of white-owned newspapers' stereotyping, ridiculing, and ignoring blacks. The black newspaper "is a tool of African American leaders to inspire, inform, and create a sense of unity among people of African descent."[90] It has a long history in America.

Early History of the Black Parallel Press

The first newspaper produced by and for blacks, *Freedom's Journal*, began publishing in 1827. This New York paper arose out of two black freemen's frustration at the mainstream newspapers' vilification of blacks and refusal to publish their letters to the editor. This paper, much like the other pre–Civil War black newspapers that followed, aimed "to report the accomplishments of Blacks, to encourage Blacks to strengthen their characters, and to seek 'by reason of persuasion' the abolition of slavery."[91] Some writers, like David Ruggles, were abolitionist activists who also worked against oppression in other forums, such as the Underground Railroad, which assisted runaway slaves. Another group was the Committee of Vigilance, which confronted slave catchers and provided legal assistance to those accused of being runaway slaves.[92]

After the Civil War, black papers flourished and pursued other political goals. Diversity of opinion within the black community was reflected in newspaper copy, including debate over whether blacks should support the U.S. Constitution; use violence or restraint in fighting oppression; support the Republican party or third parties; pursue equality through integration or accept and work within a segregated society (a position called "conciliation"); and return to Africa or stay in the United States.[93]

Prior to 1908, when black newspapers started to appeal to a mass readership by being politically independent, they were partisan. Both sides of major issues that divided the black community "had a publication to trumpet their views."[94] Booker T. Washington, an advocate of conciliation, subsidized certain black newspapers; integrationists supported other papers. These financial ties influenced the papers' positions and the degree to which they challenged white authority.[95]

The Antilynching Campaign and the Black Press

While black newspapers publicized intragroup debates on some issues, they reflected and encouraged the unity of the black community on other issues, such as the problem of lynching. Not only did the black press challenge the practice of lynching and call for antilynching legislation, but it also criticized the coverage this problem received in the mainstream press. It claimed that simply reporting the fact that whites tortured and murdered more than 4,000 blacks between 1880 and 1947 was not enough.[96] They saw white reporters as hiding behind the ethic of objectivity when they simply reported the facts of these executions. Black newspapers argued that the claim to objectivity was used to justify white reporters' lack of moral outrage over lynchings, but it did not stop them from asserting the guilt of the black victims who were lynched for crimes that they had not been convicted of.[97]

Unlike these white reporters, Ida B. Wells-Barnett, co-owner and editor of the weekly *Memphis Free Speech*, investigated the facts surrounding lynchings. She wrote an editorial that questioned the legality of lynchings, the racist and economic motivations for these acts, and the evidence used by the executing mobs and reporters covering the murders. Shortly after it was published, her newspaper was destroyed.[98] Yet, she continued to write against lynching and the mainstream press's silence on the issue in the *New York Age* and later from Europe in a weekly column, "Ida B. Wells Abroad."[99] She and her criticisms received a sympathetic reception in Great Britain. Yet, the *New York Times* characterized her as an emotional, dogmatic, self-interested deviant outside of the realm of the "'rational' sphere of discussion."[100] Journalism and mass communications professor David Mindich explains the reasons for this response:

> Wells was thwarted in her attempts to be heard because the idea that whites were more civilized than blacks was deeply ingrained in mainstream journalists' belief systems. Understanding lynchings as white terrorism of blacks would undermine these beliefs. The second barrier against Wells was that she herself was considered less reliable because she belonged . . . in the three categories that the elites used to define non-"objectivity": she was an outsider, a woman, and member of an "uncivilized race."[101]

The active campaign against lynching in the early 1930s was the first major civil rights initiative that involved the black press and an activist African American organization, the National Association for the Advancement of Colored People (NAACP). Major black newspapers covered the NAACP's efforts to lobby for the Costigan-Wagner (antilynching) bill. It also helped build the organization by urging readers to become members. Hundreds of columns were written on the topic, and international newspapers covering the debate used many of them.[102]

Civil Rights Advocacy and the Black Parallel Press

One newspaper that gave a lot of attention to lynching was the *Chicago Defender*, founded in 1905, a year in which there were fifty-seven documented cases of blacks being lynched. This problem was only part of the newspaper's civil rights agenda. "The *Defender* was a forceful advocate for civil rights since its earliest days of publication, and provided commentary on all aspects of racial discrimination, including prejudice of the white press."[103] Langston Hughes called the paper the "journalistic voice of a largely voiceless people."[104] It went from being a weekly to a daily newspaper in 1955 and continues to publish today.[105]

During World War I, the *Defender* was monitored by the FBI for its outspoken criticism of President Woodrow Wilson's support of segregation. The editor of the paper was threatened with jail time under the Espionage Act of 1917 after he published a cartoon in which African American troops were being shot in the back by white American troops. The government continued to monitor the paper after the war, claiming that it might have communist leanings and could incite racial violence. Although the paper became more circumspect and prudent during the war, intimidation failed to deter the *Defender* from its political agenda.[106]

Covering and commenting on racial-issue concerns was the primary aim of other black newspapers. An analysis of sixty-four black newspapers in the early 1920s indicated that three-fifths of the articles were about racial struggles.[107] The black papers did not just complain about inequality; they advocated political remedies to the problems they covered.[108]

The number of black newspapers and their readership size varied over time. They gained readership after periods of social and economic instability.[109] The late 1920s and early 1930s were a period of low circulation, even for the *Defender*, which started an annual contest in 1934 to help sales. The contest was the election of a mayor of Chicago's black South Side community known as "Bronzeville" during a time when blacks were politically disempowered. The symbolism of the mayoral elections and the process of voting for black candidates helped promote black pride and cultural identity across the country.[110]

Black newspapers were at their peak in the 1940s. At that time, they were covering black servicemen, critiquing segregation in the armed forces, and promoting the Double V Campaign—victory over racism at home and fascism in Europe.[111] Some black publishers and the government criticized the Negro Newspaper Publisher's Association decision to continue criticizing racism at home during the war as unpatriotic. Yet, they held firm to the position that they were committed both to supporting the war and to criticizing discriminatory policies.[112]

Many black newspapers closed or decreased the frequency of their publication after the civil rights movement, when mainstream news hired their reporters and increased coverage of the black community.[113] Yet, the black press survives today with fewer newspapers.[114] These remaining publications have relatively stable circulations.[115] For the most part, its agenda has become less political as it has struggled for advertising and a middle-class audience.[116]

"Blacks depicted in the pages of black newspapers are still generally either heroes whose career advancements, civic achievement, or fame are hailed as strides for the entire race, or victims of an unjust America."[117] Readers are less likely to rely on these papers exclusively than they were in the past. Now, the black press is more of a supplement than an alternative to the mainstream press for black readers.[118]

Differences still remain between the parallel press and the mainstream. Black newspapers continue to cover information left out of the mainstream news and to provide alternative interpretations to stories found in both.

A comparison of coverage of the Los Angeles riots/rebellion in white mainstream and black papers revealed both differences and similarities. Both presses used a tragic frame to interpret the riots. The major black newspapers in Chicago and Los Angeles saw the tragedy as self-destructive and were more critical of rioters than the mainstream press was. The papers' interpretation of the cause of the crisis differed. The black press blamed an unjust legal system and criticized the lack of leadership and political participation in the black community. The mainstream newspapers saw the tragedy as the result of inescapable racial divisions in society.[119] Of the articles in the black press, 20 percent used terms like "revolt" or "uprising" to describe the events, while only 9 percent of the white press did. Also, slightly more paragraphs claimed that rioting is a legitimate form of social protest in the black press (6.6 percent versus less than 1 percent in the white press).[120] Both presses were pessimistic about the future of race relations.[121]

One study compared the coverage of a Supreme Court decision on a federal affirmative action program in 1995 (*Adarand v. Pena*) in the *New York Times*, *Washington Post*, and *Los Angeles Times* to that found in twenty-two black newspapers. The mainstream newspapers' coverage relied heavily on legal jargon and said that the Court had decided that reverse discrimination was unconstitutional. Black newspapers framed the decision as a dramatic setback. They criticized the decision, the Court's conservative majority, and Justice Clarence Thomas for undermining social justice. While the mainstream newspapers generally did not differentiate Thomas from the other justices he voted with in the majority, the black press gave him extensive (and unfavorable) attention. One black newspaper referred to him as "Justice Buffoon."[122]

Black Radio and Television

Although the first radio news program aired in 1927 in New York City, the first black-owned commercial station did not get its license until 1949. It was WERD in Atlanta, Georgia. Despite the many black-owned radio stations that followed, these commercial stations had little political content. "As a teacher, leader, guide, unifier, and advocate of self-help and superior citizenship, Black radio was slow to prove itself."[123] However, today's community (or independent) black radio is growing[124] and speaks with a distinctively alternative political voice.[125] Community radio tries to reach a particular audience and give it access to the airwaves in order to strengthen its identity.[126]

Catherine Squires conducted a participant observation study of WVON, a black talk radio station in Chicago, Illinois, in 1995.[127] She worked at the station, interviewed its workers, analyzed its content, and surveyed its listeners. Her extensive study revealed the community-building role of the station. "WVON serves as a locus both for information critical to community activities and political education and for the formation and sustenance of a Black identity. Not only does WVON speak to 'Black issues,' it also seeks to address issues with a Black framework."[128]

Both KUCB Radio in Des Moines, Iowa, and Black Liberation Radio, in Springfield, Illinois, provided forums for social-issue discussions, tried to increase black pride, and investigated issues generally neglected in the mainstream press (such as police brutality). Black Liberation Radio was a pirate station operating without a license and ordered to stop by the FCC.[129] The station's founder, Mbanna Kantako, resisted the order, arguing that the FCC was "a symbol of domination and control."[130] "Mbanna Kantako argues that the key to self-determination is the control over knowledge, so he devotes much of his radio time to producing and circulating counterknowledges of the white social order and the way it insinuates its power into Black consciousness, Black bodies, and Black everyday life."[131] One example of "counterknowledge" is the argument that AIDS is a weapon of genocide against blacks and the evidence that supports this claim.[132]

Radio stations do not have to be owned by blacks to include shows with black perspectives. The *Tom Joyner Morning Show* is syndicated on hundreds of radio stations across the country and serves over five million listeners; because it is an entertainment-oriented program with commercial appeal, it has been able to thrive under media consolidation. Yet, it also includes political commentary, voter registration drives, black college scholarship fundraising, and campaigns against companies that racially discriminate.[133]

From 1968 to 1970, the Emmy-winning *Black Journal* appeared on PBS once a month, providing provocative discussions among blacks on urban issues. Executive producer William Greaves wanted issues discussed in black barbershops to have a place on television. The show included black-nationalist symbols, including the dashikis worn by the hosts and Swahili salutations. It also offered solutions to racial problems and gave artistic freedom to black filmmakers. It inspired black documentaries, which found audiences in independent movie houses.[134]

Black Entertainment Television (BET) started in 1980. It illustrates how cable television's ability to target a segmented audience can serve racial-minority audiences, as well as how commercialism can compromise political messages. BET's public affairs programming originally covered racial issues and black history that were not routinely part of mainstream channels. Viewers drawn to BET tended to have high "racial orientations" (a sense of racial distinctiveness and pride) that the programming reinforced.[135] After twenty years of black ownership, the network was sold to Viacom (owner of CBS, MTV, UPN), a conglomerate that looked to profit off of the black market.[136] After the sale, BET's news continued to diminish in quality.[137]

CONCLUSION

Although blacks receive more news coverage than other racial minorities in the United States, much of this coverage is negative. They are ghettoized into stories about urban problems, including drugs, crime, and poverty. Not only are blacks visually attached to bad news stories about these subjects but they are more often shown as the villains, and their victimization is ignored. In the ways they celebrate black achievement and interpret social disorder, stories lay the fault for inequality at the feet of individuals rather than institutions. The black press has challenged these representations and the sensibility that the mainstream media bring to racial issues. It has challenged government policies and advocated political reforms since its inception, reflecting both the debates and the consensus issues in the black community.

Native American Mass Publics in the News

NATIVE AMERICANS RECEIVE LITTLE NEWS COVERAGE. STEREOTYPES FOUND IN entertainment media are used to justify the changing government solutions to the "Indian problem." This coverage serves status quo interests, justifying and protecting the political and economic interests of the establishment. Native Americans have created their own communication networks to combat this exclusion and bias.

EXCLUSION AND SELECTIVE EXCLUSION OF NATIVE AMERICANS FROM THE MAINSTREAM NEWS

In her analysis of Native Americans in the news throughout American history, Mary Ann Weston finds that aside from stories about their colorful uniqueness or their having got in the way of what whites wanted, Native Americans receive very little coverage.[1] She argues that they can do little about this because of their peripheral status and lack of political and economic power.[2] Topics important to Native Americans (such as land claims) are not typically covered in the mainstream press, which considers the audience for this news small and unimportant.[3] The *Washington Post* included only eight articles during a ten-year period about Native Americans' legal battle with the Washington Redskins football franchise over the use of a derogatory term.[4] Often, white reporters lack basic knowledge about Native American history and legal arrangements with the U.S. government. This makes it difficult for them to report events in context and with depth and accuracy.[5]

Even stories about Indians rarely include their voices. They are talked about, rather than talked to. This is particularly true in the national press.[6] Even when the U.S. government's Indian policy was in flux (such as in the 1920s) and their coverage was most extensive, white sympathizers rather than Native American leaders articulated their positions. An exception to this was the 1960s during the American Indian movement (see chapter 13).[7] The news coverage Native Americans do receive overlooks differences between individuals and between tribes. One study of the *New York Times* found some improvement over time in this area. By the early 1990s, almost 50 percent of the articles about Indians identified them by tribe.[8]

Throughout the years, the national and local news has presented Indians in substantially different ways. National news is attracted more to stories involving Native Americans that are sensational, vivid, and conflictual. For example, the Lumbee tribe in North Carolina drew national news attention when it broke up a Ku Klux Klan rally in 1958.[9] Even the prestigious *New York Times* has given little coverage to Native Americans.[10] Local coverage contains more detail and treats Indians as part of the community. In areas where Indians live, they are more likely to appear in the local news and more likely to speak for themselves.

Even newspapers from the same state can cover local indigenous groups differently. This is illustrated in the coverage of Project Chariot, a 1958 federal government plan to detonate nuclear bombs in Alaska without notifying or consulting Eskimos living close to the proposed site. Early coverage did not mention that the plan was to use Native lands; nor did it include what the people living there had to say about it. Instead, the Alaskan mainstream press supported the plan enthusiastically because they thought it would booster the economy.[11] Eskimo voices were finally shared in the *Fairbanks Daily News-Mirror* after the American Energy Commission reported environmental dangers. The *Anchorage Daily News* provided less coverage of their criticisms.[12]

STEREOTYPES OF NATIVE AMERICANS IN THE MAINSTREAM NEWS

Anti-Indian sentiment has a long history in newspapers that once explicitly promoted negative stereotypes.[13] The terms "buck," "chief," "brave," "squaw," and "papoose" were common in newspapers until the 1960s.[14] Stereotypes of the "noble savage," the "exotic relic," and the "degraded Indian" endured for decades in the news, adjusted to fit the events of the day.[15] Reoccurring images "of Indians as exotic, warlike, childlike, or improvident" are still common.[16]

The "good Indian"/"bad Indian" (or "good tribe"/"bad tribe") dichotomy found in films has also dominated news coverage of Native Americans. Who was "good" and who was "bad" depends on how much trouble particular Indians were giving whites in power at particular times. Neither stereotype considers Indians as complex and unique individuals. An examination of how the good/bad Indian dichotomy has been used over time illustrates a variety of simplistic stereotypes.

Indian Stereotypes in the Media of the 1800s

The good/bad Indian dichotomy dominated coverage in the 1800s as whites disagreed about what to do about the Indians. One side saw the bad Indian as a barbaric savage to be battled into submission or extinction so that whites could be safe and progress could be achieved. This stereotype "was a product of newspapers aligned with both government and business interests, a view that saw Indians as obstacles to economic growth and national expansion."[17] Coverage was particularly negative prior to the 1870s.[18] A sentence from Denver's *Daily Rocky Mountain News* of that time period illustrates the blatancy of this bias: "That the North American Indians are hopeless savages is the most clearly established fact in the history of man."[19]

The other side also thought that government action was needed, but they used the good Indian stereotype to justify their approach. They romanticized Indians as children who needed to be "saved," not from the government but by the government. They needed to be civilized through education and religion. The image of a "civilized savage" was common in the news by the late 1870s, justifying the workability of this approach. For example, in 1879, when the Poncas tribe was arrested for not relocating as ordered by the government, much of the coverage was sympathetic, showing them as civilized and progressive.[20]

Much of the good Indian coverage resulted from the political advocacy of a white journalist. Thomas H. Tibbles, of the *Omaha Daily Herald*, helped the Indian reform movement with his writing and organization of an eastern lecture tour featuring Poncas. "Sympathetic newspapers in Chicago and New York, relying on information from Tibbles and other Ponca supporters, treated the Poncas as an exceptional case, a tribe readily distinguished from less civilized tribes."[21]

Being "civilized" meant emulating whites by going to school, attending Christian churches, and speaking English. The *New York Times* repeatedly characterized the Delawares, Potawatomies, and Poncas as "semicivilized" and the Oglala, Sioux, and Utes as "wild and predatory."[22] The reform movement's publicity used the good Indian/bad Indian dichotomy to build support for reform legislation that was more "pro-Indian" since it challenged military solutions. Although progressive at the time, these assimilationist solutions are now seen as undermining Native cultures.[23]

Indian Stereotypes in the Media of the Early to Mid-1900s

In the early 1900s, the debate changed, and cultural pluralists who wanted Indian ways of life preserved challenged assimiliationist solutions. Opposed to laws restricting Indian cultural expressions (such as ceremonial dances and religious rituals), these white reformers successfully promoted romantic images of Native Americans to the press. The noble part of the noble savage stereotype was emphasized in newspaper coverage of the Pueblos. Both sides of the debate also used imagery of Indians as children to make their cases in the press. For the assimilationists, Indians were childlike and vulnerable, needing to be protected from the modern world by being taught "white ways"; to the cultural pluralists, Indians were innocent "children of nature" whose uniqueness needed protecting.[24]

During this debate about preserving Indian cultures, the press often used inaccurate terminology that homogenized Native customs. Reporters assumed that they all lived in wigwams or used wampum.[25] Distinctions were made between tribes in terms of how close they were to white customs and values. Of the little coverage Indians received, the most assimilated tribes were given the most sympathetic treatment.[26] How cooperative a tribe was with U.S. government policies and economic interests also influenced which stereotype was used to describe them; thus, the Paiutes were presented as bad Indians and the Pueblo as good Indians.[27]

One common stereotype was that of the "degraded Indian pagan." These images emphasized Native American inferiority to whites. In the 1920s, the focus was on drunken, sickly, and dirty Yaquis or Plains tribesmen. In the 1930s, it was the Osage tribe, who were presented as stupid spendthrifts; the Seminoles and Hill Indians of Montana were shown as losers.[28]

Even after the lives of Indians changed in the 1930s with the Indian Reorganization Act, the press's images did not change much. They still "frequently built and reinforced inaccurate images of Indians as lazy, drunken, exotic, naive, and ignorant. Native religious practices, particularly, suffered in the press, often being rendered as bizarre entertainment, somewhere between a circus act and a museum exhibit."[29] At this time, the bad Indian became an object more of ridicule than fear.

In the 1930s, another stereotype, the "involved Indian citizen," was added to the noble savage, the degraded Indian, and the exotic relic. Since new policies gave some Indians official status in government institutions, the press considered these individuals legitimate sources. Their coverage lacked the colorful stereotypical terms used when describing other Indians.[30] This was another version of the "good Indian" who helped maintain the preestablished racial hierarchy.

The magazine *Arizona Highway* used Indians to market the Southwest to tourists. An analysis of the magazine from 1925 to 1940 showed how two contradictory images of Indians were used to promote the region. Indians were presented as "traditional" (exotic, primitive, and colorful) and as "progressive" (giving up traditional ways for modern technological advancement and assimilation). Both versions were oversimplified. The traditional Indians were covered for the exoticness of their rituals. These rituals were sometimes described as "weird," and their meanings were rarely explained. The progressive Indians were covered for their accessibility and eagerness to modernize. They were used as proof that "white ways" were superior.[31]

> The colorful, traditional Indian who lived an "authentic" and apparently contented life in the desert, and the competent, progressive Indian, not so exotic or bizarre as to be inaccessible. This two-sided figure was the perfect tourist creation—romantic and colorful, but not frightening or hostile, seemingly content, timeless, and well off the political agenda.[32]

The good Indian/bad Indian dichotomy was also present in the magazine in how it distinguished Pimas ("peace-loving and industrious friends of the White man") from Apache (violent and hard to control).[33]

The 1940s press continued to treat Indians as exotic without explaining much about their traditions and practices. However, the war made another version of the "involved Indian citizen" possible. The press treated Native Americans who fought in World War II as "noble warriors."[34] Since their stereotypic savagery now served the dominant ideology and institutions, it became a good thing. Indian service in the war was characterized as patriotic, loyal, and brave. It helped justify the 1950s "termination" policy of the federal government.

The termination policy was a plan to withdraw government support and services from tribes in favor of integrating them into white society and relocating them to cities. The good Indian, sometimes called the "new Indian" in the 1950s press, had assimilated into white culture without government assistance. The bad, degraded Indian was characterized as too lazy, stupid, or drunk to stop living off of the federal government. The exotic images continued but were presented alongside "modern" and ironic images (such as a traditionally dressed Indian chewing gum).

Indian Stereotypes in Today's Media

Many of these stereotypes persist today. Some more varied representations are joining the stereotypical ones even in the national press.[35] Yet, troublesome language and images continue. News coverage still includes phrases like "circle the wagon," "on the warpath," and "powwow." Story titles like "Indian Men's Love Secrets Aren't for Sale" continue to exoticize Indians. News about Indians is typically negative, focusing on the problems of bad Indians, such as alcoholism, poverty, and gambling.[36] Coverage of the sports team mascot issue also trivializes them.[37]

When the Lac Courte Oreilles band of the Chippewa Nation tried legally to block the establishment of a mine in rural Wisconsin in 1990 and 1991, newspaper coverage presented them as "'the other,' as spiritually mysterious and embracing anti-technology and anti-progressive values."[38] Warlike symbolism resonated "with stereotypical images, in which Indians are depicted as losers in military and cultural battles."[39] Stories also delegitimized the Chippewa by characterizing them as outsiders, interviewing them less often than mining officials (Indians made up 9 percent of the sources quoted; mining officials made up 16 percent), and relegating coverage of their position to sidebars. They were also presented as primitive, irrational, and mysterious.[40]

SYSTEM-SUPPORTIVE THEMES ABOUT NATIVE AMERICANS IN THE MAINSTREAM NEWS

Since their arrival in North America, whites have wrestled with how best to deal with the problem of indigenous populations. Solutions to the so-called Indian problem have included extermination, forced assimilation, cultural pluralism, and self-determinism. The news coverage has reflected the vicissitudes of the government's approach to Indians and the self-interest of local elites.

Journalism and mass communications professor Patricia Curtin argues that, virtually overnight, the mainstream press characterized similar events differently to serve the changing interests of the government. She demonstrates this with an analysis of coverage during the government's battles with the Plains Indians. When South Cheyennes were killed in 1864 in the Sand Creek Massacre, New York newspapers were critical of the horrible butchery.[41] However, four years later the same papers characterized a similar event as a "justified solution to a long-term problem."[42] Reporters experienced in covering the Civil War who accompanied military troops on their missions to solve the Indian problem, no longer saw Indians as "helpless children."[43] The need for a "renewed sense of [national] purpose" after the Civil War resulted in ethnocentric media coverage that redefined the murder of Indian families as necessary rather than horrible.[44]

Stories that focused on the conflicts between Native Americans and whites serve to problematize Indians and justify government policies. Sensational and graphic detail of white-Indian conflict made coverage in the 1800s primarily violent and simplistic. It emphasized and exaggerated Indian violence against whites in part to justify government policies.[45]

> Violent encounters between evil Indians and innocent whites made compelling, page-one stories; peaceful relations and gentle Indians did not. Moreover, Indian-white conflicts could be easily reduced to a standard set of sensational "facts," ready-made for telegraphic transmission to every AP newspaper. . . . Year in and year out, the press looked for—and found—simple tales of violence and evil on the Indian frontier. These stories were journalistically "true," but they were never the full story of Indian-white relations in the West. For Native Americans, already viewed as savage and uncivilized, this emphasis on violence worked to reinforce Indian inferiority and ensure that the news would continue to emphasize conflict over benign ideas about Indians.[46]

Contemporary Coverage of Indians as Problems

The theme of Indians as a problem did not go away once the West was "won." Native Americans are still characterized as a problem in three ways—as a problem for the government and businesses, a problem to themselves, and a problem for whites.

Native Americans are seen as a problem for the government in stories that emphasize the demands they make and the dangers they pose. When FBI agents died in a shootout on an Oglala Sioux reservation in 1975, wire services, television, and newspapers quickly characterized the event as an "ambush" and an "execution." Reporting was mistakenly "based on the assumption of premeditated treachery by Indians" stemming from historical stereotypes.[47]

The idea that Indians present a problem to themselves is evident in news about poverty, alcoholism, and poor education. These topics dominate the *New York Times'* coverage of Indians.[48] News of an outbreak of the fatal hantavirus on a reservation in the Southwest in 1993 was an example of problem coverage. The press was quick to characterize the disease as peculiar to Navajos, despite the fact that other people had contracted it. *USA Today* and the *Albuquerque Tribune* called hantavirus "the Navajo Flu," while *The Arizona Republic* labeled it "the Navajo Epidemic."[49]

The hantavirus stories characterized Indians as diseased and dirty, since the virus was thought to be contracted through contact with rodent excrement.[50] A content analysis of three mainstream newspapers in the West revealed that 35 percent of the references to Navajo in hantavirus stories were negative rather than neutral.[51] The intrusiveness of the press during the epidemic angered many members of the tribe, who put up signs reading "No News Media Allowed."[52] In part, this opposition resulted from reporters' violating Navajo customs and traditions that required private, spiritual rituals and for the dead person's name go unspoken for a year after his or her death.[53]

The notion of Indians as a problem is promoted when they are accused of having special rights or interests opposed to the general interest of the white community. These stories are given an "us-versus-them" conflict frame. Stories about profits reservations earn from casino revenue illustrate this frame. A study of Albuquerque, New Mexico's local television news found extensive and superficial coverage of Indian gambling, but no coverage of other subjects important to Indians. For example, it overlooked "cuts in the Bureau of Indian Affairs' budget that could impact local Pueblos, including cuts in new housing construction, remedial education, and education job training and employment programs."[54]

Similarly, a January 19, 1992, story about Chippewa spear fishing rights on KARE-TV (NBC's Minneapolis–St. Paul affiliate) illustrates how stories that use the conflict frame employ historic stereotypes.[55] The issue was whether Indians should be allowed fishing rights denied to whites. The news coverage marginalized the Indians and their position through source selection, the use of sound bites, and a lack of historical perspective. No Chippewa were interviewed and the Court's decision to uphold their right to fish was not explained. "Three white journalists report on the events, a white state official describes the agreement, a throng of white protesters represents the dissatisfaction of 'sports fishing' enthusiasts, and local hero Bud Grant, a white man, serves as the commonsense champion of their cause."[56]

Journalism and mass communications professor Cynthia-Lou Coleman found conflict frames in ten Wisconsin newspapers' coverage of a dispute over mining rights in the early 1990s. When the Lac Courte Oreilles band of the Cippewa (Ojibwa) Nation and environmentalists tried to stop the Flambeau Mining Company, the issue was described as a battle using warlike metaphors. References to the history of Indian–U.S. government wars connoted that the Indians would be the inevitable losers.[57]

THE NATIVE AMERICAN PARALLEL PRESS

Reservation papers and radio stations constitute a parallel press that serves Native American interests by spending substantial time and space on topics important to Native Americans. It also provides a place for Native American voices to be heard. These media provide a counterpoint to the stereotypes and limitations of the mainstream press by focusing on positive aspects of the Native communities.

Newspapers and Magazines

Indian newspapers and magazines were born of social forces that threatened Native Americans' lives and property. Publications "owned or managed by, intended for, and speaking for American Indian people" were used in the 1800s prior to the Civil War and served an educational role for their readers. Native Americans were provided with community news, advertising, and strategies to survive their encounters with whites. Cherokees originated the first Native newspaper (the *Cherokee Phoenix*, 1828) and magazine (the *Cherokee Messenger*, 1844).

> Throughout its brief history, the *Phoenix* was at the center of Cherokee national life, portraying the standards of its civilization, carrying letters that discussed problems and politics, and reflecting the persistent problem of alcoholism among Cherokees.[58]

Despite the harassment and arrest of its reporters, the *Phoenix* was an outspoken critic of a 1829 Georgia law that took away Indians' rights in court.[59] As early as 1843, Indian nations were investing in official papers. The *Cherokee Advocate* was financed in part by the Cherokee government.[60]

In the parallel press, Native Americans are at the center of the news, and their issues, problems, and successes are shared with their communities.

Indian newspapers and newsmagazines do not take monolithic political positions, as is illustrated by two major magazines from the 1920s that differed in their views on Indian-white relations. The *American Indian Magazine* promoted assimilation and pan-Indianism, whereas *American Indian Life* supported cultural pluralism and self-determinism.[61] During the hantavirus epidemic, 32 percent of the references to Navajo in the *Navajo Times* were negative.[62]

Tribal newspapers are independent from the U.S. national government and are free of the pressure to conform to the expectations of a commercial white audience; however, they are not necessarily "free presses."[63] Despite the Indian Civil Rights Act of 1968, which guarantees a free press, tribal officials control some of the reservation newspapers.[64]

About six hundred weekly or monthly Indian newspapers are divisions of their governments, and the editors are extensions of the tribal councils.[65] Since the tribal government subsidizes these newspapers, they are expected to reflect its views.[66] Reporters who do not report what leaders demand can be censored, threatened, fired, banned from meetings, or denied access to documents. Sometimes their newspapers are shut down.[67] Stories about battles within the tribe and its leadership for control of the reservation, as well as those about corruption, are often cut from the papers by tribal leaders.[68] Some authorities demand to read stories before they are printed,[69] thereby exercising prior restraint. Therefore, while the Native American press may challenge national hegemony, it may also support local elites who can be unrepresentative and corrupt.[70]

Most reservation newspapers are good at providing positive news about Indians. This contrasts greatly with the poor coverage of Indian tribes in the mainstream media.[71] In 1981, Jennette Henry observed that these papers were "Indian to the core," with little coverage of international or national news that did not directly affect Indians.[72] Since then, Native American newspapers have cast wider nets for news.[73]

Some reporters (and tribal leaders) resist the assumption that reservation papers are "house organs" for the Indian government. They try to make these newspapers serve the community better by including bad news about reservation leaders.[74] Also, there are more independent, Native-owned newspapers with national circulations, urban magazines, and newsletters than there once were.[75] In the early 1980s, Indian underground newspapers such as the *Cherokee Wildfire*, written by unnamed reporters, provided a counterpoint to tribal policies and acted as watchdogs to officials' corruption.[76] The *Carolina Indian Voice* claims to be a "voice of the silent majority" in Pembroke, North Carolina. It routinely criticizes the local mainstream press as racist for ignoring and stereotyping Indians.[77]

One of these is the national *Indian Country Today*, which began in 1981 and has been operated by the Oneida Nation of New York since 1989. Originally called the *Lakota Times*, the paper changed its name after receiving funding from the Gannett Foundation.[78] Advertising itself as "The Nation's Leading American Indian News Source," it covers news and provides political commentary, claiming to offer a Native American perspective.[79] This can be seen in its strong stand against the use of sports mascots that dishonor Native Americans.[80] It provokes debate within the Native American community with investigative reporting, such as its indictment of medicine people as frauds.[81]

Sometimes the parallel press can find its way into the mainstream. The *Tundra Times* was started in Alaska to provide Eskimo news for the mainstream media.[82] To combat the lack of Native voices in Alaska's newspapers, a student-writing project out of the University of Alaska's rural branch campus, Chukchi College, distributed writings of Alaskan natives. The Chukchi News and Information Service provides authentic community voices to newspapers such as the *Anchorage Daily News*, which runs the articles as a biweekly feature. This information service has won journalism awards despite its inherent challenge to the traditional conventions of newsworthiness, which privilege conflict, controversy, exceptions, and timeliness. Instead, the service practices cultural journalism, which focuses on the daily experiences of a community.[83]

Radio and Internet

Native broadcasting made major advancements in the 1970s. "Radio—the spoken word carried afar—blends well with the tradition of oral communication in Indian culture."[84] Most of these stations were in the Western rural communities. Some broadcast to large areas; others with only a few hundred watts serve a small geographic area.[85] Native radio stations' mission statements include the following ideas:

1. The preservation of Native language and culture is of paramount importance.
2. Educational and informational programs, especially those that promote literacy, are also important.
3. Entertainment programs should target the interests of Natives.[86]

Tribal governments hold the licenses of nearly half of these stations; others are independent, but are routinely pressured by Native leaders. Some are government funded; others are commercial. For most stations, programming is bilingual. In fact, some channels primarily broadcast in Native languages. For example, Apache is spoken during 70 percent of airtime on Whiteriver, Arizona's KNNB. The Alaskan radio stations are traditionally the only local media providing up-to-date news, and they provide a lot of it. In 1987 the National Native News radio service began daily broadcasts. It is distribu to National Public Radio affiliates, allowing Native news to be heard in are outside of individual stations' signal ranges.[87]

Native Americans have also used the Internet in their efforts to take control of presenting the news about themselves. The Native News Network, established in 1991, buys and sells news and features on Native American issues using Internet technology. The Internet is used for intragroup communication and to provide the general public with information.[88] Both the eastern and western bands of Cherokees have websites that serve their communities (www.cherokee-nc.com and www.Cherokee.org). While both sites help to enlarge and inform their communities, the western band's page is more political and contains more hard news.[89]

CONCLUSION

This chapter illustrates that the perceived political and economic interests of the white majority determine the amount and type of coverage that Native Americans receive in the mainstream press. When these interests are debated, the coverage reflects alternative views. Some of these positions and the coverage of them are more sympathetic than others. However, they still draw on stereotypes using the good Indian/bad Indian dichotomy to advocate whatever "solutions" to the "Indian problem" are in vogue. Since the early 1800s, Native Americans have resisted these solutions and stereotypes through their parallel press. While not always independent of Native governments, these media provide a place of empowerment and alternative views to those of the mainstream press.

10

Hispanic Mass Publics in the News

~~~~~~

THIS CHAPTER DISCUSSES EXCLUSION, STEREOTYPES, SYSTEM-SUPPORTIVE themes, and the parallel press in terms of news about Hispanics. It shows how, relative to their percentage of the population, their exclusion is worse than that of other racial minorities. At the same time, Hispanics share some of the same stereotypes imposed on other racial minorities, which are used to justify their inequality. Finally, the chapter examines Spanish-language media as a potential parallel press that is larger than other minorities' media and less radical.

EXCLUSION AND SELECTIVE EXCLUSION OF HISPANICS FROM THE MAINSTREAM NEWS

Although Hispanics are the largest growing minority in the United States, their news coverage remains small.[1] Studies of 1990s coverage consistently found that 1 percent of the news dealt with Hispanics, which is less than blacks and Asian Americans receive.[2] This neglect was true of leading newspapers[3] and network television news.[4] The frequency of Latinos' coverage in the *New York Times* from 1934 to 1994 was much more similar to Native and Asian Americans' than blacks'. Even though they received four times more *New York Times* coverage in the 1990s than in any other decade, they still only got a meager nineteen column inches a year.[5]

Geographic Exclusion of Hispanics

How does the size of the Hispanic community affect the amount of coverage they receive in local news? Studies provide different answers to this question. There is some evidence that communities with small percentages of Hispanics provide little or no coverage of them. At a time when Hispanics made up about 5 percent of the community served by the Raleigh, North Carolina's

News & Observer, they were included in 0.14 percent of its stories. Yet, news exclusion is also present in places with large Hispanic populations.

In southwestern papers published in 1980, Hispanics were virtually ignored on the editorial pages and only prevalent on the sports pages.[6] An analysis of newspapers from forty cities with at least 10 percent–Latino populations revealed infrequent coverage: every three papers had about two articles that included Latinos. The coverage frequency varied greatly, with the *Miami Herald* giving the most coverage and the *Gary Post Tribune* the least.[7]

Some research indicates that there is more local news coverage of Hispanics on the West Coast and in the Southwest, where many Latinos live.[8] A study of news media content in cities with 20 percent–Hispanic populations found that newspapers and television gave Hispanics space and time equivalent to their population proportion, but that radio did not. This study's threshold for counting coverage as including Hispanics was low. Most of this coverage qualified as Hispanic because it included a Spanish surname rather than because it provided substantive coverage of Hispanic individuals or racial issues.[9]

Exclusion by Story Type

Even when the frequency of newspaper coverage is proportionate to the Hispanic population, as it is in a few cities (for example, San Antonio, Texas, and Albuquerque, New Mexico), it tends to portray them negatively.[10] Most news about Hispanics focuses on crime[11] and conflict.[12] Stories featuring Hispanics are about gangs, poverty, and drugs.[13] Immigration makes up a large percentage of network news coverage of Hispanics.[14]

Of the few national television news stories aired in 1995 focusing on Latinos, half were about singer Selena's murder.[15] Local television coverage of Hispanic events or issues is also rare.[16] These stories are often soft news and are rarely found in the business section.[17] One explanation for this is that the news treats race as a "black-versus-white" issue rather than recognizing diversity.[18] Such is the case with affirmative action reporting[19] and the Los Angeles riot/rebellion coverage.[20]

Despite the heavy involvement of Hispanics in the Los Angeles riot/rebellion as both the perpetrators and the victims of crimes in the heavily Hispanic-populated parts of the city, the story was covered as a black-white problem.[21] Lost in the news was the fact that 52 percent of the first five thousand people arrested during the event were Latino, compared to the 39 percent who were black,[22] and that one of the policemen who beat Rodney King was Hispanic.[23] Even in news about riots occurring in predominantly Hispanic neighborhoods, newsmagazines use photographs of blacks.[24]

Hispanics are practically invisible as authorities in the news,[25] even in news about affirmative action.[26] In fact, Hispanic individuals only appear in half of the network news stories about Hispanics.[27] Their leaders and organizational spokespeople are rarely contacted for comment on stories. Journalist Jorge Quiroga laments that there are "no Hispanic names in the newsroom Rolodex."[28] Latinos quoted in Raleigh's *News & Observer* stories were not usually experts, but "ordinary people talking about their personal experience." This might give them visibility and even empathy, but it does not legitimate their authority vis-à-vis white experts.[29]

Exclusion by Subgroup

The press also ignores the diversity in the Hispanic community.[30] The terms "Hispanic" or "Latino" are used to represent a multitude of people: legal and illegal aliens, the native born and the foreign born, Mexican Americans and Puerto Ricans. Although this projects a greater national presence and image of solidarity,[31] it overlooks the uniqueness of the subgroups. Treating Hispanics generically is misleading in many ways. Not only do subgroups have different political agendas, but most Hispanics identify with their national-origin group (rather than with "Hispanics" as an entity).[32] Assumptions made by reporters about the homogeneity of Hispanics can result in distortion, as was demonstrated by local coverage of civil unrest in 1991 in Washington, D.C., as a result of a black police officer shooting a Salvadoran immigrant. Reporters referred to these events as the "Cinco de Mayo riots," despite the Hispanic residents of the area being primarily from Salvador and Columbia, therefore unlikely to be celebrating the Mexican independence day.[33]

Coverage of the different national-origin groups reveals another type of selective exclusion. Events that occur in the Cuban American community in Florida and issues identified with Cuban Americans are more likely to get national coverage than those concerning other Hispanic subgroups.[34] Despite comprising only 5 percent of the Hispanic population, Cuban Americans received 46 percent of coverage that mentioned a single national-origin group in large circulation daily newspapers in 1989.[35] This percentage was likely much higher in 1999 and 2000 when the relatives of refugee Elian Gonzalez fought to prevent his being sent back to Cuba and immigration authorities took him from their house to send him back to his father. The imbalanced attention paid to Cuban Americans over other Hispanics might be because they read newspapers more frequently than other Hispanics[36] or because their conservative political ideology distinguishes them from other minorities (and thus creates the perception that they are more newsworthy).[37] Perhaps because Cuban Americans are the most assimilated of the Latino group,[38] they are given more coverage by an Anglocentric press.

STEREOTYPES OF HISPANICS IN THE MAINSTREAM NEWS

Film stereotypes of Hispanics also find their way into newspapers. For example, a study of newspaper cartoons revealed examples of Mexican men as lazy and Mexican women as "easy."[39] Generally, news coverage treats Hispanics as "problem people"[40] and as "a caste of subservient, inferior people."[41] They are also presented as dangerous and criminal. All of these attributes are embedded in the most common representation of Hispanics as illegal aliens.

Immigrant Stereotypes

Hispanics of Mexican or Central American descent are often stereotyped as immigrants and illegal aliens. Illegal aliens are perceived as outsiders and lawbreakers, a bias inherent in the terminology. These images of Mexican Americans are not isolated to immigration stories. Coverage of welfare policy is tainted with images of "brown-skinned illegal immigrants crashing the border and the legal immigrant milking his green card for all its worth."[42] Consistently, the media stereotype Mexican immigrants as poor, criminal drains on society.[43]

Leo R. Chavez analyzed all major newsmagazine covers related to immigration from 1965 to 1999. Latinos made up 26 percent of the images of people on seventy-six covers. Visuals of Mexican immigrants "stress their backwardness, peasant-ness, and lack of modern sophistication. They appear as a metaphor for the 'Third World.'"[44] They were characterized as invaders threatening the United States economically (by taking jobs and social services), linguistically, and physically (by compromising national security).

The dominant images of immigrants in coverage of the debate over California's Proposition 187 (to cut government benefits to undocumented immigrants) were negative. They characterized Mexican Americans as criminals and economic units, as diseased, dirty, and dangerous. This was the case in print and television, in local and national publications, and in the arguments made in editorials on both sides of the debate. An "us-versus-them" narrative permeated the discussion, drawing on suspicion of outsiders and on racism.[45] The reoccurring metaphor for immigrants in this debate was that of animals.[46]

Dangerous and Criminal Stereotypes

Almost all of the coverage of Mexican Americans in national magazine coverage from 1890 to 1970 treated them as threats to society and in need of government and police control. "In these periods, symbols such as 'zoot-suiters,' 'wetbacks,' and 'Chicanos,' in the militant sense, dominated the headlines of national magazines."[47] Although some of these terms are no longer used, there is some evidence that the media continues to promote the image of Hispanics as dangerous.

Local television news shows black or brown criminals more frequently than white ones.[48] Reality-based programs (like *Cops*) often feature Latino criminals.[49] Newsmagazine coverage shows Latinos as the instigators of racial conflict even more frequently than it shows blacks in that role.[50] Of the coverage Latinos received in the *New York Times*, 38 percent portrayed them as victims or perpetrators of crime.[51] Other major newspapers cover Mexican immigrants in the context of crime.[52]

Is this enough evidence to say that a criminal stereotype is imposed on Hispanics? The prevalent images of them as victims indicate that it might not be and that noting Hispanic's presence in crime news is not the best way to measure dangerous stereotypes. In fact, there is some evidence that Hispanics are not shown disproportionately as criminals.

A study of Los Angeles television news concluded that although Latinos appeared more often than whites as the perpetrators of crimes, the frequency was less than their arrest statistics.[53] Another analysis compared coverage in the *Orlando Sentinel* with perceptions of its coverage voiced in focus groups. It found little support for Hispanic readers' widely held assumption that the paper showed them primarily as criminals. Only 10 of the 115 individuals with Hispanic surnames who appeared in the newspaper in 1997 were identified as criminals.[54] Less than 4 percent of the Latinos appearing in four years' worth of Raleigh's *News & Observer* stories were identified as criminals.[55]

Covering of Hispanic criminals is not the only way the media can promote the stereotype. The context and placement of criminal images is also important. Crime stories featuring Hispanics received more prominence in the *Orlando Sentinel* than many of the other routine, public-record listings that included Hispanic names.[56] All of the Hispanic crime stories in the Raleigh paper were prominent, and one of the longest stories published in the four years analyzed concerned a Mexican immigrant with a criminal background. It lamented the Immigration and Naturalization Service's (INS) poor record of deporting people like him.[57] The lack of other news about Hispanics on Los Angeles's television news shows might still present an exaggerated impression of their criminality, especially since they were underrepresented as figures of authority upholding the law.[58] For example, only 10 percent of the police appearing in Los Angeles television news crime coverage were Latino despite their comprising 25 percent of the force there.[59]

SYSTEM-SUPPORTIVE THEMES AND MESSAGES ABOUT HISPANICS IN THE MAINSTREAM NEWS

What larger messages about the government and the status quo does coverage of Hispanics send? Their presentation as problem people can legitimate the system if it leads white audiences to blame them for their difficulties and unequal status in society. It can make members of white audiences feel better about themselves in comparison. Negative coverage can be used to justify restrictive immigration policies because in the minds of white Americans, the contemporary immigrant is a Mexican.[60]

Immigration Themes

Mainstream media coverage of immigration reflects public opinion and policies that provide an ambivalent welcome to émigrés.[61] On one hand, a nativism narrative scapegoats immigrants through stereotypes and binaries that characterize them as different and inferior (i.e., backward to "our" civilized; primitive to "our" modern; dirty to "our" clean). On the other hand, the popular national mythology of America tells us we are a "melting pot," a "race-blind society," and a "land of opportunity."[62] This ambivalence can be promoted in a single editorial that advocates tolerance toward individual newcomers but characterizes immigration as a problem overall.[63]

The lack of immigration beat reporters with expertise on the subject and the tendency of the news to use the "flashiest figure available" help explain inaccuracies.[64] The nature of the times also explains coverage. Immigrants are reviled during times of economic stress and promoted as exemplifying the American Dream during good financial times.[65] During bad times, news coverage quotes scholarship that is more ideological than empirical on the costs of immigration.[66]

Inconsistent messages in national newsmagazine's covers from 1965 to 1999 reflected this ambivalence toward immigration. Some of the covers celebrated a nation of immigrants; others emphasized the threat to national identity. While most of the covers were identified as "alarmist" (66 percent) compared to "affirmative" (25 percent) or "neutral" (9 percent), fifteen of the sixteen covers that dealt specifically with Mexican immigration were alarmist (the other was neutral). These covers "metaphorically invoke crisis, time bomb, loss of control, invasion, danger, floods, and war."[67] The immigration crisis shown on the covers of the major ten newsmagazines was portrayed as a racial crisis, as a "perceived loss of whiteness."[68]

Whether immigrants are shown as virulent or as somewhat sympathetic, their coverage serves hegemonic national interests. Coverage showing them as different and threatening can be used to justify racial exclusion and discrimination. Coverage of them as legitimate and useful members of society portrays them as living examples of how wonderful America is and defuses criticism of the government. Either way, national unity is promoted.

Raleigh's *News & Observer* provided an example of how a specific immigration story can serve the system. On March 8, 1998, an article about Julio Granados appeared on the front page. It provided viewers with a look into his life as an undocumented grocery store worker and included the story of how he crossed the Mexican-American border. It also stated his name and place of employment. The INS used the article to raid the store and arrest him (and five others). He was eventually deported.[69] As a result, the newspaper apologized, hired more Hispanic reporters, and improved its coverage. Of course, this did not help Mr. Granados.[70]

Crime Themes

The reliance on visuals to tell crime stories on television news contributes to "stereotypical beliefs that advance racism and discrimination."[71] Because of the pictures it provides, television news crime coverage routinely identifies crime suspects by race.[72] The reoccurring image of Hispanic suspects portrays them as "dangerous outsiders" and whites as their "all-American" prey.[73] This coverage lays the blame for racial inequality at the feet of Hispanics for not "playing by the rules," thereby justifying restrictive policies.

A study of newsmagazine coverage of black-Latino interaction from 1980 to 1992 also emphasizes conflict and violence.[74] Because the conflict is characterized as far away from whites, temporally, physically, and culturally, "readers are reassured that the problems would remain isolated in the territory designated for interminority interaction and not spill out into other parts of the community."[75] By ignoring the structural and historical causes of racial conflict in both groups, the coverage gave the impression that the conflict arose from the "emotional outbursts of individual blacks and Latinos" who wanted to hold each other back. "This framing absolves whites of any responsibility in interracial conflict."[76]

SPANISH-LANGUAGE MEDIA AND THE HISPANIC PARALLEL PRESS

Between 1848 and 1942, there were about seventy-five Spanish-language newspapers in California alone.[77] Nationally, the number grew from 232 in 1970 to 504 in 1997.[78] Radio Unica, a twenty-four-hour Spanish-language talk and news network, broadcasts nationwide reaching 83 percent of the Hispanic market.[79] Two million Hispanic viewers watch the major Spanish-language television news shows (*Noticiero Univisión* and *CBS Telenoticias*).[80] Surveys indicate that native Spanish speakers prefer Spanish-language newspapers, magazines, radio stations, and television stations to English-language ones.[81] Spanish-language papers present more positive images of the Hispanic community[82]; this is also true of Spanish-language inserts into mainstream newspapers.[83] The journalists, the subjects, and the sources in these media are more likely to be Hispanics. The Hispanic News Link has offered syndicated columns to news organizations seeking Hispanic voices since 1990.[84] On *Noticiero Univisión*, 35 percent of the news sound bites featured Latinos.[85]

History of the Hispanic Parallel Press

Early Spanish-language newspapers were used to empower Hispanics, as their names alone evidence. In 1835, the weekly *El Crespusculo de la Libertad* ("the dawn of liberty") was published in Taos, New Mexico, to champion Mexican and Indian rights.[86] Los Angeles's *El Clamor Público* ("the public outcry"), created by activist Francisco P. Ramírez in 1855, was a "forerunner of today's progressive press."[87] He infused the paper with a "courageous editorial tone," condemning lynchings, supporting reforms, opposing slavery and squatters, and encouraging Californios to emigrate to northern Mexico.[88] In keeping with the idea of a parallel press, he "used the press to inform his readers of their rights, expose injustices and inspire action."[89]

In the early twentieth century, Spanish-language newspapers in the United States turned their attention to Mexico to cover (and take sides) in its war of independence. Yet, there was still room for activism on behalf of the Mexican American community. While the newspapers shared a concern for this community, they expressed it in different ways. To some extent, this was based on the publisher's sociopolitical identity and that of his audience.

Los Angeles's *El Heraldo de Mexico* called itself the "Defender of Mexicans in the United States." It advocated for the rights of recent immigrant workers fighting their exploitation and discrimination. San Antonio's *La Prensa* newspaper was geared toward middle-class exiles who planned to return to Mexico. Rather than promote the development of a Mexican American identity, it tried to provide its diasporic audience with connections to their homeland. In a nonconfrontational style, it also advocated nondiscriminatory policies and better education in South Texas. *El Espectador* (serving the San Gabriel Valley) promoted integration into American society. It advocated traditional political activism, cooperation with Anglos, and inclusion of Mexican Americans in mainstream institutions.[90]

Radio also served as a political tool for the Hispanic community. White frustration over the limited number of jobs during the depression led to the deportation of more than half a million Mexican Americans (many of them citizens). Pedro González challenged this on his Spanish-language radio show. He informed his listeners about employment opportunities and sang ballads about injustice.[91] As an "influential troublemaker," he became the target of the Los Angeles district attorney. After unsuccessfully trying to have González broadcasting license revoked, the district attorney succeeded in shutting him down by having him sent to prison for a crime he did not commit. As the authors of *Border Radio* put it, "Pedro González was taken to San Quentin, where he served six years in the state penitentiary for making trouble in Spanish over an L.A. radio station."[92]

Foreign-language radio was under attack in the early 1930s, with government reforms of licensing laws ending many Spanish-language broadcasts. By the 1950s, there was a surge of Spanish-language radio programming. As mass audiences moved to television, radio tried to retain audiences through narrowcasting.[93] Although radio was largely a vehicle for music, there were still examples of political advocacy on radio. The nonprofit Radio Bilingüe network brought peasants, artists, and activists together to "use radio to improve life and sustain the cultural identity of farm workers in California's San Joaquin Valley."[94]

The Parallel Press in Miami, Florida

Although the *Miami Herald* has been accused of succumbing to intimidation by the local Cuban American community,[95] this has not been the impression of most Cuban American readers. Members of the Cuban exile community in Miami claim that the press is biased against them and their political positions and that they are portrayed as extremists.[96]

> The exiles frequently take exception to the paper's coverage and editorials, and the [*Miami*] *Herald* is routinely accused of being antagonistic to the cause of a liberated Cuba and the Cuban community. In October 1987 the Cuban American National Foundation, a prominent exile organization, took out a full-page ad in the *Herald* to accuse the paper of "ignoring" [the] political and civil well-being of the Cuban American Community.[97]

Over time, the Cuban American community has been able to use its growing economic and political clout to alter some of the editorial positions of the *Miami Herald*.[98] It has also led the *Herald* to create a Spanish-language supplement called *El Nuevo Herald*. In 1998, the papers could be bought separately.

Stylistically, the *El Nuevo Herald* embraces the *"People* magazine concept"* and has become one of the fastest growing newspapers in the country.[99] In terms of content, some of it is translated *Miami Herald* stories, but it has its own news and editorial staff who create its own political message. Along with coverage of celebrities and a flashy style, this paper has an anti-Castro political voice (in both editorials and news slant) in keeping with the views of its Cuban American audience.[100] Its coverage of the Elian Gonzales immigration/child custody case was passionate and partisan, as exemplified by the headline "How Shameful" when federal agents took the boy from Miami.[101]

In order to influence the issue positions expounded on Miami radio in the 1970s, Cuban Americans picketed stations, insulted opponents on talk shows, car-bombed a broadcaster, and threatened radio personnel with guns. In addition to trying to change the mainstream radio representations, the Cuban exiles in Miami have developed a parallel radio. They use Spanish-language radio as "a source of information and a forum for assembly and militancy, especially against Castro."[102] This has been especially true of the AM talk and news channels whose "programming is devoted to Cuba, and [whose] tone is usually combative and strident."[103] *Univisión*'s WLTV-TV in South Florida focuses on immigration stories, includes political advocacy, and promotes Cuban and Cuban American culture and history.

For Profit or Politics?

It is debatable whether Spanish-language newspapers and inserts really constitute a parallel press. Many Spanish-language media are owned by mainstream publishing companies and are produced to profit from a growing market rather than for political goals. The publications offer news about Latino celebrities, rather than critical public-affairs information.[104] The companies that own these newspapers take over minority-owned newspapers or simply put them out of business.[105] For example, the largest Spanish-speaking daily in the Southwest, *La Opinión*, was originally founded in Los Angeles in the 1920s by a Mexican political refugee. The Times-Mirror Company bought it in 1990.[106] Times-Mirror also killed *Nuestro Tiempo*, a Spanish-language weekly.[107]

Spanish-language newspapers can lack a political bite, even when run by Hispanics. *El Nuevo D'a*, Puerto Rico's Spanish newspaper, "seldom takes positions on issues of the day."[108] The *Dallas Morning News* offers a supplemental bilingual section, *La Fuvente*, which covers soft news.[109] *La Opinion*'s 1996 election coverage was less extensive than that of the *Los Angeles Times*, leaving the 57 percent of its readers who rely on no other newspaper in the dark politically.[110] The *Univisión* and *Telemundo* television networks offer proportionately little news.[111] The news that does appear on *Univisión* usually lacks advocacy, relies on the same official government sources as the mainstream news, and is overtly patriotic and system supportive.[112] It focuses on Latin America in about half of its stories and on U.S. Latino communities in about a fifth.[113]

Coverage of U.S. Latino stories on *Noticiero* also includes mainstream news stories presented in Spanish (on topics like the national economy). It also includes, however, some topics that are less extensively covered in mainstream English-language news, such as civil rights and immigration. Since a "heritage of immigration" is assumed of the audience, the reporters are "defenders of Latin American immigration" and provide useful information about immigration reforms (fulfilling a "service orientation").[114] In this way, *Noticiero* looks like a parallel press.

Spanish-language television promotes itself as providing Latino-oriented news. It speaks to (and helps create) an imagined community of Hispanic Americans. As America Rodriguéz explains, it "symbolically denationalizes its intended audience as it renationalizes them as U.S. Hispanics."[115] In this way, it rejects an assimilationist model and promotes a panethnic identity.[116]

This identity has not been easily forged. Mexican American activists who protested the replacement of a Mexican American with a Cuban American at Los Angeles's KVEA and Puerto Ricans who protested comments made about them by a Cuban American commentator on *Univisión* demonstrate impediments to this panethnic identity.[117] The concern over Cuban American voices drowning out other Hispanic groups' voices has merit. For example, a study of 1984 election coverage in Spanish-language daily newspapers indicated that Hispanics were largely Republicans, reflecting Cuban Americans' partisanship, but not the orientation of the majority of the Hispanic community.[118]

Other newspapers very self-consciously reflect the politics of their communities. For example *La Opinión* in Los Angeles uses Latino think tank sources, puts Hispanics at the center of the stories, uses international wire services, has news bureaus in Mexico City and Tijuana, and covers local Latino culture and entertainment and small Hispanic-owned businesses.[119] While much of the Spanish-language news is without a political edge, the advocacy that remains reflects the Spanish-language newspaper's roots.

CONCLUSION

Hispanics do not receive coverage commensurate with their growing population. This tends to be true even in communities where they live in large numbers. Their presence in the news does not show them as powerful or having authority, as they are underrepresented as both experts and police. Unlike black authorities, Hispanic authorities are even left out of stories about race. Hispanics are stereotyped as "problem people," and negative stereotypes dominate immigration stories, in which Mexican immigrants are shown as bad for public health (because they are sick and dirty), for the economy (because they take other people's jobs and government benefits), and for public safety (because they are criminal and violent). While the prevalence of the criminal stereotype is debatable, there is some evidence that coverage of Hispanic lawbreakers is given prominence. While it does not perhaps live up to its history of political advocacy, Spanish-language news provides more frequent and uplifting images of Hispanics and stories that focus on issues of concern to them.

11

Asian American Mass Publics in the News

~~~~~~

NEWS COVERAGE OF ASIAN AMERICANS EXCLUDES, STEREOTYPES, AND PRESENTS them in ways that support the dominant ideology. They have a history of foreign language newspapers that serve as their parallel press. This chapter illustrates how coverage of Asian Americans has stigmatized them even at times when they are treated as a stereotypically "model minority."

EXCLUSION AND SELECTIVE EXCLUSION OF ASIAN AMERICANS FROM THE MAINSTREAM NEWS

Little research has been done to document the prevalence of Asian Americans in the news. Studies examining multiple racial-minority groups in the news have found that Asian Americans, like other minority groups, get far less coverage than blacks. Even in major newspapers, articles including Asian Americans are less frequent than those including Hispanics or blacks.[1] From 1934 to 1994, the *New York Times* gave Asian Americans very little coverage, less than it gave Latinos and Native Americans. During most of those years, there was not even one column inch of news dedicated to Asian Americans.[2]

In addition to the infrequent coverage Asian Americans receive generally, certain national subgroups get most of the attention. Of the 635 articles about Asian Americans found in twenty newspapers from across the country in 1994 and 1995, Chinese Americans got the most coverage (58), followed by Japanese Americans (53), Vietnamese Americans (52), and Korean Americans (47). Other groups were covered in between one (Burmese Americans) and twenty-four (Filipino Americans) articles. Those with Southeast Asian origins other than Vietnamese (Laotian, Thai, Cambodian) received almost no coverage.[3] It is hard to generalize from this study that Chinese Americans get the most coverage because other newspaper studies do not support this finding.

Another study of articles in twenty-eight other newspapers from 1989 to

1995 found that Japanese Americans received more coverage than any other Asian American ethnic group, with the exception of Korean Americans in 1993 (the year of the Los Angeles riots/rebellion).[4] A study of the *New York Times* from 1934 to 1994 found that 32 percent of the coverage of Asian Americans focused on people of Vietnamese origin, 27 percent on Chinese Americans, 11 percent on Hawaiians, 8 percent on Koreans, and 2 percent on Japanese Americans.[5] These Vietnamese American stories concerned new immigrants.[6]

Attention depends to some extent on the events of the time. International crises help explain why certain groups get attention at certain times. For example, Chinese Americans received their greatest attention in 1989, the year of the Tiananmen Square protests.[7]

The newspaper's audience also helps explain coverage differences. Newspapers on the West Coast tend to cover Asian Americans more than those on the East Coast and in the Midwest.[8] The *Seattle Times* stands out as providing extensive coverage of a great range of Asian ethnic subgroups. There is some evidence that California papers represent Asian Americans less simplistically and negatively than other states' papers.[9] However, having a reasonably sized Asian American population is no guarantee of media coverage. Local television news coverage of Samoans is rare even in Honolulu, Hawaii.[10]

A study of four Oregon newspapers' coverage during the late 1800s looked at the relationship between population size and news coverage. It found that in towns where Chinese Americans made up half of the population, they received little coverage.[11] For example, the *Daily Astorian* served a town with a 47 percent Chinese population, but in 108 stories, they were mentioned only twenty-two times. In fact, only twice were any Chinese mentioned by name.[12] Most Chinese mentioned in stories were simply called "John Chinaman," "Chinaman," or "Celestial."[13]

Asian Americans most commonly appear in entertainment and human-interest stories.[14] Although these are not necessarily negative stories, they are less important than hard news. Asian American organizations are not typically contacted for comments about stories on racial issues.[15] Instead, white political actors are used to discuss issues related to Asia or stories about Asian Americans.[16] Asian American "voices and perspectives are virtually absent" from the news.[17] For example, blacks and whites, not Asian Americans, were asked to talk to the press about the actions of Korean merchants during the Los Angeles riots/rebellion.[18]

Selective exclusion also promotes the impression that Asian Americans only live on the West Coast. A study of 217 articles appearing in twenty-eight newspapers between 1989 and 1995 found that only 17 (7.8 percent) concerned events occurring east of California. This finding is especially glaring given that only a few of those analyzed were West Coast newspapers.[19]

STEREOTYPES OF ASIAN AMERICANS IN THE MAINSTREAM NEWS

Stereotypes of Asian Americans in the news have much in common with those in entertainment media. They appear as evil, dangerous, foreign, odd, and nerdy. The desexualized "houseboy" of television entertainment and films becomes the "model minority" in the news.

Criminal Stereotypes

Asian Americans often appear in crime news as suspects or gang members.[20] Gang stories were common in the 1970s, when dramatic events like the 1977 Labor Day Massacre in a San Francisco Chinese restaurant were covered.[21] The television news special *Asian Gangs: Terror in the Streets* (1992) primarily used white police sources to characterize Southeast Asian gangs in Orange County, California, as uniquely terrible, and the reporter indicted the Vietnamese community in general for its "wall of silence."[22]

A study of twenty newspapers' coverage of Asian Americans in the mid-1990s revealed that crime was the third most frequent story topic (behind entertainment and human interest). These crime-related stories were most commonly associated with Vietnamese Americans.[23] Between 1934 and 1994, the *New York Times* dedicated 20 percent of the space it used to cover Asian Americans to crime news, almost all of which focused on criminal Chinese Americans.[24] A *Newsday* article applied the label of gang to an entire racial class of young people when it noted that children of Asians in America turned to gangs as an alternative family.[25]

Dangerous Foreigner Stereotypes

Some news representations of Asian Americans demonize them. The image found in entertainment of Asian Americans as evil and manipulative is also evident in news coverage.[26] References to their inscrutability and manipulativeness abound.[27] For example, the vast amount of coverage in the 1970s of Rev. Sun Myung Moon of the Unification Church represented him as powerful and sinister.[28]

The dangerous and sinister images were evident during coverage surrounding the Los Angeles riots/rebellion. First of all, one event that fueled the frustration that in turn led to the uprising was the shooting of a black teenager by a Korean American. Like the Rodney King beating, this injustice was recorded on videotape. A store surveillance camera showed merchant Soon Ja Du kill Latasha Harlins without clear provocation. The light sentence imposed on the shopkeeper helped incite anger in the black community. This event was repeated frequently on local television and interpreted in terms of the women's races.[29] "Headlines in the *San Francisco Examiner* and the *Los Angeles Times* on 16 November 1991 blared 'Korean Shopowner Freed' or

'Korean Grocer Receives Probation.' Such identification of ethnic backgrounds in criminal cases violates standard journalistic practices."[30] The coverage racialized an event that could have been handled in another way, such as an unfortunate tragedy or an opportunity to initiate a conversation about community relations or mental illness.

Korean Americans were also portrayed as dangerous during the Los Angeles uprising by the frequent images of them toting guns and acting as vigilantes. They were shown as cold, as more interested in property than black lives.[31] The coverage failed to provide a context in which to understand their behavior.

Sometimes Asian Americans are represented as posing an economic, rather than a physical, threat. The stereotype of greedy foreigners stealing jobs from "real Americans" is an old one. It was expressed virulently in an editorial in the *Oregon Sentinel* on May 23, 1868: "Nothing could so much damage and degrade the labor interests of Oregon as the introduction of these yellow vermin."[32] Over one hundred years later, in less strident language, Korean Americans in Los Angeles were described as "economic exploiters, profiteering from the poverty of African Americans."[33] Asian Americans "are frequently depicted as resented outsiders—foreign newcomers—competing for employment, business opportunities, and political power."[34]

News also presents Asian Americans as a threat to national security by focusing on their "foreignness" and promoting the idea that they have "divided loyalties." The fear of Asian Americans as foreign agents and spies, common in entertainment, is also found in news. The coverage of the arrest and detainment of Wen Ho Lee illustrates this. Lee designed computer codes for the Department of Energy in a top-secret division of the Los Alamos National Laboratories. He was arrested and indicted for improperly downloading classified nuclear weapons information. He received extreme treatment from the courts and criminal justice system due to political pressure. The media coverage of his case emphasized his Chinese heritage. Despite the fact that he was from Taiwan (rather than mainland China) and had been an American citizen for twenty-five years, the news defined Lee by his foreignness and promoted the impression that "the involvement of Chinese Americans in espionage is inevitable."[35]

The extensive focus on Asian Americans in immigration stories also reinforces the idea that they are foreigners.[36] The use of phrases like "Asian invasion" in discussions about Asian Americans conveys this stereotype.[37] The invasion rhetoric has deep roots in discussions about Japanese immigration and was used in major newspapers to ban their immigration entirely. The dominant theme supported the Immigration Act of 1924 that set stricter national quotas based on national origin by treating Asians as "incompatible aliens." This characterization tried to sidestep its inherent racism by claiming that Asians were not necessarily inferior; they were just "too different" from whites.[38]

The words "Asian" and "Asian American" are often used interchangeably in news stories.[39] The media frequently refer to Korean Americans as Koreans, new immigrants, or foreigners, and the Korean government is referenced on issues involving Korean Americans.[40] This notion of Asian Americans as "not American" was clearly illustrated in the headline "American beats out Kwan" for a story about (white American) figure skater Tara Lipinski winning a gold metal over (Asian American) Michele Kwan.[41] The assumption that people of Asian descent are unable to assimilate seems to underlie this coverage.[42]

Coverage of the 1996 campaign finance controversy provides another example of how Asian Americans are treated as perpetual foreigners and scapegoats for domestic problems. Rather than defend or ignore the right of Asian Americans to participate in the flawed campaign finance system, people like John Huang and Charlie Trie were blamed for taking advantage of the system.[43] The language used in stories about the campaign finance scandal was extensively and explicitly racial. It made references to the "Asian connection" and referred to the Clintons as "the Manchurian candidates."[44] In fact, over 60 percent of the stories about the subject in six major newspapers analyzed in one study referenced the "yellow peril."[45] Another content analysis of five major newspapers and *Newsweek* revealed that articles on the subject did not differentiate between Asians and Asian Americans, that they treated the people involved in the scandal as representatives of their race rather than as individuals, and that they used cultural assumptions to explain behavior.[46] Ethnic studies professor L. Ling-chi Wang argues that the extensive and racialized coverage of campaign fund-raising essentially "denaturalized" Asian Americans by presenting them as "unscrupulous aliens" trying to "subvert democracy and national security" through influence peddling.[47]

Ridiculous and Irrelevant Stereotypes

Media coverage also trivializes Asian Americans.[48] Some news demeans Asians by underestimating their credentials or mocking their (real or imagined) accents. For example, Sen. Alphonse D'Amato mimicked Lance Ito, the judge in O. J. Simpson's trial, on the *Imus in the Morning* radio show.[49] Los Angeles Dodger Chan Ho Park was described in *Sports Illustrated* as "so foreign" and was compared to a "flying saucer on the mound."[50] Another news story referred to an Ivy League–educated landscape architect as a gardener.[51]

The trivialization of Asia Americans went much further in the late 1880s, when stories treated Chinese lives as irrelevant. For example, a report of an accident involving Chinese miners included the statement, "It's a pity they were only injured," and an article about a miner buried alive was entitled "Well-Planted."[52] These mocking comments were not uncommon in the Oregon newspapers studied.[53]

The Model Minority Stereotype

Another stereotype promoted in coverage of Asian Americans is the "model minority." The model minority is hardworking and intelligent, but also docile and deferential.[54] Asian Americans, according to this stereotype, are successful, patriotic, and law abiding and have stable families.[55] The stereotype denies the discrimination and hardships experienced by this group by focusing on individual successes in the areas of employment and education.[56] It disregards differences between and among Asian Americans and treats them as a generic group.[57] The assumption that all Asian Americans are high achievers makes it harder for members of the group who do not fit the model minority stereotype.

While Asian American readers and journalists complain that this stereotype is prevalent in the news, scholars disagree over its extensiveness. One study found that only 3 percent of the coverage of Asian Americans in twenty newspapers presented them as model minorities.[58] When sociologist Setsuko Matsunaga Nishi used stories about recipients of awards and honors to quantify the stereotype, he found few newspaper stories between 1989 and 1995 that fit the criteria. Attention to Asian American students and entrepreneurs lent more support to the stereotype since newspapers exaggerated their numbers in the population. Nevertheless, attention to achievers paled in comparison to the focus on Asian Americans and crime.[59]

Qualitative analysis has been more productive at understanding the model minority stereotype. These studies demonstrate the subtle ways that the stereotype infuses news stories. An analysis of newsmagazines found that they "unselfconsciously produced and perpetuated this stereotype from about the 1940s to the 1970s."[60] In the 1980s and 1990s news, more complex discussions of the model minority stereotype acknowledged ways that it hurt Asian Americans. However, the coverage still assumed that Asian Americans were successful; it simply asked why.[61] Communications professor Thomas K. Nakayama examined fifteen newsmagazine articles that characterized Asian Americans as model minorities (the first in 1966). He demonstrated the ways that the image can be linked to a foreign threat.[62]

Another study looked at how Hideo Nomo was covered as a model minority in sports sections after he left Japan to pitch in the major leagues. Descriptions of him emphasized his hard work, self-sacrifice, humility, and silence. "Resisting the Japanese media, attempting to emulate American players, and turning his back on Japan, Nomo conformed as the quintessential model minority."[63]

SYSTEM-SUPPORTIVE THEMES AND MESSAGES ABOUT ASIAN AMERICANS IN MAINSTREAM NEWS

There are two main ways that news about Asian Americans supports the system. The first is by using the model minority stereotype to affirm U.S.

policies and national pride. The second is extensive use of a conflict frame that supports a racial hierarchy with whites at the top. This conflict focus includes clashes between Asian Americans and other racial groups and their opposition to America itself. Conflict coverage of racial minorities is system supportive because it serves to justify their oppression and the stereotypes about them.

How the Model Minority Stereotype Complements America and Hurts Asian Americans

The model minority stereotype is inherently system supportive. It can be used in conjunction with fear of the "yellow peril" to justify racial exclusion. In 1924, the idea that Japanese were model workers was part of the rationale used in the press to justify support for the immigration act of that year, which banned all Japanese immigration[64]: they were referred to as "overachieving hard workers" who would hurt American workers.[65] This coverage tried to characterize the exclusionary immigration policy as a complement, using the model minority stereotype as justification.

Once Asians are allowed into the country, their success stories are used to affirm "the workability of American social institutions."[66] The model minority image celebrates the American Dream and equalitarianism. It equates the experiences of Asians Americans with those of European immigrants, ignoring the additional challenges that race brings to assimilation and the costs of assimilation. This image contrasts Asian Americans' successes with other racial-minority groups' failures in order to undermine the legitimacy of their claims of institutional racism.[67] Nakayama argues that the model minority stereotype provides a comforting vision of American institutions as unbiased, rewarding merit and hard work, and that it ultimately serves "the interests of white Americans whose families, work ethic, and cultural beliefs do not come under media scrutiny."[68] The way that the model minority serves the dominant ideology of American superiority was clear in the sports articles that quoted pitcher Hideo Nomo as saying that the American major leagues were "real" and Japan's were subpar.

Journalism and mass communications scholar Patricia A. Curtin's study of the coverage of Japanese American combat troops in World War II demonstrates how model minority coverage can be a mixed blessing. She analyzed newspaper stories about the 442nd Regimental Combat Team made up of Japanese Americans (primarily from Hawaii). The newspapers "supported a larger-than-life stereotype of Japanese-American troops."[69] The coverage served the government's desire to look fair and racially sensitive to loyal Japanese Americans at the same time it was interning the Japanese American population. However, it was also a source of pride for the troops, their families, and their communities. The coverage of the troops as patriotic and self-sacrificing might also have helped combat some of the anti-Japanese hostility

Japanese Americans encountered when they returned from internment camps.[70]

The government orchestrated the generally positive coverage of these troops by restricting access to them and providing press releases that shaped the coverage. To Americanize the soldiers, they made only those who spoke English well available for interviews and referred to them as "honorary Texans" after they rescued members of a Texan division. The army also promoted the troops as "good soldiers" rather than "heroes" and as "willing to sacrifice" rather than as "martyrs" or "cannon fodder" by limiting coverage of their greatest feats and heaviest losses.[71]

This stereotype has also led to a backlash against Asian Americans by whites and other racial minorities. Whites accuse them of breaking the curve and stealing jobs. Because the stereotype appeals "to a racist fear that Asians might illegitimately take power within America," it has led to resentment and anger that have in turn resulted in violence.[72]

Conflict Coverage That Reinforces Racial Hierarchy

The model minority stereotype can be used to compare Asian Americans with, and thereby discredit or criticize, other minority groups. This can fuel interminority resentment, and the resulting tensions can serve as evidence that a racially diverse society is a contentious one and the racial status quo is preferable.

Coverage of the Los Angeles riot/rebellion dramatically illustrated the way the media use interracial conflict themes to pit one minority group against another and to distract viewers from each group's subordination by whites.[73] Even before the riot/rebellion, most *Los Angeles Times* coverage of Korean Americans focused on racial tensions.[74] "Utilizing various examples of 'black/Korean conflict,' the media disproportionately emphasized the conflictual aspects of the two groups' relations, strongly implying that the Korean-Americans had been asking for this kind of looting and destruction due to their repugnant relations with African Americans."[75] Attention to black boycotts of Korean American businesses and looting was more commonly covered than intergroup cooperative efforts.[76] Also lost in the conflict coverage was a discussion of the historical and institutional processes that help explain it.[77]

Due to the pro-American bias of the press,[78] coverage of foreign Asian countries often includes an "us-versus-them" conflict theme that has implications for Asian Americans. International tensions between the United States and Asian countries guide attention to particular Asian American communities.[79] American's historical relations with the countries people come from shape news coverage of Asian Americans. The wars in Japan, Vietnam, and Korea, China's communism, and economic competition with Japan have a negative impact on coverage of Asian Americans.[80] For example, coverage of the fiftieth anniversary of Pearl Harbor included many Japanese Americans and was framed in terms of contemporary economic competition with Japan.[81] Anti-Japanese bias in news about the anniversary of Pearl Harbor may have fueled anti–Asian American hate crimes.[82]

Coverage Justifying Japanese American Internment during World War II

"The American press helped shape public opinion against Japanese Americans during World War II that permitted more than 100,000 ethnic Japanese living on the West Coast, most of them U.S. citizens, to be hauled away into internment camps, without due process."[83] Analyses of newspaper and magazine coverage following the evacuation in 1942 demonstrate the different ways that the media supported the government instead of the civil liberties of the Japanese Americans.[84]

Many newspapers enthusiastically endorsed the policy. Walter Lippmann was one of many prominent media personalities to endorse the action.[85] Of the more than one hundred editorials that ran in California during the two-month period after the mass evacuation, 77 percent supported restrictive measures against Japanese Americans.[86] "When the government said evacuation was a military necessity, editorial discussion of the constitutionality of the incarceration was minimal. The press issued few challenges to government's right to suspend the writ of habeas corpus."[87] An analysis of seven Western newspapers and the *New York Times* indicated that 87 percent of the editorials published in the first four months after the decision were supportive of the policy. Only the *New York Times* offered some critical editorials, but its criticisms were mild and pointed to inconveniences the internment caused whites rather than challenging the legitimacy or morality of the decision.[88] The power of the government to lead media opinion in periods of crisis can be seen in the abrupt shift in positions taken by newspapers like the *San Francisco Chronicle.* In six weeks, their editiorial position went from opposing restrictions on Japanese Americans prior to evacuation to supporting the government's policy.[89]

Other newspapers ignored the event, failing to criticize the action. Some news outlets helped justify the situation by making the hardship on Japanese Americans seem more benign. For example, the national magazine *Life* "described the Japanese Americans at the camp at Manzanar, California, as generally happy, adapting quickly to their situation, planting flowers in window boxes and enjoying the 'scenic loneliness' of their surroundings."[90] The *New Republic* reported that the relocation was humane, and the *Atlantic* defended it as "a good example of democracy in action."[91] Some newspaper editorials supported a more extensive internment policy to include Japanese Americans further inland.[92] Overall, newspapers in the Midwest and the East were more passively tolerant of the policy compared with the outspoken support of newspapers on the West Coast, where the policy's victims lived.[93] Letters to the editor of western papers were more often supportive than critical of the policy. Those who favored internment often used racist language (terms such as "yellow peril," "wild Jap," and "monkeylike") to voice their support.[94]

THE ASIAN AMERICAN PARALLEL PRESS

Asian Americans created a parallel press for the same reasons as other racial groups: they wanted to protest their representation in and exclusion by the mainstream news and to provide alternative views that were more sympathetic and relevant to their community. Because recent immigrants spoke their respective native languages, the Asian American parallel press was more focused around the needs of the various ethnic groups rather than a panethnic one.

History of the Asian American Parallel Press

The first Asian American newspaper was the *Golden Hills News* in San Francisco in the 1850s. Since it was bilingual, its audience included both the underpaid and outcast Chinese immigrants and non-Asian Americans. Editorials advocating better treatment of Chinese Californians were written in English, while business news and commercial notices were written in Chinese.[95]

Joki Sen ("steamship") was the first Japanese-language newspaper in the United States. It was started in 1887. By 1922, there were twenty Japanese-language newspapers published on the West Coast. They served to build community and identity.[96] *Doho* ("comrade") was a progressive weekly newspaper published in English and Japanese in the late 1930s.[97] Before the United States entered World War II, three Japanese-language newspapers in California served 73 percent of the Japanese American population.

Before Pearl Harbor, most Japanese-language newspapers supported Japan.[98] Immediately after the bombing, the government required all Japanese American newspapers to stop publishing, arguing that they might contain secret enemy messages. When they were allowed to resume at the end of 1941 (until evacuation in May 1942), they did so under the watchful eye of the government.[99] Not only did the government monitor the publications (requiring that translations be provided), but it supplied content. Official announcements, policy statements, and military orders filled these newspapers. Too fearful and financially strained to challenge the censorship, the newspapers took on editorial policies of "Americanism." For example, one Japanese American paper stated that its goal was "to foster a deeper appreciation among resident Japanese of American ideals and democracy."[100] Patriotic self-censorship led them so far that they voiced "cheerful compliance with the government's decision to intern."[101] Although the newspapers lost their ability to criticize the mainstream press under the restrictions, other functions of the parallel press remained, since they continued to provide much needed practical advice to the community preparing for relocation.

The War Relocation Authority required that newspapers be established in each internment camp. It believed that these would help the government spread information while fostering a sense of community among the camp residents. The papers were primarily in English and published biweekly. Because overt censorship was rare, criticism of the government appeared from the beginning. At first, it was subtle, often appearing in cartoons, but became more obvious and terse over time. The newspapers show how the group struggled to keep (and adjust) their cultural identity as both Japanese and American while experiencing extreme discrimination. Initially, they emphasized their American identity, stressing loyalty and patriotism, and rarely referred to Japanese cultural or religious events or ideas. They called themselves "colonists" and the government "Caucasians." This allowed them to avoid labeling themselves or their oppressors as "Americans." After some of the internees were recruited to fight in the war and the Supreme Court decided that those who were loyal should be freed, the newspapers' criticism of the government intensified, and aspects of the internees' Japanese cultural identity appeared in the papers.[102]

Contemporary Asian American Parallel Press

Following a boom in the Asian American population, the 1990s saw an increase in Asian-language media and English-language media directed at Asian Americans.[103] By July 1995, Asian-language media nationwide included more than three hundred newspapers, fifty radio stations, and seventy-five television programs.[104] The first Chinese-language television program in San Francisco started in 1973. Leo Chen purchased airtime, then created, produced, and appeared as newscaster on *Asia-Am TV*.[105]

Ethnic newspapers, such as the *Korean Times Los Angeles*, are integral parts of Asian American communities that protect "ethnic culture and interest in a community which previously lacked well-organized social institutions."[106] Ethnic radio can do the same. Radio Korea (KBLA) in Los Angeles was used to coordinate efforts to protect Koreatown businesses during the riots/rebellion.[107]

Communications scholar Rick Bonus conducted an ethnography of producers and readers of Filipino American community newspapers in southern California during the early 1990s.[108] The circulation for these weekly newspapers was estimated at 350,000. He found that the editors and publishers of the newspapers saw themselves as building pride in the community in addition to providing information omitted from the mainstream media. Readers described the value of the papers as helping them feel at home in the United States.[109] The newspapers served the diasporic community by covering the

Philippines and Filipino Americans. In letters to the editor and commentaries, disappointment over the gap between the promise of America and the reality immigrants experienced was voiced, and racism in the mainstream media was exposed and critiqued. Local news coverage focused on activities of Filipino social organizations. The editorial pages included disagreements between Filipinos. This contrasted with the monolithic portrayal of ethnic groups found in the mainstream media. Bonus concluded that "in the minds of Filipino Americans who write and read about themselves and their larger world in their newspapers, it is a kind of self-determination that could potentially change the world around them—a kind of participation that for now will not be allowed space in mainstream press but later may be emulated by a more multivocal local and even national press."[110]

Asian Americans have also created documentaries, such as *Asian America* (1989) and *The Color of Honor: The Japanese American Soldier in WWII* (1991).[111] *Who Killed Vincent Chin?* (1988) stands out as one of the most provocative documentaries of the 1980s. It uses a collage structure and a fast-paced editing style to create a variety of moods and points of view. The film examines the murder of a Chinese American by a white, unemployed autoworker and the structural conditions that surrounded it. "Through its form, *Who Killed Vincent Chan?* challenges us to intuit, sense, or inferentially grasp, and therefore understand, the frame or perspective that gives this act of 'random' violence its fullest meaning."[112]

CONCLUSION

Asian Americans have been excluded and selectively excluded in the news media. They have been characterized as "different," as inferior to whites, or as threatening competition by highlighting their "foreignness" and associating them with danger. In times when the external threat from Asian countries was high, the media acted aggressively to support the government's agenda, as the media's complicity in the Japanese internment illustrates. The more favorable characterization of Asian Americans as a model minority depends upon their conforming to expectations of the mainstream quietly and deferentially. This stereotype has many negative implications. Conflict frames are also used to support the status quo. Although the Asian American parallel press has a long history, it has not served to explicitly politicize its audiences into a Pan-Asian entity. Instead, the Asian ethnic press supports the various Asian cultures and helps to maintain their respective communities, even in times of censorship and repression.

III

News Coverage of Racial-Minority Social Movements

Atlanta City councilman John Lewis holds the March 1965 issue of Life Magazine *in his office, August 7, 1986. Courtesy of AP/Wide World Photos.*

Social Movements and the Media: An Introduction

∿∿∿∿∿∿∿∿∿∿∿∿∿∿∿∿∿∿∿∿∿∿∿∿∿∿∿∿∿∿∿

SOCIAL MOVEMENTS TRY TO USE THE MEDIA AS A TOOL TO ACHIEVING THEIR goals of racial justice. As sociologist Harvey Molotch explains, "the mass media represent a potential mechanism for utilizing an establishment institution to fulfill nonestablishment goals."[1] But using an establishment institution for political change has inherent problems. Not only do the media often ignore movement efforts, but they frequently undermine them by providing negative coverage. This chapter examines the media goals of social movements, the obstacles that get in the way of their achieving them, and the type of coverage that results. It explains why coverage varies over time, between movements, and in different media.

MEDIA GOALS OF SOCIAL MOVEMENTS

Social movements try to use the mass media to broaden the scope of conflict. When new political actors are drawn into a dispute, the balance of power can change, and losers can become winners.[2] Public demonstrations are one major way that social movements try to draw attention to social problems and the solutions that they prefer.[3] Movement communication targets supporters, opponents, the general public, and policy makers. The goal is to change public opinion, activate participation, and ultimately change policies.

Movement events attempt to inform and persuade people outside of the movement.[4] Activists try to persuade politicians by demonstrating the intensity of their commitment to certain ideas by taking the time and assuming the risks that boycotts, marches, and civil disobedience entail. The more people who take these risks, the clearer and more salient their messages will become to government.

Movements communicate indirectly with politicians by mobilizing public opinion. The idea here is that even if politicians are willing to ignore an intense minority of people, they will not dismiss the will of the majority. Of course, this strategy assumes that a democratic model of government responsiveness is at work. The belief that "the people matter" is a fundamental premise for protest politics. This idea is debatable,[5] and if it is untrue, then elite unresponsiveness to public opinion would be an obvious obstacle to any social movement's success.

Activists in a social movement can best use media to talk to each other by creating a parallel press. This allows them to control their own messages. The parallel press varies in sophistication, depending upon the skills and resources available to movement. Some groups might simply issue position papers and manifestos to be distributed at meetings. Others create newsletters or even newspapers or magazines to send to their supporters. "Modern communication technologies, especially the Internet, allow for a more decentralized channeling of information about public demonstrations than is possible through mass media outlets."[6]

The parallel press can be used to motivate and organize followers. Practical information can be shared about where to go, what to do, whom to contact, and how to recruit new supporters. Aside from an occasional short news story about where and when a march will be, the mainstream news does not typically provide this information. Parallel press coverage can be used to reinforce allegiance to the group and build solidarity[7] through educating supporters about the cause. This might include publishing information about the organization, its efforts, its history, or its philosophy. The parallel press also helps build community among activists by putting them in contact with each other and reinforcing their sense of being "in this together." Emotional support is also provided with inspiring stories, recognition, and thanks and by reassuring activists that success is possible. Mainstream news coverage can also mobilize and validate supporters and bring in new members and donations.[8]

OBSTACLES TO ACHIEVING THESE GOALS

It is difficult for movements to use the media successfully to inform and persuade. "For a variety of economic, political, and institutional reasons, journalists and their employers tend to denigrate those out of the mainstream."[9] These reasons include news-making routines, newsworthiness criteria, reporting techniques, and ideological considerations.

Media organizations follow routines and standard operating procedures that create news affordably and quickly. These processes make reporters jobs easier, but they also result in certain ways of covering stories. One example of a standard operating procedure is the "beat system." Beats are places that reporters are routinely assigned to cover because newsworthy things are expected to happen there. The White House is a beat. Social movements are not. This obviously results in more coverage of the president than of activists. Beat systems are just one of the factors that result in a dependence on official sources. As a result, the government officials whom the reporters are used to talking to, or the reporters themselves, define the meaning of protests rather than the activists.[10]

Because the news is produced for profit, organizational understandings of what appeals to its audience determine what is considered newsworthy. Conflict, violence, familiarity, and novelty are newsworthy criteria relevant to reporting protests. When protests are dramatic, colorful, action-filled, and conflictual, they are considered "good copy" and get coverage, but that coverage does not usually contain the group's substantive agenda. Protests with arrests and violence are more likely to get coverage, but the coverage focuses on the violence and arrests, which undermines the protesters' legitimacy and clouds their messages.[11]

Journalists fit the various events performed, statements made, and actions taken by protest groups into their own way of telling stories. News stories are not told in ways that tend to serve the interests of movements. They focus on individual events and people rather than general themes and conditions.[12] This type of framing leaves viewers and readers confused as to why people are protesting. By their nature, the media are "covering the event, not the condition; the conflict, not the consensus; the fact that 'advances the story,' not the one that explains it."[13] In addition, issues important to movement activists are not those that tend to interest the media.[14] So, they do not get discussed.

An ideological explanation for why social movements do not get the kind of coverage they seek is that their goals are critical of the values held by the mainstream media. As an establishment institution, news organizations are invested in the status quo; they are either part of a ruling class[15] or protectors of that class.[16] As a result, they "are reluctant to report or be viewed as sympathetic to community activities that might undermine their profit-making potential, threaten the community [business or otherwise] and their own position."[17] Counterarguments produced by government officials refute activists' claims and easily find their way into news coverage.[18] In this way, reporters combat system critiques made by social movements while still appearing neutral.

HOW MEDIA COVER SOCIAL MOVEMENTS

Most protests do not receive any coverage.[19] When they do, the protest news focuses on actions.[20] The coverage tends to characterize protesters as a problem. This problem is controlled through news framing and the use of official sources that demonize, marginalize, and delegitimize the groups and their actions.[21]

Protests that are covered in the news tend to be only part of a story otherwise dominated by institutional perspectives. A study of national television news coverage of a variety of protests found that 80 percent of the news including them did not focus on the protests. Instead, they were part of another story. This meant that the event was treated as a "sideshow," as simply a "quick flash of a picket line or rally."[22] "Protest scenes are usually the backdrop or 'props' for introducing a debate that reflects elite, as opposed to grassroots, perspectives."[23]

Activists are treated as deviant, dangerous, and sometimes even insane in press coverage. "A focus on the quirky or odd nature of protest relegates it to amusement or ridicule."[24] The activities that earn activist groups the most attention tend to be those extraordinary techniques that end up reinforcing the deviant label and hurting their movement's legitimacy, which further undermines their ability to communicate substantive concerns.[25] Sociologist William A. Gamson and political scientist Gadi Wolfsfeld warn activists, "Those who dress up in costumes to be admitted to the media's party will not be allowed to change before being photographed."[26]

Protest-story frames are cliches that communicate the events of the protest in a way that leads to a certain interpretation of the event. Journalism and mass communications scholars Douglas M. McLeod and James K. Hertog identified eight types of protest-story frames that marginalize protesters. These emphasize violent crime, property crime, random acts of violence ("riot frame"), the carnival nature of the activities, the graphic oddities of the protesters ("freak show" frame), the immaturity of the deviants ("Romper Room" frame), the possible threats posed ("storm watch" frame), and the evidence of general social decay ("moral decay" frame). Another frame used for protesters, the "futility" frame, emphasizes the unlikelihood that what they are doing will make a difference.[27] All of these frames tend to trivialize or demonize the groups.[28]

Coverage minimizes the perceived threat posed by an outside group by normalizing its critiques. Political communications scholar W. Lance Bennett claims that the media has a "normalization bias" that "makes sense" of disruptive events in a way that reassures people. We are told that the system works because the threat is being handled by the establishment.[29] Even violent frames and stereotypes can be normalizing when they are used to justify a forceful response from the establishment (usually the police, army, or criminal justice system).

WHY MEDIA COVER SOCIAL MOVEMENTS DIFFERENTLY

The view that the media serve "primarily as guard dogs for powerful interests and mainstream values"[30] seems to dominate research on movements and the press. However, Molotch concludes, "I do not think it can be said as a generality that media help movements or that media destroy them."[31] Instead, he views the relationship between them as a dance where certain conditions will help or hinder the movement's ability to lead. What conditions influence the amount and kind of coverage a movement will receive?

Characteristics of the movement influence coverage. A group can employ certain tactics to improve its coverage: it can communicate clear and narrow goals through consistent messages;[32] it can have a single spokesperson to direct the media's attention;[33] it can develop professional organizational structures (with coordination and strategic planning);[34] it can plan large protests, which get more attention than small ones;[35] and it can create the new and changing images that the media want.[36]

Groups sometimes have to compromise their beliefs to meet the media's priorities and coverage. For example, a group's commitment to equalitarianism can result in a decentralized leadership structure (or no leadership at all) that ends up getting in the way of communicating with the press.[37] Deciding how to address the media can tear a movement apart and exaggerate its internal divisions.[38] Some activists might want to deal only with "trusted" media (parallel press or targeted publications)[39] or to forego coverage[40] rather than compromise their principles. Others might find the media's spotlight too hard to resist, even though its glare can cause internal organizational problems.[41]

Movements should also avoid certain things, even though they result in coverage. Internal rivalries can attract attention to a movement, but the coverage is about the rivalry, not the issues and events.[42] These rivalries can actually be created and fueled by competition for press coverage or reactions to the coverage received.[43] Similarly, the more violent protests gain the most attention, but the attention is on the violence, not the goals of the group.[44]

Not all media outlets treat movement activities the same way. The more elite the media outlet's audience, the less likely control the movement will have over the interpretation of the events. Some scholars contend that the more visual media give more attention to action strategies.[45] Alternatively, others find that television provides more description of the protesters goals than print.[46] Even the same publication can give different slants to coverage of the same movement. For example, newspapers' science sections have been more supportive of the anti–nuclear weapons movement than the news sections.[47]

HOW COVERAGE CHANGES OVER TIME

Coverage of a movement can change over time. "As a rule, media coverage of an emerging social movement is either highly restrained or nonexistent until the movement has been legitimized in the system."[48] Once the movement is established, it can experience a short, intense period of attention that inevitably wanes as the press and public's attention moves on to something else.[49] Once media personnel perceive that a movement has used them to become stronger, there can be a backlash. The movement either loses publicity or gets negative coverage.[50]

Changes in coverage can also stem from fundamental changes in the movement. As its goals, membership, and techniques change, so does the media's response to it.[51] Movements that become more radical get increasingly worse coverage.[52] Groups that adapt to the expectations of the media can get more coverage because their message has become more conventional or simplistic.

> Movement-media communication is like a conversation between a monolingual and a bilingual speaker. The media speaks [sic] mainstreamese, and movements are pushed to adapt this language to be heard since journalists are prone to misunderstand or never hear the alternative language and its underlying ideas. But it is a common experience of movement activists to complain that something has been lost in translation.[53]

The "issue-attention cycle" also helps explain changes in coverage. There is an inevitable cycle of attention paid to issues in the media and by the public. Political elites and activists have long-term interests in particular issues, but the public and the media do not. Instead, the public's interest is stimulated by the media's alarmed discovery of a problem. Enthusiasm in the public and the press for finding a solution to the problem is intense and short-lived, lasting until they grow discouraged and bored and move on to another problem.[54] When social movements organize events that are relevant to the issue during the time that it is considered newsworthy (during the "discovery" and the "euphoria" phases), they have a better chance of getting coverage.[55]

Perhaps the most important explanation for how movements get covered and why coverage changes over time is "hegemony theory," which argues that a dominant ideology exerts power in societies. This power is not based on an elite imposing its will on the masses through force and threats. Instead, elite power is secured through the consent of the masses. Consent is built and maintained through ideological state apparatuses, promoting values and expectations. These values are shared and promoted through mainstream media. Public consent comes from the belief that the status quo is inevitable, unchangeable, and desirable. But this consent is not absolute; it can be negotiated through struggle and challenges from below. As a result of this struggle, the dominant ideology can change.[56] These changes can be incremental adjustments and occur slowly.[57] They can also be the result of political crises and social disruption that make it harder for elites to maintain quiescence.[58]

Typically, when a movement's goals resonate with values articulated by the mainstream, coverage is more sympathetic.[59] If the movement is radical and seeking major change, coverage is harsh.[60] Movements that are the "most threatening to the existing socioeconomic order" either get no coverage at all[61] or coverage that focuses on events rather than goals and issues.[62] However, when the hegemony is shifting, voices critical of the existing dominant ideology become more acceptable, are more visible, and can facilitate the shift.

A shifting hegemony can be seen in elite disagreements over major issues or questions. These cleavages in the ruling class allow political outsiders' voices to be heard.[63] Political scientist Daniel Hallin's study of news coverage of the Vietnam War illustrates this point well. He found that when the elites were unified in their support for the war, antiwar protesters were ignored or characterized as deviant in the press. When the elite consensus broke down and the hegemony was broken, the media treated the issue as one with legitimate controversy. At that point, protesters were covered as reasonable.[64] Similarly, disagreement within the administration over nuclear weapons testing and treaties opened the door for the anti–nuclear weapons movement.[65]

CONCLUSION

The goals and limitations of media strategies for social movements help explain media coverage of racial minorities in the 1960s and 1970s. Chapter 13 discusses coverage of the black civil rights movement, describing and critiquing the conventional wisdom about the media as the movement's friend and advocate. It also looks at coverage of events leading up to the protests, events during the movement, and the riots and black power movement that followed. Hegemony theory is used to explain the change in coverage.

Chapter 14 looks at coverage of other racial social movements that occurred in the late 1960s and early 1970s. While these movements were not monolithic,[66] they had more in common with the black power phase of the civil rights movement than with the nonviolence stage that preceded it.[67] Rhetoric like "red power," "brown power," and "yellow power"; groups like the Brown Berets and the Red Guard; the influence of Malcolm X and Mao on theories and actions—all of these help to illustrate this.[68] Chapter 14 demonstrates that the more radical the critique and its expression, the more negative the coverage.

13

The Civil Rights Movement
and the Mass Media

~~~~~~

CONVENTIONAL WISDOM HOLDS THAT THE MEDIA SERVED AS AN ALLY AND A
tool of the black civil rights movement. Journalists, activists, and historians
have asserted this position widely. Yet, this conclusion runs counter to expectations of the racial status quo–oriented mainstream institution this book
describes. Nor does it jibe with what we know about the media as a reflection
and reinforcer of the national consensus rather than an agent of change. To
reconcile these disparate views, this chapter describes the conventional wisdom and the evidence upon which it is based; it then presents information
that complicates these claims.

Research into news coverage of particular civil rights events reveals a
messier version of the media–civil rights movement relationship than that
which has been mythologized. Systematic content analysis of national and
local media illustrates that actions seen today as unambiguously "right" or
"wrong" were not presented that way at the time. While some coverage promoted black activists' goals and actions, much of the news ignored, criticized,
and even demonized them. The direction of the coverage depended on the
event, the time it occurred, the elite responses, and the media outlet. The
media did not always act in concert. Not only did the parallel and mainstream
press differ, but so did national and local coverage. At times, the three major
national newsmagazines, *Newsweek*, *Time*, and *U.S. News and World Report*, interpreted events differently.

THE CONVENTIONAL WISDOM

The notion of the news media as an ally of the civil rights movement rests
on the assumption that the media gave the movement extensive, favorable
coverage, which resulted in mobilized public opinion and policy makers.

Rodger Streitmatter states this position clearly in *Mightier Than the Sword: How the News Media Have Shaped American History*, a book about the power of the press:

> By covering the movement's various events, television news awakened people throughout the nation to the realities of black oppression in the South. By pushing those realities into the face of the American people, television news propelled the Civil Rights Movement into the American consciousness and onto the national agenda. . . . When those images became imbedded into the nation's consciousness, public opinion suddenly galvanized in support of the Civil Rights Movement.[1]

Streitmatter believes that television had the greatest impact because it has "the power to transmit the experience of actually being part of the event."[2] It is widely believed that television images of peaceful protesters and their angry (often violent) opponents were inherently persuasive on behalf of the movement.[3] The movement's success is credited to Martin Luther King Jr.'s strategy of provoking a violent response from white segregationists for all the world to see.[4]

> The stream of violent scenes from the front lines of the American Civil Rights movement during the 1960s—freedom marchers being attacked by fire hoses, snarling police dogs, and "Bull" Connor's cattle prods—aroused the long dormant consciences of whites and mobilized mass support for the most far-reaching civil rights legislation in the nation's history.[5]

While television gets more of the credit for bringing images of injustice into people's living rooms, Northern newspapers are also remembered as covering the movement "with courage and commitment."[6] Journalists and observers have proudly asserted that reporters at the time sided with the movement explicitly in their coverage.[7] William Drummand, a newspaper reporter in Kentucky during the 1960s, claims to have "firsthand experience of how civil rights workers and newsmen thought they were in it together."[8] Frank Stanton, president of CBS, "called upon broadcasters to launch a 'mighty and continuing editorial crusade' in support of civil rights" at a conference of broadcasters in July 1964, echoing many TV executives' feelings about the issue.[9] Activist Julian Bond believes that the first corps of reporters and editors were liberal, "eager to support the struggle," and not mired in the cynicism of later generations of journalists.[10]

Although this advocacy seems to run counter to the notion of a neutral press, political scientist Michael Robinson explains that "the South was so far out of step with non-Southern cultural values and opinion about race relations that television journalists could be civil rights advocates, and get away with it."[11] Communications professor Mary Ann Watson agrees that the nature of the story gave reporters license: "Not every story had two sides with equal merit. Balance was not a journalistic prerequisite in matters of human decency. Villains deserved excoriation and good guys rightfully earned sympathetic coverage."[12]

Some news personnel may also have felt an affinity with the movement because they, too, had been attacked by white segregationists and could therefore relate to the protesters. Southern politicians and police accused them of being propagandists.[13] They were physically assaulted by white mobs while covering events.[14] CBS News cameraman Lauren Pierce carried a gun for protection against white mobs.[15]

The conventional wisdom goes beyond claiming that the reporters and the news they created supported the movement and covered it sympathetically. It also holds that this coverage had an important, favorable impact on the movement itself, on public opinion, and on the politicians who enacted civil rights policies. It was said to mobilize, unify, and energize those already supportive of racial equality and to inform and encourage people who wanted to protest by showing them how and where to focus their energies.[16] Stories about white Northerners leaving their homes to work for civil rights in the South after seeing television coverage of what was going on there illustrate this claim.[17] News coverage also served as a catalyst for increased financial contributions to civil rights organizations.[18] Media attention helped legitimate leaders within the black community.[19]

According to the conventional wisdom, news coverage of the movement also had three effects on public opinion. First, it increased awareness of racial oppression outside of the South. Second, it increased the saliency of the civil rights issues through agenda setting. Third, it pushed attitudes about these issues in more liberal directions.

We have anecdotal evidence of the first point. Documentaries and memoirs report Northerners' shock at what they saw on television.[20] An analysis of responses to the question, "What is the most important problem facing the nation today?" on national polls provides some support for the second. Answers to this question between 1946 and 1976 reveal that "civil rights was virtually unrecognized as a problem area until 1956," the year after the Montgomery, Alabama, bus boycott started.[21] Perceptions of the importance of the civil rights issue rose again in the fall of 1957 during the Little Rock, Arkansas, school-desegregation efforts. It substantially increased again in 1963 after the March on Washington and the rally in which King gave his "I Have a Dream" speech. Civil rights were on or near the top of the list of most important problems from late 1963 to early 1965.[22] This data shows changes in public opinion coincide with current events. Other scholars go further in crediting the press with leading the public to establish these priorities.[23]

In terms of the third point, attitudes became more supportive of civil rights legislation over time. For example, support for a nondiscriminatory public accommodations law rose 12 percent (from 54 percent to 66 percent) between June 1963 and January 1964. Some public-opinion scholars believe that the movement's media coverage explains some of these changes. Benjamin Page and Robert Shapiro conclude, "There can be little doubt that the civil rights movement and Southern whites' highly visible 'massive resistance' to it had a major impact on public opinion."[24] Donald Kinder and Lynn Sanders use more cautious language, claiming, "Presumably some of the change [in white opinion on equal treatment of blacks] was a direct reflection of what whites saw."[25]

Conventional wisdom also contends that the media coverage affected politicians and policymaking. News coverage of police violently reacting to young black marchers in Birmingham, Alabama, is credited with influencing the Kennedy administration. Television coverage is said to have moved President John F. Kennedy to propose civil rights legislation, when he had been reluctant to do so before.[26] He was particularly concerned about how the violent images would be interpreted and used overseas. In fact, the news of police using fire hoses and dogs against marchers in Birmingham had led African heads of state gathered in Addis Ababa, Ethiopia, for a meeting of the Organization of African Unity to debate whether they should break relations with the United States. The Soviet press showed these images from Birmingham extensively to illustrate American hypocrisy. Since copies of the text of President Kennedy's June 11, 1963, speech to the nation on civil rights were distributed to diplomatic posts with special directions on how they should be used, it is not hard to claim that concern over how the nation looked abroad was important to the president.[27] According to communications from American diplomats in many developing nations, the president's speech claiming that civil rights was a moral issue served one of its goals by turning negative opinion toward the United States around in many foreign countries.[28]

News coverage of the movement's march in Selma, Alabama, is also thought to have facilitated the passage of the Voting Rights Act of 1965 by leading members of Congress to support the legislation. During congressional debates, representatives read from newspapers and talked about how they felt and how their constituents said they had felt watching television coverage of "Bloody Sunday," the name given to the day police reacted violently to civil rights marchers gathering at the Edmund Pettus Bridge in Alabama. Coverage President Lyndon Johnson saw of the incident pushed him to propose the bill.[29] Newspaper editorials urging Congress to pass voting rights legislation appeared in newspapers read by legislators (*New York Times*, *Washington Post*, and *Washington Evening Star*).[30] Reporters interviewed in the late 1960s attributed passage of civil rights laws to network news. They believed that coverage changed public opinion and that public opinion changed Congress.

In a typical explanation, one NBC correspondent stated, "Before television, the American public had no idea of the abuses blacks suffered in the South. We showed them what was happening; the brutality, the police dogs, the miserable conditions they were forced to live in. We made it impossible for Congress not to act."[31]

CHALLENGES TO THE CONVENTIONAL WISDOM

The conventional wisdom's characterization of the media's relationship to the civil rights movement rests on many accurate facts. Media coverage of Birmingham and Selma was extensive. The police did use violence against peaceful activist at these events. The Civil Rights Act and the Voting Rights Act were passed soon afterward. Politicians claim to have been moved by coverage and the effect they thought it would have on national and international audiences. However, the conventional wisdom also overgeneralizes, oversimplifies, and overlooks too much in making the case for the media's importance. Coverage was less extensive, positive, and clear-cut in defining the movement as "good and noble" and those who stood in its way as "bad and morally bankrupt" than is remembered. Looking at more coverage (and polls) from a longer period of time illustrates the media's much more complex and contradictory role. Only *part* of the mass media allied itself with *some* types of efforts to overcome racial oppression at *certain* times. Furthermore, the impact of this coverage on the public is debatable.

Extent of the Coverage

Examination of the major newsmagazines' coverage of race relations between 1960 and 1970 shows that the most extensive coverage took place not during the marches for voting rights (prior to 1964), but in 1967, then 1969, the years not of peaceful protests but of race riots. Counter to the agenda-setting hypothesis, the years (between 1964 and 1970) with the greatest number of articles about race relations in the three major newsmagazines do not coincide with the years when the greatest percentage of people said that civil rights was one of the most important problems facing the nation.[32] Another study that looked at *Newsweek*'s coverage over a longer time period (1950–1994) found that the civil rights movement did coincide with an increase in coverage. The number of stories about racial issues peaked in 1963. After that year, coverage decreased until it went up again in the mid-1970s during disputes over school busing.[33]

Many Southern papers chose not to cover the movement,[34] particularly events occurring in their own cities[35] or regions.[36] James Forman, executive secretary of the Student Nonviolent Coordinating Committee (SNCC), claims that it was hard to get local news coverage of violence against protesters because reporters deferred to local authorities who did not want the publicity.[37]

An extensive study of the coverage of blacks in the two major Los Angeles newspapers found that relative to blacks' percentage of population in the city, coverage of them actually declined from 1893 to 1965. Rather than peaking during the civil rights movement, coverage of blacks remained the same between 1952 and 1962 as it had been in the decade following World War II.[38] The authors of this study concluded that "the press had increasingly contributed to black invisibility for more than a half century, failing to redress it even when civil rights activism became commonplace across the country."[39]

Although the black press had once had the civil rights beat to itself, this changed during the 1960s.[40] When the movement received mainstream attention, some black newspapers folded, others turned away from political news, and still others remained to provide long-range perspectives and interpretation of events that were given summary and descriptive coverage in the mainstream.[41]

Nature of the Coverage

A government commission (Kerner Commission) looking into explanations for the urban rebellions issued a 1968 report indicating that the press showed a general indifference toward blacks, failing to cover blacks as a normal segment of society. Instead, it promoted stereotypes and focused on conflict and unrest without explaining the reasons behind the protests. Only between 3 and 11 percent of the black news coverage in the *Atlanta Constitution*, *Chicago Tribune*, *New York Times*, and *Boston Globe* discussed the reasons for black protests.[42] "The newspapers' scanty explanation of the causes of black protest during the 1960s, plus their relative inattention to black problems, combined to convey a picture suggesting that blacks were aggressive and demanding."[43] In some ways, the press contributed to readers' annoyance with racial issues first by treating race as a Southern problem (rather than a national one), then by celebrating the problem's "solution" when the Civil Rights Act was passed.[44]

Blacks were largely excluded in news coverage of the civil rights movement. In television news stories about civil rights, whites were still the major sources. "Even when the messenger was black, in fact, the message was usually from a white point of view."[45] When sociologist Herbert Gans accompanied a national magazine reporter to a civil rights movement event, he observed that the reporter never spoke to any marchers.[46] Newspaper coverage of desegregation relied almost exclusively on government sources and whites.[47]

Most of the coverage of the civil rights movement in the *New York Times*, *Washington Post*, and *Los Angeles Times* appeared in what was called the "Negro Affairs" section of these papers, while riot coverage appeared on the front page.[48] The *Chicago Tribune*'s news coverage and editorials were unsympathetic to the civil rights movement in the 1950s and 1960s.[49] Its editorials "showed hostility toward any persons or groups seeking a change in the status quo on racial matters, accusing them of being agitators, lawbreakers, the tools of communist interests, or, at best, wrong-headed."[50] Coverage also tended to focus on dramatic, unusual, and violent events, while ignoring complex issues.[51] This resulted in news that was both shallow and erratic: shallow because the underlying causes of the conflict were not explained—"It seemed as though the papers regarded the civil rights movement as a kind of drama to be followed and described, rather than as a manifestation of a severe societal maladjustment that cried out for thorough exploration and discussion by the media"[52]—and erratic because civil rights disappeared from the news when there were no dramatic events to cover. This sometimes worked to the movement's benefit when activists were able to provoke a violent response from local officials. At other times, it worked against them, confusing their messages, misrepresenting their concerns, and reinforcing the impression that political dissention and social disorder go together. An analysis of the *New York Times* coverage of the SNCC in 1966 indicated that once the more militant Stokely Carmichael became the group's leader, coverage increased, appeared more frequently on the front page, and was more critical.[53]

The historic Montgomery bus boycott lacked a dramatic visual moment and therefore received less coverage than other, less historically significant movement campaigns.[54] The coverage that the boycott did receive portrayed it as a spontaneous act by a previously meek community momentarily inspired by a charismatic leader, rather than as part of a continuous effort.[55] Communications scholar Carolyn Martindale claims that by focusing on conflict and ignoring the causes of protests, coverage led readers to see activists as "threatening and unreasonably demanding, thus contributing to distrust and hostility between races and classes in the United States."[56]

The degree of support that coverage gave the movement varied over time (from the late 1950s to the 1970s) by media (e.g., television, radio, newspaper, newsmagazine), by outlet (i.e., particular newspapers), and by setting (local versus national, Southern versus Northern or Western). In addition, the black newspapers differed substantially from the mainstream press and sometimes from each other. The bottom line is that there was more than one civil rights movement narrative in the news; multiple, conflicting stories were being told.

Impact of the Coverage

Recall the conventional wisdom's contention that media coverage of the civil rights movement affected public opinion and directly or indirectly influenced policy makers and changed public policy. This assumes that all people interpreted what they saw in the same way. In fact, people tend to perceive the news selectively, to recall and interpret it in ways consistent with their prior attitudes.[57] Given the research on attitudes, it is more likely that media coverage polarized the public than that it converted people.[58]

It is inaccurate to assume that the now familiar video clips of dramatic events, like the fire hoses turned on black protesters, were shown and interpreted in the same way then as they are in today's documentaries or coverage of Martin Luther King Jr.'s birthday. "The events in Birmingham and the March on Washington were not so simple as they have become in memory."[59] Our responses to images are not uniform; instead, they are influenced by the interpretations of the press, by leaders' opinions, and by the attitudes we already hold when we view them. Watching the now-familiar images of water hoses and dogs turned on black children in the streets of Birmingham is not the same as watching them then.

It is easier to say which opinions changed and when than it is to know why. Did the media change public opinion, or were changes in public opinion reflected in the media coverage? Did newspaper articles change politicians' attitudes, or were politicians using these articles to articulate positions they already had? Did elite opinion change because of the media coverage of the movement, or did the coverage change because elite opinion had?

Three systematic studies conducted empirical tests to disentangle causes from effects. Political scientists Benjamin Page and Robert Shapiro did the first study, which examined the timing of changes in public opinion over a forty-three-year period.[60] They found that the trend toward support for civil rights began in the 1940s, rather than as a response to a few weeks of television coverage.[61] They argue that "something more long-lasting and fundamental was occurring than any series of particular events or even the organized civil rights movement, which did not get under way with any vigor until the late 1950s and then faded after the 1960s."[62] In fact, it was in the South, where the newspaper and local television coverage was least supportive of the movement, that attitudes changed the most during the late 1950s and early 1960s. The authors also point out that the public tended to think that demonstrations hurt the advancement of black rights and the percentage of people who said this increased during the mid-1960s (to 80 percent in 1966).

The second study by political scientist Paul Kellstedt concurs with the notion that public opinion on racial attitudes changes gradually rather than in response to specific events or their coverage. He found that generational replacement (people born into more progressive times replace those born in more conservative times, who are dying), rather than individuals' changing their minds, explains the aggregate attitude change. He found that the media's framing of stories had a subtle impact on racial-policy attitudes. Stories using equalitarianism (rather than individualism) to frame racial issues primed the ambivalent public to emphasize that core value when considering them. The equalitarian framing was more common in *Newsweek* stories about race during the 1950s and 1960s than it was afterward.[63]

The third relevant study, by sociologist Paul Burstein,[64] looks at the complicated relationship between news coverage, public opinion, civil rights activity (pro and con), and congressional action from 1940 to 1972, using statistical tests to see how the factors relate to each other. Burstein acknowledges that movement activity resulted in media coverage but warns "against exaggerating the extent to which Congress was directly influenced by collective action and media coverage."[65] He finds demonstrations and their coverage did not directly correlate to the passage of civil rights laws. While many civil rights laws were passed in Congress over a fifteen-year period, some followed demonstrations, but many did not. He also concludes that public opinion did not change because of dramatic events, demonstrations, or news about them; instead, it had been growing more supportive of civil rights legislation for years.

Direction of the Coverage and Hegemonic Shifts

As the conventional wisdom claims, some events received a great deal of coverage, and some of that coverage was positive. The positive coverage tended, however, to reflect the positions of national public officials and national public opinion at that time, rather than leading the reaction, as some journalists and scholars assume. For a time, the national elite and mass opinion (reflected in the national media) were at odds with the dominant regional ideology in the white South (shared by Southern politicians, the white public, and the Southern press). This helps to explain why Pulitzer prizes were awarded to Southern newspapers that published editorials urging compliance with Supreme Court decisions on desegregation.[66] While those papers were espousing progressive racial social policies in their communities and challenging the local ideology, they were following the national dominant ideology, and they were rewarded by a mainstream institution for doing so. Media coverage reflected a shifting hegemony. Because the shift took time and occurred at different times across the country, news coverage was not unified.

The racial ideology in the United States in the 1950s and early 1960s endorsed legalized segregation and black exclusion. Challenges to these inequalities prior to the mid-1950s contradicted the dominant ideology and were characterized as radical and even unpatriotic.[67] News coverage reflected this. When officials (police and politicians) characterized blacks as threatening and unreasonable, that was in the papers.[68] At the national level, the dominant ideology began to shift *before* the major protests of the civil rights movement when in 1954 a national political institution, the Supreme Court, declared in the *Brown v. Board of Education* that the dual-school system was unconstitutional. The decision was controversial and ahead of its time, remaining unenforceable until other political actors caught up with it. This shifting hegemony was reflected in the mixed coverage the decision received. Since local segregationist leaders in the South resisted changes to the repressive racial status quo, they provided alternative (but still "official") voices that allowed the Southern newspapers to continue to present civil rights reforms and protesters negatively.[69]

Indeed, coverage of the civil rights movement, rather than instigating changes in attitudes, reflected a hegemonic shift that was already underway and the ambivalence in public opinion. Once prominent national leaders (Presidents Kennedy and Johnson and some congressmen) interpreted black nonviolent resistance in the face of violent opposition in moral terms using equalitarian ideals,[70] the mainstream national news media adopted that interpretation. President Johnson gave a forty-five-minute nationally televised speech in which he spoke the words "We Shall Overcome," referred to Selma twelve times, and addressed a joint session of Congress urging them to pass a voting rights bill.[71] His commitment to voting rights for blacks was not created by his having watched television coverage of the march. The events did influence the timing of his speech, which provided an "official voice" of support that the media could use in framing news coverage about the issue and events. They could support racial equality without abandoning their system-supportive institutional position.

Protests seen as consistent with American principles were acceptable to the elite, the media, and the public. However, once riots broke out five days after the Voting Rights Act was signed, the protests were interpreted differently, and news frames became consistently critical of blacks and their political agenda.[72] The dominant ideology supported some moderate reforms (voting rights, abandoning forced segregation), but it was not open to a wholesale critique of racism in American economic and social institutions. Even the tone of King's coverage fluctuated based upon how moderate his goals were at the time; the media found his support of voting rights and desegregation far more acceptable than his pursuit of economic justice and an end to the Vietnam War.[73] After his assassination, the radicalism that brought him negative coverage was "interred with him" and replaced by a "benign, reformist image" that could be used to celebrate America.[74]

Positive coverage of the movement during the Birmingham demonstrations, the Selma March, and the March on Washington can be reconciled with a view of the media as a system-supportive, elite-dominated institution by recognizing that this was a time of hegemonic change. National elite opinion and public opinion were in transition on matters of race. Therefore, sympathetic coverage of the civil rights movement during the mid-1960s might have been challenging the short-term status quo, but it was not outside of the sphere of legitimate controversy. Reforms advocated by the civil rights movement (desegregation of public facilities and voting rights) were not radical in a national mainstream. Instead, they were part of the emerging ideology that would soon become the dominant one.

The media reflected Southern elites' and publics' resistance to this change. Newspapers "put their own survival first and tried not to offend local sensibilities. Often in moments of crisis, their instinct would be to protect the community against its critics, to soften accounts of its failings and, above all, to blame outsiders."[75] Consequently, media institutions acted as we would expect them to by reflecting the values of those whom they served: the white public and the political establishment. Only because the United States was in a period of hegemonic change and because the mainstream's emerging values accorded with (some) black activists' values and advocated (limited) reforms did the media *appear* to be acting differently than we would expect. Without transforming into crusaders for political outsiders, the media helped create this new dominant ideology.

COVERAGE OF EVENTS THAT PROCEEDED THE MOVEMENT

During the 1950s, events occurred that facilitated the civil rights movement. The media coverage of two major ones demonstrates how the news treated black oppression and resistance before the more progressive national elite consensus had emerged. The first event was the Supreme Court's decision in *Brown v. Board of Education* to overrule the "separate but equal" doctrine that allowed for school segregation. A variety of efforts to desegregate public schools followed. The second was the Mississippi trial of two white men who lynched a black boy in Mississippi.

Coverage of *Brown v. Board of Education*

In *Brown v. Board of Education*, the U.S. Supreme Court declared that separate schools were inherently unequal and therefore had to be desegregated. The National Association for the Advancement of Colored People (NAACP) had initiated the case as part of its legal strategy to dismantle the dual-school system. Studies that examined coverage of the decision focused on Southern newspapers and found that most of them were silent or voiced opposition to the decision.[76] Southerners who supported desegregation were ridiculed, and the federal government's involvement in the issue was portrayed as illegitimate.[77] The decision failed to push civil rights onto the pages of the *New York Times* or national newsmagazines.[78]

In Mississippi in the 1950s, the media was for the most part "a monolithic force united behind the efforts of the [Mississippi State Sovereign] Commission," an organization established by the state legislature to defend state's rights and maintain segregation.[79] A study of twenty daily newspapers published in Mississippi between May and August 1954 showed extensive coverage and commentary on the *Brown* decision in keeping with this committee's directive. Mississippi press coverage criticized the Court's decision, saying that it infringed upon state and individual rights. Reports claimed that Mississippians (both black and white) were not ready for integration.[80] Although some newspapers criticized Mississippi politicians who advocated closing down the state school system in order to circumvent the decision,, the local press did support ignoring the Court's mandate to desegregate.[81] The papers also said that blacks opposed desegregation but failed to provide evidence to support that assertion. The mainstream Mississippi press quoted widely one editorial in the black newspaper the *Newark Telegraph* that suggested blacks might be hurt by the decision.[82]

Articles in the state's two largest newspapers (the *Jackson Clarion-Ledger* and the *Jackson Daily News*) were among the most virulent.[83] They slanted stories in favor of segregation and "aggressively defended the 'Southern way of life'" in editorials.[84] Despite Jackson's large black population (approximately 40 percent at that time), its television stations also openly advocated segregation and refused to air opposing viewpoints or give time to civil rights organizations.[85]

> To most of the white editors and reporters of the Mississippi daily press in 1954, and to most white Mississippians, socially responsible editorship during the time meant endorsement and protection of Mississippi society as they had always understood and defended it—racially segregated with blacks in subservient roles as second-class citizens.[86]

Even the few Mississippi papers that took more progressive positions on the decision did not advocate integration. The *Natchez Democrat* was one of the few Mississippi newspapers to support the decision initially in an editorial published on May 17, 1954. However, two days later, the editorial's author equivocated.[87] One Mississippi newspaper that stood apart was Greenville's *Delta Democrat-Times* published by the locally maligned Hodding Carter. Although the newspaper gave extensive and sympathetic coverage to the desegregation issue,[88] Carter was determined not to be labeled an integrationist. He claimed to support a "gradual approach."[89]

The limited studies of newspapers in other Southern states have revealed more varied responses. Although some small dailies in Tennessee endorsed the *Brown* decision and a few vocally opposed it, most newspapers in the state did neither. Only 32 of the 151 white newspapers in the state published editorials on the Court's decision. "In 1954, the great majority of Tennessee's newspapers that did comment editorially on the *Brown* decision did so in a fashion that encouraged a calm and responsible—if stoic—acceptance of the new doctrine."[90] Yet, no Tennessee schools were desegregated a year later.

North Carolina newspapers were divided equally between supporting segregation, integration, and gradualism. However, prosegregation newspapers devoted more space and more front-page attention to the issue. Nondaily newspapers were the most slanted toward segregation.[91] More Virginia papers were opposed to the decision than in favor of it. The *Norfolk Virginian-Pilot* "was the only white newspaper in the state and one of the few in the South to oppose massive resistance" to the *Brown* decision.[92] In fact, the editor of the *Richmond Times-Dispatch*, considered a friend to the NAACP during the antilynching campaign, opposed the Court's decision to overturn the "separate but equal" doctrine.[93]

These studies provide more evidence that the Southern media did not champion civil rights and that news coverage varied according to audience ideology. Elites and the white public were more racist in Mississippi than in Tennessee, as coverage of the *Brown* decision in those states' newspapers reflected.

Coverage of School Desegregation Efforts

Efforts to desegregate schools got more attention than the Court's decision. As rhetoric became action and white resistance hit the streets, the issue became more newsworthy. Media scholars have studied two dramatic confrontations that received national attention: the attempt by a few black students to attend public school in Little Rock, Arkansas (1957), and James Meredith's effort to attend the University of Mississippi (1962). White mobs formed at both schools, requiring federal intervention to protect the students.

Little Rock

National network news covered the school desegregation efforts in Little Rock daily. It was "the first all-out confrontation between the force of the law and the force of the mob, played out with television cameras whirring away in black and white."[94] This coverage showed black students walking into the school amid angry white mobs.[95] The event was ideal for television coverage because it "had drama, tension, and the ever present whiff of real and threatened violence, all concentrated into a manageable geographic area and relatively brief time frame."[96] The event also demonstrated the clash between the national government's antisegregation position and the position of state governments. While it might have appeared to sympathize with blacks, television coverage of 101st Airborne troops escorting black children into school reflected the national elite position on civil rights and defended the legitimacy of the Supreme Court and the Constitution.[97]

National newsmagazine cover stories focused on white violence against the movement but also blamed blacks for the incidents. Neither side was portrayed as criminal, but the "real victims" were said to be the uninvolved moderates.[98] *Time* magazine did a feature on Gov. Orval Faubus, calling him a "slightly sophisticated hillbilly" and a "mountain Populist." The national media used Southern stereotypes, marginalizing and angering white Southerners.[99] Reporters for the black press inadvertently became part of the national story when the Associated Press wrote that when angry whites attacked black reporters, the students were able to get into the school.[100]

Although the *Arkansas Gazette* took a stand against Faubus's decision to

defy the court order to desegregate, its rival, the *Arkansas Democrat*, ultimately supported the governor.[101] Tennessee newspapers continued to disagree over school desegregation policies, and many looked for a middle
ground. Five of the largest dailies supported the federal intervention, and
three opposed it. "The presence of federal paratroopers in Little Rock pleased
no newspaper—again, excluding the Negro press—in Tennessee."[102] Once
again, Tennessee's weekly newspapers took the most conservative stance. Of
these, twenty opposed and only four supported President Eisenhower's decision to send troops to the school.[103] The *Delta Democrat-Tribune* was not
only at odds with the Mississippi media; it was one of the few newspapers in
the South to support the use of federal troops to desegregate in Little Rock,
Arkansas.[104]

University of Mississippi

Television coverage of the University of Mississippi desegregation effort was
also extensive. It included stories on the evening news, bulletins and special
reports during entertainment shows, and coverage of President Kennedy's
(unsuccessful) effort to quell violence in a televised speech. CBS also produced a special *Eyewitness to History* program on the event, featuring interviews with James Meredith and Mississippi governor Ross Barnett.[105] They
also appeared on separate *Meet the Press* shows.[106]

Local elites used all three media (television, radio, and print) to oppose
James Meredith's attending the all-white university. "Mississippi radio stations were giving play-by-play reporting on the riot, treating it as if it were a
football game. All across the state, static-riddled radios hummed with news
about the riot."[107] The governor made a statewide television address calling
for the support of Mississippians in his opposition to the federal government.[108] Governor Barnett "fanned the flames by framing the conflict in a
Civil War motif" during his speech. He also revealed that Meredith was on
campus, further jeopardizing the student's safety.[109] For the most part, Mississippi newspapers supported Barnett,[110] and "their news and editorial pages
reflected—and contributed to—the segregationist fanaticism which culmi-
nated in violence and bloodshed."[111] Once again, the *Delta Democrat-Tribune* took a stand against the governor's position, resulting in the burning of a
cross on the publisher's property.[112]

Southern papers had a long-standing habit of characterizing white mobs'
violence and defiance of the law as an exception to the mostly law-abiding
behavior of a public said to deplore the actions.[113] However, the violence surrounding the efforts to integrate the University of Mississippi led the *Chatta-
nooga Times* to question this assumption. "Editors of Tennessee's four
moderate dailies had never been warm admirers of defiant Southern politicians. But in the fall of 1962, Mississippi officialdom could find precious little
support even among Tennessee's traditionalist press."[114] By this time, Ten-

nessee's newspapers "were nearly unanimous in their conviction that prudence, if not conscience, dictated a bowing to the inevitable."[115]

Once again, we see variation in the media coverage. Reports all focused on conflict but disagreed on who was right and wrong. Mississippi coverage reflected the dominant ideology of the state. National media gave the drama extensive coverage that identified the disagreement between the national and local elites (Kennedy and Barnett). The Tennessee press reflected a gradual change in hegemony.

Murder of Emmett Till and Coverage of His Assailants' Trial

Emmett Till, a fourteen-year-old black boy, was lynched by the husband and friend of a white woman to whom he had said, "Bye baby," in a store in rural Mississippi in 1955. An all-white jury found the men "not guilty," despite evidence to the contrary. The defendants later sold the story of how they had killed Till to a reporter. Lynchings were nothing new in America and were typically not big news stories. Till's death got more attention than most because he was from Chicago (instead of the South) and because of a bold decision made by his mother and a national black magazine.

With the approval of his mother, who wanted the world to see what had happened to her son, a picture of Till's mutilated body was printed on the cover of *Jet*.[116] This horrifying photograph and the story that accompanied it illustrated the power of the black press to create a "cause celebré nationwide, especially among the black middle class."[117] Many blacks his age, who would go on to fight at the forefront of the civil rights movement, claimed that his murder politicized them.[118] Sociologist Joyce Ladner refers to them as the "Emmett Till generation."[119]

Reporters from the major Northern black newspapers of the time endured abuse in order to cover the trial. They were called names and segregated in the courtroom.[120] Black journalists were instrumental in the trial. They sought out witnesses and evidence after the local white police failed to investigate the case thoroughly.[121]

In addition to extensive coverage in the black press, Till's murder and the trial that followed received national mainstream and international attention.[122] *Life* magazine published a full-page editorial condemning the "not guilty" verdict and praising the bravery of blacks who had testified.[123] Pictures of the white defendants and their families, Till's mother addressing a black crowd, and his uncle's shack brought attention to the story in *Life*'s pictorial way. However, like much of the coverage of injustice against blacks, the story was framed as a social aberration rather than as representative of a systemic problem.[124] The *Jackson Daily News* (a Mississippi newspaper) ran a story refuting national news reports that Till's father had been killed fighting in World War II. They reported that he had been hung during the war for a murder/rape.[125]

This case illustrates variation in news coverage. The local press reflected the overtly racist ideology of Mississippi's elites and white public. The national media spoke to an audience critical of racial brutality but unwilling to see the problem as endemic. The black press put the murder in social, political, and historical context, arguing that it was not an individual act of violence but indicative of widespread and institutionalized racism.

COVERAGE OF CIVIL RIGHTS MOVEMENT ACTIVITIES

In the first half of the 1960s, civil rights movement activities had their heyday. Direct action tactics included sit-ins, marches, rallies, and civil disobedience organized by a variety of organizations and individuals. This section first looks at the media coverage of student-led efforts to desegregate public facilities in the South and to liberate blacks in Mississippi through education programs and voter registration drives. Next, it examines the coverage of events most central to the conventional wisdom that the press allied itself with the movement, including the Birmingham protests, the March on Washington, and the Selma March.

Coverage of Student-Led Activities

Efforts to desegregate public facilities came from college students who organized challenges to laws and norms they considered unjust. By sitting at lunch counters, riding interstate buses, and organizing poor blacks in Mississippi, they fought at the front lines, enduring ridicule, harassment, and violence. While this abuse periodically earned them press coverage, the attention given to King overshadowed that paid to their organizations (Congress of Racial Equality and Student Nonviolent Coordinating Committee).[126] In fact, the timing and form of their protests were sometimes at odds with the recommendations and desires of King and the organization he led (the Southern Christian Leadership Conference).

Sit-ins

Students orchestrated numerous sit-ins in 1960 and 1961 to integrate lunch counters. Southern papers provided more coverage and more diverse sources than Northern ones; yet, editorials were generally critical of students' unlawfulness and their motivations.[127] These actions were also unpopular with the border state press in Tennessee. With the exception of a few small weeklies, Tennessee papers argued that "worthy ends do not justify unworthy means."[128] Reporters sought out the leader of the sit-ins, and finding none, turned to King, even though he was not involved in organizing the sit-ins.[129]

National newsmagazine coverage varied. *Time* magazine covered the sit-ins by contrasting King's rhetoric with students' actions. It also provided a positive spin by contrasting the studious, orderly black students with the "degenerate" whites who opposed them.[130] Coverage in *U.S. News and World Report* was more negative, implying that sit-ins were a step toward widespread violence and holding King up as an alternative symbol of restraint.[131] This coverage reflected the growing divide in the civil rights movement between the more conservative King and the more radical youth who would become the black power movement.

The *Atlanta Daily World*, a black newspaper, provided descriptions of the tactics used by students in Greensboro, North Carolina, providing local college students, like Julian Bond, a model to emulate locally when they conducted sit-ins in Georgia.[132]

Freedom Rides

CORE volunteers organized the Freedom Rides of 1961 to challenge segregation on interstate buses. They did this by putting both blacks and whites on interstate buses traveling from Washington, D.C., to the South. When the buses got to Alabama, angry whites attacked them. Images of a burning Greyhound bus and hospitalized riders received extensive national coverage.[133] There was speculation that coverage was secured because middle- and upper-class white Northerners (including the son-in-law of Sen. Nelson Rockefeller) had taken part in the event.[134] Although the violence against the two Freedom Rides might have forced President Kennedy's hand,[135] the coverage did not lead to public support for the event. Nearly two-thirds of people polled disapproved of the rides, and a larger percentage thought they would hurt the fight for civil rights.[136]

National newsmagazines varied greatly in their accounts of the Freedom Rides. *Time* wrote that "the stinging rebuke to the officials of Alabama was matched by the cold disdain for the agitators of CORE."[137] *Newsweek* established King as the leader of the rides, presented the riders as brave, but voiced sympathy for Southern moderates. *U.S. News and World Report* presented four unsympathetic themes in its coverage of the rides:

> They were an invasion of the South; they were characterized by near-anarchy, implying that they were fomented or encouraged by the federal government; the government was unconstitutionally and unnecessarily intruding into the affairs of a sovereign state; and finally, the likely result would be a bloody racial war.[138]

Mississippi newspapers predictably condemned the rides.[139] Tennessee newspapers were ambivalent.[140] On one hand, they condemned the effort as "outside agitation"; on the other, they acknowledged that the bus stations were illegally segregated.[141]

The response of the black press to the Freedom Rides was not unified. The *Jackson Advocate*, a conservative, Mississippi black newspaper, opposed it.[142] Other Southern black newspapers, such as the *Birmingham World*, remained silent on the topic. Major Northern black papers (such as the *Chicago Defender* and the *Pittsburgh Courier*) covered the violence against the riders on their front pages and sided with the protesters.[143]

Freedom Summer

During the summer of 1964, college students and their supporters went to parts of rural Mississippi to work in black communities and register voters. Voter registration drives were less visual than protests and lacked the large-scale dramatic confrontations needed to get national news coverage. Despite efforts by the SNCC to get press coverage, little attention was gained until the murder of three civil rights workers.[144] Because two were Northern whites whose relatives actively pursued justice, the story received national attention.[145]

While no systematic studies have investigated how the mainstream press covered these events, research is available on how black newspapers in Jackson, Mississippi, did.[146] The conservative *Jackson Advocate* criticized the workers and their efforts toward civil rights, even blaming them for the violence they experienced. It parroted white conservative opinions and reprinted a *Wall Street Journal* article "that questioned the need for the civil rights volunteers in Mississippi."[147]

The *Mississippi Free Press* gave extensive coverage to the efforts of the volunteers and graphically described the obstacles they and blacks in Mississippi faced. It described bombings, harassment, mutilations, and lynchings and ridiculed white bigots aggressively (including those holding government positions).[148] This paper fulfilled "the traditional advocacy role of the black press by championing the cause for blacks and arguing passionately for social change and equal justice."[149]

The SNCC created its own newspaper, the *Student Voice*. It was "a forum for the exchange of news about SNCC and the violence and achievement surrounding the movement that the mainstream press frequently ignored."[150] By focusing on the individuals who worked in Southern communities and the dangers they faced, the *Student Voice* was able to recognize and encourage grassroots participants who were invisible in other media. It used bold headlines and photographs of violent responses to their activities to increase sympathy and financial support from its readers.[151]

The differences in these newspapers' content stems in part from economics. The *Advocate* relied on white businesses' advertising; its support for segregation allowed it to survive financially. The *Mississippi Free Press* used donations from Northern whites to subsidize its distribution to a local, poor black audience. The *Student Voice* also relied on donations.[152]

Coverage of the Birmingham Protest and Police Response

Commissioner of Public Safety Eugene "Bull" Connor got a court order to prohibit demonstrations against segregation in Birmingham, Alabama. When King was jailed for violating this order, the movement responded with what was called the "children's crusade." Students (from six years old to college age) marched, picketed, and demonstrated peacefully. They were arrested in a dramatic confrontation that received extensive coverage nationally and internationally.[153] More than 250 media personnel went to Birmingham to cover the teenagers' arrest.[154] The television coverage of this event holds a central place in the conventional wisdom. Some of the video clips from this coverage remain, but the audio portion of the coverage is lost to history, and no systematic analyses of it exist.

The images of fire hoses and attack dogs being turned on black demonstrators hold a less ambiguous place in recollections of the event today than they did at the time. We now interpret these pictures as a dramatic illustration of good versus evil, King's shrewdness, the media's progressiveness, and the public's emerging enlightenment. While there is some truth to these interpretations, it is not the whole truth. The media frames at the time were mixed, reflecting a still-shifting racial ideology.

Prestige newspapers, such as the *New York Times* and *Washington Post*, gave front-page space to the story for twelve consecutive days.[155] As we would expect from the research on social movements and the media, the coverage focused on the conflict rather than the demonstration's various goals. While the police violence was part of the story, "news accounts of the confrontations at Birmingham were laced with references to how some black onlookers, if not actual marchers, bombarded police with stones, bottles, and other objects."[156] Those opposing civil rights could use this information to justify the police response, which our contemporary eyes might see as unjustifiable.

Time and *Newsweek* shared a distaste for confrontation and a confidence in Southern moderates that led to explicit criticism of the movement's efforts in Birmingham. *Time* characterized King's presence in Birmingham as unwelcome to local blacks who were already making progress there. *U.S. News and World Report* saw it as an example of the federal government "conspiring to usurp the rightful authority of the Southern states."[157] The magazines criticized the use of children and the timing of the protests (after a new mayor had been elected but had not yet taken office). *U.S. News and World Report* went so far as to characterize King as sinister and ruthless—an "intruder inciting racial hatred."[158] It also downplayed Connor's violence and focused on violent blacks. One story in *U.S. News and World Report* "showed that any action taken by the police was justified because blacks were one step removed from savagery."[159]

Coverage of the March on Washington

The March on Washington, a rally held on August 28, 1963, was originally intended to promote jobs and a higher minimum wage, but its purpose was changed to advocating a voting rights bill.[160] Consistent with the conventional wisdom, the March on Washington has been characterized as "a historic gathering rendered all the more significant because television made it a national manifestation. Sharing equipment and personnel, the networks showed more than 200,000 marchers crowded into the national capital to make known their sympathy with the cause of minority rights."[161]

Coverage of the event was expansive by 1960s standards. Networks used "pools" stationed at various sites, allowing them to share recorded pictures and expand coverage. One network used seven cameras to cover the Washington Monument; another used a cherry picker to cover the crowds. Images were sent to Europe using the Telstar satellite.[162] Coverage started on NBC's *Today* show with a thirty-minute report and continued throughout the day with updates, a two-hour recap in the afternoon, and a final report at night. The network lost money on the venture by airing a three-hour show with no advertising sponsors.[163] Speeches were covered live on CBS for three hours, followed by an hour-long special.[164] The *New York Times* reported that March coverage "rivaled that given to astronaut launchings."[165]

The event and its coverage were criticized from the right and the left. On the right, the Mississippi governor called the television coverage propaganda, and South Carolina senator Strom Thurmond argued that CBS gave the event too much coverage.[166] Coverage in the black conservative *Jackson Advocate* focused on traffic jams, disorganization, and the arrest of a Nazi.[167] On the left, the *Student Voice* complained about the moderation of the speeches, which had been censored by organizers in order to stifle criticism of the government.[168] Most black newspapers reported favorably on the eagerness and intentions of the marchers and claimed that the event had great significance.

Positive coverage in the mainstream media applauded the new hegemony that offered moderate reforms. The nature of the event helps to explain this sympathetic coverage. It had been "conceived as a confrontation with American practices" but "became a celebration of American principles."[169] *Newsweek* originally opposed the planning of the march, characterizing it as too militant, but then provided favorable coverage along with *Time*.[170] "The March was respectable enough for almost anyone's taste, fine words and good feelings in abundance, effects on congressional deliberations of the civil rights bill almost nil."[171] But it was apparently not respectable enough to endear King to *U.S. News and World Report*.

U.S. News did its utmost to ignore King and, when he could not be ignored, took care to strip him of this dream, to depict him as an ineffectual leader and, most important, to label him the author of more of the threats that *U.S. News* believed were coming from most quarters of the black movement.[172]

Coverage of the Selma March

On March 7, 1965, a march from Selma to Montgomery was planned as part of an effort to register blacks in Alabama and draw the nation's attention to the need for federal intervention to guarantee voting rights. The day became known as "Bloody Sunday" because of the violent response of local officials to the march.[173] The goal of the action was clear, the violence used against protesters was dramatic, and it got extensive coverage[174] that was not universally positive.

Prestige newspapers gave front-page coverage to the march and the thwarted efforts to register to vote that had led up to it.[175] Sociologist Todd Gitlin claims that the *New York Times* treated the march to Montgomery seriously by using ominous wording in such statements as, "The Reverend Dr. Martin Luther King, Jr. led 25,000 Negroes and whites to the shadow of the state Capitol here today and challenged Alabama to put an end to racial discrimination."[176] Local Alabama newspapers (the *Montgomery Advertiser* and the *Birmingham Post Herald*), however, defended the state officials' conduct, and Alabama representatives read these opinions into the *Congressional Record*.[177]

Initial coverage of the Selma campaign in newsmagazines was unsympathetic. Both *Time* and *Newsweek* argued that the blacks intentionally provoked Sheriff James Clark unnecessarily. *Newsweek* "was beginning to get edgy about King and his tactic of filling the streets with marchers."[178] *Time* presented Clark as a "man of common sense seeking only to maintain a necessary degree of public order, not as a club-swinging segregationist."[179] Once the marchers were charged by horsemen and beaten with clubs on national television, these magazines changed their tunes, defending King and criticizing Clark. *Time* took great care to distinguish Selma from America at large. By making this distinction, the magazine could take the side of the blacks without siding against the system.

U.S. News and World Report was far more negative. It created a "narrative of unlawful defiance and just retribution."[180] The magazine's "long standing crusade for states' rights and against mob rule" was sustained in the coverage of an event that some argued to be incontrovertible.[181] "*U.S. News* raised the specter of government by ignorant blacks, of ignorant blacks, and for ignorant blacks" and voiced fears of black insurrection.[182] This magazine (along with the *New York Times*, the *Wall Street Journal*, and the *Washington Evening Star*) was later critical of the proposed Voting Rights Act, which passed after the Selma March.[183]

Despite these negative national newsmagazine stories, the Selma March is remembered as one of the best examples of the media's instrumental role in helping the movement. Rep. John Lewis (D-GA), an activist at the time, was beaten unconscious by the police on that day. He claims that the movement owes a debt of gratitude to television for helping pass the civil rights legislation. That gratitude cannot include coverage that was soon to follow, for days after the Voting Rights bill was signed, race rioting, which would become the major racial story of the rest of the decade, started.

COVERAGE AFTER PASSAGE OF THE VOTING RIGHTS BILL

Riots that broke out in Watts (Los Angeles), California, in 1965 drew the media's attention away from nonviolent protests in the South.[184] This event was only the beginning. Major riots occurred in other cities in following summers. In the summer of 1967, seventy cities saw urban rebellions,[185] including Detroit, Michigan, and Winston-Salem, North Carolina.[186] Many cities, including the nation's capital, were burned following King's assassination in April 1968.

These events received extensive coverage, dominating the news about blacks during that time.[187] Criminal justice professor Melissa Hickman Barlow argues that they had the lasting effect of "racializing" criminals. Public discourse continues to equate criminals with young black males.[188] The bulk of coverage was unsympathetic to blacks and ignored the problems that led to the violence.[189] It depoliticized the urban unrest, equating it with crime in general.[190] Although mainstream newspapers varied in how far they would go to characterize the police as heroic and the rioters as irrational, the major interpretive differences were between the black press and the mainstream press, rather than within the mainstream press.[191]

Mainstream Coverage of Urban Unrest

Because the mainstream assumed that race relations were primarily a Southern problem, the riots caught the press off guard.[192] When the Watts riot started, the *Los Angeles Times* checked its "morgue" (the library of articles previously published in the paper) and found nothing under "Watts."[193] When editors realized that they knew nothing about those areas of their cities then in turmoil or how to cover them, some hired black reporters, who were to "blend with the crowd and report back to the office so that others could write a story they had not in most instances witnessed."[194] The press failed to explain why the riots were occurring.[195]

> For one long hot summer after another, Americans watched what appeared to be the coming apart of their own country. On the front pages of their morning newspapers and on their television screens in the evening appeared dramatic and frightening pictures of devastation and ruin: cities on fire, mobs of blacks looting

stores and hurling rocks at police, tanks rumbling down the avenues of American cities.[196]

In addition to these visuals, the riot story was framed with conservative themes (such as "law and order" rather than "equalitarianism") that promoted white anxiety. Coverage was in sync with national surveys of the time, which showed that "62% of whites declared that looters should be shot, 72% said that civil rights leaders were pushing too fast, and 79% agreed that blacks shouldn't push themselves where they're not wanted."[197]

Government officials (leaders, police, and army) and their perspectives dominated the coverage. In 1967, *Newsweek* "devoted four times as much text to police and army attempts to restore order as to descriptions of the disturbances."[198] The injuries of white police got more newspaper attention than those of blacks.[199] Police brutality went unreported.[200] Damages were exaggerated.[201] Police statements were taken on their face.[202]

During the Watts riots, Los Angeles newspapers "tended to reflect the interpretation of the riot expressed by white public officials and white public opinion. The *Los Angeles Times* treated the Watts riot as a threat to public safety, not a symptom of inadequate conditions and urban problems."[203] Local newspapers presented the Winston-Salem riot from the perspective of law enforcement and city officials in part because reporters used their official beats to gather information, rather than going to the scene of the events.[204] Reports characterized police as the good guys and blacks as the enemy. On television news, "the police were depicted as a strong, forceful body which dealt adequately and successfully with the challenges that beset them."[205] Both the *Los Angeles Times* and the *Chicago Tribune* carried the theme of "police as heroes" during Watts, whereas the *New York Times* characterized national politicians as the potential heroes. The mainstream papers described the rioters as hysterical and "evil enemies of civil society."[206] Their actions were attributed to communist influence, irrationality, and even insanity.

Despite the frequency and intensity of the riots, prestige newspapers like the *Washington Post* and the *New York Times* failed to acknowledge that racism might be a cause of inner city blacks' actions.[207] Although the media would often acknowledge that living conditions were bad for blacks, they were careful to include with this admission a defense of America's political and economic institutions. This served to normalize the coverage so that it would not be antiestablishment. These events were also normalized, and their potential to cause systemic change minimized, by saying the problem was caused by a "criminal few."[208] The newspapers' efforts to contain the psychological and ideological threats from the Winston-Salem riots included pointing to the large peaceful areas of the city, emphasizing police control of the situation, avoiding inflammatory language, and talking to moderate blacks who advocated calm.[209] The news media promoted the interpretation that any problems would be taken care of by the "powers that be."[210]

This kind of coverage does not contribute to an understanding of the nature of Afro-American grievances or of conditions in that community. Blacks lose because their self-assertion is not fully respected; whites are deceived as to the extent and nature of black discontent and, therefore, of the potential or actual danger their city faces. In both cases the newspaper fails to provide a truthful, comprehensive, and intelligent account of the day's events.[211]

Parallel Press Coverage of Urban Unrest

The three major black newspapers in New York, Chicago, and Los Angeles all provided a historical context for critically interpreting these events and the role of the police and public officials in them. The *Los Angeles Sentinel*'s coverage of Watts criticized the rioters, calling them "lawless" and "shameful," but did not portray them as "insane" or "unprovoked," like the *Los Angeles Times* did. Instead, the *Sentinel* discussed how the city's past of police brutality and racism had contributed to the rioting.[212] The (black) *New York Amsterdam News*'s interpretation was even further from the white mainstream's. It claimed,

> Rioting was the *most rational* strategy of ghetto residents. It was not enough to wait for federal intervention, because mainstream society had historically only been motivated to act on the basis of "sudden and terrified fear" brought on by events such as Watts.[213]

Most black newspaper columns opposed extremism and violence in the streets, but they expressed an understanding of why riots were occurring.[214] These papers "served a protective function   providing alternative interpretations against the most damaging representations made in the dominant public spheres"[215] Whereas the white press blamed the protesters, avoiding critiques of the system, the black press pointed to white indifference and racism as the cause.[216] Exceptions included the conservative voices of George Schuyler of the *Pittsburgh Courier* and Percy Greene of the *Jackson Advocate*, who both blamed the riots on the civil rights movement and supported segregation.[217]

Coverage of the Black Panthers

The Black Panther organization was created in 1966 to promote black power and self-determination.[218] Although they organized community programs, such as free breakfast programs for black children, they became known for their militancy.[219] In part, this image was their own creation. Their rhetoric, garb, and pseudo events made them easy to identify with guns and force. However, the national press had "difficulty differentiating between rhetorical threats of violence and real actions; between what the Panthers meant to the nation symbolically and any real threat they posed."[220] For example, when

Stokely Carmichael held a press conference after King's assassination and said that Americans were incapable of handling race problems, that there would be more violence, and that King's death was a declaration of war on blacks, the *New York Times* called him "psychotic" and characterized him as similar to King's killer.[221] Newspapers condemned the slogan "black power" at its inception.[222]

Despite disapproving of them personally, reporters were attracted to the Panthers because they fit newsworthiness criteria.[223] Their novelty and confrontational style led to extensive, but negative, coverage.[224] This coverage characterized the group as a problem.[225] On television news between 1968 and 1970, black militants got worse coverage than white racists.[226]

The most extensive study of media coverage of the Black Panthers is an analysis of the *New York Times* and the three major newsmagazines from May 1967 to the summer of 1968.[227] This study revealed three dominant thematic frames that characterized Panther coverage: fear, condemnation, and celebrity. The fear theme was evident in the frequent use of words like "armed," "roamed," "barged," and "shouted" to characterize their actions and in pictures showing them with guns and wearing berets.[228] This fear was also sexualized in *New Yorker* essays about the Panthers.[229]

The condemnation theme was found in editorials that compared them to white segregationists and quoted government sources who claimed they were a threat. *Time* magazine's first story about the Panthers included this example of condemnation: "'Thinking black' is Huey Newton and his rage—a rage so blinding he can look on white America comfortably only through the cross hairs of a gun."[230]

The celebrity theme, seen in feature stories in the *New York Times*, characterized the Panther personalities (i.e., "the charming thug") and focused on their fraternizing with Marlon Brando.[231] Overall, the coverage was full of black stereotypes (violent, criminal, and irresponsible, with an irrational hatred of whites) and failed to recognize the Panthers' contribution to the black community.[232] These characteristics were also evident in newspaper coverage of leader Huey Newton's death.[233]

The Panthers' coverage was not limited to the mainstream press. They produced their own weekly newspaper, the *Panther*. Founded in the 1970s, it "decried police treatment of Blacks and called for various programs for Black self-determination."[234] Its circulation was greatest in the early 1970s (200,000). It published the group's platform, speeches, programs, slogans, and symbols and used terms like "pigs" and "lackeys" to refer to officials.[235] An analysis of the newspaper's content in 1968, 1970, and 1973 indicated that the use of aggressive imagery and rhetoric decreased over time and was replaced by pictures and messages of community building.[236] The *Panther* served its organization's interests better than other black newspapers that were editorially opposed to militancy and failed to give them favorable coverage.[237]

CONCLUSION

The conventional wisdom claims that the media helped the civil rights movement by showing the American public images of racial repression on television, providing a forum for blacks to articulate their grievances, and articulating their own social justice ideals. On the surface, this picture of the media is at odds with the mainstream mass media described in other chapters, one that is fundamentally unreceptive to racial minorities and alternative perspectives. Yet, a closer look at the conventional wisdom, the evidence used to support it, and the mainstream ideology of the time enables us to reconcile these divergent images. Still, the rationale for the conventional wisdom is fragile. Much of it is built on assumptions, memories, and wishful thinking rather than on hard data. Most of the assertions of favorable media coverage of the movement are not based on content analyses.

The coverage of the civil rights movement in the late 1950s and the 1960s actually varied in focus and favorability. While some of the visual images on national television news may have served the movement's agenda, the interpretations offered of what the pictures depicted might not have. The slant taken in national newsmagazines and local newspapers and on television was often more critical than favorable.

There was no consensus about who were the good guys and who were the bad guys; opinion varied depended upon goals, tactics, timing, and audience. Nonviolent demonstrators could be characterized as brave, self-sacrificing, and morally upstanding. Or, they could be shown as impatient outsiders who unconstitutionally defied states rights and intentionally provoked the violent responses they received. These alternative characterizations depended upon whether demonstrators were seen as threatening the status quo from outside the dominant ideology or if they were seen as peacefully working within it by asking for fundamental rights consistent with the American creed. The second interpretation became more viable as the national political elite advocated reform; the first interpretation remained dominant in the Southern media and some national media (i.e., *U.S. News and World Report*) for longer than the conventional wisdom would lead us to believe. Regional and national media differences virtually disappeared once peaceful demonstrations were replaced by riots, and the Black Panthers (judged as dangerous outsiders who threatened the system) entered the picture. Mainstream and parallel press continued to differ.

14

Native Americans, Chicanos, and Asian Americans: Social Movements and the Media

~~~~~~

UNLIKE CIVIL RIGHTS COVERAGE, MASS MEDIA COVERAGE OF OTHER RACIAL-minority groups' movements is not remembered according to a particular conventional wisdom. The centrality of the civil rights movement is demonstrated by the way American history is taught inside and outside of the classroom. For example, the public holiday celebrating Martin Luther King Jr.'s birthday teaches us that "times have changed" and that we are living up to our creed of equality, fairness, and freedom. The protest movements of the other three racial-minority groups do not hold a similar place in the nation's mainstream collective memory. In fact, many American are unaware that these other racial social movements ever existed. Yet, as time went by, the way the media covered events would influence what these groups fought for, how they expressed their grievances, and the perceived legitimacy of their claims. That coverage has been the focus of a limited amount of academic scholarship that primarily concentrates on key events. This chapter reviews that research.

THE AMERICAN INDIAN MOVEMENT AND THE MEDIA

Although Native Americans engaged in some direct action tactics in the late 1950s, their social movement followed the civil rights movement in the mid-1960s with some of their most visible activities occurring in the 1970s. In the 1960s, more than sixty events dramatized their desire for self-determination, that is, for control over their own institutions (such as schools and reservation governments) and to be able to express their values and traditions.[1] They also made claims on land the U.S. government had taken from them through unfair and broken treaties.[2] They often expressed these goals by occupying lands or buildings.[3] Forty-five occupations occurred between 1969 and 1974.[4]

After briefly overviewing the movement's coverage, this section discusses three of the major events of the time: the takeover of Alcatraz Island, the occupation of the Bureau of Indian Affairs (BIA) building, and the confrontation at Wounded Knee. These cases are featured because of their importance in the movement, their prominent news coverage, and the availability of research on their coverage. The occupation of Alcatraz Island was "the most symbolic, the most significant, and the most successful Indian protest action of the modern era."[5] It catalyzed the pan-Indian social movement.[6] The extensive destruction to federal property during the occupation of the BIA makes it worth looking at. The seventy-one-day standoff with the government at Wounded Knee received the most extensive media coverage of all of the movements' events.[7]

Coverage of the Indian Rights Movement Overall

The strategies used by the American Indian rights movement took into account the media's newsworthiness criteria of conflict and novelty. This sophistication helped them gain coverage but not control over the message in the news. As a result, their political messages tended to get lost in colorful and dramatic imagery. We can see this as a form of selective exclusion.

Stereotyping was also common due to mainstream news conventions and ideology and the way the group played to the media. Movement events drew on widely held stereotypes, which the activists were trying to poke fun at; yet, the media covered them in predictable ways by maintaining the "good Indian"/"bad Indian" dichotomy. They presented activists as romantic, mystical, exotic relics *and* as dangerous, uncivilized warriors and savages.[8] The American Indian Movement (AIM), an urban-based organization, had an "outlaw image"[9] comparable to that of the Black Panthers.[10] For example, the *Chicago Tribune* referred to AIM activists as "outlaws," "militants," and "armed insurrectionists" with "no scruples."[11]

By far the most dominant theme in national television coverage of the movement between 1968 and 1979 was that of Indians as "militant."[12] A full 90 percent of the stories about Indian protests on national television news "mentioned or showed the breaking of laws, the use of weapons, gunfire, injury to individuals, and destruction of property."[13] The movement wanted to talk about civil and treaty rights, but the news' focus on militancy overshadowed these issues. At the same time, violence against the movement received little publicity. The media also tended to ignore movement events that took place on reservations.[14]

Claiming Alcatraz Island Coverage

On November 11, 1969, eighty-nine American Indians landed on Alcatraz Island in San Francisco Bay and claimed it for all Indians.[15] They said that they had discovered the land and offered the U.S. government $24 in glass beads and red cloth for it.[16] For many of the activists, the goal was to gain publicity for Native Americans' rights rather than to acquire the island.[17] They claimed that the event was a success because it "tapped the potential of media-fueled, spectacular protest on a grand scale" and got extensive coverage.[18] However, some were determined to win the land from the government,[19] a goal they did not achieve as federal marshals removed the last fifteen Indians from the island on June 11, 1971.[20]

Although the event received coverage in the European press, national magazines, and prestige newspapers like the *New York Times*,[21] the bulk of the attention it garnered was local. During the entire nineteen months of Alcatraz's occupation, the three national television news shows carried only four stories on the event.[22] Yet, between November 20, 1969, and January 10, 1970, more than 125 articles about the event appeared in the *San Francisco Chronicle* and the *San Francisco Examiner*.[23]

The amount of local coverage varied over time, with the initial coverage being both extensive and supportive. Newspapers in the Bay Area showed support by providing the activists with a forum for their views. They also helped sustain the occupation by encouraging people to make donations to the effort.[24] This early local coverage may have been favorable because the political establishment of San Francisco was liberal, and the media reflected this ideology.[25] Or, it may have been favorable because the event was organized and promoted with the media in mind and initially fulfilled both the media's objectives and its own goals by providing an interesting story, visuals, and accessibility to reporters.

Media accessibility was high from the beginning. In fact, a reporter for the *San Francisco Chronicle*, Tim Findley, helped to arrange for the boats that took the Indians to the island. The event was actually planned during a party at his house.[26] The Indians also established a press office on the island and readily talked to reporters and posed for photographs.[27] LaNada Boyer acted as the public relations representative on the island and eventually appeared on news programs and the *Dick Cavett Show*.[28]

> The young Indians on the island initially invited the press to accompany their landing and visit their makeshift habitations. The news media, in turn, covered the story extensively, publicizing virtually without question the Indians' demands that the island be turned over to them and used for a Native American cultural-educational center.[29]

The originality and creativity of the peaceful event made it an appealing contrast to the usual bad-news stories.[30] Yet, the coverage had limited usefulness for explaining the Indians' agenda. Most of the coverage was superficial and light-hearted.[31] It focused on the novelty and suddenness of the Indians politicization, rather than on the event as part of a long struggle for Indian rights and recognition.[32] One local newspaper article used the word "wacky" to describe the act.[33]

Eventually, as the situation changed on the island, coverage, even by previously sympathetic local reporters, turned negative.[34] "Bad Indian" stereotypes of violence and savagery replaced the more "romantic portrayals."[35] After a fire on the island destroyed three historic buildings, a local news editorial on KCBS radio called for the Indians' removal.[36] At this point, one-time advocate Tim Findley compared the chaos and dissension on the island with *Lord of the Flies* in a series of articles.[37] He describes his change in reporting as follows:

> I had become too close to the whole story to write about it with professional objectivity. What I had written had helped to create it, and what I had chosen not to write had helped to perpetuate it. I am not really sorry about that. . . . But by mid-December 1969, I did feel obligated to correct some illusions I had helped to create, not just among white readers, but among Indian occupiers and their supporters as well.[38]

The parallel press created by Indians on the island challenged the negative news framing in the popular press. One of the island occupiers, Sioux John Trudell, had a radio show, *Radio Free Alcatraz*, aired on a leftist radio station in Berkeley (KPFA-FM) and rebroadcast in Los Angeles and New York City. On the show, Trudell conducted interviews, told stories, and reported on events on the island. He read a letter his wife wrote to the newspapers contradicting their hopeless characterization of the situation.[39] On this radio show "for the first time Indian broadcasters reached people nationally on the critical issues in Indian affairs as the Indians saw them. The broadcasts also promoted cultural and political awareness among Indian people."[40] The island's parallel press also included a short-lived *Indians of All Tribes* newsletter that contained occupation news, history, and poetry.[41]

Occupation of the Bureau of Indian Affairs Coverage

Various Indian activist groups organized caravans of hundreds of people to travel from three West Coast cities through large Indian communities on their way to Washington, D.C. The plan was to present a position paper to the White House. The plan lacked the support of the National Congress of American Indians and the BIA. Poor advance work that included a failure to secure accommodations in Washington and miscommunication with government officials resulted in the activists' flooding the BIA building once they arrived in town. When police tried to evict them, a fight broke out. What was supposed to be the peaceful presentation of a document turned into a battle with police and resulted in the takeover of a federal office building. The protesters occupying the BIA renamed the building the Native American embassy and welcomed all Indians who wanted to come in. A surrender agreement was eventually reached after the protesters had vandalized the building extensively.[42]

Members of the AIM organization thought that the confrontation with the police and the occupation of the building would result in coverage that would voice their criticism of the government for failing to work with Indians.[43] This was not the case. First, the attention the group received was largely limited to Washington, D.C.[44] This can be explained in part by bad timing. The event occurred during the final week of a national election and had to compete with campaign news.[45] Second, the coverage emphasized the destruction of federal property.[46] The "televised images of Indians with clubs, the ruined bathrooms and the upended file cabinets, and the rumors of the entire building wired with Black Panther–supplied bombs" promoted a dangerous image of Indian activists.[47] Third, the White House handled the event carefully so as not to reinforce the activists' message.[48]

Some useful coverage eventually resulted when a nationally syndicated columnist published information from documents stolen from the BIA during the event. Jack Anderson used this information to write about the mismanagement and corruption in the bureau. However, when a researcher for the columnist was arrested for possession of stolen documents, the coverage became focused on freedom of the press rather than Indian affairs.[49]

Confrontation at Wounded Knee Coverage

AIM joined two hundred Lakotas on February 28, 1973, to seize a trading post and a church at Wounded Knee, South Dakota, on the Oglala Sioux Reservation.[50] The reasons for the action were complex. Activists sought federal government reform, treaty enforcement, and the dismissal of a locally elected tribal leader.[51] This standoff between the Indians and local and federal officials resulted in open combat. Coverage of the seventy-one-day event was intermittent, but at times extensive.

"Wounded Knee was a fixture on the national evening news for weeks."[52] It received more coverage during the first week than Indian activism had received in a decade.[53] After the first month, coverage dropped off dramatically. After that, even the most dramatic confrontations resulted in minimal coverage. When an FBI helicopter opened fire on Indians retrieving food that had been dropped for them from a plane, their gunfire was returned. Other law enforcement officers shot back and injured four people. This exchange only aired for ten to twenty seconds on the evening newscasts.[54]

The coverage the confrontation received was rich in symbolic imagery but poor in explanation.[55] Because the setting was the site of the 1890 U.S. military massacre of two hundred Native Americans,[56] the media initially "found the second Wounded Knee theme compelling."[57] Early *New York Times* coverage invoked "a romantic view of the Indians as heroic, noble warriors trying to hold out against a superior federal force."[58] But before long, stories looked and sounded like war coverage[59] and focused on shootings.[60] Then, the stereotype of the bad Indian renegade from Westerns was used to tell the story.[61] The final visuals of the village showed the vandalism committed by the Indians but not the bullet holes they sustained from the authorities' assault.[62]

Activists used visual symbols to please reporters and get coverage.[63] For example, activists posed as warriors for photographs, located a teepee for a televised negotiation scene, and restaged events for cameramen who missed them.[64] Although this resulted in ample coverage, it also invited cynical framing. The images and the issues they were meant to communicate were sometimes dismissed as theatrics by the very news media that used them.[65] Reporters even attacked the authenticity of the Indians at Wounded Knee because they did not know how to butcher cattle.[66]

Originally, reporters had ample access to the Indians. In fact, an NBC affiliate filming a documentary was present from the beginning. Within the first week, three hundred journalists were at Wounded Knee, including representatives of the wire services, networks, newsmagazines, and prestige newspapers.[67] Indians allowed sympathetic reporters into the town.[68]

Realizing that this access was not serving the government's interests, the Justice Department shut down journalists' access after claiming that they could no longer guarantee reporters' safety.[69] Although some journalists got into the village by slipping past marshals and FBI agents, government restrictions worked well to diminish coverage.[70] Most news organizations relied on feeds from the reporters who remained rather than keeping crews at the remote site.[71] On the final day of the occupation, television networks returned, "but only CBS managed to get in, and they could only observe the beginning of the stand-down before they were discovered and then arrested by the marshals. The rest were kept miles away and saw nothing of what happened."[72]

Although William Hewitt acknowledges that some reporters "got it right," he blames both the activists and the press for the problematic coverage of Wounded Knee. He argues that "rather than clearly defining issues involving Native Americans, Indian activists exploited stereotypical images of Indians in their quest for media recognition" and "the media also fell short of its acknowledged obligation to investigate events and tell the whole story as accurately as possible."[73] English professor Robert Allan Warrior argues that the press "did their collective job fairly well. Reporters from the mainstream press pieced together the puzzle."[74] He acknowledges, however, that they missed "one of the occupation's biggest stories: the illegal presence of the military."[75]

In addition to the national coverage, there was also local coverage of the event and coverage in Indian papers. Prominent and extensive local press coverage in the *Rapid City Journal* continued throughout the standoff. It presented "a cumulative image of AIM as outsiders, armed interlopers who had descended on a peaceful village and dispossessed the residents, upsetting the tranquillity and economy of the region."[76] The *Akwesasne Notes*, a national Indian newspaper with a circulation of fifty-six thousand at that time, covered the occupation extensively. Its stories were quoted in smaller Indian papers across the country. Its coverage was sympathetic and explained the conditions leading up to the incident. These stories were nominated for a journalism award in 1974.[77]

Summary of the American Indian Movement's Coverage

There was little sustained coverage of the Indian's social movement of the 1960s and 1970s in the national mainstream press. What coverage it did receive focused on certain dramatic events and contained the kinds of stereotypes seen in fiction and the news generally. Sometimes the Indian activists used these stereotypes to draw attention to their events. However, the dominance of the "violent Indian" image served to undermine the movement's legitimacy and justify the government's responses to its actions. There is some evidence that the Native American parallel press's framing was sympathetic to the movement. Despite some high-profile events and accusations that the Native Americans manipulated the media, studies of coverage have revealed that the movement had more success at the beginning of events than as they continued and that, ultimately, the movement had little control over framing.[78]

THE CHICANO MOVEMENT AND THE MEDIA

Scholars and journalists disagree over when the Chicano movement started, who participated, and what its primary goals were. Historian Juan Gómez-Quinones argues that in the early 1960s, Mexican American political activity entered a social-movement phase, with various activities "loosely identified" as a movement.[79] Others locate the movement in the activities of working-class youth[80] and see it as a generational response to alienation.[81]

Author Francisco J. Lewels Jr. identifies September 17, 1965, as the day the Chicano movement started in rural California with striking grape pickers.[82] While ethnic studies scholar and civil rights activist Carlos Muñoz Jr. acknowledges that the farm workers involved in these strikes were mostly of Mexican descent, he contends that these protests were part of a labor movement and union struggle that should not be considered part of the Chicano movement. He argues that the people involved did not support Chicano nationalism or define their quest in terms of Chicano identity and power.[83] Rather than focusing on identity or particular methods of activism, others consider any efforts of Mexican Americans to challenge their subordinate position in society to be part of the Chicano movement.[84]

Because so little has been written on the Chicano movement and the mass media,[85] this chapter uses the most inclusive definition of the movement and reviews the available studies of its media coverage. It starts by looking at the unionizing of California farm workers, then examines coverage of the Crusade for Justice, its leader, and its activities, paying particular attention to the Poor People's Campaign coverage. Finally, it discusses media coverage of the Chicano youth movement and two of its most visible events: the National Chicano Moratorium and the occupation of Santa Catalina Island.

Organization of Farm Workers' Coverage

Cesar Chavez organized a labor union in 1962 in Delano, California, by mobilizing the farm worker community and leading an international grape and lettuce boycott.[86] Although financial support from outsiders helped pay for organizers and strike funds, the boycotts provided the necessary pressure on growers to result eventually in union contracts in 1970.[87] Overall, Chavez was successful at using the media to help achieve these goals.

Chavez was aware of the media as a potential resource. He sought support from outsiders through "a variety of rhetorical tactics," some of which included the media (writing letters and articles and appearing on television).[88] When the Senate Subcommittee on Migrant Labor's public hearings were held in Delano, California, in March 1966, reporters from national media covered the event. While they were there, Chavez led farmers in a 230-mile protest march to the state capitol. The heavy media presence stopped the police chief and city manager from blocking the march through the center of town.[89] The march received national evening news coverage for twenty-five consecutive days[90] and helped earn the movement visibility and give it cohesion.[91]

Chavez's rhetorical appeals relied heavily on moral and religious rhetoric and imagery. He called the march from Delano to Sacramento a "pilgrimage," demanded "God-given rights," and used Catholic symbols.[92] He held a twenty-five-day fast that ended with a Communion ceremony for eight thousand supporters.[93] "His willingness to live a stoic existence, his strict adherence to nonviolence, and his deep religious beliefs, many believe, were the main elements in transforming his unionization efforts into a national movement."[94] National newsmagazines compared Chavez positively to Gandhi and Martin Luther King Jr.[95] He even appeared on the cover of *Time* magazine in 1967.[96] Through his national recognition as a Mexican American leader, Chavez brought attention to other worker strikes. For example, when he visited the Upholsters' International Union in Austin, Texas, their petition to proclaim it "Cesar Chavez Day" received extensive news coverage.[97]

National publicity was particularly important when the National Farmworkers Association called for a grape boycott in 1967.[98] Some celebrities and politicians, including Democratic presidential candidates Robert Kennedy and George McGovern who supported the national grape boycotts, were used to bring visibility to the boycott.[99] Sen. Walter Mondale joined one of the marches; Sen. Edward Kennedy spoke at a rally.[100] Just one year after the grape boycott began, sales dropped 12 percent.

Despite these successes, the support of the mainstream media should not be exaggerated. Compared with the coverage that the civil rights movement received, these protests got little national news coverage.[101] Local news coverage was against the union. The *Coachella Valley Sun* called the movement's leaders "threatening agitators" and published a petition used by the John Birch Society to try to deny the union use of public facilities.[102] Union leaders eventually picketed the newspaper, protesting its biased coverage.[103]

The movement relied on its own union newspaper, *El Malcriado* (the voice of the farm worker), to articulate its claims and educate workers. This newspaper began publishing in 1963 and had eighteen thousand subscribers by 1969.[104] Eventually, sympathetic documentaries were created, including *Sweatshops in the Sun* (1974), *Food—The Next Crisis?* (1974), and *The Fight in the Fields* (1997).[105]

Crusade for Justice Coverage

The Crusade for Justice was a Denver, Colorado–based, civil rights–oriented action organization founded in 1966 by Rodolfo "Corky" Gonzáles.[106] Gonzáles's poem (*I Am Joaquin*), play (*The Revolutionist*), proclamations (*Plan for the Barrio*), and other speeches and essays formed part of an "extensive rhetorical campaign." They were designed to alert people of Mexican descent to their oppression and to inspire young people to political action.[107] Gonzáles's writings explicitly criticized the media for ignoring violence inflicted on Mexican Americans and for stereotyping them as villainous and inferior.[108] Before he became a national figure, a Denver newspaper referred to him as "almost a thief."[109]

The Crusade for Justice was "a vehicle to unify Chicanos, train leaders, and control mass actions in the community."[110] It organized and participated in demonstrations, marches, school strikes, and other creative efforts to illustrate the neglect of the Hispanic community. For example, to dramatize how Denver had neglected the swimming pools in poor neighborhoods, it held a "splash-in" at white neighborhood pools.[111]

Not only did the Crusade talk about Chicano nationalism and the need for alternatives to Anglo-dominated institutions,[112] but it created some. Esculela Tlatelolco was the Crusade's own school where volunteers taught three hundred children about Chicano culture.[113] Colorado La Raza Unida was an alternative political party.[114] *El Gallo* was the Crusade's newspaper.[115]

No academic research has been conducted into how the mainstream press covered the Crusade or most of its activities, with the exception of its involvement in the 1968 Poor People's Campaign (or March). Martin Luther King Jr. organized the Poor People's Campaign as a multiethnic march to Washington, D.C., intended to call attention to the needs of poor people. The plan was to bring the capitol to a standstill and force a response by the federal government.[116] King invited Gonzáles as one of the seventy representatives of various ethnic groups to a conference to help organize the campaign.[117] The Crusade for Justice led four hundred people (mostly of Mexican descent, as well as some blacks and Native Americans) to Washington for the rally where they helped build a temporary encampment on the mall ("Resurrection City").[118] It was here that Gonzáles issued his "Plan for the Barrio," which called for reforms in housing, education, business ownership, and land ownership.[119]

The coverage of the Poor People's Campaign in the national newsmagazines underestimated the Hispanic presence there and characterized it as a "black event," despite a press release by the Southern Christian Leadership Conference publicizing Hispanic groups' involvement.[120] When Chicanos were covered, they were shown in conflict with blacks. Chicano leader Reies Lopez Tijerina was quoted as saying that "brown, red, and white Americans were being bossed around by the Negroes and shouted down at the meeting" in *Time* in a story titled "Turmoil in Shantytown."[121] Even the Hispanic columnist for the *Los Angeles Times*, Ruben Salazar, drew attention to conflict between the groups. He characterized Gonzáles as having "feuded with the black leadership during the Poor Peoples' March on Washington."[122]

Even when the participants from various racial groups acted as a bloc, as they did outside the Supreme Court one day, the newspapers emphasized disorder. The coverage failed to explain the issues the activists were trying to call attention to.[123] "The net impact of the newspaper treatment of the demonstration was almost totally negative (presumably reinforcing the attitudes of those who believe that the poor are criminals and eroding the positions of others who aren't sure yet)."[124]

Chicano Youth Movement Coverage

Student organizations led protests, school strikes, and walkouts focused on educational reform and the Vietnam War.[125] The Crusade for Justice sponsored a National Chicano Youth Conference to help direct some of this energy into organizing around racial issues. Students and members of the Brown Berets (the Chicano counterpart of the Black Panthers) organized the largest Chicano antiwar demonstration,[126] called the National Chicano Moratorium.

The moratorium was held on August 29, 1970. Approximately thirty thousand people attended the demonstration in Los Angeles. When police tried to disperse the crowd, fighting broke out. In the end, forty officers were injured, four hundred people were arrested, and three people were killed.[127] *New York Times* coverage of the moratorium relied heavily on official points of view and treated the rioting as street crime from "roaming gangs."[128] One of the dead was the Hispanic reporter and columnist Ruben Salazar.[129]

Salazar was the first Mexican American to work at the *Los Angeles Times* and the first to have a regular column in an American English-language paper.[130] His columns drew whites' attention to the Hispanic community.[131] Since the *Times* covered Los Angeles' large Mexican American population less frequently than it did the smaller black community, Salazar "provided a voice for the millions of Chicanos who had been denied a public forum for years by institutions such as the *Times*."[132]

Salazar claimed that he could maintain journalistic professionalism while still advocating for the Chicano community "in the same way that general media advocated the Anglo power structure."[133] He did not identify himself as a member of the Chicano movement. In fact, the movement often criticized him for not being militant enough.[134] Yet, since he was a highly visible, successful, Latino journalist slain by a sheriff's tear gas projectile, Salazar became a martyr for the movement.[135]

Salazar's death was investigated in a sixteen-day inquest that was televised on KMEX-TV.[136] A grand jury ruled that Deputy Thomas Wilson had killed Salazar, but the district attorney chose not to press criminal charges, and the Department of Justice refused to investigate.[137] The ruling received only two sentences in the *New York Times*, stating that Salazar "died at the hands of another."[138] Many activists claimed that this was a government conspiracy and an assassination,[139] a belief fueled by Salazar's investigative reporting on police brutality, records of local police and FBI investigations of him, and the police department's efforts to get him fired from the *Times*. Skepticism persists today in Los Angeles's Hispanic community.[140]

Coverage of another event organized by the Chicano movement demonstrates how novelty gets movements news coverage.[141] In August 1972, members of the Brown Berets occupied Santa Catalina Island and claimed to liberate it (and other offshore islands) for Mexico.[142] After renaming the island, they stayed there for twenty-four days before armed sheriffs removed them.[143] Although the event was short-lived and involved only twenty-five people, it received more prominent news coverage than the development and success of a Latino third political party in Texas.[144]

Movement Challenges to Negative Coverage

The Chicano movement perceived unfair coverage and fought it with protests and the use of a parallel press. On September 16, 1972, one hundred Chicanos demonstrated and sat on the sidewalk across from the *El Paso Herald-Post* building to pressure the editors to meet with them to discuss coverage and staffing issues.[145] In the early 1970s, the movement also challenged FCC license renewals for television stations in Texas, Colorado, and California. "Many stations, rather than become involved in lengthy litigation, succumbed to the pressures and signed formal agreements to provide more access to Chicanos."[146]

The movement also produced a lively parallel press. Some were news arms for political organizations like *El Malcriado* (the union newspaper for the National Farm Workers Association), *Agenda* (the magazine of the National Council of La Raza), *El Gallo* (Crusade for Justice's newspaper), *La Causa* (newspaper of the Brown Berets), and *Sin Fronteras* (the paper of Centro de Acción Social).[147] Others were independent newspapers sympathetic to the fight: *El Grito del Norte* (Espanola, New Mexico), *La Guardia* (Milwaukee, Wisconsin), *Adelante Raza* (Appleton, Wisconsin), *El Pocho Che* (Oakland, California), *La Raza* (Los Angeles, California), and *Basta Ya!* (San Francisco, California).[148]

A Chicano Press Association was formed in the 1960s to facilitate communication among these and other newspapers. They shared articles and editorials focusing on police brutality, prison reform, and opposition to the Vietnam War.[149] Photographs of police misconduct during the moratorium taken by *La Raza* photographers and published in that paper provided an example of the use of the alternative media to challenge oppression.[150] The parallel press was particularly active during this time, but it was not to last.

> After the 1970s, practically all of the most activist press declined due to the divisions and transformations of the political movements, the increased costs of production and distribution, and most certainly as a consequence of the repressive efforts of state and/or federal government agencies.[151]

Summary of Chicano Movement Coverage

It is difficult to make overall assessments of the coverage of the Chicano movement because so little scholarly work has been done on it. Perhaps there was too little national coverage to study. The exclusion of Hispanics from the mainstream contemporary news discussed in chapter 10 might explain this. Or, there may have been coverage that simply awaits systematic analysis. Analysis that has been done indicates that the distinctions between "good" and "bad" minorities found in the civil rights reporting (Martin Luther King Jr. versus Stokely Carmichael) were also evident in this coverage (Chavez versus Gonzáles). It also appears that disruptive and violent stereotypes were common.

THE ASIAN AMERICAN MOVEMENT AND THE MEDIA

The Third World Strike at San Francisco State University from November 1968 to March 1969 marked the beginning of the Asian American movement. It demonstrated the group's potential for political activism.[152] The Third

World Liberation Front organized the strike, which was the first campus revolt to bring Asian Americans together to voice their collective concerns.[153] Although the immediate goals of the strike were to institute an ethnic studies program and an open admissions policy at San Francisco State University, the movement it launched dealt with more than educational reform.

The movement was a "quest for identity as Asian Americas."[154] The students' efforts linked them to their working-class communities, a history of resistance, and other liberation movements (both domestic and abroad).[155] The black power movement had heightened their racial consciousness and informed their political strategies, while the antiwar movement drew Asian Americans together.[156] In addition to political changes, the activists sought cultural transformation. They wanted to redefine the Asian American experience through panethnic confrontations with dominant institutions.[157]

One idea at the core of the movement was controversial among Asian Americans: that they had more in common with each other and with African Americans than they did with European Americans.[158] This idea mobilized students to participate in sit-ins, strikes, demonstrations, and rallies.[159] In addition to students, the Asian American movement was made up of urban youth involved in community-service programs and older community and labor activists focused on economic injustice.[160]

> In the decades following the strike, several themes would reverberate in the struggles in Asian American communities across the nation. These included housing and antieviction campaigns, efforts to defend education rights, union organizing drives, campaigns for jobs and social services, and demands for democratic rights, equality, and justice.[161]

Mainstream News Coverage of the Movement

With the exception of a few references to newspaper articles reporting on specific events, scholars have paid no attention to how the mainstream press covered the Asian American movement. This inattention might mirror the press's. The lack of a national leader, the concentration of supporters in a few geographic areas, and the lack of a specific plan of action would help explain a lack of visibility.[162] In an article on the strike, urban studies professor Karen Umemoto notes that "there were many efforts to split the ranks of the student coalition by administrators, media, and others." Unfortunately, she does not elaborate on how the media tried to do this or what the coverage of the Third World Strike looked like.[163] Historian William Wei's *The Asian American Movement* provides the most extensive analysis of the movement. In this book, he refers in passing to mainstream news coverage of three movement events.[164]

First, an East Coast pan-Asian organization, Asian Americans for Action (also called "Triple A") voiced its opposition to a U.S.-Japan security treaty by organizing a rally in Washington, D.C., in November 1969. They demonstrated in front of the Japanese embassy, and twenty of the three hundred demonstrators were arrested. Wei claims, "As a media event, the demonstration was a success: Not only did it receive front-page coverage in the *Washington Post* and *Washington Star*, but it was reported by journalists from Japan as well."[165] Unfortunately, Wei does not describe the content of the coverage, so how successful activists were at getting sympathetic news frames of the event is unclear. Second, Yisho Yigung, a group in Ann Arbor, Michigan, received coverage in the *Michigan Daily* in the fall of 1971 by staging "guerrilla theater" to depict crimes against Vietnamese civilians. Again, the nature of the coverage is not assessed.

Third, a disturbance between police and young people at the 1969 Chinese New Year's festival in San Francisco's Chinatown resulted in sensational coverage in the national magazine *Esquire*. The article, written by Tom Wolfe, focused on the violence and attributed the activities to the "Red Guard" before the group even existed in the United States. "Some of the youths [involved in the event] went to the *Berkeley Barb*, a famous alternative newspaper of the period, to explain how the riot had occurred. In their side of the story, the riot was a struggle between the police and a revolutionary group—until then unheard of—called the 'Red Dragons.'"[166]

Parallel Press Coverage of the Movement

Much more scholarly attention has been paid to the alternative press created by the movement than to the mainstream press's coverage of it.[167] Wei claims, "These publications made Asian Americans aware of the social forces that influenced their communities and called for militancy toward those with political power."[168] Student organizations, such as the Asian American Political Alliance, produced their own newspapers and alternative campus newspapers covered protests.[169]

The most widely circulated movement publication was *Gidra*,[170] "the first radical Asian American newspaper."[171] Founded in Los Angeles and published from 1969 to 1974, *Gidra* was used to help organize and publicize movement events and articulate ideas about self-determination, identity, and Asian American opposition to the war. It led to other Asian American newspapers and magazines.[172]

Another important publication was *Bridge*. Although run by and focused on Chinese Americans, this magazine also promoted solidarity among Asian Americans and between the native born and foreign born.[173] *Bridge* frequently addressed the topic of Asian and Asian American stereotypes in the media.[174] Overall, the alternative press, even when short-lived, played a key role in the movement.

In the course of reporting on the day-to-day activities of Asian American women and men and commenting on their actions and concerns, alternative press publications promote the pan-Asian concept; in researching the past and discussing the present circumstances of Asian Americans, they provide a historical and contemporary basis for a collective identity. By serving as cultural media, they contribute to the definition of who is an Asian American, giving the term shape and unity, in the process creating a constituency for themselves.[175]

CONCLUSION

As we would expect from the status quo–oriented press, news coverage of these three social movements was limited and generally negative. When novel events and violence attracted coverage, that coverage was fleeting and not particularly supportive. The nature of the coverage was more violent and superficial than the activists would have preferred.

The most favorable coverage was given to the least radical events and individuals. When Chavez evoked religious symbols and practiced nonviolent protest for an outcome supported by many politicians, his received sympathetic coverage. When Indians were willing to accommodate reporters with access to events and appealing stereotypical visuals, they too received short-term sympathetic coverage. However, when these groups strayed greatly, either in action or rhetoric, from the establishment ideology, coverage turned harsh. This can be seen in Wounded Knee and the Poor People's Campaign.

Local coverage varied according to the nature of the public and elites in a given area. It was worse than national coverage for the farm workers because important local economic interests were threatened. However, local coverage was more extensive and favorable than national coverage for the Alcatraz occupation because of San Francisco's liberal establishment.

Television was drawn to dramatic conflict, especially when it became violent. Thus, events like Wounded Knee received more television coverage than other, more peaceful events. Each movement had a parallel press that helped combat the mainstream news spin, mobilize its supporters, and articulate its objectives. These presses were particularly active during the time in their respective movements when the groups were most politicized.

IV

News Coverage of Racial-Minority Candidates and Politicians

Governor Gary Locke speaks to Asian-Pacific Islander immigrants at the Capitol rotunda in Tumwater, Washington, February 26, 1999. Courtesy of AP/Wide World Photos.

15

Media Coverage of Candidates and Politicians: An Introduction

~~~~~~

SO FAR, THIS BOOK HAS CONVEYED THE MESSAGE THAT THE MAINSTREAM MEDIA support political elites and the status quo against political outsiders and racial minorities. What happens when racial minorities are not outsiders but political insiders? Do racial minorities who become part of establishment institutions "earn" establishment coverage? Or does "white privilege" trump positions of authority and allow racial-minority status to block the media access and coverage? This part of the book will look at coverage of minority politicians and candidates compared with how the media cover politicians and candidates in general.

Candidates and politicians accuse the media of being biased against them. They claim that the media distort their messages and hinder their ability to communicate with the people. Their advertisements and speeches are efforts to "get around" the media. At the same time, reporters claim that politicians and candidates manipulate and use them for ends inconsistent with the purpose of a free and open press. Despite these complaints, there is more cooperation than conflict between politicians and the media.

Candidates and politicians consider the media daily and offer reporters assistance. They routinely provide information to the press through briefings, press conferences, statements, photo opportunities, and press releases. Politicians and their staffs control and limit access, leading reporters to certain stories and interpretations of events and away from others. Since reporters are aware of this, they take what the politicians and candidates give them but incorporate counterpoints, criticism, and their own cynical spin into their stories. In this way, they can follow a procedure that makes their jobs easier and still think of themselves as independent government watchdogs.[1]

This chapter examines how the news covers politicians and candidates, why they are covered this way, which factors influence coverage, and what consequences the coverage has.

CANDIDATES AND MEDIA COVERAGE

Media coverage of campaigns focuses on style over substance, strategy over ideals, and people over processes. Generally, issues are given less coverage than horse race and campaign strategies. Candidates who are actually outsiders, not just campaigning as such, are given less and worse coverage than insiders.

The focus is on the candidates as personalities rather than as potential leaders with issue agendas, ideologies, and party identifications. Not only is it easier to cover people rather than ideas, but doing so fits into the way that the media define news. Conflicts, scandals, mistakes, and misstatements that supposedly reveal who the candidates really are appeal as subjects to reporters.[2] Candidates and politicians become characters in a giant political play or sitcom.[3] They are presented as two-dimensional, known by their flaws (inarticulate, clumsy, folksy) and characterized with catchy names like "Tricky Dick" (Richard Nixon), "Slick Willy" (Bill Clinton), and "The Teflon President" (Ronald Reagan). Knowing how these simplistic labels appeal to the press, candidates promote their more appealing personas: "The Gipper" (Ronald Reagan), "The Comeback Kid" (Bill Clinton), and "The Compassionate Conservative" (George W. Bush).

Dominance of Horse Race Coverage

Perhaps most frequently lamented is the media's preoccupation with the horse race. Horse race reporting considers which candidate is ahead and which is behind, primarily using public opinion polls.[4] Changes in these polls are reported much as a sports reporter covers a race. Even when these changes are small and statistically insignificant, they are used extensively.[5] This coverage helps the press winnow the field of candidates, allowing them to devote their scarce resources to those candidates whom the polls determine are the most viable.[6]

Candidates that are ahead in the polls get more coverage, and those trailing behind in the pack do not get much.[7] This lack of visibility can doom their campaigns by preventing them from getting enough support to change their poll results and subsequently earn more coverage. In this way, their lack of legitimacy becomes a self-fulfilling prophecy. Essentially, candidates argue that by not giving them coverage, the media prevent them from succeeding. Reporters agree that candidates who do not do well in the polls are not viable enough to cover.

Being ahead in the polls is not a sufficient condition for victory or even for positive media coverage. The front-runners (those ahead in the polls) get more coverage, but that coverage brings with it the criticism of other candidates (parroted in the media) and the scrutiny of reporters. Not wanting to be accused of helping any candidate, the press may cover the front-runner with negative spin,[8] meaning that reporters look for trouble and report any they find. The desire for an interesting and exciting race also pushes reporters to attack the front-runner and provide useful coverage to any challengers who might catch up.

The strategies of the front-runner and any challengers get a lot of attention: where they are going, what they are doing, whom they have hired, what ads they are running, and how they are pitching their messages in speeches and debates are all reported with "strategic frames."[9] This means that rather than report on the meaning of a speech, the media discuss its political purpose and its potential effect on the race. For example, rather than reporting that "Candidate Jones said he supports gun control because . . ." they say, "Candidate Jones is talking about gun control to convey the impression that he is 'tough,' but this might backfire by turning the National Rifle Association against him." Interpretive campaign stories, rather than stories that describe events, have become more prevalent over time and have increased the negativity on the news.[10]

Factors That Influence the Amount and Type of Coverage

Coverage depends on where candidates stand in the race (front runner, viable challenger, long shot) and the characters they play in the drama (spoiler, survivor, surprise). It also depends upon how conventional the candidates are. Those who are authentically outsiders receive less and worse coverage than insiders. Sometimes candidates who are not ideologically extreme and who have political experience, resources, and connections that make them insiders successfully campaign as "outsiders." Gov. Jimmy Carter did this to differentiate himself from politicians "inside the beltway" stained by Watergate and the public distrust emanating from it. Bill Clinton did this in 1992, and George W. Bush did it in 2000. The media find outsider rhetoric appealing as long as those using it are not really outsiders.

Candidates from third parties (such as Libertarians, Communists, Greens), or those who create parties in order to run virtually independently (like Ralph Nader in 2004), tend to get little coverage overall, and the coverage they do receive treats them as novelties. The exception is when a third-party candidate appears to be having an affect on the outcome of the race; then he or she will receive some coverage. The reporting tends to be positive for a short time as reporters marvel at the surprising showing; then it turns negative and protective of the two-party system as reporters look for the candidate's "dark side." This was the case for Ross Perot in 1992 and John Anderson in 1980.[11]

Short of being a third-party candidate, some candidates, by virtue of their positions, can be more "outside" than others. This influences the coverage they receive. For example, media coverage of local politics and House of Representative races focuses on incumbents, sometimes to the complete exclusion of their challengers. Studies of congressional races have found that incumbents are not only given more coverage, but their coverage is more positive than their challengers'. They are more successful at leading the press to their issue agendas.[12] Of course, there are exceptions when incumbents make campaign mistakes, or challengers' attacks are compelling.[13]

There is also some evidence that female candidates get less coverage than males and have a harder time getting reporters to cover their issue agendas.[14] Reporters tend to see women challengers as less viable, which the coverage reflects.[15] Anecdotal evidence suggests that female candidates are stereotyped and trivialized in the press, with attention placed on their familial relations, appearances, and emotions.[16]

Why Media Coverage of Candidates Is Important

For a long time, political scientists argued that campaigns did not make a difference because party identification, incumbency, and "the nature of the times" (peace and prosperity) determined election outcomes. Therefore, the media were not an important enough factor in election outcomes to merit much scholarly attention. While these are important factors, they do not tell the whole story. Campaigns have always been important in close races, and their significance has increased as the electoral environment has changed. The decline of political parties as organizations and groups to identify with has made the electorate more volatile and open to persuasion.[17] Some of this persuasion comes directly from the candidates' strategic efforts; some of it is filtered through the media.

The treatment of candidates in the press is important because the media can influence campaigns and election outcomes. First, exclusion from the news can hurt a candidate's chances because name recognition is an important factor when voting.[18] When party identifications were strong, most people automatically voted for candidates of their own party; who the individuals were was not as vital. Now, party identification is no longer as important, and more people call themselves Independent, rather than Democrat or Republican.[19] They want to know more than the party label before they vote for a candidate. Sometimes just recognizing a candidate's name is enough.

Second, the media can influence or destroy a candidate's legitimacy with the coverage's tone and treatment.[20] When voters perceive a candidate as a long shot, they are less likely to vote for him or her. The media play an important role in these strategic voting decisions by presenting some candidates as viable and having momentum.[21] Campaign organizations tend to be led by a professional consultant who understands news conventions, rather than by a party apparatus. Such consultants organize media strategies to try to lead the press to certain issues and images.[22] These strategies have electoral and governing consequences, boxing candidates into certain policies and promises.[23]

Third, just as they interpret news about racial mass publics, the media set agendas and "prime" audiences during elections. Agenda setting tells voters "not what to think, but what to think about." For example, in 1984, Walter Mondale wanted to talk about the deficit, but Ronald Reagan did not. Because the issue was complicated, reporters stayed away from it, and Mondale's arguments were lost to most voters. If one candidate's issue agenda is ignored, and another's gets extensive coverage, then the media's agenda-setting role will help the first candidate.

Recall that the term "priming" refers to the media's identifying the dimensions according to which voters will evaluate candidates by focusing on certain information.[24] A good example of how priming hurt a candidate took place in 1980 when television news gave extensive coverage right before Election Day to the one-year anniversary of the captivity of American hostages in Iran. This coverage primed undecided voters to make up their minds based on this issue; they voted against the incumbent, President Jimmy Carter.[25]

MEDIA COVERAGE OF POLITICIANS

Once candidates get elected, their media coverage remains important. They are in effect running a permanent campaign in which they are selling themselves and their ideas to the public, other politicians, and the press.[26] Their aim is to remain popular to win reelection and get their policies enacted. Politicians have created organizational structures to help them do this. The tools at a president's disposal for managing the media and examples of their use are well known. The resources available to those at the other end of Pennsylvania Avenue might be less apparent; yet, legislators also utilize press secretaries and recording studies.

Congressional leaders have followed the presidents' lead in going public to achieve their policy goals.[27] Members of Congress do not have to be leaders to use outside strategies for mobilizing public support and drawing media attention to issues.[28] These tactics pressure their colleagues to support their legislation. Of course, with 100 senators and 435 representatives, not everyone will get airtime or space in major newspapers; while national media coverage is valuable for influencing policy decisions and personal prestige, it is a rare commodity for most legislators. The representatives who get the most national news coverage tend to have seniority or leadership positions or are running for higher office.[29] Positions of authority within the institution help reporters decide which of the legislators eager to be a news source are worthy of attention. Ordinary legislators can get fleeting national media attention as a news source when stories deal with areas in their policy specializations.[30] Over time, the perceived importance of having a base of operations in Congress to get publicity has grown.[31]

Local news coverage is a different story. Depending upon how well the media market and the congressional district match, local news coverage can be extensive.[32] In fact, most representatives consider getting attention there a higher priority than getting it in the national news because local coverage serves their reelection and representation goals. Local coverage promotes name recognition essential for victory and tends to be more positive, treating the legislator as "our advocate" rather than "another self-interested politician."[33] The local press and the legislator have a symbiotic relationship that allows him or her to shape much of the news through press releases, newsletters, local columns, and interviews.[34]

This does not mean that the local media will ignore a scandal. The structural biases toward conflict and an adversarial approach to politics are also present in local news.[35] Scandals give legislators without positions of leadership national press.[36] Of course, this is not the kind of coverage that helps them achieve the goals of reelection, prestige building, and policy making, since the reporting becomes a feeding frenzy, and they are the fresh meat.[37]

CONCLUSION

Despite the importance of media coverage to campaigns and governing, media coverage of minority politicians has received very little systematic attention, and almost all that has been done has focused on blacks. Case studies of specific campaigns do contain some observations about media and minority candidates. Even less attention, however, has been given to the coverage of elected officials of color and how it differs from that of white politicians.

The following chapter on black candidates and politicians in the media uses (like the chapters before it) the scholarly literature to describe what is currently known about this coverage. The rest of part IV of this book will look directly at newspaper coverage of a few Native American, Hispanics, and Asian American candidates and politicians. The research is organized into sections on visibility (coverage extensiveness), favorability (tone of coverage), and racialized coverage (reference to race, stereotyping).

Visibility deals with whether the media exclude minorities. It is important that minority candidates not be excluded from coverage since voters learn most of what they know about candidates from the media. While it is true that a candidate lacking news coverage can purchase advertising to address voters directly, the resources this requires can be hard to come by, especially without the funds that come from news visibility. In addition, news coverage carries credibility that self-interested, paid advertising does not.[38] Although media attention is particularly important in national and state-level races where the candidates cannot effectively run grassroots campaigns, it is also important in lower-level races.

While the amount of attention a candidate receives speaks to the question of exclusion, the types of stories in which candidates appear relate to selective exclusion. Are the stories that minorities appear in less prominent or about less important subjects? Candidates who are talked about without being talked to lack control over their messages.

The favorability of coverage relates to its direction or tone and can be measured as "positive" or "negative" (as opposed to the more prevalent "neutral" coverage). We can assess the positive or negative nature of the news by looking at the topics covered. Scandals are "negative" news; endorsements are "positive." What the direct quotes used in the story say about candidates and politicians can also be used to assess favorability.

Racialized coverage can take different forms. It might simply include references to the race of candidates or their constituents. Or, it might include speculation as to the impact that the candidate's race will have on white voters. It will include coverage of racial issues and might include the explicit or implicit use of the stereotypes identified in earlier chapters.

Overt racism is unlikely to appear in contemporary news coverage of politicians and candidates since racist statements and terminology have become unacceptable in mainstream American culture. Racism has not gone away; it has gone underground, and subtle racism has taken its place.[39] Old-fashioned racism has been replaced by code words that imply race-based threats to traditional values.[40] Reporters may no longer explicitly demean racial minorities, but subject selection, implicit stereotyping, and story framing and emphasis can draw negative attention to race.

The chapters on the news coverage of Native American, Hispanic, and Asian American candidates and politicians will rely on case studies. These case studies analyze newspaper coverage of particular candidates and politicians, assessing their visibility, favorability, and the racial nature of the coverage. The candidates were chosen so as to provide a diverse group. The Asian American chapter includes a Chinese American, a Korean American, and a Japanese American. The Hispanic chapter includes Mexican Americans, a Puerto Rican, and Cuban Americans. The Native American candidates and politicians are from various tribes. Some of the case studies focus on women, others on men. Politicians and candidates from various states are included. Some of the minority candidates won and others lost. Some of them are Republicans; most are Democrats.

These case studies provide some contemporary examples of coverage of nonblack racial-minority politicians and candidates. They help us consider questions like, Is the incumbency advantage still evident when the incumbent is a racial minority? Are minority candidates treated as outsiders, even when they are competing for inside positions? Who initiates racial references—reporters or candidates? While these cases will be instructive for addressing these questions, they may not be representative of other newspapers' coverage of other races. Larger random samples would need to be drawn to ensure that findings are generalizable. These case studies are simply a first step toward taking a look at a subject that scholars have yet to study.

16

News Coverage of Black Candidates and Politicians

〜〜〜〜〜〜〜〜〜〜〜〜〜〜〜〜〜〜〜〜〜〜〜〜〜〜〜〜〜〜〜〜〜〜

POLITICAL SCIENTISTS AND COMMUNICATIONS SCHOLARS STUDY NEWS COVER-age of black candidates and politicians using qualitative and quantitative content analysis. Qualitative case studies look comprehensively at specific campaigns, describing news coverage and speculating, based on an understanding of the entire race, what role it played in the election results. Quantitative content analyses can focus on a particular race or on many races. They try to identify factors that influence the kind of coverage black candidates or politicians get. This chapter shares the findings from this research in sections on visibility (coverage extensiveness), favorability (tone of coverage), stereotypes, and racialized campaigns. It concludes with a brief look at coverage of black candidates and politicians in the black press.

VISIBILITY OF BLACK CANDIDATES AND POLITICIANS IN THE NEWS

Candidates' and politicians' visibility can be measured by the extensiveness of their coverage. If one candidate gets more coverage than another, then he or she has more visibility in the press. We can think of candidates who get little or no coverage as suffering from exclusion. The type of stories that candidates and politicians are in and their placement tell us about how they may be selectively excluded. Candidates might appear in different types of stories or play limited roles in them. For example, if stories about white candidates are more likely to be on the front page than stories about black candidates, blacks are selectively excluded from the most important news stories.

Coverage of Black Candidates Overall

The most comprehensive studies to compare the amount of news coverage that black candidates receive to the amount whites get tell different stories.

Journalism professor Anju G. Chaudhary analyzed election coverage of winning candidates for U.S. congressmen, state senators, state representatives, mayors, and council members from nineteen daily newspapers for cities with substantial black populations. The 2,786 newspaper items were drawn from the period between 1970 and 1977. Chaudhary's results indicated that black candidates received significantly more coverage in longer articles than whites; however, white candidates' coverage was more likely than blacks' to be prominent (on the front page and above the fold).[1]

When political scientists Nayda Terkildsen and David F. Damore examined newspaper coverage of congressional elections occurring in 1990 and 1992, they found that black candidates received less coverage than whites. However, the extensiveness depended on whom the black candidates were running against. Overall, whites received 1.5 times as much coverage as blacks because whites running against each other got twice the coverage that black candidates running against other black candidates got. There was no difference in the amount of coverage received when a black and a white candidate ran against each other.[2]

Another study of four black mayoral candidates found that each got more coverage than his white competitor.[3] These campaigns took place over a twenty-three year period (between 1967 and 1990) in three different cities that varied in size and region: Cleveland, Ohio (Carl Stokes/Seth Taft), Los Angeles, California (Tom Bradley/Sam Yorty), New York City (David Dinkins/Rudolph Giuliani), and Shreveport, Louisiana (C. L. Simpkins/Hazel Board). Not only did these black mayoral candidates get more coverage, but they received twice as much prominent coverage (above the fold on the front page). The average length of the stories about whites did not differ significantly from that of blacks.[4]

Coverage of Harold Washington for Mayor (Chicago, 1983)

In 1983, Harold Washington and Bernard Epton competed in the general mayoral election in Chicago. Because of an aggressive voter registration drive in the black community, black registrants outnumbered whites (by 6 percent) for the first time in Chicago's history. Washington barely won, getting 90 percent of the black vote and 12 percent of the white vote.[5] Two studies looked at the media coverage of this race.[6] Both considered the amount of coverage the candidates received and came to different conclusions.

Political communications scholar Doris Graber coded newspaper stories as primarily about one candidate or the other. She found that the black candidate (Washington) got "the lion's share of coverage."[7] In the *Chicago Tribune*, 70 percent of the coverage went to Washington and in the *Sun-Times*, 61 percent went to Washington.[8]

The other study categorized stories according to twenty different subjects. It found that Washington's campaign activities received a little more coverage in the *Chicago Tribune* than Epton's. However, the *Sun-Times* devoted slightly more attention to Epton's campaign activities than to Washington's (13 percent versus 11 percent).[9] Obviously, this study shows more balanced coverage than Graber's study.[10]

Coverage of Jesse Jackson for the Democratic Presidential Nomination (1984, 1988)

Reverend and civil rights activist Jesse Jackson ran for the Democratic presidential nomination in 1984 and 1988. The field was particularly crowded in 1988 with eight major contenders. Since national evening news time is scarce, they could not all be covered extensively. Overall, Jackson fared well in the amount of national television coverage he received.[11]

Coverage was measured by calculating the number of times a candidate appeared or was noted as a source in a story and converting these frequencies into a relative percentage for the eight candidates during various stages of the Democratic nomination campaign. The results showed great variation between candidates over time. Jackson's visibility started and ended high but was limited during the period when the major decisions were being made.[12]

From February 8 to December 31, 1987, Jesse Jackson had the second highest visibility after Gary Hart (13 percent to 22 percent); he was just ahead of Richard Gephardt, Bruce Babbitt, Paul Simon (each with 12 percent), and Michael Dukakis (11 percent). Al Gore and Joe Biden each got 9 percent. For the period starting with the beginning of 1988 and running until the Iowa caucuses, Jackson's coverage dropped to sixth. He received only 8 percent of the total. For the period ending on Super Tuesday (February 17 to March 8), he was in fourth place with 19 percent of the coverage (behind Gephardt, Dukakis, and Gore). During a time when many candidates dropped out of the race (March 9 to April 5), Jackson was in first place with 34 percent of the coverage (followed by Dukakis with 26 percent).[13]

Which Candidates Get Excluded and Why?

Although the results of these studies are inconsistent in some ways, none of them indicates that the press ignores black candidates. They are not, as a group, victims of exclusion. That does not mean that the press does not overlook individual black candidates. Alan Keyes called journalists racist because they did not ask him questions after a Republican primary debate in 2000;[14] yet, other declared candidates were not even invited to the event. Candidates who have low poll numbers, minimal funds, and lack endorsements from party leaders get little coverage, regardless of their race.

Candidates are excluded when they are perceived as ideologically extreme. Beyond getting the *Progressive* magazine's endorsement, African American Ron Daniels and his running mate, Native American Asiba Tupahache, received little attention in the mainstream press when they ran for president under the National Black Independent Party (NBIP). When Lenora Fulani ran for president as the New Alliance Party nominee in 1988 and 1992, she only received headlines for "shouting down Bill Clinton and Jerry Brown in Harlem and Brooklyn" as they tried to give speeches during the New York primary.[15]

Extent of Coverage of Black Politicians

Once black candidates are elected, how does their coverage compare to white officials'? Interviews with black representatives in the U.S. House reveal their belief that the press does not take them as seriously as it does whites.[16] Three studies address this question by comparing the amount of coverage of black representatives with that of white representatives.[17]

One found that metropolitan daily newspaper stories published between 1979 and 1983 gave more coverage to black representatives and that blacks were more frequently named in headlines than whites. It also found that blacks were less likely to be quoted in stories dealing with congressional, international, national, and state affairs. They were more likely than whites to be quoted on local matters.[18]

Another study that looked at more than twenty-five hundred newspaper articles from the late 1990s indicated that there was no significant difference between black and white representatives' coverage in terms of frequency, article length, or placement. Yet, there were more photographs in *Newsweek* and the *New York Times* of black activists than of black elected and appointed officials.[19] It is unlikely that the same could be said of white officials and activists.

The third study examined local television news coverage in 1999. It included data from sixty different media markets (including 168 television stations), covering parts of 370 congressional districts. The amount of news that black incumbents in the House of Representatives received was compared to that of nonblack representatives. Regardless of how well the media markets overlapped with congressional district lines, black House members received more coverage than other legislators. Television news mentioned the black members in an average of 21 stories compared to 14.3 for the others.[20]

FAVORABILITY OF COVERAGE OF BLACK CANDIDATES AND POLITICIANS

One approach to examining content is to evaluate how favorably or unfavorably a candidate is treated in news stories. This is sometimes referred to as "tone."[21] Despite norms of objectivity, news organizations have been known to play favorites—matching their news coverage to their editorial endorsements. Sometimes newspapers develop reputations for clearly favoring or opposing a candidate or politician. In the 1970s, Gary, Indiana's *Post-Tribune* constantly criticized the city's black mayor, Richard Hatcher, and his three successful reelection campaigns. The mayor claimed that the attacks were racially motivated.[22] The relationship between the *Washington Post* and Mayor Marion Barry was "a running battle for years."[23]

Studies that analyze tone can get beyond speculation by documenting favorable and unfavorable coverage of candidates. Five studies compared the coverage of black candidates to that of whites, but only two looked at more than one election.[24]

Chaudhary analyzed winning candidates' coverage in nineteen newspapers from across the country between 1970 and 1977, coding stories as "unqualified positive," "qualified positive," "balanced," "qualified negative," "unqualified negative," and "neutral." The results showed a slight, but significant, difference in the coverage of black and white officials. Of the blacks' coverage, 18 percent was coded as "negative" or "unqualified negative," compared to 15 percent of the whites'. In addition, whites' positive coverage was more likely than blacks' to be "unqualified" than "qualified."[25] Newspaper coverage of four mayoral campaigns also indicated that black candidates received a bit more negative coverage than whites (23 percent versus 19 percent). However, they received the same percentage of positive stories (31 percent).[26]

The studies of local newspaper coverage of Harold Washington and Bernard Epton measured tone differently with conflicting results. One holistically coded stories into topics that were positive or negative to each candidate. It revealed that both Chicago newspapers' coverage was generally impartial.[27] The other study coded the negative and positive themes in articles and looked at the ratio of friendly to unfriendly sources quoted. It showed that the black candidate's coverage was more favorable than the white's.[28]

Direction of Coverage of Black Candidates for President

Regardless of their color, presidential candidates often accuse the press of being biased against them. Republicans' claims of a "liberal media" help them dismiss any bad news about them. Richard Nixon and George Bush used this strategy extensively.[29] When campaigns are biracial, debate about ideology shifts to accusations of racism or reverse discrimination. Complaints also come from white candidates who say that that the press applies a double standard that favors black candidates.[30] The logic behind this allegation is that reporters do not want to appear racist, so they resist criticizing blacks.[31]

Time magazine made the question, "Has He Got a Free Ride?" the headline of a story about Jesse Jackson's 1988 press treatment.[32] Although the author of this article indicated in the third paragraph of the story that he thought the answer was no, he reported the vast speculation that the press was not holding Jackson to as tough a standard as it was the other candidates.[33] Meanwhile, Jackson's supporters complained that the press was biased against him.[34] These same conflicting accusations arose during the 1984 primaries, when ample attention was paid to anti-Semitic comments Jackson made, including a reference to New York City as "Hymietown."[35]

A study measuring the tone of television coverage of the 1988 Democratic primary addressed this debate over Jackson's coverage. Its authors created a good press/bad press variable based on assessments made on television news of candidates' character, job performance, issue positions, campaign performance, and general desirability. Of the eight candidates in the Democratic primaries, Jackson's percentage of positive assessments was second only to Bruce Babbitt's (74 percent versus 88 percent). The eventual nominee (Michael Dukakis) was third, with 56 percent of his assessments being positive.

Since Babbitt's high percentage was based on relatively little coverage, the authors concluded that Jackson had received the best coverage. Jackson's percentage of positive assessments was higher than the average for the other candidates' throughout the nomination campaign (from before the Iowa caucuses until after the New York primary). The authors attribute this positive coverage to Jackson's skills as a campaigner and the reluctance of both reporters and sources (both partisan and nonpartisan) to criticize him.[36]

Direction of Coverage of Black Politicians

Despite the different techniques used to measure coverage favorability, none of the studies showed rampant negative coverage of black candidates. There is some evidence of differences in tone once blacks are elected, which lends support to the perceptions expressed by black officeholders.[37] Two-thirds of the black politicians interviewed in a survey said that they thought that blacks were treated differently than whites by the press. They complained that the coverage of blacks was "insufficient, incomplete, and inappropriate."[38]

A study of coverage of black representatives in the early 1980s showed that blacks were presented more positively than whites in terms of compassion and less favorably in terms of leadership and morality.[39] While a study of newspaper coverage of representatives in the House in the 1990s found that a mostly neutral tone was used for both blacks and whites, the ratio of positive to negative stories was greater for whites.[40] Blacks were covered more negatively when morality was the topic, which resonates with stereotypes of blacks in entertainment and the news.

Clearly, there is no consensus that the tone of coverage for black candidates and politicians is worse then it is for white candidates and politicians. More sophisticated analyses are needed to determine what factors influence the tone of coverage, how race influences tone, and under what conditions race leads to a better or worse tone.

BLACK STEREOTYPES IN NEWS COVERAGE

Stereotypes found in the public imagination and popular culture also appear in news coverage of blacks. Are they also used in news coverage of black candidates and politicians? No systematic content analyses have been performed to document racial stereotyping of black candidates in the media; however, case studies provide some examples of characterizations that present black candidates as dishonest and immoral, dangerous and threatening, or novel and different.

Dishonest and Immoral

The stereotypes of blacks as dishonest and immoral are common in film and television.[41] They also find their way into news coverage of black candidates and politicians. Communications professors Robert Entman and Andrew Rojecki found that more than half of ABC's television news stories that mentioned black leaders during a twelve-month period (1990–1991) included an accusation of wrongdoing or the leader's denial of having committed crimes.[42] Of the newspaper stories about four black mayoral candidates, 23 percent were about ethics, compared to 18 percent for their white opponents.[43]

Black candidates can suffer under stereotypes of corruption and dishonesty. These two examples illustrate how. Political scientist James M. Glaser examined the special election campaign for Mississippi's second congressional district in 1993.[44] Five black Democrats, two white Democrats, and a white Republican competed to be in the runoff in this black-majority district. Glaser noted that the "corrupt black politician theme" was used against Bennie Thompson (a black candidate) by Republicans, who used mock newspaper headlines with the words "indictment" and "corrupt" in their advertisements against him. They leaked a story that authorities had once considered investigating Thompson to newspapers. Eventually, articles with headlines like, "Friends in High Places Saved Thompson," appeared on two Delta newspapers' front pages, giving legitimacy to the white candidate's advertisements.[45]

Political scientist Sheila Collins claims that the press's preoccupation with Jesse Jackson's "Hymietown" comment "suggests a double standard among whites on the matter of moral purity—a double standard linked to their need, in a racist society, to project their own moral turpitude onto a debased 'other.'"[46] Empirical evidence supports the conclusion that Jackson's anti-Semitic comments were given a lot of attention. During the 1984 Democratic primaries, forty-three reports on television news about Jackson were coded as "negative role model," compared to only ten for Gary Hart and fifteen for Walter Mondale.[47] In the television coverage, Jackson's comments were interpreted as evidence of his "unsuitable personality," which then became the focus of many stories.[48]

Dangerous and Threatening

The prevalent stereotyping of blacks as dangerous reflects white anxiety over their potential threat to the status quo. Because candidates and politicians are acting "within the system," they should be less susceptible to this stereotype. However, it simply takes a subtler form in news coverage about black politicians and candidates. Rather than present black candidates or politicians as violent, they are shown with dangerous people, accused of promoting threatening ideas, and portrayed as angry.

One way black candidates are made to appear threatening in the news is by identifying them with the controversial Louis Farrakhan. Farrakhan "is the subtext in the news coverage of scores of political campaigns involving black candidates across the country."[49] Black candidates are "required" to publicly condemn Farrakhan. Even moderate David Dinkins was put through this ritual as part of his campaign to be mayor of New York. No similar requests are made of white candidates to attack inflammatory whites just because they share a skin color.[50]

In fact, the news media are preoccupied with Louis Farrakhan. National television news exaggerates his influence among African Americans and gives him extensive coverage. During Jesse Jackson's 1984 campaign for president, 68 percent of major news stories about black political activity focused on Farrakhan (as did more than half of the coverage in 1985). A clip of Jesse Jackson and Louis Farrakhan embracing at a rally became a visual symbol that was repeated throughout the campaign and used to interpret Jackson's popularity and his priorities as frightening.[51] An analysis of newspaper coverage of Farrakhan's speech at the Million Man March in 1995 tended to ignore his messages of reconciliation and unity in order to malign his character instead.[52] According to scholars Entman and Rojecki, this focus on Farrakhan has dire consequences:

> [The media] misinterprets and magnifies the significance of incidents that give shape to latent fears and suspicions born of segregated lives and misunderstanding, and thus construct a plausible reality that changes the structure of political opportunity.[53]

Opponents use this technique of associating more extreme blacks with a moderate black candidate to frighten white voters. In the last debate of the 1982 California gubernatorial campaign, white Republican George Deukmejian insinuated that his moderate black opponent (Tom Bradley) was extreme by saying that Bradley was an ally of the more radical black state legislator, Willie Brown.[54] North Carolina's Senator Jesse Helms ran an ad against his black opponent, Harvey Gantt, that showed Gantt accepting a campaign donation from Jesse Jackson.[55]

"Anger" can be thought of as a surrogate term for "violent" or as a precursor to violence. More television airtime goes to black leaders when they use angry rhetoric. This is also true of local television news coverage, which includes a lot of angry sound bites uttered by African Americans.[56] In contrast, white leaders are rarely shown shouting.[57]

Novel and Different

Blacks are also stereotyped as "novelties" because whiteness is assumed to be the "norm," which makes racial minorities the exception; it "otherizes" them.[58] Media studies professor Arnold Gibbons argues that Jesse Jackson's coverage during the 1988 presidential campaign presented him as "a media toy, to be played with, sympathized with, perhaps admired, but never to be taken seriously."[59]

The press was less preoccupied with reporting on Jackson's chances of winning than it was for his competitors in 1984. Even when Jackson had strong poll numbers, the press did not consider him viable. Only 13 percent of his television news coverage included assessments of Jackson's chances of winning, compared to between 27 percent and 38 percent for the other candidates. In fact, his exit poll numbers and vote tallies were often left out of reports, even when he came in second or third in state primaries. Perhaps this was the case because reporters saw Jackson as a novelty and not as a serious contender for the nomination.[60]

Novelty coverage treats blacks as different. It reports on their "uniqueness" rather than their competitiveness, then blames them for being a distraction. In 1984, Jackson was characterized as an "outsider" more frequently than the other candidates (seventy-six times), and as a "spoiler" (six times). "For a candidate who is thought to have no chance of winning, an Outsider Role makes him (or her) seem obtrusive and brash."[61] Even after they are elected, blacks are more likely to be presented as outsiders, lacking independence and power.[62]

Additional Stereotypes of Black Women Candidates and Politicians

Since the media do not take women candidates and politicians as seriously as they do men,[63] black women have both racial and gender stereotypes to worry about. When Shirley Chisholm ran for the Democratic presidential nomination in 1972, she was accused of trying to split the vote to help another candidate rather than seriously running for office.[64] Third-party presidential candidate Lenora Fulani's only press attention focused on conflict and flamboyance in a way similar to coverage of protest groups.[65] While the former were candidates with little chance of winning, demeaning stereotypes also characterized coverage of a successful black female candidate, Illinois senator Carol Moseley-Braun.

Moseley-Braun's portrayal in her campaign coverage fit black stereotypes of laziness, tardiness, stupidity, and dishonesty.[66] She went from "outsider" to "novelty" (as the first black women in the Senate) to "unethical."[67] Journalism scholar Carmen L. Manning-Miller contends that more judgments were made about Moseley-Braun's campaign behaviors than about her male opponent's. She received attention for shopping for panty hose and was judged as "cracking under pressure" and verging on a nervous breakdown when she cried in front of the press.[68] As an incumbent, she was left out of national political news coverage in the *Chicago Tribune*, although this may have had more to do with her press strategy of avoiding questions and giving few interviews than with her race.[69]

RACIALIZED CAMPAIGN COVERAGE

Black candidates can also be undermined in news stories when they receive attention for being the "black candidate," which itself brings a certain amount of baggage. Race can become an election issue when a candidate is black, regardless of whether he or she talks about race.[70] Racialized coverage can take a variety of forms. It includes references to the race of candidates, to the potential impact of race on the election outcome, to the race of voters, and to racial-issue positions. Race has consequences for how the campaign is run and sometimes for election results.

Quantifying the Coverage of Race

Studies differ in their approaches to quantifying the presence of race in campaign coverage. These methodological choices have important consequences for how much racial coverage they find.

One approach is to code a story as "about race" or not. Two studies that did this found that race was present but not a major topic in three campaigns. Even though Washington and Epton insisted that race was not an issue in their campaign, the topic received 14 percent of the campaign coverage in the *Chicago Tribune* and 9 percent of the *Sun-Times*'s coverage, which was more coverage than each of the seven major policy issues.[71] Of the campaign stories in the *New York Times* about the 1989 David Dinkins/Rudolph Giuliani mayoral race, 20 percent focused exclusively on race, and 9 percent of the stories in the *Seattle Times* about the 1989 Doug Jewett/Norm Rice mayoral election in Seattle were about race.[72]

Attention to race appears more prevalent when measured by references made to race in stories that are not necessarily about race. Using this approach, race was mentioned in 44 percent of the stories about four mayoral campaigns between blacks and whites. This attention to race did not wane over the twenty-three years the campaigns spanned. In fact, references to race were least frequent in the 1967 campaign in Cleveland, appearing in only 27 percent of the stories; race was referred to in 63 percent of the coverage of the 1990 race in Shreveport.[73]

What was the nature of these references? Of the *New York Times* stories, 20 percent, and of the *Seattle Times* coverage, 63 percent referred specifically to the candidates' race or ethnicity. In addition, 75 percent of the *New York*

Times stories and 33 percent of the *Seattle Times* stories contained references to racial and ethnic groups in the electorate.[74]

A study of coverage of House races indicated that for biracial campaigns, newspaper stories were more likely to highlight African American candidates' races and the percentage of blacks in the districts than stories about white candidates. The frequency of the media's references to race was highest in competitive races.[75] The race of the candidate is also signaled through photographs. A study of blacks who ran against whites for Congress in 1990 and 1992 revealed that blacks were shown in newspaper photographs more often, thereby reminding readers of their race.[76]

Rather than code story subjects or references to race within stories, another study quantified "racial framing" by looking at word use.[77] Newspaper stories that included words and phrases identified by the authors as "racial code words" were counted in two biracial Senate campaigns—the Carol Moseley-Braun/Richard Williamson race in Illinois (1992) and the Alan Wheat/John Ashcroft race in Missouri (1994). Many (36.6 percent) of the 202 postnomination campaign news stories in the *Chicago Tribune* and the *St. Louis Post-Dispatch* contained racial code words. The presence of racial code words was greater in the Illinois race, especially in articles focusing on the horse race. Stories about the black candidates in both campaigns contained significantly more racial code word than stories about their white competitors.[78]

An analysis of newspaper coverage of twenty-one House races in the early 1990s went beyond quantifying racial references to examine who made them.[79] By looking at source use, this research was able to see who drew attention to race—the candidates or the media. It found that the media made the majority of the racial references, and that they were not located in quotes from the candidates or other sources. Therefore, the media do more than simply amplify the candidates' racial campaign strategies. The media racialize campaigns. According to the study, even when black candidates ran against each other, the media provided ample racial references.[80]

Once black candidates take office, the media continue to focus on race in their coverage of them. In newspaper coverage of U.S. House representatives from 1979 to 1983, blacks were quoted more often then whites on racial issues.[81] The study of U.S. House representatives' coverage in the late 1990s found that "African American members get coverage that suggests they are interested only in African American concerns and coverage that emphasizes that they are locked out of the power structure."[82] An examination of the members' Web pages and interviews with press secretaries indicated that the emphasis on race originated with the media, rather than with the members. In fact, black representatives were likely to talk about race as "a commitment to inclusion," and the media talked about it as "a preference for exclusion."[83]

These findings are consistent with an analysis of 1999 local television news coverage. This study found that 13 percent of the stories that included black U.S. House Representatives were "race oriented" compared to only 3.3 percent for their white colleagues. This coverage was not based on their legislative agendas. In fact, blacks representing less racially diverse districts received *more* race-oriented news. The authors concluded that "local television coverage is race oriented in markets where it might hurt African-American legislators most. Where African-American legislators could most benefit from an image of an effective lawmaker, they are instead portrayed as narrowly focused on minority issues."[84]

Accusations of Representing Only Blacks

By focusing on black candidates' and politicians' positions on racial issues, the media serve some white candidates' strategy of suggesting that their black opponents will only represent blacks to the exclusion and detriment of whites. There are numerous examples of how this idea has made its way into campaign coverage.

During the North Carolina Senate race of 1984, white incumbent Jesse Helms characterized his black opponent, Jim Hunt, as "prounion" and "pro-black" in radio and small-town newspaper ads.[85] Helms also manipulated video images and sound in his advertising against Harvey Gantt in 1990 to trigger white fears. Gantt's image was darkened on screen, and his voice was slowed to make him sound ignorant. Helms also played on white resentment over affirmative action in the infamous "hands ad," which showed white hands crumpling a job rejection letter while the voice-over claimed, "You needed that job, and you were the best qualified. But they had to give it to a minority because of a racial quota. Is that fair? Harvey Gantt says it is."[86] Although Gantt did not support racial quotas, Helm's effectively pushed undecided white voters away from the black candidate by leading them to "think about race rather than beyond race."[87]

The press does not always wait for white politicians to introduce the question of whom black candidates represent. The media have also led white voters to suspect minority candidates by identifying them as "antiwhite" or as allies of those who are. In Mississippi's 2nd district runoff in 1993, editorials harshly criticized Bennie Thompson for saying that he did not need white farmer support (a statement he denied making, but that his opponent accused him of).[88]

During Jesse Jackson's 1984 campaign's coverage, "The constant references to Jackson as a 'black presidential candidate' may have enforced an impression among whites that Jackson was a candidate *only* for blacks."[89] To the media,

> Jackson was the candidate of African Americans and that stereotype persisted to the very end. It was as though the media could not bring themselves to consider

any other possibility; and the more he was identified that way, the more it limited his appeal to the wider electorate.[90]

This impression that Jackson spoke exclusively for and to blacks was reinforced in other ways throughout his campaigns. For example, televised reaction shots during speeches made at the 1984 Democratic National Convention suggested to whom the speaker was talking or whom he was affecting. During Jackson's speech, CBS used 115 reaction shots of blacks in the audience (63 percent of the total shown) compared to only nine shots of blacks (6 percent) during Gary Hart's speech.[91] The press also ignored Jackson's effort to build a multiracial "Rainbow Coalition" of supporters.[92]

Focusing on the Race of the Black Candidate

Media attention to the race of a black candidate and the effect race might have on the election outcome can push issues about governing off the front pages and reinforce white voters' fears. For example, a candidate's issue positions took a back seat to his race in the 1982 California gubernatorial race between Tom Bradley and George Deukmejian.

The *Los Angeles Times* made frequent references to Tom Bradley's being black. Bradley's white support eroded over the course of the campaign as the paper published numerous stories about his strong support from black voters and questioned whether whites would support a black for governor. When George Deukmejian's campaign manager got extensive publicity for saying that his candidate would win because of a "hidden antiblack vote," the statement "served to invite, dignify, and legitimize the presence of race as a proper dimension of campaign coverage."[93]

Despite Bradley's efforts to downplay the topic, the race issue dominated media coverage and contributed to his defeat.[94] Although the Deukmejian campaign blamed the press for making race an issue,[95] his campaign advertising and mailings included "racially charged code words and slogans."[96] The slogan "He can represent all Californians" clearly implied that Bradley could not.[97] This message was reinforced by the publication of a poll indicating that 6 percent of the respondents supported Deukmejian because they thought Bradley would favor minorities.[98]

When Andrew Young ran for governor of Georgia in 1990, the press raised the issue of race more than the candidates.[99] Issues and public-opinion polls were discussed in terms of race. The press went from characterizing Young as a "conciliator" to characterizing him as a "long shot" with white voters.[100] Reporters could claim that they were simply covering the results of polls that showed white support for Young diminishing; however, in so doing, they continuously reminded undecided white voters that other white voters had problems with the black candidate.

> The reduction of election analysis to race—a reduction no doubt resulting from its saliency in the population—serves to keep the issue alive in the minds of voters and fails to provide alternative ways of looking at the political process.[101]

Jesse Jackson's color was also prominent in news about him during his presidential bids. One question asked of him by Marvin Kalb on *Meet the Press* illustrates how the legitimacy of a black candidate can be called into question in a way that seems unimaginable for a white candidate. Kalb asked, "Are you a black man who happens to be an American running for the presidency, or are you an American who happens to be a black man running for the presidency?"[102]

Race was a frequent topic in media coverage of the Harold Washington/ Bernard Epton race for mayor of Chicago.[103]

> After his victory in the primary, television interviewers kept asking people how they felt about the possibility of a black as the next mayor. When answers skirted the race issue, reporters kept pressing for racial statements. Newspapers and television stations started a series of special features describing how other major cities had fared under the administration of black chief executives.[104]

Here, once again, the candidates claimed that the media kept bringing up the race issue, but race was certainly part of their campaigning. When Epton complained that he was a victim of reverse discrimination because the media were being too soft on Washington because he was black, he injected race into the campaign. So did his supporters who distributed racist handbills, defaced black churches, and yelled racial slurs at a campaign event. In turn, Washington responded with ads that mixed images of jeering Epton supporters with images of a Ku Klux Klan rally.[105]

The Washington/Epton campaign provided a good example of how the media play on both sides of the street by reporting extensively on race while claiming to act as "racial ombudsmen" by criticizing the veiled racial appeals of the white candidate.[106] The slogan "Epton for mayor—before it's too late" did not explicitly refer to Washington's blackness, but it was criticized by the *Chicago Tribune* for its racial undertones.[107] Yet,

> hardly a story failed to refer in some way or other to the fact that Harold Washington was black and that his primary base of support came from members of his race; the phrase "the black candidate" became almost a part of his name.[108]

The media's focus on race in a campaign can have serious consequences. White sensitivity to the worry that black candidates will not represent white interests fairly makes it possible for media to hurt black candidates without carrying explicitly negative messages. Experimental research has revealed that subtle racial cues can trigger uneasiness and apprehension among whites, discouraging them from voting for black candidates.[109] Political scientists Jeremy Zilber and David Niven attribute black U.S. House representatives' inability to win Senate election to media coverage of them that has primed white voters to see black representatives as interested only in black constituents' concerns.[110] As a result, whites make assumptions about black candidates that contradict their actual issue agendas.[111]

Black Candidates' Double Bind

Black candidates are in a double bind when it comes to campaigning. If they talk about race, they suffer consequences; if they do not talk about it, they suffer other consequences. It seems that avoiding race is a better strategy for winning white votes; however, it can backfire and comes with a price.

Political science and black studies professor Sharon D. Wright speculates that African American candidates receive "increased and at times more favorable media coverage" when they enter into interracial coalitions and run deracialized campaigns.[112] A deracialized campaign is one "in which racial issues and themes are minimized, if not avoided, in order to attract increased white electoral support."[113] Political scientists Charles E. Jones and Michael L. Clemons suggest that a deracialized strategy can get the media to police "race-baiting."[114] They do this by trying to "blunt the manipulation of racially laden campaign tactics" by condemning them, thereby helping black candidates.[115]

The press can help establish the legitimacy of black candidates in their news coverage and editorial pages[116] and encourage crossover voting among whites.[117] Charles Bullock shows that endorsements in the *Atlanta Journal* and *Atlanta Constitution* had a positive impact on crossover voting for black candidates in citywide, countywide, and 5th congressional district races between 1970 and 1982.[118] The *Cleveland Plain Dealer*'s endorsements of Carl Stokes in 1967 and Michael White in 1989 "played the role of assuaging the fears of the white community and touting them as candidates for *all* the people."[119] When Doug Wilder ran a deracialized campaign for governor of Virginia in 1989, he received more newspaper endorsements than his opponent.[120] In 1991, Troy Carter was endorsed by the *New Orleans Times-Picayune* when he ran a deracialized campaign for the Louisiana state legislature.[121]

Other studies indicate that regardless of the strategies used, black candidates will receive potentially damaging coverage that emphasizes race.[122] In the 2002 senatorial race in Texas, African American Ron Kirk avoided policy messages directed at minority interests. He talked about working with both parties and all races. Yet, the press contradicted this message by focusing on his campaign stops at minority rallies and churches. This press attention became a "cue" that he was trying to mobilize minorities and that their interests were important to him. These campaign appearances also became a source of negative news attention. He was criticized for attending a hip-hop festival, where a rapper known for his antipolice lyrics performed, and accusing his opponent of being more comfortable with the possibility of striking Iraq militarily because a disproportionate number of minorities would be on the front lines.[123]

Avoiding race also can open a minority candidate up to criticism. Carol Moseley-Braun received negative coverage in the *Chicago Tribune* for there being too little racial diversity at a fund-raising event.[124] Shirley Chisholm was criticized in the *New York Times* for not having "overwhelming support among women, blacks, and youths."[125] Even if the media do actively police candidates' race baiting, they can inadvertently make race an issue just by talking about it.[126]

Deracialized campaign strategies can also diminish black voter turnout needed for the candidate to win.[127] This proved to be the case when Andrew Young ran for governor of Georgia; his efforts to appeal to white voters cost him support of black leaders and voters.[128] When politicians represent congressional districts in which the majority of voters are black, it makes sense to talk about race. It not only serves their electoral and representational goals, but it can also help them secure national news coverage.

Talking about race can have positive consequences for media coverage. House representative Maxine Waters (D-CA) received considerable coverage by becoming a policy spokesperson on racial issues. She received more national television news coverage in 1993, 1994, and 1998 than any other woman in the House of Representatives. Her visibility rose when she advocated reforms after the Los Angeles riots.[129] Her vocal criticism of *USA Today*'s misrepresentation of gang members surrendering their guns received publicity and an apology.[130] Carol Moseley-Braun got front-page coverage on major newspapers and national evening news coverage when she filibustered to stop the congressional seal from being placed alongside the Confederate flag on the United Daughters of the Confederacy's logo.[131] "She enjoyed a newfound national reputation as a spokesperson for the issues affecting African Americans."[132]

COVERAGE OF BLACK CANDIDATES AND POLITICIANS IN THE PARALLEL PRESS

Black newspapers can be important tools for mobilizing minority voters to vote for black candidates.[133] Little research has been done on how the black press covers candidates, possibly because their campaign coverage is assumed to be positive and therefore "preaching to the chorus." However, the lack of study leaves unanswered some questions about how black candidates use the parallel press and what impact it has.

First of all, it would be interesting to see how black newspapers treat races between black candidates. A case study of the Democratic primary in Mississippi's 2nd district indicated that when black candidates competed there, the local black press endorsed the most ideologically extreme one.[134] Second, the degree of enthusiasm that the black press shows for a candidate might be important in shaping his or her agenda and influencing black voter turnout. Third, black newspapers can be critical of black candidates. While Tom Bradley's deracialized campaign succeeded in getting him elected, it also got him much negative coverage in the black press. The *Los Angeles Sentinel* repeatedly referred to him as "Uncle Tom" and accused him of abandoning the black community.[135]

There are examples of the parallel press's usefulness for black candidates and politicians. The African American Media Coalition in Washington, D.C., monitors coverage of elections and successfully prevented NBC from showing a two-hour special on Mayor Marion Berry prior to his trial.[136] The D.C. black press also played an important part in Eleanor Holmes Norton's election as a delegate to the House of Representatives. The black press helped her overcome a tax evasion scandal to get reelected. "Norton, attacked by the mainstream media, began courting the black press—a press that had editorially supported her throughout the campaign and continued to do so, even after the disclosure."[137] Adam Clayton Powell, who represented New York's Harlem district in the U.S. House of Representatives, was also editor of the *People's Voice*. He saw these two roles as complementary in promoting black society.[138]

CONCLUSION

Research does not support the conclusion that the media exclude black candidates and politicians as a group. There is some evidence that their coverage portrays them as less important (giving them fewer pictures, less prominence, less coverage in "important stories"). Black candidates (like white ones) who are outside of the mainstream are not given much coverage.

It is difficult to assess the nature of the coverage because studies disagree about the tone of black candidates' coverage. Some studies point to blacks getting slightly worse coverage. Yet, Jesse Jackson's presidential campaign coverage from 1988 was more positive than negative. Still other studies find similar tones for candidates regardless of race. There is some evidence, however, that the tone is worse for black politicians than white ones, particularly on topics of morality and leadership. Although some of the evidence is anecdotal, the stereotypes of blacks as corrupt, immoral, dangerous, and different seem to be present in some of the news coverage of black candidates and politicians. This stereotyping also seems to shape story selection, pushing Farrakhan to the forefront.

The media's focus on race is clearly the most consistent finding in research on coverage of black candidates. The media focus on race when it is part of candidates' rhetoric and when it isn't. News programs sometimes amplify racial campaign discourses, and sometimes they try to police them. Regardless of the reason, it seems that attention to the race of black candidates reinforces fears among white voters that he or she will not represent them.

17

Newspaper Coverage of Native American Candidates and Politicians

~~~~~~

How are Native American candidates and politicians covered in the media? We currently have no research on the topic with which to answer this question. While we might suspect that coverage will follow the pattern observed for black candidates and politicians, this is only speculation. Therefore, this chapter describes and analyzes news coverage of some Native American candidates and politicians to provide a preliminary answer to the question.

The first analysis looks at the 1992 newspaper coverage of U.S. Senator Ben Nighthorse Campbell and his white opponent Terry Considine. The second looks at three Democrats, Native American state senator Ron Volesky and two white aspirants, who sought the party's nomination for governor of South Dakota in 2002. Finally, 2001 newspaper coverage of Native American state legislators is analyzed. Both quantitative and qualitative content analyses identify the extensiveness, favorability, and references to race in coverage of Native American politicians. Some examples of news in the parallel press *Indian Country Today* are also described.

BEN NIGHTHORSE CAMPBELL FOR SENATE (COLORADO, 1992)

Ben Nighthorse Campbell is the highest-ranking Native American government official. This was true even before he won a seat in the Senate in 1992, because prior to that election, he had represented Colorado in the House of Representatives for five years. No other Native American currently serves in the U.S. Congress. Early in the 1992 race, Campbell's victory to replace Democratic senator Tim Wirth looked like a sure thing; polls showed Campbell ahead of Republican Terry Considine by more than a thirty-point margin.[1] However, after negative campaigning and combative debates, the race became too close to call. How did Colorado's largest newspaper, the *Denver Post*, cover the candidates? How did race factor into coverage of the rich white businessman and the Native American jewelry maker?

Visibility of Campbell and Considine

A LexisNexus search revealed ninety-three *Denver Post* stories between September 1, 1992, and Election Day (November 3) that named either or both Campbell and Considine. Of these, 14 percent (13) were on the front page. Four factors were used to compare the visibility of the white candidate to that of the Native American: the number of stories that named them, how often they were quoted directly, the number of times their names appeared, and how central they were to these stories. Campbell appeared in more stories than Considine (80 versus 72). He was also quoted more frequently (in 117 sentences compared to Considine's 94). Yet, Campbell's name appeared less frequently than Considine's (425 times versus 475).

Campbell was also less central to the stories he was included in than was Considine to those that named him. Centrality was determined by coding the candidate's involvement in the story as "very high" (the story was about him), "high" (he played a major role), "medium" (he played a role of medium centrality), "low" (he played a minor role), "very low" (he was mentioned in passing), or "nonexistent" (he was not mentioned).

Including all of the stories in the analysis demonstrates that the candidates received relatively equal centrality in their stories. Campbell was either excluded or mentioned in passing in 43 percent of the stories, compared to 36 percent for Considine. Twenty-five of the stories were coded as about Considine, compared to twenty-three for Campbell.

When only stories including each candidate were considered, Considine was more central. Consider that 34 percent of the stories including Campbell made only passing mention of him; only 17 percent of Considine's stories treated him in this way. More central coverage does not mean better coverage, however; therefore, the nature of the coverage needs to be considered.

Favorability of Coverage of Campbell and Considine

Favorability measures the number of statements made about the candidates that were "friendly" and "unfriendly" and evaluates whether stories were "good news" or "bad news." Statements made by the candidates were not included in the count; however, quotes from their supporters or campaign workers were. The good news/bad news assessment considered the topic of the story and its treatment. For example, stories about a candidate's being behind in the polls, questioned about a scandal, or criticized in an editorial or advertising analysis would be considered bad news. Good news would include stories about a candidate's being ahead (unless the focus was on him being not as far ahead as he used to be), achieving legislative successes, or getting endorsements from members of the other party or by the media. Endorsements by groups closely identified with a particular issue or interest (such as abortion) would not be coded as "good" or "bad" because their value would be based on the reader's position toward the group.

Considine received much more bad news and much less good news than Campbell. Four stories were coded as "good news" for Considine, compared to twenty for Campbell. Eighteen were considered bad news for Considine, compared to nine for Campbell. Thus, Campbell got twice as many good news as bad news stories, and Considine got four and a half times more bad news than good news stories.

Ten stories concerned scandals involving Considine, including a land dispute, his partnerships' loan defaults, and his having profited from the savings and loan failures. These stories questioned Considine's business practices and were brought up by the media, not by Campbell. Similarly, the one story to question Campbell's business dealings was also media driven. The candidates criticized each other a lot, but the coverage treated these attacks (about issue positions, use of incumbency perks, and absenteeism) as "negative campaigning" rather than legitimizing them. While the newspaper noted (and sometimes criticized) the nastiness of the debates and television advertising, it did not indict one candidate or the other for the tone.

Most of the poll reporting coded as "good news" was good for Campbell because he was ahead. However, once he slipped dramatically in the polls, and the decline was attributed to his poor campaigning, the poll reporting was coded as "bad news" for him. Nonpartisan endorsements supported Campbell, including the *Denver Post*'s endorsement.

Considine faired better when direct quotes from sources were considered. He received twenty-three "friendly quotes," compared to eighteen for Campbell. They both received about the same number of "unfriendly quotes" (twenty-nine for Campbell and thirty for Considine). Considine's campaign was more successful at getting quoted directly in the stories. In fact, many of the favorable quotes for Considine appeared in bad news stories for him. They provided a way for the report to appear objective by providing a rebuttal to negative news.

Racialized Coverage of Campbell

Eleven stories included some reference to race. Two of these were not specifically about Native Americans. The first was in a bad news story that asked Considine to explain his use of the term "wetback" in a 1986 interview.[2] The second nonspecific racial reference appeared in a story that covered Campbell's speech at an African American church, which quoted him as saying, "We've seen a backsliding of civil rights. . . . There's been gender bashing, gay bashing, ethnic bashing. . . . We've got to change."[3]

Nine stories referred to Campbell's race. One article called him "a Northern Cheyenne chief."[4] In other articles, he was referred to as "part-Indian,"[5] "a Native American,"[6] "part Northern Cheyenne,"[7] "one of the nation's best-known Native Americans,"[8] and "the only American Indian in Congress."[9]

Three stories questioned the authenticity of his racial identity. One story about Considine's campaign momentum simply noted, "Even his [Campbell's] Korean War stories and the extent of his American Indian heritage have come under question."[10] The other two stories give more extensive attention to Campbell's race.[11] Both quoted a Smithsonian specialist on American Indians who claimed to have verified Campbell's heritage and statements made by members of a tribe that claimed him. In each of these stories, the quotes served to counterbalance the dominant frame that Campbell was not "Indian enough." One article implied that he did not represent Indian interests; the other accused him of exaggerating his Indianness for political reasons.

The first story, "Campbell Peaceful Style Irks Activists," discussed his estrangement from Native American activists[12] and included their claims that he was an "apple" (red outside, white inside) and "not radical enough" and that his background "may be phony." Yet, the story also allowed Campbell to disparage the activists as unrepresentative of Indian America. He called them "militants" and compared them to the Ku Klux Klan. Campbell was directly quoted in thirteen sentences, and only one direct quote by others explicitly criticized him (and the criticism was embedded in neutral comments). The story seemed to reify the dichotomy found in literature between the "good" and the "bad" Indian.

Campbell came off worse in the second story, "Campbell's Images Are Not Always Jeweled."[13] It implicitly asked, "Is he 'playing Indian' to benefit electorally?" This story began,

> Ben Nighthorse Campbell is a creator of images, in silver and semiprecious stone jewelry. He's also a crafter of his own image, as a Democratic candidate for the U.S. Senate.
>
> Some would accuse him of being an image, too: "The Outsider," a Native American, Western, romantic. Take away that evocative second name—a sort of one-word poem—and you've got a guy who sounds about as Indian as a can of tomato soup.
>
> Then you look at him: fifty-nine, with long, graying hair, a brusque speaking style and the kind of Western clothes they don't sell in Santa Fe.

The article went on to talk about the candidate's race as if it were simply an image used to distract voters from his "real" identity (that of a political insider). The authors also seem to confuse class and race by insinuating that having money (even if it was earned by designing Native American jewelry) jeopardized Campbell's "Indianness."

Campbell's goal was to be even more of an outsider than GOP nominee Terry Considine, a former state senator who led a 1990 Colorado ballot drive to limit politicians' terms.

Campbell apparently realized that being in Congress six years, voting moderately, wouldn't say "outsider" to most folks. Having been in the Colorado House for four years prior to that wouldn't say it either, even if Campbell was the only man in the House with a ponytail.

So Campbell focused on his earlier life history: a difficult childhood in the California home of an alcoholic, three-quarters-Indian father and a tubercular mother.

His aids described [his] getting into judo and taking that experience to the Olympics; serving in the Korean War; confronting—and eventually embracing—a heritage he says his father taught him to hide to avoid discrimination.

The "Horatio Nighthorse Alger" ads carried Campbell into the public imagination as atypical of the congressional stereotype. They also showed he had experienced ordinary people's hardships in a year [when] the economy has elbowed aside other issues.

Questions have been raised about how real the Campbell image is, especially when his combined congressional salary, horse-ranching and jewelry-making income gave him overall assets worth—in the broad categories of official congressional reports—between $680,000 and $1.6 million last year. Even Campbell's Indianness—the heart of his image and the Teflon coating on his years as a politician—has been called into question, by critics who suggest a three-eighths Indian background isn't enough to back up the "Nighthorse" persona.[14]

The minimal attention to Native American interests in the newspaper coverage of Campbell's campaign was inconsistent with this story's claim that Campbell was actively promoting an Indian image for electoral reasons.

The candidates did not seem to racialize the campaign. Campbell refused to wear "American Indian regalia" when he was grand marshal in the Denver Labor Day parade because "he doesn't like to wear the regalia in an election year because it might be seen as exploiting his heritage."[15] Campbell did not make an issue out of Considine's decision to march in the Columbus Day parade, which Native Americans planned to protest.[16] Ultimately, Considine spoke at a rally that took place in lieu of the parade.[17] Campbell participated in neither the parade nor the rally protesting it. When asked about the event, he said, "I support any Indian's right to peacefully protest."[18] He refused to introduce legislation that Columbus Day be abolished, despite requests from Native American interest groups that he do so.[19] He did not even add "Native American" to the long list of descriptors he provided for a background story.[20] The only story that quoted Campbell's advocacy for Native American interests was one about a possible "Little Bighorn Theme park." It noted that Campbell "complained that the old name [the Custer Battlefield National Monument] glorified the losers of the battle."[21]

Overall, Campbell got about the same amount of attention as his white competitor. He was included in more stories but played less central roles in them. Stories were generally more negative toward Considine, although he received more friendly quotes than Campbell. Most troubling about Campbell's coverage were the challenges to his racial authenticity.

RON VOLESKY FOR DEMOCRATIC NOMINEE
FOR GOVERNOR (SOUTH DAKOTA, 2002)

On June 4, 2002, James Abbott, the president of the University of South Dakota, became the Democratic Party's nominee for governor, beating, among other candidates, Native American state senator Ron Volesky. A LexisNexus search for coverage of this race in the state and local Associated Press found forty-eight stories that included the names of one or more of the three major candidates. All stories including Abbott, Volesky, or James Hutmacher (the third place Democratic candidate) that appeared between January 1 and the election were coded for visibility of, focus on, and tone of coverage toward the three candidates. Special attention was given to the use of direct quotes by or about the candidates. Stories that included any racial references were identified for qualitative analysis.

Visibility of Volesky, Abbott, and Hutmacher

The visibility of each candidate was assessed in five ways. First, the number of stories naming each candidate was counted. Second, the order in which they were named was noted. Third, the candidate's centrality to the story was assessed. Fourth, the number of times each candidate's name appeared was counted. Fifth, the number of times each candidate was quoted directly was counted.

The three candidates names appeared almost the same number of times. Volesky and Hutmacher were named in forty-seven stories, and Abbott was named in forty-eight. In the forty-seven stories that included all three candidates, the Native American candidate's name appeared before the others' 43 percent of the time (it appeared last only 28 percent of the time). Of course, inclusion in stories does not guarantee balanced attention to each candidate since one might only be named and another covered at length. Therefore, the centrality of each candidate in the stories was evaluated.

To measure centrality, each story was evaluated for whether the candidate was the primary focus of the piece, a major player in it, a medium player, a minor player, or simply mentioned in passing. Table 17.1 shows that Ron Volesky was more central to the stories that named him than the other two candidates. Of his stories, 43 percent were coded with the two most central categories ("primary focus" and "major player"), compared to 31 percent for Abbott and 32 percent for Hutmacher. He was mentioned "in passing" less frequently than the other two (19 percent compared to 29 percent and 23 percent, respectively).

Table 17.1   Centrality of Coverage by Candidate

| | Candidate | | |
Category	Volesky	Abbott	Hutmacher
Primary focus	11%	10%	9%
	(5)	(5)	(4)
Major player	32%	21%	23%
	(15)	(10)	(11)
Medium	26%	33%	30%
	(12)	(16)	(14)
Minor player	13%	6%	15%
	(6)	(3)	(7)
In passing	19%	29%	23%
	(9)	(14)	(11)

No exclusion bias against the Native American candidate was revealed by the number of times the candidate's name appeared since Volesky was named a few more times than Abbott (154 versus 150) and many more times than Hutmacher (154 versus 116). Hutmacher also lagged behind the other two candidates in terms of the number of sentences that quoted him directly in the articles (sixty-three compared to seventy-four for Volesky and seventy-six for Abbott). Overall, there is no evidence that the Native American candidate was given less visibility than the white candidates. In fact, he played a more central role in the campaign stories.

Favorability of Coverage of Volesky, Abbott, and Hutmacher

The favorability of each candidate's coverage was evaluated by the overall tone of the article toward him and by the number of "friendly" and "unfriendly" quotes about him. Most stories were neutral toward the candidates. Thirteen of the stories were positive toward one candidate, and five were negative. Abbott and Volesky were each targeted by two negative stories, and Hutmacher was the target of the remaining negative story. Positive stories were also balanced between Abbott and Volesky (with each receiving five positive stories). Hutmacher was complemented in three stories.

Volesky's negative stories appeared early in the campaign. One concerned his not filing his financial reports on time.[22] The other included criticism from House Democratic leader Mel Olson, who endorsed Hutmacher, saying "I'm not here to speak poorly of Ron Volesky. But some of the bills he supported over the years make him less electable."[23] The only negative reference toward Hutmacher concerned his taking "potshots" at the governor.[24] Of the two stories coded negative for Abbott, one accused him of having too many Republican ties;[25] the other suggested that his presence on the Board of University Physicians might be a conflict of interests.[26] Even bad news stories provided information to help balance the accusations. None were aggressively critical or biased.

Positive stories included one in which thirteen legislators endorsed Hut-macher[27] and another in which five legislators endorsed Volesky.[28] All three candidates were complemented in another story for running a cleaner race than the Republicans.[29] Two stories praised policies proposed by Abbott and Volesky.[30] The sole poll story was coded as favorable news for Abbott since he was ahead.[31] Each candidate received a complementary profile. Abbott's focused on his popularity, energy, and straightforward answers.[32] Hutmach-er's showed him as a down-to-earth, tough, hard-working South Dakotan.[33] Volesky's portrait described him as a passionate speaker, friendly volunteer, and dedicated family man.[34]

Favorability can also be measured by evaluating what is said about a candidate or his plans in direct quotations used in the story. Forty-nine direct quotation sentences made either positive or negative claims regarding the three candidates. Abbott was the target of twenty of these statements, 75 percent (15) of which were negative (almost half appearing in the story about his Republican ties). Volesky and his proposals were evaluated in eighteen quotes, of which 56 percent (10) were positive. Six of these appeared in the portrait article, and the rest were about his proposals (i.e., a state income tax to better fund education). Hutmacher was evaluated in eleven statements, 64 percent (7) of which were positive (three of these appearing in his endorsement article). The comparison of friends' versus foes' statements does not reveal a racial bias in either direction. Instead, Abbott received the most negative commentary, perhaps because he was the front-runner.[35]

Racialized Coverage of Volesky

Only 13 percent (6) of the articles made any reference to Native Americans. Three of these talked about Volesky's being a Native American. In one he was called "an Indian born on the Standing Rock Reservation."[36] In another he was "the sole Native American candidate for the governor's seat" who was "originally from the Standing Rock Sioux reservation."[37] That article noted that he had raised campaign funds by auctioning a painting by Dale Iron Cloud (for $400). The profile of him on the campaign trail identified him as "a member of the Sanding Rock Sioux Tribe" and described his sharing stories about Sitting Bull with his daughter's kindergarten class and getting a campaign contribution from Kevin Costner, who "has long been interested in South Dakota and Indian issues."[38]

Four articles referred to Native American issues. Three articles dealt with Volesky's plan for the state to work with tribes to develop a meatpacking plant.[39] The fourth article concerned a debate during which the candidates were said to have agreed that "the racial division between whites and American Indians in South Dakota must be bridged."[40] Volesky was quoted as saying that this would not be easy but could be accomplished if people committed themselves to it. The article also stated, "Volesky said that state's tribes can be an important economic force. But he said something must be done about rampant alcoholism, domestic abuse and poverty on Indian reservations." Abbott, the only other Democratic candidate referred to on this issue, indicated that "state government should look at tribes as sovereign governments."

Overall, race seems not to have played a role in the extent and favorability of these candidates' campaign coverage. Volesky got equal coverage and slightly more centrality in his stories. The media did not racialize the campaign as few stories mentioned race, and most of those that did reflected statements made by the Native American candidate. The question of whether Volesky's race would influence the election outcome was never voiced, nor was his authenticity challenged.

NEWSPAPER COVERAGE OF NATIVE AMERICAN STATE LEGISLATORS (2001)

In 2001, there were thirty-five American Indian and Alaska Native state legislators,[41] ten in the state senate. They served in Alaska, Arizona, Arkansas, Colorado, Montana, New Mexico, Nevada, North Carolina, North Dakota, Oklahoma, and South Dakota. Their tenure in office ranged from one to thirty-seven years.

A LexisNexis search of state and local newspaper and wire services for these states was conducted to see how much visibility the Native American state legislators received. The number of stories naming politicians, their centrality in stories, purpose they served in them, and whether they were quoted directly were used to assess visibility.

Visibility of Native American State Legislators

The story count revealed that eleven legislators received no coverage (see table 17.2). One or more of the other twenty-four were mentioned in 183 newspaper articles.[42] The number of stories per person ranged from one to forty-three. Only five received mention in more than nine stories in 2001.[43] The legislators who received the most coverage were from South Dakota (Ron Volesky, 43), North Carolina (Ronnie Sutton, 16), and New Mexico (Leo Tsosie, 15). Although the greatest number of stories that included Native American legislators appeared in South Dakota (47), Alaska (41), and New Mexico (23), the stories in Alaska were dispersed among more politicians (7).

The centrality of the member in a story that included him or her was evaluated as "high," "medium," or "low." In 62 percent of these stories, legislators played a medium role, meaning they were not the focus of the story (as they were in 9 percent of stories); nor were they simply mentioned in passing (as in 29 percent of the stories).

The centrality of the coverage was related to three variables: party, cham-

Table 17.2   Newspaper Stories of American Indian and Alaska Native State Legislators, 2001

Name (Party, State)	Tribe	First Year	Number of Stories
Ron Volesky (D, S. Dakota)*	Standing Rock Sioux	2001	43
Ronnie Sutton (D, N. Carolina)	Lumbee	1991	16
Leo Tsosie (D, N. Mexico)*	Navajo	1993	15
Carol Juneau (D, Montana)	Mandan Hidatsa	1999	12
Suzanne Williams (D, Colorado)	Comanche	1996	11
Bill Williams (R, Alaska)	Tlingit	1993	9
Albert Kookesh (D, Alaska)	Tlingit	1996	8
John Oceguera (D, Nevada)	Walker River Paiute	2001	8
Dennis Bercier (D, N. Dakota)*	Ojibwa	1999	7
Lyman Hoffman (D, Alaska)*	Yup'ik	1994	7
Jack Jackson (D, Arizona)*	Navajo	1999	7
Mary Kapsner (D, Alaska)	Yup'ik	1999	5
Paul Valandra (D, S. Dakota)	Rosebud Sioux	2001	4
Jo Ellen Carson (D, Arkansas)	Apache	1999	4
William Eggers (D, Montana)	Crow	1999	4
Beverly Masek (R, Alaska)	Athabascan	1994	4
Carl Moses (D, Alaska)	Qawalangin Tribe of Unalaska	1965	4
Leo Watchman (D, N. Mexico)	Navajo	1993	4
Reggie Joule (D, Alaska)	Inupiat Eskimo	1996	3
John Pinto (D, N. Mexico)*	Navajo	1977	3
Joey Jayne (D, Montana)	Navajo	2001	2
Sylvia Laughter (D, Arizona)	Navajo	1999	1
James Madalena (D, N. Mexico)	Jemez Pueblo	1985	1
Carl Morgan (R, Alaska)	Yup'ik	1999	1
Ray Bagay (D, N. Mexico)	Navajo	1999	0
Norma Bixby (D, Montana)	North Cheyenne	2001	0
Richard Foster (D, Alaska)	Tukawa	1989	0
Richard Hagen (D, S. Dakota)	Ogalala Sioux	1982	0
Kelley Haney (D, Oklahoma)	Seminole Creek	1987	0
Georgiana Lincoln (D, Alaska)*	Athabascan	1992	0
Debora Norris (D, Arizona)	Tohono O'odham	1997	0
Donald Olson (D, Alaska)*	Fish River Chinik	2001	0
Gerald Pease (D, Montana)*	Crow	2001	0
Frank Smith (D, Montana)	Assiniboine	1999	0
Albert Tom (D, Arizona)	Navajo	2001	0

* State senate

ber, and tenure. Republicans were given less central coverage: 64 percent of stories that included Republicans mentioned them in passing, compared to 26 percent for Democrats. Members of the lower chamber received less central coverage than senators (see table 17.3). Freshmen were given more central coverage than members who had served longer (see table 17.4).

Direct quotes from the Native American legislators were included in 62 percent (114) of the stories. Once again, Republicans received less attention than Democrats. Republicans were only quoted in 36 percent of their stories, whereas Democrats were quoted in 65 percent of theirs. Chamber also had an impact on the presence of quotes. State senators were quoted more often in

Table 17.3   Relationship between Chamber and Legislator's Centrality in Story

Centrality	Chamber		Total
	House	Senate	
Low	42%	15%	29%
	(40)	(13)	(53)
Medium	53%	71%	62%
	(51)	(62)	(113)
High	5%	14%	9%
	(5)	(12)	(17)

their stories (72 percent) than house members were in theirs (54 percent). Tenure made no notable difference.

Favorability of Coverage of Native American State Legislator

The favorability of the coverage was assessed in three ways. First, the story was coded as "neutral," "positive," or "negative" toward the legislator. Second, negative and positive content in neutral stories was analyzed. Third, the legislator's role in the story was considered.

The data showed that the tone of the coverage was balanced, with 90 percent "neutral," 5 percent "negative," and 5 percent "positive." Positive stories were typically found on the editorial page and included letters to the editor, such as one thanking Carl Moses for sponsoring a bill to reinstate the state income tax[44] and another supporting Mark Kapsner's bill to require students to study Alaska's history.[45] Positive stories also included editorials such as one praising Jo Ellen Carson for opposing a bill that would ban homosexuals from adopting children[46] and another calling Leonard Tsosie's appointment as cochair of the redistricting committee "a hopeful sign."[47] One columnist wrote, in reference to John Oceguera, "courage was shared by four lonely Assembly members who voted against" a measure to graduate students who failed their proficiency exams.[48]

Some positive news appeared in news stories about events lauding members, such as a speech in which Gov. Judy Martz praised Carol Juneau for

Table 17.4   Relationship between Tenure and Legislator's Centrality in Story

Centrality	Tenure		Total
	Freshmen	Other	
Low	18%	34%	28%
	(10)	(42)	(52)
Medium	68%	59%	62%
	(39)	(74)	(113)
High	14%	7%	9%
	(8)	(9)	(17)

sponsoring an education bill.[49] Two stories concerned a ceremony honoring John Pinto and other Navajo code talkers—marines during World War II who created a code from Navajo that the Japanese were unable to crack.[50] Occasionally, good news appeared in news stories that attributed success to programs promoted by members. For example, a bill by Carol Juneau to educate teachers about Indian cultures was referred to as "good progress."[51]

Negative stories were also most often found on the editorial page. One editorial said, "we're frankly perplexed" by an element of Suzanne Williams's bill on character education.[52] Another mocked Ronnie Sutton for his disparaging remarks about a bill to provide Spanish ballots.[53] Negative stories included those portraying the legislators as confused, "too political," enjoying personal gain from their positions, or breaking protocol or laws. For example, John Oceguera was labeled as one of four legislators who "head the list of lawmakers wined and dined by lobbyists."[54] Some negative stories covered government officials disparaging each other: Ronnie Sutton was called "extraordinarily hostile to open government";[55] the State Fair Commission said they wished Ron Volesky "would have come to us first" about a bill he introduced; another member accused Leonard Tsosie of being rude.[56] Others stories were judged as negative because of what the legislators said or did. Bill Williams' admission, "We're trying to deal with that issue. . . . I don't know how,"[57] and news that Jack Jackson switched his vote and "was caught unaware" cast both in a negative light.[58] Probably the worst news about a legislator was Leo Watchman's sentencing for battery.[59]

Some stories not coded as "bad news" still contained negative comments; however, these were offset by positive comments or delegitimized by the reporter's framing. For example, one story evaluating new members gave John Oceguera the lowest marks of the three freshmen (a B–) and criticized him for being "too eager to please";[60] however, it also called him "clever" and quoted a leader as saying that "the talent in the three of them is extraordinary." Another article identified Mary Kapsner as "the best-paid member last year, claiming more optional pay for work during the interim." Her explanation that she served a district that lacked a strong municipal government, together with evidence of this statement's truth, offset any possible implications of impropriety.[61] An article concerning Leonard Tsosie's appointment as cochairman of the Redistricting Committee provided another good example of negative information appearing in a story coded as "neutral."[62] One member accused the senate president pro tem of paying Tsosie off for his earlier support with this appointment, and another member called Tsosie "kind of a bird brain." However, positive comments about Tsosie in the story, the appointment itself, and his own quotes offset these accusations.

In 80 percent of the stories, legislators took a position on an issue or problem. In 4 percent of the stories, the legislator spoke about legislature processes from a position of leadership (about issue scheduling or the chances of something's getting done). Republicans were more likely to fill this role than

Democrats due to Bill Williams' news coverage as cochair of the Finance Committee. Native American legislators were included in 5 percent of the stories for nonpolitical reasons (i.e., being on a corporate board). In 9 percent, legislators were identified for factors relevant to their political role that did not deal directly with policy issues (i.e., redistricting; receiving x amount of money in per diems). Furthermore, 2 percent of the stories discussed members' political disputes (running for office; angering the party). Stories about issues and leadership are inherently more favorable than those about politics.

Racialized Coverage of Native American State Legislators

The presence of race in the stories was measured by looking at four things. First, any reference to Indians was included, its focus analyzed, and the subject of the story considered. Second, stories were examined to see if they indicated that the legislator represented Indian interests. Third, stories that identified members as Indians were counted. Fourth, the use of stereotypes from popular culture to characterize Native legislators was qualitatively assessed.

Some reference to Indians appeared in 30 percent (54) of the stories. These were primarily references to Indian issues, the implications of policies for Native American constituents, redistricting/voting, ceremonies/events, and identification of the legislator's race.[63] In addition, 20 percent (36) of these stories dealt with policies under discussion in the legislature. In all of these stories, Native American legislators advocated the positions that reflected Indian interests. It would be hard to argue that the media racialized the coverage of these members when the legislators actively advanced these positions by sponsoring bills and speaking about them.

Of these issues, 14 percent (25) dealt explicitly with Indians. These included issues of racial discrimination (including profiling and hate crimes), establishing tribal delegates to the legislature and representation on state boards, renaming places that include the word "squaw," gaming compacts, Indian education issues (including building schools and bilingual education), support for medicine men, financing Native fishing/hunting programs, supporting an Indian cultural center, and allowing the use of tribal identification cards in place of birth certificates. The other six percent (11) of these stories dealt with more general issues like the budget, abortion, environment, subsidies, taxes, and child custody. The legislators who discussed the implications of these policies for their constituents or advocated the issue agenda made the connection between these general issues and Native Americans.

Representing Indian Interests

In 21 percent (38) of the stories, the legislators were shown representing Indian interests.[64] Most of the coverage of Joey Jayne, Reggie Joule, Paul Valandra, and Carol Juneau presented them as representing Native American interests. None of these stories was about Republican members. Eleven of the legislators were never identified with Indian interests in their news coverage.

Representation of Indian interests was related to seniority. Members who had served six or fewer years were identified as representing minority interests in 26 percent of the stories, compared to 13 percent for those who had served longer. Half of the time, legislators quoted in a story were speaking on behalf of a particular group of people. Of fifty-eight such quotes, twenty-nine had specifically to do with racial minorities.

One story referred to one of these legislators as promoting Indian interests but did not include a quote from him or other clear indications that he was publicly taking the position. This article concerned a change in leadership in the New Mexico senate. Speculation as to why Leonard Tsosie supported a change in leadership included a reference to Native Americans that he had not voiced to the reporter: "Tsosie declines to say why he broke ranks with the former Senate leader (Manny Arragon). Arragon has said Tsosie was concerned about the way Indian needs were being addressed."[65]

Identifying Legislators as Indians

Of the stories that referred to race, 12 percent (21) identified members as Native Americans. These references appeared most commonly in stories in which the legislators played a central role. Only 6 percent of the stories in which members were mentioned in passing included their race, compared to 10 percent for stories with moderate centrality and 35 percent for those with high centrality. The race of thirteen members was never identified in the sixty-seven stories they appeared in.

Some racial references appeared in articles that noted the novelty of Indians in government. These included comments like, "one of the few legislators in state history to have an American Indian heritage,"[66] "the first time we've had a Native American chair a key committee,"[67] and "one of six Indian legislators—a record number in Montana—representing five of the state's seven reservations."[68] The members themselves made other references to race. For example: "Rep. Joey Jayne, D-Arlee, said that as an attorney she had concerns about the measure, but as a Navajo woman she supported it."[69]

In other stories, a legislator's remarks were clarified by referring to his or her race. For example, when Rep. Carol Juneau opposed language in a resolution that said that the Missouri Breaks were "first traversed by the Corps of Discovery in 1804" because "I think they forgot who the first people of Montana were," the reporter added that Juneau was a member of the Mandan-Hidatsu tribe.[70] Other racial identifications were essential to understanding stories, like the two articles about Sen. John Pinto's being honored as a Navajo code talker[71] and another about Navajo senators welcoming former Navajo chairman Peter MacDonald home from prison.[72]

Using Racial Stereotypes

Racial stereotypes were neither common nor explicit; yet, a few of the stories reinforced stereotypes drawn from popular culture. It seemed as though three stereotypes were evoked subtly: the wooden Indian,[73] the sidekick/Tonto,[74] and the drunk.[75]

Although no article included any direct reference or picture to identify Carl Moses's ethnicity, and although the reporter may have been stating a fact, a reference to Moses's reticence evoked the "silent Indian" stereotype:

> As he tried vainly to increase the Department of Public Safety's budget for Alaska State Troopers, Veteran Representative Carl Moses, who rarely speaks in committee except to say "yes" or "no," argued fiercely for more law enforcement in rural areas.[76]

Another story evoked a sidekick, or "Tonto," stereotype when John Oceguera was characterized as "too eager to please his own colleague."[77]

References to alcohol were also present in some stories. Seven stories dealt with policy issues involving alcohol (DWI or alcohol taxes). In most of these, Native American legislators were quoted as advocating leniency toward DWI offenders. Jack Jackson was noted as being the only dissenting vote against lowering the legal intoxication limit.[78] Paul Valandra's opposition to a law forcing chronic drunk drivers to serve more jail time was noted in another story.[79] Leo Tsosie was one of only two senators to vote against a bill that charged drunk drivers with the cost of installing ignition interlock devices in their cars.[80] However, two stories did discuss Ron Volesky's bill making it easier for the state to prosecute drunk drivers for vehicular homicide.[81] None of these articles made reference to the legislators' race or explicitly connected alcoholism to Indians.

Two stories referred to alcohol abuse by these politicians. One story covered Leo Watchman's sentencing for battery and included a reference to his drinking. The other appeared in an article covering Rod Volesky's announcement that he would run for governor:[82] "Volesky was dogged by personal problems as the 1986 session ended, including missing roll call votes after a night of drinking." The article also referred to his treatment for a chemical imbalance and juvenile delinquency. References to how he turned his life around balanced these negative references. The article also noted, "Volesky brought up his past during his candidate announcement." It is interesting to note that this information was not repeated during the months of campaigning studied in the case study above.

Parallel Press Coverage of Native American State Legislators

Five articles mentioning two Native American legislators appeared in *Indian Country Today* in 2001. These were looked at separately to see how the parallel press's coverage differed from the mainstream's.

Stories in *Indian Country Today* were longer than mainstream stories, and legislator were more central to them. Legislators were coded as "highly central" in two stories, "medium" in two, and "low" in one. The biggest difference was the presence of race in the stories. Each story made it clear that the legislator was a Native American, often providing additional personal information about him. For example, in a story about the lack of nursing homes on or near reservations, readers learned that Sen. Paul Valandra's mother was in the White River Nursing Home owned by the Rosebud Sioux tribe "because she wanted to be close to American Indian people."[83] Another story about Volesky's gubernatorial bid shared information about his heritage (American Indian and German) and his education.[84]

Three stories including news about Volesky's campaign provided more extensive coverage of his issue positions than any of the mainstream newspaper articles.[85] They included his agenda on health care, long-term elderly care, economic development, racial profiling, and tribe-state relations. An article covering his keynote speech at the Tetuwan Oceti Sakowin Treaty Council Conference noted that he "vowed to create a panel that would study the impact of state laws on tribal communities."[86] Another story discussed at length his position on the State-Tribal Relations Committee and his plans to improve state-tribe relations; these were not even mentioned in the mainstream press.[87] The question of whether Volesky's race would prevent voters from supporting him was broached in *Indian Country Today*, but not in the mainstream newspapers. In an extensive article about gaming contracts that prohibit tribes from contributing money to political campaigns, Volesky voiced his commitment to tribal sovereignty and political clout for Native Americans: "I'm the first one who believes in campaign finance reform, but I guess I'm a little irked as to why it should start with Indian tribes."[88]

CONCLUSION

These case studies provide no evidence that newspaper coverage excludes Native American politicians. Nor do they indicate that Native Americans receive worse coverage than their white opponents. It is less clear what role race plays in their coverage. There are certainly references to race, but the candidates and politicians invite many of these as they seek to establish their images and represent their communities. Still, some of the racial content seems to draw on stereotypes.

The role that race played in these case studies varied. The Colorado senatorial race included troubling accusations that challenged Campbell's Native American authenticity. Yet, the South Dakota governor's Democratic primary campaign largely ignored race. More of the news coverage of Native American state legislators contained racial references, but most of these seemed to reflect the politicians' agendas. There is no evidence that reporters pushed them into this advocacy or that media framing was the reason for the coverage. In fact, it seems more likely (based on parallel press coverage) that rather than overemphasize racial issues, mainstream newspapers failed to cover much of these politicians' Native American issue advocacy. Although a few stories included subtle Indian stereotypes, it is interesting that Volesky's drinking problems (noted briefly in the 2001 data set's articles) did not find its way into any of his 2002 campaign coverage. If that's the good news, then the bad news is that neither did his extensive racial-issue agenda.

18

Coverage of Hispanic Candidates and Politicians

~~~~~~

MOST OF THE RESEARCH ON HISPANICS, ELECTIONS, AND THE MEDIA FOCUSES on how white candidates market themselves to Hispanic voters rather than on coverage of Hispanic candidates. It also illustrates how there has been an increased use of ethnic news media for promoting white candidates through advertising and news releases. In presidential campaigns, Republicans took the lead in reaching out to Hispanic voters in 1984 and 1988 by using Spanish-language media.[1] The Democratic National Committee developed its first "Latino Communication Strategy" in 1994.[2] This research is beyond the scope of this book, which focuses on Hispanic candidates and voters rather than appeals to Hispanic voters.

This chapter begins reviewing the limited research on Hispanic candidates and the media, then looks at how local newspapers covered a few Mexican American, Puerto Rican, and Cuban American candidates for the U.S. House of Representatives. As in the previous chapters, these articles were analyzed for visibility, favorability, and racial content. Given the extensive and growing number of Hispanic politicians and candidates across America, it is imperative that more studies investigate the patterns of their coverage and the factors that influence differences in coverage. While the following analysis will not take into account the use of Spanish-language media, it is important to remember that the parallel press participates in electoral media environments in districts with sizable Hispanic populations.

RESEARCH ON HISPANIC CANDIDATE COVERAGE

Although no systematic studies have been done of how Hispanic candidates and politicians are covered in the news, some case studies of campaigns provide insights into the process. They reiterate some of what we learned about the coverage of black candidates and politicians.

First of all, third-party candidates are largely ignored because of a bias toward the conventional major parties. When Hispanics created the La Raza Unida party in the 1970s, it had some success at winning local elections in Crystal City, Texas, in spite of the media giving their candidates little coverage and treating their victories like flukes.[3]

Second, at the local level, newspapers can act as advocates for or obstacles to particular candidates, based on the ideology of the publishers or their friendships. In the 1957 mayoral campaign in El Paso, Texas, the *Herald-Post* openly advocated Raymond L. Telles, whereas the *El Paso Times* harshly criticized the Mexican American candidate.[4] When Mexican American George Cordova ran against Republican Rick Renzi for Arizona's 1st house seat in 2002, the typically conservative *Arizona Republic* endorsed the Democratic candidate. However, the paper probably did him more harm then good because it also published accusations of business failures and failure to pay taxes. This information came out of opposition research done by the Republican's campaign and was leaked to a reporter. "The charges against Cordova had essentially been 'laundered' by getting them into print in the states' largest newspaper and they took on a mantle of legitimacy."[5]

Third, the wisdom of emphasizing ethnicity in campaign themes depends upon the context of the race and the individual candidates. Federico Peña's mayoral victory in Denver, Colorado, in 1983 was attributed to his ability to attract news coverage and legitimacy by running a deracialized campaign.[6] Although Hispanic candidates might make the choice to run broad-based campaigns and avoid racial issues in order to get white votes, their names or appearance can undercut this approach by presenting racial cues.[7]

Fourth, ethnic newspapers can assist minorities in securing their bases. In Miami, Spanish-language newscasts have more viewers than those in English. Radio stations provide political forums for the Cuban American community. The disdain many Cuban Americans feel for the *Miami Herald* enhances the political influence of these outlets.[8]

Winning without Media Attention: Loretta Sanchez in California's 46th District (1996)

Loretta Sanchez's victory in 1996 illustrates how effectively grassroots campaigning can mitigate the lack of media attention given to a long shot. Sanchez chose to use her Hispanic maiden name in her bid for California's 46th house seat in 1996. In 1994, she had come in eighth in the Anaheim City Council race using her married name (Brixey). The nature of the district, her issue agenda, and the context of the time explain why this was a wise choice.

The district had changed from Anglo and Republican in 1980 to ethnically mixed and Democratic by 2000. In 1996, 40 percent of the district's population had been born outside of the United States. It had a growing Latino and Asian American population. Sanchez ran a campaign focused on knowing the neighborhoods and meeting the people in them. Her campaign worked hard to register voters and convince them to vote. In addition, the 2000 election came "at a moment of ethnic instability" in California, when the anti-immigration Proposition 187 had politicized Latinos.

Without the help or endorsements of party insiders, Sanchez won an upset victory in the Democratic primary. She had virtually no press coverage. After her primary victory, she continued to focus on face-to-face campaigning rather than running an aggressive television advertising campaign or releasing poll results to the media. Because she had flown under the radar, Sanchez's opponent, incumbent Robert Dornan, failed to raise the necessary money to campaign hard against her once it became clear that he needed to. Eventually, Sanchez ran cable advertisements that helped her raise enough money to buy some late-cycle commercial television ads and drew some news coverage. Using this campaign strategy, the nontraditional candidate beat the Republican incumbent by fewer than a thousand votes.

> Sanchez' deep personal involvement in the campaign was a source of constant inspiration for unpaid volunteers, and in news coverage—what little there was of it—earnest electioneering helped to differentiate Sanchez from a distant, doom-saying opponent fond of knife-edged rhetoric.[9]

HISPANIC CANDIDATES AND THEIR COMPETITORS IN THE SAN ANTONIO EXPRESS-NEWS

Henry Bonilla became the first Hispanic Republican elected to the House of Representatives from Texas in 1992. Prior to his campaign, he was an executive news producer for KENS-TV. He represents the 23rd district; the largest in Texas, it is bigger than the state of Massachusetts and includes twenty-three counties and eight hundred miles of the Texas-Mexico border. The district was originally drawn for a Democrat, and 56 percent of its voting population is Hispanic. While Mexican Americans are more likely to vote for Democrats, they are also drawn to Hispanic candidates. This makes Bonilla an interesting case for examination.

In 1996, Democrat Charlie Jones, a San Antonio lawyer and Vietnam War veteran, challenged Bonilla. With the help of labor organizations, Jones ran an aggressive grassroots campaign. The Democrats were hopeful that President Bill Clinton's popularity and large turnout might help Jones win. However, the advantages of incumbency (money, experience serving constituents, and name recognition) gave Bonilla a clear advantage. In the end, he won easily. Did he also win the battle for superior newspaper coverage?

A LexisNexus search identified the thirty-seven articles that appeared in the *San Antonio Express-News* during the general election campaign of 1996 and included either of the candidates' names. Twelve of these were editorials. Each article was examined to evaluate the extent and tone of each candidate's coverage. The extent of coverage was determined by looking at who was mentioned in the articles, whose name came first, the number of times the candidates were mentioned, and how many of their direct quotes appeared. Each candidate's centrality to the story was also considered. The tone of the coverage was measured by counting the number of favorable and unfavorable direct quotes about each candidate, and whether each article was good or bad news for the candidate was determined. For example, an endorsement would be good news. News about a campaign blunder or scandal would be bad news. Stories that included any racial references were identified for a qualitative analysis of how race played a part in the news coverage.

Visibility of Coverage for Bonilla and Jones

The Hispanic Republican incumbent received more extensive coverage than his challenger. Bonilla was named in all of the articles, while Jones was only named in 35 percent. Of the thirteen articles in which both candidates appeared, Jones was named first in 77 percent (10) of the stories. In all of the articles combined, Jones's name appeared 51 times and Bonilla's appeared 107 times. In the articles that named Jones, his name appeared more frequently (3.9 times) than Bonilla's did in articles naming him (2.9 times). However, the large number of articles that did not include Jones's name at all indicates that he was less visible in news coverage of the campaign.

Jones was more central in the articles in which he appeared than Bonilla was in the articles that named him (see table 18.1). Jones and Bonilla were both quoted directly in four stories; however, ten of Jones's statements appeared in these four articles whereas only four of Bonilla's did. Despite this exception, it seems the Hispanic candidate enjoyed the incumbency advantage in terms of visibility.

Favorability of Coverage of Bonilla and Jones

While Bonilla got more attention, it contained more bad news than good; 35 percent (13) of the stories were coded as "bad news" for Bonilla. Only one story (3 percent) was coded as "bad news" for Jones, when the designation was based on negative things said about the candidate. Of these articles, 19 percent (7) were coded as "good news" for Bonilla, and 8 percent (3) were coded as "good news" for Jones.

The *San Antonio Express-News* endorsed Bonilla and repeated this position in five articles. Only one of these articles included the rationale for endorsing local house incumbents: "Their opponents, who did appear for interviews, did not convince us that voters in these districts should turn out

Table 18.1 Centrality of Bonilla and Jones in Stories

Centrality	Candidate	
	Bonilla	Jones
Primary focus	5%	3%
	(2)	(1)
Major player	22%	14%
	(13)	(10)
Medium	8%	8%
	(3)	(9)
Minor player	27%	11%
	(10)	(4)
In passing	38%	—
	(14)	(0)
Not mentioned	—	65%
	(0)	(24)
Mean for all stories (range 0–6, lower is more prominent)	3.7	4.9
Mean for stories including candidate	3.7	2.8

the incumbents."[10] Overall, however, the incumbent had more directional (positive or negative) coverage than the challenger, and it leaned toward the negative. The little directional coverage for Jones was more positive than negative.

In terms of "friendly" quotes in the stories, the candidates faired about the same. Four direct quotes (appearing in four articles) said positive things about Bonilla, and five (appearing in two articles) said positive things about Jones. However, Bonilla was the target of many more "unfriendly" quotes than Jones. Sixteen negative direct quotes about Bonilla appeared in five articles, compared to four about Jones in two articles. Slightly more positive than negative statements were made about Jones (5:4), compared to four times more negative than positive statements made about Bonilla (4:16). A look at this negative coverage reveals how race played a part of the campaign coverage.

Racialized Coverage of Bonilla

Some of the bad news for Bonilla questioned his support for House Speaker Newt Gingrich and accused him of not answering questions about his issue positions.[11] However, the bulk of the bad news and unfriendly quotes appeared in eight stories that referred to a comment made by Democratic U.S. Senate candidate Victor Morales that Bonilla was a "coconut" (meaning brown on the outside, white on the inside). The quotation appeared first in a September 26 article coded as "bad news" for Bonilla.[12] The article included four unfriendly quotes about Bonilla (all by Morales) and one friendly quote from the spokesman of Morales's opponent. The spokesman said, "Congressman Bonilla can certainly speak well and articulately and needs no defense from me against the likes of Victor Morales." According to the article, Morales said what he did about Bonilla because Bonilla had "forgotten his Hispanic heritage" and was distancing himself from his "heritage and community." Specifically, the article read,

> "Where I grew up, we called them coconuts—white on the inside, brown on the outside," Morales said. "To me, there are certain people within the Hispanic community, who for their own reasons, seem to forget who they are . . . and that's the way he [Bonilla] strikes me," Morales said later. Bonilla declined to respond to Morales' remarks.

Seven subsequent articles referred to the "coconut" comment. Some of them were primarily about the Morales campaign and merely referred to the comment and his subsequent apology for the terminology he used. Three of these articles also mentioned that Morales had called Bonilla a "wannabe white."[13] Another article referred to a joke about the statement made in a political satire.[14]

Two articles corroborated the idea that Bonilla did not represent the Hispanic community. One of these was an editorial critical of the language used and the political strategy behind the statement but supportive of the sentiment it conveyed.

> Morales certainly is within his right to criticize Bonilla's voting record, which, some have argued, has not always appeared to reflect the best interests of his predominantly Hispanic constituency.[15]

The second article quoted the state director of the League of United Latin American Citizens as agreeing that Bonilla did not represent the Hispanic community well.

> He's voted for the best interest of the [Republican] party, and so I guess that's why even though he's Hispanic, we're a little upset," Garcia said. "It was probably that anger that [prompted] Victor to blurt out this comment.[16]

Race was referenced in 43 percent (16) of the stories. In addition to the eight stories about Morales' comment, eight others mentioned Hispanics or Hispanic issues. One identified Bonilla as Mexican American, four talked about Hispanic voters, and three mentioned immigration issues.[17] Three of the articles that included references to Hispanic voters focused on campaign strategies and the rhetoric of Bonilla, Senator Gramm, and the Democratic Party. One discussed Bonilla's ability to get Hispanic votes: "A majority of Hispanics vote Democrat, but Bonilla has disrupted that tradition and cut a deep gash in the conventional wisdom." The article also quoted Bonilla's campaign manager as saying that "Bonilla will get his fair share of additional Hispanic voters attracted to the polls by Morales."[18]

Coverage of Another Hispanic Candidate in San Antonio

The focus on race in the Bonilla/Jones campaign and the debate it provoked over what it means to be a Hispanic candidate was not present in the *San Antonio Express-News*'s coverage of another congressional race. Two years after the Bonilla victory, Democrat Charles Gonzalez was elected by a large margin to replace his father, Henry B. Gonzalez, in Texas's 20th district, which also represents part of San Antonio. Of the thirty-two articles covering the general election, only two referred to Hispanics.

In one of these articles, a single sentence noted that the Republican candidate, James Walker, would have (among other things) to "overcome the Hispanic vote" to win the race.[19] Another article provided a sympathetic profile of Walker, noting that, "unlike his opponent, Charles Gonzales, whose father is an icon in the 20th congressional district, Walker lacks a built-in constituency." It also included a friendly quote that called Walker *buena gente* (good people) and provided one of Walker's arguments for why Hispanics should vote for him:

> His [religious] background will be an asset in the largely Hispanic, working-class district. He said he hopes his antiabortion stance will win him votes among the predominately Catholic constituent base. This week, he launches an ad on Spanish-language television noting his opponent's abortion-rights beliefs.[20]

Overall, Gonzales received more coverage (he was included in all thirty-two articles, compared to Walker's inclusion in only eighteen), was named more often (ninety-four to eighty-three times with twenty-three of Walker's mentions occurring in one profile), and was directly quoted more frequently (thirty-one to twenty-six times). His race was not a primary focus of the articles or quotations made about him.

Perhaps the differences can be explained by the idea that when Mexican American candidates fulfill certain racial expectations, their ethnicity is not an issue. Since Gonzales was a Democrat and supported progressive racial issues and Bonilla was a Republican who did not, Bonilla's ethnicity became an issue, and Gonzales's did not. Another viable interpretation is that the newspaper simply followed the lead of political actors. Once another Hispanic candidate made Bonilla's race an issue, the press amplified it. Perhaps Gonzales's race was not an issue because he was following in the footsteps of another Hispanic, his father, who had represented the district for years.

NEWSPAPER COVERAGE OF NYDIA VELAZQUEZ FOR DEMOCRATIC NOMINATION FOR NEW YORK'S 12th DISTRICT (1992)

Nydia Velazquez became the first Puerto Rican woman to serve as a U.S. House representative in 1992. She beat Stephen Solarz, a white incumbent who had spent eighteen years in Congress. The race was for part of Solarz's old Brooklyn district after redistricting split it into six pieces. Solarz spent more than $1 million in two months of campaigning, about ten times as much as his five opponents spent. In the end, Velazquez won the primary with 33 percent of the vote.[21] She went on to win the general election easily in this Democratic district.

The candidates competed in New York's 12th district, which included parts of Manhattan, Brooklyn, and Queens. Solarz chose to run in the new 12th instead of other districts because polls indicated that he had a better chance of winning. Solarz was vulnerable because he had overdrawn 743 checks in the House banking scandal. The district had been drawn to promote Latino representation. Now 54 percent of its residents were Hispanic,[22] but only 49 percent of the registered Democrats were Hispanic. With six Latino candidates competing for their votes against a well-financed Solarz, it was considered "the hottest congressional race in town."[23]

Velazquez's resume included serving as head of the Commonwealth of Puerto Rico's office in New York. She had been a professor at the University of Puerto Rico before resigning when the conservative government there accused her of being a communist.[24] She distinguished herself from the other Latino candidates by getting the endorsements of labor groups and Mayor David Dinkins.[25] Her ethnicity played a prominent part in her campaigning. She started her victory speech in Spanish saying, "My first words are going to be in our language. . . . Today we write a new page in the development of our community."[26]

Marie Braden observes that there was little coverage of Velazquez in her bid against Solarz.[27] In fact, a LexisNexus search revealed only fifteen articles in *Newsday* including either candidate's name during the campaign period. Race played a major part in that coverage.

Racialized Coverage of Velazquez

In a district drawn to represent Latinos, with ethnically identified liberal candidates, it was not a surprise that much of the campaign coverage focused on race. In fact, all of the articles that included either Solarz's or Velazquez's name talked about it. Yet, only one of these stories dealt with issues, an article with brief profiles of each candidate that included thumbnail sketches of their issue agendas. Some of these included Hispanic issues: for instance, candidate Ruben Franco "vow[s] to fight 'English Only' movement," and Velazquez "promises to fight against AIDS in the district and in Puerto Rico." If race and ethnicity were not infused into the coverage through the issues, then how was it introduced?

Almost all of the stories made a point of referring to NY-12 as a "Latino district." Three of the stories described the racial/ethnic composition of the voting population. Candidates were repeatedly referred to by their ethnicity. Solarz was identified as white (and a few times as Jewish); the others were called Latino (and sometimes Puerto Rican). The Latino candidates were often not distinguished from each other; instead, they were discussed as Latino alternatives who might split the vote, allowing Solarz to win. A few articles discussed endorsements of candidates by politicians, interest groups, and Latino community leaders.

The newspaper provided a tepid endorsement for Solarz, noting that the most important language to understand was not Spanish but "urban policy." The endorsement was for "one more chance" and acknowledged the candidate's "warts." It concluded by saying,

> Placing our bets on Solarz was a close call. The three Latin candidates in the 12th—Elizabeth Colon, Ruben Franco, and Nydia Velazquez—have promise. Velazquez' days teaching politics courses, her stint on the City Council, her work for the Commonwealth of Puerto Rico and her role in pushing voter registration and AIDS prevention means she knows her way around the mean streets and the offices where local and federal policy are made. Colon, too, has community and government experience. Franco, a tireless civil rights lawyer, is bright and able.[28]

One article covered a "Spanish-language candidate debate" and highlighted combativeness rather than issues. It described a shoving match between candidate Franco's daughter and a Velazquez supporter and an anti-Semitic slur shouted from the audience at Solarz. Like many other articles, this one noted criticisms of Solarz for running in a district designed for Latino representation. A major focus of the article was language. Velazquez was said to have criticized Solarz for caring less about local issues than foreign affairs and saying, "You don't know our language, and I don't mean Spanish, but the language of oppression." Language was the topic of another paragraph:

> While Velazquez chided Solarz—who had an interpreter behind him—for speaking no Spanish, candidate Elizabeth Colon charged Velazquez has a limited command of English that could hurt her in Congress. "I know how Daniel felt in the lion's den, but Daniel survived and I will again," Solarz said. He said he would study Spanish if re-elected, but noted, "Down in Washington, they speak English." Colon directed her fire at Velazquez, saying she has "strings attached to her that are pulled from Puerto Rico." Velazquez has worked for the Puerto Rican government and made several fund-raising forays to the island.[29]

Race and Postelection Coverage of Velazquez

Velazquez's association with Puerto Rico was even more prominent in the postprimary coverage. Because the district was heavily Democratic, she was virtually assured the seat after winning the primary. Therefore, coverage after the primary was not about campaigning; instead, it provided more information on the imminent "Representative Velazquez." This information had been generally lacking in the primary coverage, probably because *Newsday* characterized the result as a "stunning upset." The paper had also focused on the conflict in the campaign, rather than on getting to know the candidates. *Newsday* claimed the primary had been noted for its bitterness and "dissonance among Hispanic politicians."[30]

Celebrations of her victory emphasized her ethnicity and were covered as doing so. She gave her victory speech in Spanish.[31] A supporter said, "At last there's a real Puerto Rican of the people going to Congress."[32] One interview focused on her commitment to Puerto Ricans in New York and Puerto Rico,[33] an approach subsequent articles referred to as her "double mission."[34] She "received a heroine's welcome" in Puerto Rico a week after the election.[35] Her father was interviewed in a story about her upbringing on the island.[36] The media repeatedly noted her status as the "first Puerto Rican–born woman in Congress." Only the last-hour revelation that Velazquez once attempted suicide drew attention away from this fanfare, and even after this fact made the news, *Newsday* gave it little attention.

While much of the coverage of Velazquez's being a Puerto Rican reflected her own campaigning, it still tended to paint her as an outsider. Issues that were discussed dealt more with Puerto Rico than New York. To some extent, this idea of her as a foreigner resulted from what other candidates said about her; however, it was reinforced by the news coverage and editorial endorsements. Although newspapers gave some attention to the criticism that Solarz was running in a district drawn for Hispanic representation, their coverage never got to the heart of what it meant to represent a largely Hispanic district or discussed the substantive alternatives the candidates offered.

The ways in which the Hispanic candidates' agendas differed and offered voters a choice about how they would be represented was largely lost in coverage that treated them merely as alternatives to Solarz's agenda. The newspaper's coverage and endorsement of Solarz reinforced the idea of racial minorities as "other," in opposition to whites at the center. In this case, Solarz shared the center with black Mayor Dinkins, whose endorsement of Velazquez was portrayed as distinguishing her from the pack of Hispanic candidates.

NEWSPAPER COVERAGE OF CUBAN AMERICAN POLITICIANS IN SOUTH FLORIDA

Republican Ileana Ros-Lehtinen became the first Cuban-born Miami resident to win a seat in the House of Representatives by beating white Democrat Gerald Richman in a contentious special election in the summer of 1989. The district included Miami, Miami Beach, and parts of other surrounding towns (such as Key Biscayne, Hialeah, and Coral Gables). No racial or ethnic group held a majority in the district at that time, although blacks and whites together made up a slight majority, compared to Hispanics. White senior rights advocate Claude Pepper had previously held the seat for twenty-six years. When Pepper was first elected, the district consisted primarily of retired white Democrats. By the time of his death in 1989, only 54 percent of the registered voters were Democrats.[37]

National Republican Party chairman Lee Atwater claimed that this was now the "Cuban American seat" and worked to get Ros-Lehtinen elected. When Richman responded to this rhetoric by saying that it was an "American seat,"[38] Ros-Lehtinen refused to debate him. She said that she intended to "unify the community," rather than divide it, and stated, "Bigotry is not debatable. As the father of a racist campaign, Gerald Richman must campaign alone."[39] Ros-Lehtinen used Spanish-language mailings urging Cuban American voters, "Tell Mr. Richman that we too are Americans."[40] This resonated with her claim that running for Congress was "the epitome of realizing the America Dream."[41]

The race was described as "bitter," with "polarized voters," with blacks and Jewish voters supporting Richman and Hispanics voting for Ros-Lehtinen. Although she won the election 52 to 48 percent, she was accused of utilizing ethnic divisions rather than "rising above them," as Claude Pepper had.[42] Since her first election, Ros-Lehtinen has retained this seat and accumulated seniority in Congress.

The daily newspaper that serves her district, the *Miami Herald*, has been criticized for not reflecting the politics and priorities of the Cuban American community. It has responded to these criticisms by claiming that when it objectively reported news reflecting poorly on Cuban Americans, it was accused of bias. The paper has, however, hired more Spanish-speaking journalists and created a Spanish supplement.[43]

A LexisNexus search of articles that included Ros-Lehtinen's name in the *Miami Herald* over five years (1998–2002) yielded twenty-one stories, which were analyzed to assess her visibility in the media, the tone of the coverage, and the topics covered, with particular attention to the issues and people the articles characterized her as representing.

Visibility and Favorability of Ros-Lehtinen's Coverage

In the five years worth of coverage that included her name, Ros-Lehtinen's centrality was relatively low in the stories analyzed (see table 18.2). Visibility in these stories was coded as "major," "medium," or "minor." No stories fell into "major" category, only 19 percent (4) were coded "medium," and the rest, 81 percent (17), were coded "minor." In fact, in almost half (8) she was mentioned only in passing. Yet, even when playing a minor role, she was able to voice her position.

Statements she made or wrote appeared in 57 percent (12) of the stories. All but one of these conveyed positions she was trying to promote. The exception was taken from a private letter addressed to an individual involved in a corruption trial. A story about that person, which mentioned her name, was one of three that reflected poorly on the congresswoman. The other two concerned her votes on environmental issues and trade policy. Neither of these articles quoted her. One favorable article regarded her efforts to save a district project.

Topics and Roles in Ros-Lehtinen's Coverage

Most of the stories (67 percent, or 14) that dealt with Ros-Lehtinen's issue positions either discussed her voting record or her positions. Three of these had a specific, local focus. Two concerned saving a federally funded project in the district. One dealt with a bill to help constituents get hurricane insurance. Eight regarded the Cuban embargo or trade policies that might affect it. Another discussed environmental issues. Two dealt with issues related to immigration.

Five of the other seven stories concerned political infighting. Most of these stories were high in conflict, covering disagreements within the Cuban American political community. For example, one talked about a political war between the mayor and another Cuban American representative, with a history that included Ros-Lehtinen and her husband.[44] In another, she reportedly "ripped" the antiembargo position of a Cuban American state legislator who was running in another House district. "I'm sure there will be a benefit to her financially," Ros-Lehtinen said.[45] Another article about the mayoral race said

Table 18.2   Centrality of Ros-Lehtinen and Richman in Stories

Centrality	Candidate	
	Ros-Lehtinen	Richman
Primary focus	27%	—
	(3)	(0)
Major player	36%	27%
	(4)	(3)
Medium	9%	27%
	(1)	(3)
Minor player	18%	18%
	(2)	(2)
In passing	9%	18%
	(1)	(2)
Not mentioned	—	9%
	(0)	(1)
Mean for stories including candidate	2.5	3.3

that her photograph in one of the candidates' brochures had been used to show his ability to "overcome ethnic racial tensions."[46]

Of the twenty-one stories, 71 percent (15) specifically mentioned Cuban Americans or Cuba. Most focused on the Cuban trade embargo, although some concerned immigration policy. Ros-Lehtinen's strong anti-Castro positions came through in stories about issues, events, and politics. She was reported as speaking at a conference on Cuba, holding a press conference in response to an antiembargo demonstration, attending a rally on the other side of the issue, attending a speech by President Bush in which he spoke against Castro, receiving a request for a visa from a Cuban dissident, criticizing a candidate who opposed the embargo, supporting an appointment to the Advisory Board for Cuban Broadcasting, and sponsoring bills that helped Cuban American immigrants. Overall, the coverage of Ros-Lehtinen in the *Miami Herald* was fairly minimal and racialized, focusing mostly on her issue positions related to Cuba and battles with other Cuban American politicians.

Other Cuban American Candidates in South Florida

In 2002, two Cuban American state legislators ran against each other for a newly created House seat (FL-24). Republican Mario Diaz-Balart soundly beat Democrat Annie Betancourt by winning 71 percent of the vote. Because Diaz-Balart had chaired the state legislative committee in charge of redistricting, the district lines were drawn to favor him. Republicans held a four-to-three margin over Democrats there.[47] This redistricting and its unsuccessful Supreme Court challenge received as much coverage as the campaign in the Miami press. Only four articles could be located using LexisNexus that dealt substantially with the campaign. Three of these focused on the candidates' contrasting positions on U.S.-Cuban relations.

Cuban-born Annie Betancourt criticized U.S. policy as outdated and suggested that we increase trade with Cuba. As the widow of a Bay of Pigs veteran, she argued that trading with Cuba did not endorse Fidel Castro, whom she called a "tyrant." Like most Cuban American politicians, Diaz-Balart strongly supported the embargo. Representative Ros-Lehtinen entered the debate between them by imputing Betancourt's motivations for taking this position, saying that there "was money to be made in holding these positions in favor of Castro."[48] Betancourt became the first Dade County Cuban American politician to publicly denounce the embargo.[49] With the attention this position gave her came the accusation that she was a "single-issue candidate."[50] It also led to negative coverage of other Cuban American politicians. For example, "The U.S. embargo against Cuba is the single issue that can reduce the otherwise even-tempered, somewhat eloquent Republican [Diaz-Balart] into an irrational ideologue."[51]

CONCLUSION

These case studies looked at how newspapers in three different states covered Hispanic candidates for the House of Representative. They included women and men, Republicans and Democrats, incumbents and challengers, people from four different regions (West, Southwest, South, and Northeast), and three different ethnic backgrounds (Puerto Rican, Mexican, and Cuban). With the exception of the Gonzales-Walker competition, race was highly visible in the media coverage. Race was prominent in the campaign rhetoric about issues and how candidates defined themselves and each other.

Sometimes these racial conflicts were between Hispanics and whites (like the conflict between Ros-Lehtinen and Richman over the meaning of "Cuban American seat"). Often, they were between Hispanics. Morales referred to Bonilla as a "coconut"; Colon claimed that Velazquez's English would undermine her influence in Washington; Ros-Lehtinen said that Betancourt was personally profiting from her opposition to the embargo of Cuba. These indicate a debate over what it means to "be Hispanic," to be a "Hispanic politician," and to "represent Hispanics." Any answers to these debates that these politicians may have come up with were not part of the public discourse analyzed here. Instead, they are found between the lines in the conflicts that fueled media coverage that is attracted to combativeness.

The idea of Hispanic representation seemed to be narrowly construed as "descriptive representation." Descriptive representation is literally having Hispanics elected by Hispanics. Yet, Hispanic politicians differ from each other (in terms of party, ideology, nation of birth, first language, how ethnically identified they are). Of course, the Hispanic population differs too, so finding a legislator whose issue positions reflect the Hispanic community is harder than finding one who descriptively represents them. Races that include more than one Hispanic candidate (like NY-12 and FL-24) preclude this "easy way out" of the question of Hispanic representation.

19

Newspaper Coverage of Asian American Candidates and Politicians

~~~~~~

ALTHOUGH HUNDREDS OF ASIAN AMERICAN POLITICIANS HOLD ELECTED OF-
fice, relatively few of them hold federal office.[1] In 2001, five representatives
in the House and two senators were of Asian decent. Three of them (including
both senators) represented Hawaii, where Asian Americans make up the majority. The other four congressmen represented districts in California, Oregon, and Virginia. They were Mike Honda (D-CA, 15), Robert T. Matsui (D-
CA, 5), Robert Scott (D-VI, 3), and David Wu (D-OR, 1). Multiracial or white-
majority constituencies elected these mainland politicians.[2]

With a relatively small population (4 percent nationally) and a dispersed
one, Asian American candidates need to appeal to non-Asian voters to get
elected. While more than 40 percent of America's Asian American population
resides in California, Asian Americans still make up only 15 percent of the
state's residents. In fact, districts with a relatively high number of Asian
Americans (Chinatown in New York and San Francisco) have elected Latino
politicians.[3] One obstacle to electing Asian Americans to state offices is a
lack of panethnic coalitions. In the 1991 Democratic primary for California's
46th assembly district, a Korean American, a Japanese American, and a Filipino American ran against each other. Each received attention, financial support, and votes from their ethnic communities, and all lost the election.[4]

The ethnic diversity among Asian American politicians has increased
over time. Yet, there are still more Japanese American and Chinese American
politicians than there are politicians from other groups, despite Filipinos'
being the second largest population.[5] Whereas in the 1970s most Asian American politicians were second- and third-generation Japanese Americans, there
are now immigrant officeholders. This coincides with an increase in the percentage of the Asian American population that is foreign-born (up from 48
percent in 1970 to 79 percent in 1990).[6] At the local level, the 1990s saw the
election of the first Vietnamese American, Cambodian American, and
Hmong American officials.[7]

This chapter takes a preliminary look at how two Asian American candidates (one of Chinese, the other of Korean descent) were covered in their local newspapers as compared to their white opponents. It also looks at the coverage of a senior Japanese American member of the House of Representatives. Quantitative and qualitative content analyses were used to assess the extensiveness and favorability of coverage, as well as any references to race.

GARY LOCKE FOR GOVERNOR OF WASHINGTON (1996)

In 1996, Chinese American Gary Locke beat five Democrats, including Seattle's mayor and a former U.S. representative, to win his party's nomination for governor of Washington. Then, he beat Ellen Craswell, a former state senator who had won the Republican nomination with grassroots conservative support and without running any television advertisements. By winning this election, Locke became the first Asian American governor of a mainland state.

The candidates had very different styles and philosophies. The campaigns focused on ideology not detailed policy plans. Education became a major issue, but much of the discussion was on whether the government was a positive or negative force, rather than on specific education proposals. Although Locke tried to take the middle road during the campaign, he had to defend a tax increase and the expansion of state government during his chairmanship of the Appropriations Committee of the state house. Craswell claimed she would "govern according to God's plans," which included some dismantling of government and repealing one-third of the state's taxes.[8] In addition to their different races, sexes, and ages (he was forty-six; she was sixty-four), more than one story contrasted their personal styles

> In conversation, Locke's hands swing, twist, move, the eyes locking on the questioner. He's a debater, a persuader. He's selling himself. Craswell barely moves as she speaks. The hands stay folded, neatly. She never raises her voice.[9]

Ninety-nine stories including one or both of their names appeared in the *Seattle Times* between September 18 (the day after the primary) and November 4 (the day before the election). Fourteen of these appeared on the front page of the newspaper. Thirty-seven were editorials, columns, or letters to the editor. All of these stories were coded for the two candidates' relative visibility and favorability and the inclusion of race in the coverage.

Visibility of Locke and Craswell

Looking at how many stories named each candidate, how many direct quotes each received, and their centrality in the stories determined their visibility.

Overall, the evidence indicates that neither candidate was more visible than the other.

Ellen Craswell received slightly more attention than Gary Locke when the stories that mentioned the candidates' names were counted. Craswell was named in eighty-five stories, and Locke was named in seventy-five. Locke's name appeared more often (503 times compared to 417 for Craswell).

Locke had slightly more visibility when direct quotes were counted. He was able to speak for himself in 129 sentences, compared to Craswell's 105. The key to this difference lay in a single story, which asked the candidates to answer questions posed by readers.[10] Locke's answers provided him with fifty directly quoted sentences; Craswell, who declined the newspaper's invitation, got none. If this single story were excluded from the analysis, Craswell would have been quoted more often than Locke (105 to 79).

Table 19.1 demonstrates the centrality of each of the candidates in the campaign stories. When all stories are considered, Craswell played a slightly more prominent role in the stories than Locke did. However, this difference was due to the ten stories that excluded Locke. Locke was slightly more central in stories naming him than Craswell was in stories that included her.

One candidate's slight advantage over another on specific measures of visibility was due in part to the choices he or she made. Locke seemed to rely heavily on his spokeswoman for making public statements, minimizing his direct quotes. Craswell's choice not to answer the readers' questions diminished her number of direct quotes.

Favorability of Coverage of Locke and Craswell

The tone of the coverage was better for Locke than for Craswell, which can be seen in two ways: the number of stories that were coded as "bad news" or

Table 19.1   Centrality of Locke and Craswell in Stories

	Candidate	
Centrality	Locke	Craswell
Primary focus	25%	27%
	(25)	(27)
Major player	17%	16%
	(17)	(16)
Medium	9%	16%
	(9)	(16)
Minor player	6%	14%
	(6)	(14)
In passing	6%	15%
	(6)	(15)
Not mentioned	24%	14%
	(24)	(14)
Median	3 (medium)	3 (medium)
Mean	3.26	3.13
Excluding not mentioned	2.39	2.66

"good news" for each candidate and the ratio of "friendly" to "unfriendly" quotes in the stories.

Locke got more good news stories and fewer bad news stories than Craswell did. Fifteen stories were coded as "bad news" for Locke, compared to twenty-eight for Craswell. Seventeen stories were coded as "good news" for Locke, compared to thirteen for Craswell. Thus, Locke had slightly more favorable coverage than negative coverage, whereas more than twice as many of Craswell's stories were coded as "bad news" as were coded as "good news."

The direct quotes about the candidates (excluding their own) favored Locke. He received a better ratio of friendly to unfriendly quotes (twenty-eight friendly versus nineteen unfriendly). Craswell got seventeen unfriendly quotes and thirteen friendly ones. Keep in mind, this part of the analysis does not take into account the positive and negative comments written in letters to the editor, editorials, and columns. A closer look at the content of the good news and bad news illustrates the nature of these additional stories.

Some of the directional news applied to both candidates. For example, it was bad news for both when the campaign was criticized for its lack of substance[11] and candidates' untruthfulness.[12] It was good news for both when they were characterized as "two decent, honorable candidates who work hard, thrive on challenge and are confident of their abilities"[13] and as "very fine veteran politicians, both with exceptional abilities, and both with clear differences in this campaign" who have "done an excellent job communicating their principles."[14]

Direction of Locke's Coverage

Some of the bad news for Locke concerned his style. For example, an article entitled "Locke-Craswell: The Mechanic vs. the Visionary" referred to Locke as a "micro-manager" and "a wind-up toy" who had praised his opponents in the primary "by saying what he, Locke, was doing when they first met."[15] His record also came under some fire. He received criticism from conservatives for his record of increasing taxes while in the legislature and for cost overruns during his tenure as King County executive.[16] Liberals criticized him for wanting to roll back a tax hike.[17]

A few stories challenged Locke's honesty. One quoted contradictory statements issued by Locke's campaign about his knowledge of a mailing.[18] Another reported, "There were laughs when he [Locke] argued that he wasn't a liberal and hisses when he said GOP claims that he supports an income tax and would be a lackey for organized labor were negative campaign tactics."[19] Bad news also included the question of how far he would go for labor unions and whether he was exaggerating his support of them to please one crowd or backing away from a commitment to please another audience.[20] The first two sentences of a story about his contradictory issue statements read, "Gary Locke is explaining himself. Again."[21]

Positive coverage of Locke pointed to his efficiency,[22] his "trustworthy, likable character,"[23] and his "plans to improve the economies of the nation and state."[24] News of groups and people (including prominent Republicans) supporting him constituted good news,[25] as did the *Seattle Times*'s endorsement.[26]

Direction of Craswell's Coverage

Most of the bad news for Craswell concerned her ideology, her desire to cut government radically, and the role religion would play in her governing. A number of stories pointed to her lack of mainstream Republican support because of these positions.[27] Her policy stands also received frequent criticism for their lack of clarity and their extremism.[28] These direct, at times venomous, criticisms held little back. For example:

> In a televised debate with her opponent, Gary Locke, she put herself forward as a born-again supply-side economic theorist who has no plans whatsoever to reduce government and wouldn't specify them if she did.[29]

In addition to her issue positions, her appearance and her religious fervor were attacked. Her preparedness was challenged in this example:

> Craswell stumbled over her words often and at one point, when given the opportunity to ask Locke a question, stood silently for a moment when she forgot the second part of her question.[30]

Letters to the editor more often concerned Craswell than Locke. She brought out extreme reactions in readers, who wrote in. Some feared the consequences of her religious beliefs. One letter said that she would cut the budget by firing "the ungodly people."[31] Another shared a persistent vision of the candidate

> standing proud, on a dock by a ship, with her fiery eyes gleaming and sword of victory held high. "Ahoy there, sinners . . . (i.e., unwed mothers; people with mental health problems on welfare; the unwashed, the unclean). . . . Repent and get off this ship. . . . I'm casting it adrift and anyone still aboard is shark bait."[32]

A gay reader wrote that if she legislated based on scripture, she would be advocating the death penalty for homosexuals.[33] Letters in support of Craswell challenged the negative coverage of Christian beliefs and of the candidate.[34] One reader accused the newspaper of being "Christophobic."[35] Another argued that the newspaper ignored the significance of the all-female gubernatorial ticket of Craswell (and Ann Anderson) because the candidates were Republican.[36]

When Bad News Got Personal

Some of the bad news about Craswell seemed to mock her personally, taking shots at her appearance and her religiosity. For example, one resident was quoted as saying that Craswell should respect the "11th Commandment: 'Thou Shalt Not Trespass'" by removing a campaign sign that had been placed on lawns without owners' permission.[37] One columnist described her as follows: "She has what in church might be called a beatific countenance. She looks like an old-fashioned porcelain doll, the smile etched, every hair painted permanently into place."[38] A letter to the editor referred to her as Bob Dole's "anchor" and "Pat Robertson in drag."[39] One message left on the "Rant and Rave" phone line for readers' comments said, "The picture on those [Craswell] signs is very unflattering. She needs to do something about the picture on those yard signs." The picture on the sign was actually of George Washington.[40]

Locke also came under ridicule in a column about appearances (a focus more often reserved for female candidates).[41]

The conventional wisdom is that Ellen Craswell was able to win the Republican nomination for governor because with so many people on the ballot and the electorate so fragmented, she was able to sneak through flying under the radar.

I have my own theory.

I think it's the hair.

I think we're in the midst of the Bad Hair Era of politics. Really. The candidate with the most complicated hair almost always wins. Not necessarily the most hair, or the prettiest, but hair that stands out from the crowd.

In this election, Craswell had by far the most hair in the Republican field.

Her hair is really a lovely thing, a modified beehive so tightly wrapped it would take the Willie Sutton of wasps to break in.

And Gary Locke, forget it. This guy has more hair than everybody else on the ballot combined. He gives barbers nightmares. His haircut gives bowls a bad name.

I know a lot of people won't believe this and will search for more insightful answers. One thing we know for sure is that issues did not decide this race. There were none.[42]

Racialized Coverage of Locke

Of the stories examined, 12 percent (12) included references to race. Nine of these included explicit references to Locke's race. Four articles noted that if he won, Locke would be the first Asian American governor of a mainland state. One long, front-page article ("Locke Making Heritage Pay Off in Race for Governor") focused extensively on race.[43] It talked about Locke's support among Asian Americans, provided details about his background, and speculated that there would be "some racial backlash at the polls."

Six articles contained references to, or examples of, how Locke used his race in the campaign. The three richest examples of this follow:

> Locke talks often of his youth, growing up with immigrant parents and striving for the American dream.[44]
>
> The wonkish Locke has tried to be more personal this year. Along with pending fatherhood, he has talked often about his Chinese-immigrant parents and what he has described as a tough childhood.[45]
>
> Asian-American connections are not only a key financial asset, but Locke's stump speech and television ads repeated focus on his personal story.[46]

Six of the stories made references to Asian Americans as financial backers of Locke's campaign. Some of the articles made campaign contributions sound like an automatic Asian American perk ("his heritage has produced financial rewards for the campaign").[47] Two articles discussed Locke's contributions in the context of illegal contributions made by Asian nationals to Clinton's campaign.[48] Although neither story accused Locke of campaign finance violations, the inclusion of the controversy in the stories and the use of the phrase "his own Buddhist connection" attached to him negative associations derived from racial generalizations.

At times, it seems like the model minority stereotype guided reporters' descriptions of Locke. He sounded like the "Asian American nerd" portrayed in entertainment media when described as a "wonk" and "a straight arrow known for working until midnight and lamenting that his social life consisted of remodeling his house and watching 'Magnum PI' reruns."[49] This sort of description of his personality was linked to his race only once—in an editorial endorsing his candidacy

> He is the son of Chinese immigrants who worked hard to lift themselves into the broad swatch of the American dream defined as the middle class. Beneath Locke's smartest-kid-in-the-class demeanor and political success is a genuine sense of real-life struggle, and an honest connection with the aspirations of people who want more for their children.[50]

Other stereotypes drawn from popular culture that made brief appearances in these articles included the deferential houseboy and the devious, inscrutable villain. One column described him as "bouncing and laughing and almost uncontrollably eager."[51] A profile of Locke quoted the Washington State senate majority leader as saying, "I kind of like Gary. He has an extremely bright mind. I just don't trust him." In the same article, the speaker of the Washington House referred to "another Gary Locke trick" and a state lands commissioner noted, "He's not an easy person to read because he keeps his own counsel."

Although several stories repeated the candidate's celebration of the American Dream, one story showed how Locke still faced the problem shared by Asian Americans of being considered foreign. The story noted that Locke had met with the Chinese ambassador in Washington, D.C. The article's title, "Big News in Beijing," referred to the attention that the Chinese leadership was giving to the governor's race. This message contradicted the inclusive messages about whom he would represent that the candidate was trying to send. One story about race made Locke's intended message clear. It claimed, "Locke has never been pigeonholed as an 'Asian politician,'" and quoted him as saying, "I've got to be a governor for everybody."[52]

JAY KIM FOR THE REPUBLICAN NOMINATION IN CALIFORNIA'S 41ST DISTRICT (1998)

Republican Jay Kim became the first Korean American to serve in the House of Representatives after being elected in California's 41st district in 1992. In March of 1998, he was sentenced to in-house detention for two months and to a year's probation for accepting illegal campaign contributions. Despite the timing of the conviction and his inability to leave Washington, D.C., to campaign, Kim sought his party's nomination. California state assemblyman Gary Miller beat him in the primary. Miller went on to win the general election in this heavily Republican district that crosses three southern California counties (Los Angeles, Orange, and San Bernardino).

Twenty-nine stories published in the *Los Angeles Times* included the names of Jay Kim or Gary Miller during the primary campaign (January 1 to June 2, 1998). These stories were coded for visibility, focus, and tone. Special attention was given to the use of direct quotes by or about the candidates. Stories that included any racial references were identified for a qualitative analysis.

Visibility of Kim and Miller

Miller was included in a few more stories than Kim (twenty-one versus eighteen). Only ten of these stories included both candidates' names because much of the coverage was not about the campaign. Instead, stories dealt separately with Kim's legal problems and Miller's actions in the assembly. In the nine stories that mentioned both candidates, Kim was named first in seven. Two of the stories concerned his conviction, and seven were about the campaign.

Kim's name appeared far more often than Miller's (158 times versus 47). However, what Miller said received much more attention. Only four sentences of direct quotation from Kim appeared. One concerned the passage of a transportation bill ("The days of California being a donor state are over").[53] The other quotes were in a story about his inability to campaign in person due to the restrictions of his home detention order (which limited his travel to the seventeen miles between his Virginia apartment and his Capitol Hill office). The context of these quotations made it clear that their inclusion was not evidence of the candidate's control over the stories.

While his colleagues go home to brag about their triumphs and inquire about other people's babies, Kim is reduced to mailing back three-minute videotapes of himself standing in front of a picture of the Capitol dome, taking credit for a proposed sound wall at an Anaheim trailer park.

"One of the reasons I can't be with you today," the videotaped Kim says, "is I am in Washington fighting to keep these projects on the table."

One of the reasons.[54]

Later, the article referred to Kim's not granting interviews. It quoted him by using his campaign communication:

This week, he mailed voters a glossy two-page campaign flier asking for mercy; it includes a photo of a dead woman and child from the Korean war, during which Kim's family home was twice burned down by communist soldiers.

"The humiliation and embarrassment I have faced personally have been very substantial," the mailer says. "I hope you will accept my pleas not only as an admission of guilt but also as a statement of contrition and that you will afford mercy to me in imposing my sentence."[55]

Gary Miller was quoted in twenty-five sentences. Seven of these concerned California assembly legislation. The other eighteen made reference to Kim. The following examples illustrate how scathing his comments about the incumbent were.

I think it would be difficult for Mr. Kim to run for reelection from a jail cell. . . . And I don't believe Congress would allow him to remain in office if he were sentenced to jail.[56]

How do I tell young people we want to hold you accountable when we don't even hold Kim accountable?[57]

The average citizen would love to be treated like this by the judicial system. . . . If you were the average man working in the streets, you would be wearing your little anklet by now. It's an incredible double standard.[58]

I talk about the election and I tell people Jay's running and they look at me in disbelief.[59]

If I were in Jay Kim's position. . . . I'd be running for cover, not for reelection.[60]

Kim received more prominent coverage when the candidates' roles in the stories were coded for centrality. They were coded as the "primary focus," a "major player," "medium," a "minor player," mentioned "in passing," or "not mentioned" (see table 19.2). Kim was the primary focus of 31 percent of the stories; Miller was never the primary focus. In fact, Miller was only a major player in three stories. Most often, he was named in passing or included as a minor player. Clearly, the Asian American candidate was not ignored in the coverage, although a look at the quotes above indicate a tone of coverage that would have made him wish he were.

Table 19.2   Centrality of Kim and Miller in Stories

	Candidate	
Centrality	Kim	Miller
Primary focus	31%	—
	(9)	(0)
Major player	7%	10%
	(2)	(3)
Medium	—	10%
	(0)	(3)
Minor player	14%	31%
	(4)	(9)
In passing	10%	21%
	(3)	(6)
Not mentioned	38%	28%
	(11)	(8)
Median	4 (minor)	4 (minor)
Mean	3.79	4.45

Favorability of Coverage of Kim and Miller

A look at stories coded as "good news," "bad news," or "neither" for candidates demonstrates how much worse the news was for Kim. Thirteen stories were bad news for him; only two were good news. Only one story was coded as directional towards Miller and was good news. The bad news for Kim concerned his campaign finance violations, the hearing, the conviction, and the political fallout (i.e., a letter from a Republican asking him to withdraw, news that he was not receiving key endorsements, his inability to campaign because of house detention).

Kim's good news concerned a transportation bill benefiting California. Kim headed a transportation task force and chaired the House Transportation and Infrastructure subcommittee, which were instrumental in getting the bill passed. Two articles made this clear. However, coverage of his campaign finance violations offset that of his accomplishments. Although Miller also received attention for bills he was initiating in the California assembly (against Internet spamming, age discrimination, and building contracts), the stories did not treat these endeavors as good news (or bad). His good news story included endorsements from Republicans.

There was also a dramatic imbalance in the negativity each candidate voiced about the other. Miller made eighteen disparaging statements about Kim; however, no quotes appeared in which Kim even referred to his opponent. Direct quotes of other individuals (not the two candidates) were coded as "friendly" or "unfriendly" toward each candidate. Once again, Kim received more directional attention. In fact, only one quote concerned Miller and it was friendly; state attorney general Dan Lungren called him "a man of experience and integrity who will uphold the best traditions in the U.S. Congress."[61]

Stories contained thirty-one sentences of quotes about Kim. Seven were friendly and twenty-four were unfriendly. The friendly quotes referred to his performance in Congress (i.e., working hard, getting funding for roads) and the "Greek tragedy" of his fall (about how he was "paying his dues" and his "sense of responsibility to atone for whatever happened"). The unfriendly quotes referred to the campaign finance scandal. Some of the most direct include the deputy district attorney's comment, "He's been given more than enough mercy. . . . It's an outrage";[62] a Republican consultant's comment, "I have great faith in the voters, and I don't believe that voters are going to reelect someone who has spit in the face of the democratic system of government";[63] and the former head of the Unruh Institute of Politics' remark, "Throw him out. It beats term limits."[64]

The editorial page was the natural place for some of the explicitly directional coverage to appear. Four letters to the editor referred to the candidates, three of them unambiguously against Kim. Of these, two argued that he had gotten too light a sentence,[65] and the third called him "an embarrassment to the Republican Party," who should resign immediately.[66] The fourth letter was ambiguous but more favorable than negative to Jay Kim. It suggested that while Bill Clinton had come back from his scandals after denials and stonewalling, Kim had been forthcoming. The author (Kun Jin Rhee) asked,

> But can Kim make a comeback after admitting guilt, serving the sentence and asking for forgiveness? All else being equal (both doing a great job in their elected posts), who gets the second chance, the contrite one or the lucky dodger?[67]

Racialized Coverage of Kim

Eight articles mentioned race in some way. While this number equals 28 percent of the stories about the campaign, it equates to 44 percent of the stories that mentioned Kim. Six referred to Kim's race. One used his Korean name (Kim Chang Joon). Three stories referred to him as the "first Korean American" in the House. One called him the "only Korean American" there. One article also explained that he was "born to a poor family in South Korea and rose to be one of this nation's most successful Korean Americans" and mentioned his "fifth-degree black belt in taekwondo."[68]

Five articles referred to race by specifying that the campaign finance violations included taking money from foreign nationals. Most of these articles referred to Taiwanese nationals; a few also mentioned Korean nationals. Coverage of the prosecution's memo to the sentencing judge "suggested that he [Kim] took advantage of Korean immigrants who gave him cash or corporate checks, unaware that they were breaking federal election laws."[69] Another article mentioned that the English-language edition of the *Korean Times* called for Kim's resignation.[70]

Kim's race was explicitly politicized only once by an article about an advertisement in the *Korea Central Daily News* (a local Korean-language news-paper) asking readers to donate to Kim's campaign. The ad claimed, "the Republic of Korea and President Kim Dae Jung need congressman Kim Chang Joon."[71] This language brought criticism from Charles Kim of the Korean American Coalition because "it creates the image that you're actually electing an agent for Korea. Korean Americans want someone to represent this country, not Korea." Charles Kim said he thought Jay Kim had not authorized the ad. Yet, Miller assumed that he had when he made the following virulent comments:

> I thought he represented the USA. He needs to go back to Korea if that's what his focus is. I would understand if he said he represents the best interests of the Korean American community. That's fine. But when an ad says the government of Korea . . . needs Jay Kim that bothers me a lot.[72]

These statements demonstrate the stereotype of Asian Americans as "always foreign." References in an article profiling Kim could be interpreted as reflecting stereotypes of Asian American men as "helpers" and as unemotional.[73] Kim was referred to as "grateful," "deferential," "a gentleman who pulls out chairs for his guests and seldom so much as raises his voice," and "a loyal GOP foot soldier." An unnamed colleague in the House described him as "not a real huggy kind of guy."

Columnist Steve Harvey referred explicitly to race when he made light of Kim's situation.

> There's one more example of L.A.'s multiculturalism. After a Latino judge sentenced Korean American Rep. Jay Kim to home detention for taking illegal campaign contributions from a Taiwanese national, Kim's attorney termed the case "a Greek tragedy."[74]

Not everyone interpreted the event racially. In fact, one letter to the editor focused on Kim's wealth in a way that rendered race invisible; he called him "a white-collar good ol' boy" when criticizing the lightness of his sentence.[75]

NEWSPAPER COVERAGE OF REP. ROBERT T. MATSUI, CALIFORNIA'S 5TH DISTRICT (1992–2001)

In 1978, Japanese American Robert T. Matsui was elected to the House of Representatives from California's 5th district. The Democrat was elected to represent Sacramento, the city he was born in. He had served on its city council and as vice mayor. In the House, he served on the Ways and Means Committee and as Democratic whip. He had also served as treasurer and deputy chairman of the national Democratic Party and chair of the Democratic Congressional Campaign Committee. He flirted with running for the U.S. Senate in 1992, but withdrew because of his father's health problems. Before his death in 2005, Matsui was the longest serving mainland Asian American in the House of Representatives. Local newspaper stories that mention him allow us to analyze coverage of an Asian American politician over time.

A LexisNexus search of state and local newspaper and wire services for California between 1992 and 2001 revealed fifty-six articles that mentioned Robert Matsui. These were from the *Los Angeles Times*, the *San Francisco Chronicle*, the *San Francisco Examiner*, McClatchy Newspapers (the *Fresno/Modesto/Sacramento Bees*), the Copley News Service, and the Associated Press. These stories were coded for centrality, favorability, role, and racial content.

Visibility of Matsui

Matsui was not particularly central in the fifty-six articles that mentioned him. He played a minor role (32 percent) more often than he played a major one (21 percent). He was the subject of only 13 percent (7) of the stories, whereas 18 percent (10) of the stories mentioned him only in passing. The stories that were about him dealt with his criticism of Democratic leaders (1), his work and leadership on trade issues (5), and scrutiny of him during the Bill Clinton fund-raising scandal (1).

His name appeared 216 times in these stories (an average 3.9 times per story). He was directly quoted in 161 sentences, averaging three quotes per story. The number of quotes per story varied from zero to eighteen. In three stories, he was quoted ten or more times.

Favorability of Matsui's Coverage

When stories were coded as "positive," "neutral," or "negative" toward Matsui, most (84 percent) fell into the neutral category, while 11 percent (6) were positive and the remaining 5 percent were negative. The few direct quotes about Matsui that could be counted as either "friendly" (5) or "unfriendly" (5) balanced each other.

One of the positive stories was a newspaper's campaign endorsement. The others dealt with the work Matsui was doing in Congress. One concerned promoting district interests—saving an air force base from being closed.[76] Another concerned a bill to guarantee health insurance to children and pregnant women, which Matsui sponsored and promoted in his keynote address to the American Academy of Pediatrics. This article stated that Matsui was "recognized as one of the most knowledgeable experts on health care reform in Congress."[77]

His ascent to the chair of the House Subcommittee on Trade also received favorable coverage.[78] An article about his role in fighting for global free trade described him as "an influential and respected member of the Democratic caucus."[79] Only one of the stories coded as "favorable" dealt with an issue related to race. It was a letter to the editor that applauded the congressman for his efforts to preserve the site of the Japanese internment camp Manzanar.[80]

All three of the negative stories had a racial component. One, an editorial written by a second-generation Chinese American, attacked Matsui for his "patronizing liberal rhetoric" and opposition to a welfare reform bill because he thought it would be too harsh on immigrants.[81] Another story indicated that Chong Lo, the former head of a "controversial San Francisco–based political action committee," had been convicted of real estate fraud. Even though the story noted that Lo's "conviction yesterday was unrelated to her role as an officer of the Lotus Fund," which "generated money for U.S. Representatives Robert Matsui," his inclusion could be considered negative coverage.[82]

The worst story for Matsui was also the longest.[83] The headline announces it as bad news: "Fund-Raising Scandal Hits Matsuis on 2 Sides." The story explained that Matsui and his wife were "under public scrutiny" for their involvement in an event where illegal funding-raising took place and that they were "under fire" for "not denouncing 'Asian Bashing.'" The article made strong claims supporting each problem. On one hand, it stated, "Matsui's participation in the dinner puts him at the event that was the starting point for the flow of millions of dollars of suspect—and potentially illegal—donations that triggered the fund-raising scandal." It also claimed, "A dozen leaders in California and Washington—many of them speaking only on condition of anonymity—criticized the Matsuis for not adequately defending the interests of Asian Americans." On the other hand, while the article allowed Matsui to defend himself (it included eleven sentences directly quoting him) and offered two friendly quotes to balance two unfriendly ones, its subject and implication were clearly negative.

Other stories contained friendly quotations complimenting Matsui's work on providing health care for children,[84] his bravery in "struggling against great odds" to pass the North American Free Trade Agreement,[85] and his "ability to provide leadership on the critical trade issues" as subcommittee chair.[86] Unfriendly quotes included an interest-group spokesman's calling his support of a dam project a "huge federal boondoggle" and "shakedown . . . of federal taxpayers."[87] Other unfriendly quotes came from Sen. Nancy Pelosi, who disagreed with his position on trade sanctions for China,[88] and from Newt Gingrich, who disagreed with him on the fast-track bill to renew President Clinton's ability to negotiate trade agreements.[89]

Role of Matsui in Coverage

The stories were analyzed to see what role the congressman played in each. How important did the coverage indicate that he was? Did it talk about his leadership and seniority? Was his issue agenda getting through? Did coverage make him seem powerful on an international, national, state, or local stage?

Information about Matsui's leadership or seniority appeared in 34 percent (19) of the stories. These included references to his leadership or seniority in the House, in the Democratic Party, on the Ways and Means Committee, and on the Subcommittee on Trade, characterized as "a pro-NAFTA group in the House."[90] He was referred to as the man "chosen by House Ways and Means Committee chairman Dan Rostenkowski to lead the campaign to pass the North American Free Trade Agreement."[91]

Matsui's activity in authoring a bill was mentioned in 21 percent (12) of the stories. Most of these (67 percent) dealt with national issues, and the rest with state or local issues. Of the eight articles that addressed bills of national scope and significance, the topics included a plan to provide health care for children, a more liberal welfare reform alternative to President Bill Clinton's, an end to an FCC tax break, a phone tax repeal, a modification of tax breaks for biotechnology industries, and a study of illegal gambling. Three of the four stories that dealt with local or state interests discussed a bill to fund a dry dam to protect Sacramento from flooding. Another concerned a bill to "waive steep penalties on California for failing to complete work on a centralized and automated child-support data system."[92]

Coding stories as either "party/campaign news," "international or national issue," or "local/state issue" revealed the focus on national issues over local issues in Matsui's coverage: 54 percent (29) dealt with national or international issues, 26 percent (14) dealt with party politics or campaigns, and 20 percent (11) dealt with state or local issues.[93] This data indicates that Matsui's coverage positioned him as an important leader rather than as someone interested solely in parochial issues.

Racialized Coverage of Matsui

Racial issues or representation of minority constituencies received little attention. Only 16 percent (9) of the stories included racial issues. Four of these discussed immigration policy or the impact of legislation on immigrants, one concerned a tax break to encourage minority-owned cable stations, another talked about 1992 as the "Year of the Asian American," two covered Asians and campaign finance scandals, and the last discussed preserving a Japanese internment site. Six of these expressed Matsui's concern for immigrants or Asian Americans.

Matsui's race was mentioned in 7 percent (4) of the stories. Two stories mentioned it in passing. The first, "The Year of the Asian American," speculated that President Clinton might give "a cabinet position to Robert Matsui, the Japanese American congressman from Sacramento."[94] The second, a story about China trade policy, referred to him as "a serious, soft-spoken Japanese American from Northern California."[95]

More extensive attention to his race, and experiences or insights based on it, appeared in a third story, "Immigrants Taking Bum Rap from Both Parties, Rep. Matsui Says," which covered a speech he gave to the Sacramento Press Club. A portion of it read,

> Matsui spent 3 1/2 years in an internment camp for Japanese Americans during World War II, beginning at the age of 6 months. He likened the recent anti-immigrant rhetoric to what took place just before the war.
> "You go back to '38, '38, '40—the rhetoric stated calmly about the Japanese don't share our values," he said. "By 1941, it was that the Japs will steal your property" and guide enemy planes to U.S. targets.
> Matsui said that violence is directed against minority groups because no matter how many generations they remain in the country, "people who can't blend in are subject to a backlash."[96]

The final story that included information on Matsui's race concerned the fund-raising scandal.[97] It referred to his wife as "the top Asian American staffer in the White House." It also mentioned their internment as infants "in California camps during World War II." In addition to criticizing Matsui for not standing up for Asian Americans during the campaign-finance scandal, the article acknowledged his advocacy of the group's interests in the past. The director of the National Asian Pacific American Legal Consortium noted that Matsui "has provided many services to the [Asian American] community in the past," and a leading Japanese American lawyer said that "he has voted consistently for the disadvantaged, the poor and people of color, and his impassioned leadership in the movement for redress may have been his greatest accomplishment." The article also provided this interpretation of the criticism Matsui had received:

> Part of Matsui's problem may stem from a cultural divide between American-born Asian Americans and immigrants, who are vastly more numerous and have given large political contributions. In the eyes of some first-generation donors, initial credit for the growing clout of the community went to assimilated third-generation leaders like Matsui, but now the blame for the donation scandal is falling on them.[98]

The article later quoted Matsui as saying,

> In the Asian American community, many people were riding on John Huang's coattails looking for jobs in the administration. Many were disappointed and are looking for scapegoats. I will not be their scapegoat.[99]

CONCLUSION

What do these three case studies suggest about newspaper coverage of Asian American candidates and politicians? First, they show that Asian Americans are not excluded from coverage. More stories named and quoted Locke than

Craswell; Kim's name appeared more frequently in stories than Miller's. The imbalance in direct quotations by the candidates did not appear to be a device to silence Kim but rather a result of campaign choices and circumstances. While we could not compare Matsui's coverage specifically to that of other congressmen, he did appear in newspaper stories, and this coverage often concerned his national leadership.

The favorability of the coverage for the three was mixed. Locke got more favorable coverage than his opponent, and his coverage contained slightly more good news than bad news and more friendly quotes than unfriendly ones. This seemed particularly positive in comparison to Caswell, whose problematic press coverage reflected her "outsider" status as a politically inexperienced, female, religious conservative. As one might expect given his situation, Kim received much worse coverage than his opponent. Stories and statements about him focused on his campaign scandal and conviction. Most of Matsui's coverage was neutral, but the remainder was more positive than negative. His achievements in office were given more coverage than any criticisms of him.

References to race were present in all three Asian American's coverage to varying degrees. Of the three Asian Americans studied here, the most extensive attention to race was given to the politician whose coverage was the most negative. Race played a part in 44 percent of Kim's stories, compared to 12 percent of Locke's and 18 percent of Matsui's. It makes sense that Kim's coverage would refer to the campaign-finance scandal involving Asians and Asian Americans given his own involvement in the problem. However, coverage given to Matsui and Locke, who had committed no crime but were simply of the same race as those who had, also mentioned the scandal.

A variety of racial stereotypes appeared in both Locke's and Kim's coverage. At times, both seemed inscrutable and deferential. Descriptions invited comparisons with the nerds, foreigners, and asexual helpers portrayed in the entertainment media. Locke's coverage also raised the question of a "racial backlash" among voters. Other racial references came out of the politicians' statements and activities. Sometimes these were issue related; sometimes they focused on Asian American constituents or contributors; at other times, they appeared in stories about achieving the American Dream.

These case studies analyzed mainstream media, so they say little about the parallel press. However, Asian-language newspapers do endorse candidates.[100] They can also help raise money for campaigns, as the ad in the *Korea Central Daily News* tried to do for Kim. This example illustrates how messages in the parallel press do not always stay there. Kim received negative coverage for a fund-raising effort he might not have initiated. The *Los Angeles Times* story about the ad contained some of the most anti-Asian comments found in the campaign's coverage. In this case, a message in the parallel press provided an opportunity for Kim's opponent to couch his attacks as a response. This case indicates that the risks and benefits of campaign coverage in ethnic newspapers might be a fruitful area of inquiry.

20

Conclusion

〜〜〜〜〜〜〜〜〜〜〜〜〜〜〜〜〜〜〜〜〜〜〜〜〜〜〜

RATHER THAN REVIEW THE FINDINGS OF EACH CHAPTER, THIS CONCLUSION DIS-cusses the book's major lessons. The first is that representation of race serves to protect the racial hierarchy in America. The second is that there is more similarity than difference in the ways that the media represents the four ra-cial-minority groups. The third is that there are similarities between how racial minorities are represented in news and entertainment. It also addresses some lingering questions, such as: Haven't things gotten better? What about the "liberal press"? and What can I do about this?

SIMILARITIES BETWEEN HOW ENTERTAINMENT
AND NEWS MEDIA REPRESENT GROUPS

There are more similarities in the media coverage of the four racial-minority groups than there are differences. Research that focuses on only one group and speaks only to scholars and students primarily interested in that group might miss this observation. Once research on these different groups is brought together, it becomes obvious that the mainstream media have a status quo perspective on race relations that is really about protecting whites' power and privilege, while denying that racism exists.

In both entertainment and the news, racial minorities are divided into "good" and "bad." Good minorities are to be saved and rewarded by whites; bad ones must be fought and controlled. Since these narratives reflect the fantasies and fears of whites, people of color are painted with the same broad brush. White saviors dominate American films, regardless of which racial-minority groups they include. "The movie image of the ideal white self is always pushed to the center, and is consistently a white self that is good, brave, generous, and powerful."[1]

The recent blockbuster *Spider-Man 2* (2003) features a white protagonist and an accidental white antagonist who sacrifices himself in the end. The focus of the film is Spider-Man's saving the beautiful white woman he loves, first by giving her up, then by fighting the man/machine to save her. Along the way, he saves mixed-race groups on the street, in a bank, on a train. These powerless, often cowering, crowds include whites, blacks, and Hispanics, who get little dialog and no character development. They add color to the background but make no real contributions. Spider-Man saves an Asian American child from a burning building and returns her to her parents, who express their gratitude in a foreign language that is not translated in subtitles. Essentially, the film tells us that there is no need to translate their words because they do not really matter. These people are simply tools to tell a story about a white man with special powers. In an effort to be racially sensitive, the film includes a multiracial city and avoids making minorities the heavies, but it fails to show them as important, central, or self-sufficient. This is one reflection of race relations as fantasized by whites in 2004—that minorities create a colorful background, that they need, appreciate, and try to help whites, but mostly that they should stay out of the way and not cause problems.

Even films about issues of race and racial minorities are really about whites. White men fight for black rights in *To Kill a Mockingbird*, *Mississippi Burning*, and *Ghosts of Mississippi*. White men lead battles for Native American survival in *Broken Arrow*, *A Man Called Horse*, and *Dances with Wolves*. White teachers try to save Hispanic teenagers from lives of crime and poverty in *Up the Down Staircase* (1967), *Teachers* (1984), and *Dangerous Minds* (1995). White cops try to save residents of Chinatown in *Year of the Dragon*, a white reporter and a white lawyer save an innocent Japanese murder defendant in *Snow Falling on Cedars* (1999), and an engineer tries to save a Chinese waitress from her lonely life by romancing her in *Now Chinatown* (2000). The examples go on and on.

Not only are good minorities the ones that whites save, but they are the ones that whites and white institutions find valuable in some way. The black Toms and mammies, the Native American Tontos and Indian princesses, the Hispanic "second bananas" and nameless hired hands (cooks, gardeners, maids, nannies), and the China dolls and Asian houseboys all sacrifice for and serve whites. Black coons, Hispanic buffoons and spitfires, Native American drunks, and Asian American nerds provide comic relief to amuse whites. Sexualized women from all of these racial groups serve and entertain white men in an obvious way. Black man-children, Asian mystics, and wise Indian elders "magically" serve to enhance white power. Each of these stereotypes projects a certain racially based uniqueness, but all serve the same purposes: they show that minorities are best if they "stay in their place"—behind whites. Entertainment that uses stories about successful, assimilated characters shows the rewards of playing by the rules.

The news pays less attention to good minorities than entertainment because of its inherent bias toward negativity. However, human-interest stories that report on "exceptional cases" reinforce the racial hierarchy in the same way that films portraying good minority stereotypes do. Good minorities presented in the news include the black "Person of the Week" who overcame adversity, the high-achieving "model" Asian American, the romanticized, but dead, peaceful protest leaders (Martin Luther King Jr. and Cesar Chavez), the progressive Indians who embrace modernization, and the immigrants who successfully assimilate by learning a new language and customs. These good minorities demonstrate that the American Dream is inclusive and that achievement comes from working hard and "not rocking the boat" too hard. They give readers and viewers "proof" that American is not a racist society.

Stories about bad minorities in entertainment and the news also reassure white America that the system works and that whites are not to blame for racial inequality. Movies and news tell us that all four minority groups are inferior to whites. They are more likely to be dangerous, criminal, adversarial, freeloading, dirty, diseased, promiscuous, drunken, drug-addicted, and from dysfunctional families. No wonder "they" cannot get ahead! No wonder "we" need to watch, arrest, confine, fight, exclude, or kill "them"!

Also, the more moderate the actions and goals of the different racial groups, the more sympathetically entertainment and the news portray them. This is perhaps best illustrated by social-movement coverage. The national media covered the civil rights movement more favorably than they did the black power movement; the farm workers strikes received better framing than the Moratorium; Indians who "hung out" peacefully on an island that no one else seemed to want got more sympathetic coverage than those who fought at Wounded Knee. The more a group threatens the status quo, the more aggressively the media frame it. This contrast is also demonstrated by the coverage of politicians and candidates. Those from third parties get worse coverage than Democrats and Republicans. Those who run deracialized campaigns get better press.

Since the mainstream media's exclusion and representations of all four racial-minority groups serve whites, each group has created parallel presses and independent films. While these have distinctive aesthetics and foci, they serve similar purposes and share useful information, alternative perspectives, empowering images, and a complexity lacking in mainstream communication.

HAVEN'T THINGS GOTTEN BETTER OVER TIME?

Examples throughout this book illustrate racial stereotypes and system-supportive themes in news and entertainment. As many of these examples are old, it might be comforting to think of them as out-of-date. This interpretation would be consistent with the widespread belief among whites that the "bad old days" of discrimination are over. This raises the question, Haven't things gotten better over time?

The answer is both yes and no. The examples in this book were chosen in order to illustrate that the major problems with representations transcend any particular period or genre. Racism persists, deeply embedded in political and social structures and reflected in the media. The form it takes and how it is expressed, however, have changed over time. Reporters use the dominant ideology to frame news, so as the hegemony shifts, so does the reporting. Periods of social anxiety, when there are major struggles over resources and power, can generate changes in film content, resulting in more progressive messages, new formats, and transformed genres.[2] In this way, entertainment can reflect and encourage social change.[3] But the dominant ideology pulls back toward the center to protect the status quo.

The question of how much media representations have changed relates to the question of how much society has changed. As explicit racism has become unacceptable in most social and political circles, there has been some improvement in entertainment and the news. As certain understandings of why there is inequality lose persuasive power, they are replaced with new ones. Like the advertising icon Aunt Jemima, a mammy who now looks like an executive secretary, some images have been deliberately reformed.[4] Yet, stereotypes persist, taking on subtler forms that carry the same ideology.

Change and Lack of Change in Entertainment

Birth of a Nation's white supremacist interpretation of U.S. history is long gone, and unapologetic, aggressively racist stereotypes no longer appear "natural" or acceptable to modern audiences. Hollywood no longer produces films with titles like *That Chink at Golden Gulch* (1910) and *The Wooing and Wedding of a Coon* (1905).[5] Yet, a subtle racism continues to idealize and prioritize whites and white institutions and helps "to perpetuate the deeply inegalitarian foundation of U.S. society."[6] A few studies that examined changes in film representations of race over time illustrate that improvement exists but should not be exaggerated.

One study that points to improvement in the representation of blacks in mainstream films is Brian J. Woodman's analysis of images of African American soldiers in Vietnam War films.[7] In terms of exclusion, films went from including one black soldier (*Green Berets*, 1968; *The Boys of Company C*, 1978) to including many (*Apocalypse Now*, 1979; *Platoon*, 1986; *Hamburger Hill*, 1987). These later films depict the large presence of black combat troops in the war (20 percent of the troops in Vietnam in 1968 were black). Not only does the number of black actors in these movies increase, but their roles become more nuanced and less stereotypical over time. The more recent war films are also more aggressive in confronting issues of race.[8]

The *Green Berets* does not give the black character, Doc, a racial consciousness or identity. In some ways, he fits the Tom stereotype because he is subordinate to the white leader, supportive of the war, and a dependable helpmate. Ten years later, the black soldier in *The Boys in Company C* also helps the white characters and is initially stereotypical (an angry, inner-city, black hustler), but he provides "a strong voice of black rage."[9] Critics disagree over how stereotypical the major black characters in *Platoon* are. Some see a "good black"/"bad black" dichotomy in the two main characters, with King as a "mammy" and Junior as a "black nationalist buffoon" and "irresponsible, inept, and cowardly sexual predator."[10] Others argue that the diversity in the black characters makes them less two-dimensional and stereotypical. Woodman is convinced that there has been improvement in black Vietnam War characters over time but maintains that not until the independent film *The Walking Dead* (1995) was the central character in a Vietnam War movie black. Contemporary films continue to put black soldiers in the background without character development and complexity. A fictitious love triangle between three white characters was at the center of *Pearl Harbor* (2001) rather than the real-life story of the heroic black cook (Dorie Miller).

In *Watching Race: Television and the Struggle for Blackness*, Herman Gray shares an ambivalent interpretation of television's representation of blacks. He believes a variety of "views of blackness" compete with each other on the television screen. He finds the fact that some representations are more progressive than others encouraging and identifies three discourse categories: "assimilationist discourse," in which their similarity to whites renders black characters invisible; "pluralistic discourse," in which black characters reside in "separate-but-equal" shows and worlds; and "multicultural discourse," which shows diversity within the black community.[11]

Many of the representations falling into the "multicultural discourse" category aired on FOX during the 1980s and 1990s as part of the new network's effort to compete with the three major networks by "narrowcasting." A proliferation of black situation comedies on FOX included black actors, writers, and aesthetics that demonstrated black pride and politics (such as posters of Malcolm X, African garb, black artwork). The effort paid off since blacks comprised 25 percent of the network's market in 1995.[12] Although some of the shows' "B plots" (those that were not the central stories) tackled controversial issues, they were more likely to suggest individual rather than social explanations for racial problems.[13] In 1994, FOX cut back on its black productions as it acquired more local stations and the rights to Sunday NFL games and focused on building its white audience.[14]

Progressive shows are not necessarily followed by more progressive shows. There are advances, then steps backward. For example, a show like *Northern Exposure* might have seemed like a trailblazer in terms of its modern, complex representations of Native Americans at the time, but it did not inspire the production of similar shows. The taboo against interracial romance has been lifted, although it is still rarely depicted.

The number of minority characters in positions of authority has increased. For example, the principal in the urban high school drama *Boston Public* is black; thirty years earlier, the one in *Room 222* was white. A number of black detectives and a black lieutenant appeared on *Homicide: Life on the Street* (1993–1999) during its seven-year run.[15] Some black television characters are "textured," rather than two-dimensional, individuals. Thomas A. Mascaro argues that the depictions of blacks on *Homicide* were breakthrough in their variety, richness, subtlety, and humanity.[16]

While some problematic racial images and messages have changed, others remain. Film studies professor Linda Williams illustrates how a "black and white racial melodrama" that began in theater and novels continues to dominate popular entertainment.[17] She claims that while the racial melodrama is reconfigured as the racial politics of the day change, it does not go away. Melodrama is a compelling storytelling form that defines truth and virtue by showing it in peril. The dominant racial melodrama includes two central images: black men beaten by white men and white women endangered by black men. Black men are victims and villains who alternately deserve our sympathy and our mistrust. Ultimately, "white America needs to believe in its own virtue vis-à-vis either the extreme suffering or the extreme villainy of the black male body."[18] Williams sees these melodramatic stories as reassuring to whites because they tell whites that blacks "pay for your sins" (thereby redeeming whites) or "deserve what they get" (thereby absolving whites). While earlier films might have connected race to villainy more directly (e.g., by using the term "black brutes"), black males on film and television still create "a heightened expectation for the expression of extreme good or extreme evil."[19]

While movie and television include far more black roles than they once did, exclusion is still a problem for other groups. Hispanics are particularly underrepresented in entertainment roles, compared to their numbers in the population.[20] Some old stereotypes of Hispanics are still around in new forms. Frito Lay no longer uses the Frito Bandito to demonstrate the desirability of its corn chips, but a little dog with a thick Spanish accent recently sold us tacos. Criminality was rampant among the gangs in *Zoot Suit* (1981) and remains in *American Me* (1992). The number of Native American characters in film and on television is not as large as during the heyday of the Western. As an analysis of Custer films revealed, "Modern critics should not assume a 'natural' movement toward more 'accurate,' 'authentic,' or 'balanced' representations."[21] The treatment of Asian Americans in film and television has not improved dramatically or steadily over time.[22] Highly simplistic and stereotypic representations still appear in films today.

Over time, filmmakers of color have had more opportunities to create their own films. While most are still low-budget, independent films, they are more common than in the past and provide the most innovative and varied racial messages.

Change and Lack of Change in News

Awareness of diversity issues and the desire to reach multiple audiences have generated some changes in newsrooms. Many of these deal with hiring practices and are limited in their ability to change content (see chapter 7). Some news organizations have instituted guidelines for diversifying sources and are more sensitive in their use of photographs.[23] Conscious efforts to give time and consideration to racial issues have resulted in some excellent stories. These include a series on discrimination in bank loans in the *Atlanta Constitution* and reports in Raleigh's *News & Observer* about public school discrimination.[24]

The dependence of the news on elites to define what is important and as the "go to" people for comments and interpretations affects how the coverage of racial minorities changes over time; it also explains the limited nature of these changes because the news will only be as progressive on racial issues as the dominant ideology allows.

There is no disputing that the dominant ideology on race is not the same today as it was before the Civil War or the civil rights movement. We no longer segregate news into a "Negro section" or exclude information about racial-minority communities entirely.[25] Reporters no longer mock Chinese deaths.[26] When most politicians stopped using racial epithets, papers stopped printing them. Now, racially inflammatory language or statements are interpreted as illegitimate and framed as scandalous.[27] This is a relatively recent phenomenon since racist remarks made to reporters by Agriculture Secretary Earl Butz during the 1976 presidential campaign got no coverage at the time in the mainstream press. When they were eventually publicized in *Rolling Stone*, other news organizations followed suit, and Butz was fired.[28]

At the same time, media organizations comprise and respond to elites, who are inherently status quo oriented, that is, invested in maintaining the sociopolitical system currently in place and from which they have profited. The American myths drawn upon to maintain the current system are deeply felt and central to the national identity. They help sustain a system that is inegalitarian and places whites at the top of a racial hierarchy.

The review of contemporary examples and findings about news coverage in part II demonstrates that negative stereotypes and themes are not confined to the past. Extensive attention to all four minority groups' criminality continues. Stories about conflict between minority groups are still common.[29] Coverage portrays blacks, Hispanics, and Native Americans as poor because of their own deficiencies and as benefiting unfairly from government programs and "special rights." Asian Americans' success is credited to their "outwhiting the whites."[30] Even U.S.-born Asian Americans and Hispanics are treated as foreigners who steal jobs, opportunities, and benefits from "real" Americans.

One study on racial-issue framing illustrates that coverage has not moved consistently in a progressive direction. Political science professor Richard A. Pride looked at rhetoric about school desegregation in Mobile, Alabama, from 1954 to 1997. He found that while different groups used competing narratives over time to explain inequality between blacks and whites, the "controlling myth" was one of individual responsibility for educational success and failure. This narrative used by elites, the public, and the media justified racial inequality and guided public policies. Policy changes reflected the narrative that resonated most as an explanation for racial inequality at a given time. During the period Pride studied, the dominant rhetoric for understanding racial inequality changed from blaming blacks (arguing that they were biologically inferior to whites), to blaming whites (for discriminating), back to blaming blacks (for lacking a good work ethic). In the 1980s and 1990s, a narrative of individual self-reliance successfully mobilized white resentment to change school desegregation policies.[31]

The parallel press continues to be a useful resource for racial-minority groups seeking information, community, and alternative perspectives. Its developmental trajectory is not clearly positive, however. The black press is less vast and vital than in the past. As the Spanish-language press has grown, it has become less political and independent. Some Native American newspapers are instruments of local elites. Asian-language papers are prevalent, but the degree to which they promote a political agenda varies. However, the Internet as an alternative communication resource holds great promise.

WHAT ABOUT THE LIBERAL PRESS?

This book's central argument is that the news media is a status quo–oriented institution that impedes progress on racial equality. Readers may wonder how this can be so if there is a liberal bias in the press. The answer is, it can't. Despite the claims of many best-selling books, websites, politicians, and citizens, there is no liberal bias in the press.[32] There are other biases (such as those toward negativity and personalization) that sometimes serve liberal interests; at other times, however, they serve conservative interests. That is, they may serve liberal or conservative interests as long as these interests are not too liberal or too conservative, because the press does have a "mainstream" bias.

The belief in a liberal bias in the press stems from the selective perception of conservatives who do not like to see bad news about their issues, politicians, or candidates. These conservatives are adept at getting their complaints publicized in the so-called liberal media. They point to examples that supposedly prove their case without looking at those that disprove it. They complain about the ideologies of journalists without considering the norms and procedures in newsrooms that screen out individual points of view. They ignore other explanations for why stories are incomplete or distorted.

Two recent books focusing on racial coverage claim that there is a liberal political bias in the mainstream press. One, *Coloring the News: How Crusading for Diversity Has Corrupted American Journalism*, was marketed to a mass audience. The other, *Press Bias and Politics: How the Media Frame Controversial Issues*, was directed at academic audiences.[33] Since both illustrate the weaknesses of the liberal bias argument, a closer look will be instructive.

In *Coloring the News*, reporter William McGowan claims that major newspapers have enforced a "diversity dogma" that has created one-sided news on race.[34] He describes news organizations' diversity plans for hiring and retention, practices to increase coverage of minorities (such as "race beats"), and procedures for promoting racial sensitivity in coverage (to minimize negative stereotypes in photo use and diversify source selection). He claims that these efforts have undermined newsroom morale, diminished the quality of news coverage, and exaggerated racial problems.[35]

In *What Liberal Media? The Truth about Bias and the News*, author and English professor Eric Alterman illustrates how McGowan's use of evidence is sloppy, unconvincing, and unreliable and how he ignores counterexamples.[36] The evidence McGowan uses is anecdotal, and much of it is at odds with systematic studies of the same topics. For example, he claims that crimes committed by blacks are underplayed, that the coverage of the Los Angeles riots/rebellion emphasized black oppression as the cause, and that the downsides of immigration are routinely ignored.[37] The studies reviewed in part II, which consider much more news coverage than McGowan, clearly refute these claims. Rather than illustrate a liberal bias, many of his examples demonstrate other biases. For example, the sympathetic coverage that McGowan claims Louis Farrakhan's Million Man March speech got would be due to the conservative content of his message (urging blacks to take responsibility for their problems), rather than deference to the black leader.

Rhetoric scholar Jim A. Kuypers's *Press Bias and Politics* content analyzes hundreds of news stories that reported on six political speeches (three of them about race). Comparing the coverage to the speeches, he claims that the press promotes liberal thoughts and vilifies moderate and conservative positions. The examples on race include Alabama state senator Charles Davidson's defense of the confederate flag and description of the Civil War, a commencement speech by President Bill Clinton promoting national unity through diversity, and Louis Farrakhan's speech at the Million Man March.[38] Not surprisingly, he found that the press framed Clinton's speech positively and the other two negatively. This illustrates a mainstream bias rather than a liberal one, however.

As is consistent with evidence provided in chapter 8 (and inconsistent with McGowan's interpretation of a limited number of stories), Kuypers found that the press vilified Farrakhan. "Whereas Farrakhan's march message was a complex blend of spiritual and secular action, the press only relayed Farrakhan's message through a narrow secular light that was tainted by the press's own prejudgment of Farrakhan."[39] Farrakhan, as a symbol of black anger and separatism, evokes fear and suspicion in the white mainstream.[40] Therefore, it is not surprising when news coverage of him is negatively framed, regardless of the content of his speech. Negative coverage of outsiders is common; critical coverage of Farrakhan is too.[41] Neither is evidence of a liberal bias.

State senator Charles Davidson wanted to return to the practice of flying the Confederate flag at the Alabama state capitol building. His speech defended this position by claiming that lies about the Civil War were being used to besmirch the flag. These "lies" included the assertions that slavery was about racism, that slaves were mistreated, and that the war was about slavery. Kuypers found that the press framed the speech as a defense of slavery, included few of the senator's statements, and judged him harshly.[42] Is this evidence of a liberal bias? No, it is evidence of a bias toward the mainstream, personalization, and probably negativity. Rather than cover complicated ideas at odds with mainstream understanding, reporters covered the person who voiced them and judged him for being outside of "the sphere of legitimate controversy."[43]

Kuypers' third race-related example illustrates how President Clinton got a lot of coverage when he announced his "One America in the 21st Century" initiative, which aimed to enhance educational and economic opportunity, personal responsibility, and community for all citizens. His speech was more thematic than specific and received positive coverage that quoted the president extensively.[44] Is this evidence of a liberal bias? No. It illustrates how successfully a white, elite politician can attract media coverage when he takes a position on racial issues that reinforces core American values and does not fundamentally challenge the status quo.

Refuting some of the claims made by these two books will not put to rest accusations of a liberal bias in the media. There will always be other books that offer different examples. Those who want to believe in a left-wing press will continue to do so. No amount of counterevidence or scholarship will sway people from a belief that protects their worldview and serves their self-interest. But those beliefs do not disprove the mounds of scholarship that refutes them.

WHAT CAN I DO ABOUT THIS?

What can you do about the racial exclusion, stereotyping, and system-supportive themes and messages in the mainstream media? If you work in the news or entertainment industries, you can try to create more racially inclusive, complex, and innovative communication. But you probably know how difficult that will be because institutional structures discourage change. As reporters, you can fight for stories, include more diverse sources, and avoid using racial stereotypes. As filmmakers, you can cast more minorities, consider their input about characters' authenticity, and pursue racially mixed audiences' feedback. Most likely, you do not work in the entertainment industry or for a news organization, but you are a consumer of media. As a consumer, you have some power.

You can see through the racial message in the media by becoming a critical viewer and reader. When consuming news, look for who is not included. Notice the stereotypes and the system-supportive messages. Identify the news frames. Create alternative interpretations for the news that take into account social, political, historical, and cultural factors. Be critical of the individualistic explanations for the status quo. Compare news about candidates and politicians of color to their own campaign communications and records. Sample the parallel press. Use the Internet to find news from racial-minority perspectives. Complain to producers of news and entertainment when they exclude or stereotype minorities.

When watching films and television entertainment, consider the perspectives of the minor characters. Look for stereotypes and try not to generalize from them to real people. Watch independent films and videos in addition to blockbusters. Generally, be aware of the messages you routinely receive about race in America. Cognizance can be your weapon against cultivation, priming, and internal oppression. You can join the other media consumers who actively resist the racial messages embedded in news and entertainment.

Even though mainstream media are encoded with messages that support the dominant ideology, those do not have to be the messages you decode. People come to a text with a variety of experiences and beliefs that affect how they interpret messages. Meaning is not just found in texts; it is negotiated by the readers and viewers, who can oppose intended messages with "resistant readings."[45] In a study of how focus groups interpreted news coverage of the Los Angeles riots/rebellion, Darrell M. Hunt found that black viewers actively challenged journalists' interpretations. He concluded that this resistance was meaningful in its own right, "contributing to a consciousness necessary for meaningful social action at some later moment in time."[46]

This resistance can also be brought to bear on entertainment communication. Studies show that Asian American viewers choose to recognize the positive attributes of Asian characters. For example, women in a Chinatown gang in *The Year of the Dragon* fit the stereotype of dragon women;[47] yet, some female Asian American viewers saw them as refreshingly defiant.[48] Similarly, the Ling character on *Ally McBeal* might represent a "fetishized sex symbol" to some viewers and a powerful, smart, liberated woman to others.[49] Black sitcoms, like *Martin*, while criticized as "hyper-racial" exaggerations, were popular with black audiences. Black viewers saw appealing qualities in seemingly stereotypical characters. For example, they appreciated black matriarchs for their strength and independence.[50] *Living Single* (1993–1998) may oversexualize some of its black female characters, but the role played by

Queen Latifah gives them agency and presents a feminist alternative.[51] You, too, can look for the ambiguity and contradictions in entertainment and embrace the affirming representations.

You can also help other people resist the messages in entertainment or news by sharing your insights. Write letters to the editors of papers. Talk with your friends about the racial messages in movies you watch with them. Join Internet chat rooms and discussion boards to hear and share alternative interpretations of texts and even to rewrite them.[52] Practice "culture jamming" by using the conventions of mass culture to spoof or alter texts and their meanings.[53] Scholars disagree over how resistant these activities really are. Some argue that this is pseudo resistance because it takes place in a private realm, is motivated by pleasure rather than politics,[54] and leaves the structures of domination intact.[55] Others argue that these acts directed against the dominant ideology are potentially threatening to the status quo and meaningfully subversive.[56]

Resist the idea that being in the audience renders you powerless. Audiences do not have to passively receive ideology that benefits the few over the many. The maintenance of power and social inequality in democratic societies is not forced on the public. The potential power of an audience is its numbers, which if mobilized could threaten the social order. Ideological state apparatuses routinely conceal and marginalize critics, but sometimes their challenges require elite accommodations, adjustments, or even a significant renegotiation of the conditions of acquiescence. This idea of public consent as conditional and unstable forms an important part of hegemony theory because the hegemony is shared by elites and masses.[57] It is negotiated by them, not simply imposed from above. When the dominant ideology no longer seems like common sense to the public, then it is vulnerable to change. Discourse is a "terrain of struggle." While "the struggle is not on a level playing field," it is still worth fighting.[58] Insights you gain from this book and others like it can help you in this fight.

Notes

CHAPTER 1

1. Lisa Taylor and Andrew Willis, *Media Studies: Texts, Institutions, and Audiences* (Oxford: Blackwell Publishers, 1999), 40.

2. NBC Universal is a corporation that includes a variety of news and entertainment vehicles. It was formed in May 2004. General Electric owns 80 percent of it, and Vivendi Universal controls 20 percent. See www.nbc.com.

3. Yet, many still hold antiblack attitudes and believe that blacks are too demanding. D. O. Sears, "Symbolic Racism," in *Eliminating Racism*, ed. P. A. Katz and D. A. Taylor, 53–84 (New York: Plenum, 1988).

4. Louis Althusser, *Lenin and Philosophy and Other Essays* (London: New Left Books, 1971).

5. Horatio Alger Jr., *Ragged Dick, Or Street Life in New York with the Boot-Blacks*, reissued ed. (New York: Signet Classics, 1990).

6. Stephanie Greco Larson and Martha Bailey, "ABC's 'Person of the Week': American Values on Television News," *Journalism and Mass Communication Quarterly* 75 (1988): 487–99.

7. Althusser, *Lenin and Philosophy*.

8. Gunnar Myrdal, *An American Dilemma: The Negro Problem and Modern Democracy* (New York: Harper and Row, 1962 [1944]).

9. Sut Jhally and Justin Lewis, *Enlightened Racism: The Cosby Show, Audiences, and the Myth of the American Dream* (Boulder, Colo.: Westview Press, 1992).

10. Oscar H. Gandy Jr., *Communication and Race: A Structural Perspective* (London: Arnold, 1998).

11. Teun A. Van Dijk, "New(s) Racism: A Discourse Analytical Approach," in *Ethnic Minorities and the Media*, ed. Simon Cottle, 33–49 (Buckingham, U.K.: Open University Press, 2000), 48; John Gabriel, "Dreaming of a White . . . ," in *Ethnic Minorities and the Media*, ed. Simon Cottle, 67–82 (Buckingham, U.K.: Open University Press, 2000), 80.

12. Christopher P. Campbell, *Race, Myth, and the News* (Thousand Oaks, Calif.: Sage Publications, 1995), 33.

13. See www.nbc.com/nbc/The_Apprentice (accessed August 15, 2004).

14. See www.hispeed.rogers.com/features/FeatureC.jsp?id=apprentice (accessed August 15, 2004).

15. It might have helped him parlay the show into more attention and opportunities.

16. In the boardroom during episode 6.

17. These are primarily media studies, journalism, communications, film studies, political science, sociology, and history.

18. Michael Parenti, *Inventing Reality: The Politics of the Mass Media* (New York: St. Martin's Press, 1986).

19. Ronald N. Jacobs, *Race, Media, and the Crisis of Civil Society: From Watts to Rodney King* (Cambridge, Mass.: Cambridge University Press, 2000).

20. Jacobs, *Race, Media, and the Crisis*; Susan Herbst, *Politics at the Margins: Historical Studies of Public Expression outside the Mainstream* (New York: Cambridge University Press, 1994).

21. Jacobs, *Race, Media, and the Crisis*, 28.

22. Herbst, *Politics at the Margins*.

23. Herbst, *Politics at the Margins*.

24. Jacobs, *Race, Media, and the Crisis*; Herbst, *Politics at the Margins*.

25. Michael O'Shaughnessy and Jane Sandler, *Media and Society: An Introduction*, 2nd ed. (South Melbourne: Oxford University Press, 2002).

26. Bradley W. Gorham, "The Social Psychology of Stereotypes: Implications for Media Audiences," in *Race/Gender/Media: Considering Diversity across Audiences, Content, and Producers*, ed. Rebecca Ann Lind, 14–21 (Boston: Pearson Education, 2004).

27. Tessa Perkins, "Rethinking Stereotypes," in *The Media Studies Reader*, ed. Tim O'Sullivan and Yvonne Jewkes (London: Arnold, 1997).

28. O'Shaughnessy and Sandler, *Media and Society*.

29. John Fiske, *Television Culture* (New York: Routledge, 1987).

30. Dan Nimmo and James E. Coombs, *Mediated Political Realities* (New York: Longman Press, 1993).

31. Gans, *Deciding What's News*; W. Russell Newman, Marion R. Just, and Ann N. Crigler, *Common Knowledge: News and the Construction of Political Meaning* (Chicago: University of Chicago Press, 1992); Rod Hart, *Seducing America: How Television Charms the Modern Voter* (New York: Oxford University Press, 1994).

32. W. Lance Bennett, *News: The Politics of Illusion*, 5th ed. (New York: Longman Press, 2003).

33. Darnell M. Hunt, *Screening the Los Angeles "Riots": Race, Seeing, and Resistance* (New York: Cambridge University Press, 1997).

34. Susan Douglas, *Where the Girls Are: Growing Up Female with the Mass Media* (New York: Times Books, 1995); O'Shaughnessy and Sandler, *Media and Society*.

35. George Lipsitz, *Time Passages: Collective Memory and American Popular Culture* (Minneapolis: University of Minnesota Press, 2001).

CHAPTER 2

1. Phillip L. Gianos, *Politics and Politicians in American Film* (Westport, Conn.: Praeger, 1998); Sut Jhally and Justin Lewis, *Enlightened Racism: The Cosby Show, Audiences, and the Myth of the American Dream* (Boulder, Colo.: Westview Press, 1992); Terry Christiansen, *Reel Politics: American Political Movies from "Birth of a Nation" to "Platoon"* (New York: Basil Blackwell, 1987).

2. Robert Skalar, *Movie-Made America: A Cultural History of American Movies* (New York: Vintage Books, 1994), 316.

3. Richard Dyer, *The Matter of Images: Essays on Representation* (New York: Routledge, 1993); Stuart Hall, ed., *Representation: Cultural Representations and Signifying Practices* (Newbury Park, Calif.: Sage Publications, 1997).

4. Michael O'Shaughnessy and Jane Sandler, *Media and Society: An Introduction*, 2nd ed. (South Melbourne, Australia: Oxford University Press, 2002), 189.

5. Ernest Giglio, *Here's Looking at You: Hollywood, Film, and Politics* (New York: Peter Lang Publishing, 2000).

6. O'Shaughnessy and Sandler, *Media and Society.*

7. O'Shaughnessy and Sandler, *Media and Society.*

8. Chris Jordon, *Movies and the Reagan Presidency: Success and Ethics* (Westport, Conn.: Praeger, 2003).

9. Hernán Vera and Andrew M. Gordon, *Screen Saviors: Hollywood Fictions of Whiteness* (Lanham, Md.: Rowman & Littlefield, 2003), 9.

10. O'Shaughnessy and Sandler, *Media and Society.*

11. C. Levi-Strauss, *Myth and Meaning* (New York: Routledge and Kegan Paul, 1978).

12. Jose E. Limón. "Stereotyping and Chicano Resistance: An Historical Dimension (1973)," in *Chicanos and Film: Representation and Resistance,* ed. Chon A. Noriega, 3–17 (Minneapolis: University of Minnesota Press, 1992).

13. Lillian Jiménez, "From the Margin to the Center: Puerto Rican Cinema in New York," in *Latin Looks: Images of Latinas and Latinos in the U.S. Media,* ed. Clara E. Rodríguez, 188–99 (Boulder, Colo.: Westview Press, 1997), 188.

14. Richie Pérez, "From Assimilation to Annihilation: Puerto Rican Images in U.S. Films," in *Latin Looks: Images of Latinas and Latinos in the U.S. Media,* ed. Clara E. Rodríguez, 142–63 (Boulder, Colo.: Westview Press, 1997), 142, 145.

15. Pérez, "From Assimilation to Annihilation," 142.

16. Ward Churchill, *Fantasies of the Master Race: Literature, Cinema and the Colonization of American Indians* (San Francisco: City Lights Books, 1998).

17. For more on the "construction of whiteness," see Patricia Hall Collins, *Black Feminist Thought: Knowledge, Consciousness, and the Politics of Empowerment,* 2nd ed. (New York: Routledge Press, 2000), and David R. Roediger, *The Wages of Whiteness: Race and the Making of the American Working Class,* Revised ed. (New York: Verso, 1999).

18. Carlos E. Cortés, "Chicanos in Film: History of the Image," in *Latin Looks: Images of Latinas and Latinos in the U.S. Media,* ed. Clara E. Rodríguez, 121–41 (Boulder, Colo.: Westview Press, 1997), 134.

19. Linda Williams, "Type and Stereotype: Chicano Images in Film," in *Latin Looks: Images of Latinas and Latinos in the U.S. Media,* ed. Clara E. Rodríguez, 214–20 (Boulder, Colo.: Westview Press, 1997), 216–17.

20. O'Shaughnessy and Sandler, *Media and Society.*

21. O'Shaughnessy and Sandler, *Media and Society.*

22. Charles Ramírez Berg, "Stereotyping in Films in General and of the Hispanic in Particular," in *Latin Looks: Images of Latinas and Latinos in the U.S. Media,* ed. Clara E. Rodríguez, 104–20 (Boulder, Colo.: Westview Press, 1997), 111.

23. Collins, *Black Feminist Thought;* Darrell Y. Hamamoto, "They're So Cute When They're Young: The Asian-American Child on Television," in *Children and Television: Images in a Changing Sociocultural World,* ed. Gordon L. Berry and Joy Keiko Asamen, 205–14 (Newbury Park, Calif.: Sage Publications, 1993), 206.

24. Berg, "Stereotyping in Films in General and of the Hispanic in Particular," 119.

25. Pérez, "From Assimilation to Annihilation."

26. Gloria Yamato, "Something about the Subject Makes It Hard to Name," in *Making Face, Making Soul: = Haciendo Caras: Creative and Critical Perspectives by Feminists of Color,* ed. Gloria Anzaldúa, 20–24 (San Francisco: Aunt Lute Books, 1990).

27. Jessica Hagedorn, "Asian Women in Film: No Joy, No Luck," in *Facing Difference: Race, Gender, and Mass Media,* ed. Shirley Biagi and Marilyn Kern-Foxworth, 32–37 (Thousand Oaks, Calif.: Pine Forge Press, 1997), 37.

28. O'Shaughnessy and Sandler, *Media and Society.*

29. Lisa Taylor and Andrew Willis, *Media Studies: Texts, Institutions, and Audiences* (Oxford: Blackwell Publishers, 1999), 64.

30. O'Shaughnessy and Sandler, *Media and Society*.

31. Skalar, *Movie-Made America*.

32. Margaret R. Miles, *Seeing Is Believing: Religion and Values in the Movies* (Boston: Beacon Press, 1996), 135.

33. Vera and Gordon, *Screen Saviors*.

34. Vera and Gordon, *Screen Saviors*, 33.

35. Martin Barker and Roger Sabin, *The Lasting of the Mohicans: History of an American Myth* (Jackson: University Press of Mississippi, 1995), 85.

36. Cortés, "Chicanos in Film."

37. Chon Noriega, "Citizen Chicano: The Trials and Titillations of Ethnicity in the American Cinema, 1935–1962," in *Latin Looks: Images of Latinas and Latinos in the U.S. Media*, ed. Clara E. Rodríguez (Boulder, Colo.: Westview Press, 1997).

38. Noriega, "Citizen Chicano," 89.

39. Pérez, "From Assimilation to Annihilation," 161.

40. Skalar, *Movie-Made America*.

41. O'Shaughnessy and Sandler, *Media and Society*.

42. O'Shaughnessy and Sandler, *Media and Society*.

43. Ward Churchill, "Fantasies of the Master Race: Categories of Stereotyping of American Indians in Film," in *Film and Theory: An Anthology*, ed. Robert Stam and Toby Miller, 697–703 (Malden, Mass.: Blackwell Publishers, 2000), 702.

CHAPTER 3

1. Donald Bogle, *Toms, Coons, Mulattoes, Mammies, and Bucks: An Interpretive History of Blacks in American Films*, 3rd ed., 117–40 (New York: Continuum, 1999).

2. Melvin M. Moore, "Blackface in Prime Time," in *Small Voices and Great Trumpets: Minorities and the Media*, ed. Bernard Rubin (New York: Praeger, 1980).

3. Summary taken from Linda Williams, *Playing the Race Card: Melodramas of Black and White from Uncle Tom to O. J. Simpson* (Princeton, N.J.: Princeton University Press, 2001).

4. Clint C. Wilson and Félix Gutiérrez, *Race, Multiculturalism, and the Media: From Mass Communication to Class Communication* (Thousand Oaks, Calif.: Sage Publications, 1995).

5. Michael R. Winston, "Racial Consciousness and the Evolution of Mass Communications in the United States," *Daedalus* 11(4) (1982): 171–82.

6. Wilson and Gutiérrez, *Race, Multiculturalism, and the Media*.

7. Screen Actor Guild Employment Statistics, press release, July 1, 2002, available at http://actorsnw.com/articles/sag070101.php (accessed July 7, 2004).

8. An excellent video that illustrates the evolution of images of blacks on commercial television from 1948 to 1988 is *Color Adjustment*, produced, directed, and written by Marion T. Riggs, San Francisco, California Newsreel, 1991.

9. J. Fred MacDonald, *Blacks and White TV: African Americans in Television since 1948*, 2nd ed. (Chicago: Nelson-Hall Publishers, 1992).

10. MacDonald, *Blacks and White TV*.

11. Kristal Brent Zook, "The Fox Network and the Revolution in Black Television," in *Gender, Race, and Class in Media: A Text-Reader*, ed. Gail Dines and Jean M. Humez, 2nd ed., 129–35 (Thousand Oaks, Calif.: Sage Publications, 2003).

12. Joan L. Conners, "Color TV? Diversity in Prime-Time TV," in *Race/Gender/Media: Considering Diversity across Audiences, Content, and Producers*, ed. Rebecca Ann Lind, 206–12 (Boston: Pearson Education, 2004).

13. Bogle, *Toms, Coons, Mulattoes, Mammies, and Bucks*.

14. Bogle, *Toms, Coons, Mulattoes, Mammies, and Bucks*, 24.

15. Williams, *Playing the Race Card.*

16. Bogle, *Toms, Coons, Mulattoes, Mammies, and Bucks*, 24.

17. Williams, *Playing the Race Card.*

18. Michael Rogin, "Democracy and Burnt Cork: The End of Blackface, and the Beginning of Civil Rights," in *Refiguring American Film Genres: History and Theory*, ed. Nick Browne, 171–207 (Berkeley: University of California Press, 1998).

19. Rogin, "Democracy and Burnt Cork," 177.

20. MacDonald, *Blacks and White TV*, 18.

21. Moore, "Blackface in Prime Time."

22. Bogle, *Toms, Coons, Mulattoes, Mammies, and Bucks.*

23. Jannette L. Dates and William Barlow, "Commercial Television," in *Split Image: African Americans in the Mass Media*, ed. Jannette L. Dates and William Barlow, 1–21 (Washington, D.C.: Howard University Press, 1990); MacDonald, *Blacks and White TV.*

24. Conners, "Color TV?"

25. Philippa Gates, "Always a Partner in Crime: Black Masculinity in the Hollywood Detective Film," *Journal of Popular Film and Television* 32(1) (2004): 21–29.

26. Bogle, *Toms, Coons, Mulattoes, Mammies, and Bucks*, 298.

27. Bogle, *Toms, Coons, Mulattoes, Mammies, and Bucks*, 332.

28. Hernán Vera and Andrew M. Gordon, *Screen Saviors: Hollywood Fictions of Whiteness* (Lanham, Md.: Rowman & Littlefield, 2003).

29. Bogle, *Toms, Coons, Mulattoes, Mammies, and Bucks*, 268.

30. Bogle, *Toms, Coons, Mulattoes, Mammies, and Bucks*, 314.

31. Gates, "Always a Partner in Crime."

32. Bogle, *Toms, Coons, Mulattoes, Mammies, and Bucks.*

33. B. Lee Artz, "Hegemony in Black and White: Interracial Buddy Films and the New Racism," in *Cultural Diversity and the U.S. Media*, ed. Yahya R. Kamalipour and Theresa Carilli, 67–78 (Albany: State University of New York Press, 1998); Gates, "Always a Partner in Crime."

34. Margaret R. Miles, *Seeing Is Believing: Religion and Values in the Movies* (Boston: Beacon Press, 1996), 123.

35. Jonathan Rosenbaum, *Movies as Politics* (Berkeley: University of California Press, 1997).

36. Rosenbaum, *Movies as Politics*; Vera and Gordon, *Screen Saviors.*

37. Vincent F. Rocchio, *Reel Racism: Confronting Hollywood's Construction of Afro-American Culture* (Boulder, Colo.: Westview Press, 2000).

38. Gates, "Always a Partner in Crime."

39. Bogle, *Toms, Coons, Mulattoes, Mammies, and Bucks.*

40. Pamela Wilson, "Confronting 'the Indian Problem': Media Discourses of Race, Ethnicity, Nation, and Empire in 1950s America," in *Living Color: Race and Television in the United States*, ed. Sasha Torres, 35–61 (Durham, N.C.: Duke University Press, 1998).

41. Wilson, "Confronting 'the Indian Problem'"; MacDonald, *Blacks and White TV.*

42. MacDonald, *Blacks and White TV*, 24.

43. MacDonald, *Blacks and White TV*, 182.

44. MacDonald, *Blacks and White TV*; Angela M. S. Nelson, "Black Situation Comedies and the Politics of Television Art," in *Cultural Diversity and the U.S. Media*, ed. Yahya R. Kamalipour and Theresa Carilli, 79–87 (Albany: State University of New York Press, 1998).

45. Stephanie Greco Larson, "Black Women on *All My Children*," *Journal of Popular Film and Television* 22 (1994): 44–48, 46.

46. Bogle, *Toms, Coons, Mulattoes, Mammies, and Bucks*, 9, 45.

47. Bogle, *Toms, Coons, Mulattoes, Mammies, and Bucks*; Vera and Gordon, *Screen Saviors.*

48. Dates and Barlow, "Commercial Television," 263.

49. Bogle, *Toms, Coons, Mulattoes, Mammies, and Bucks*, 5–6.

50. Bogle, *Toms, Coons, Mulattoes, Mammies, and Bucks*.

51. James Snead, *White Screens, Black Images: Hollywood from the Dark Side* (New York: Routledge, 1994).

52. Bogle, *Toms, Coons, Mulattoes, Mammies, and Bucks*, 178.

53. Bogle, *Toms, Coons, Mulattoes, Mammies, and Bucks*; David Pilgrim, "The Tom Caricature," 2000, available on the Jim Crow Museum of Racist Memorabilia website at www.ferris.edu/news/jimcrow/tom (accessed July 7, 2004).

54. Pilgrim, "The Tom Caricature."

55. Vera and Gordon, *Screen Saviors*.

56. MacDonald, *Blacks and White TV*.

57. Tracey Owens Patton, "Ally McBeal and Her Homes: The Reification of White Stereotypes of the Other," *Journal of Black Studies* 32(2) (2001): 229–60.

58. Michael A. Chaney, "Coloring Whiteness and Blackvoice Minstrelsy: Representations of Race and Place in Static Shock, King of the Hill, and South Park," *Journal of Popular Film and Television* 31(4) (2004): 167–75.

59. Bogle, *Toms, Coons, Mulattoes, Mammies, and Bucks*.

60. Bogle, *Toms, Coons, Mulattoes, Mammies, and Bucks*, 7.

61. Bogle, *Toms, Coons, Mulattoes, Mammies, and Bucks*.

62. MacDonald, *Blacks and White TV*. Murphy was on the show from 1980 to 1984.

63. Bogle, *Toms, Coons, Mulattoes, Mammies, and Bucks*, 8.

64. Bogle, *Toms, Coons, Mulattoes, Mammies, and Bucks*.

65. Bogle, *Toms, Coons, Mulattoes, Mammies, and Bucks*, 8.

66. Bogle, *Toms, Coons, Mulattoes, Mammies, and Bucks*, 41, 42.

67. Bogle, *Toms, Coons, Mulattoes, Mammies, and Bucks*, 257; Mark A. Reid, *Redefining Black Film* (Berkeley: University of California Press, 1993), 37.

68. MacDonald, *Blacks and White TV*, 28.

69. MacDonald, *Blacks and White TV*, 182.

70. Nelson, "Black Situation Comedies and the Politics of Television Art."

71. MacDonald, *Blacks and White TV*.

72. Donald Bogle, "TV's New African American Images: Good or Bad?" in *Dollars and Sense* 171 (1991): 41–42.

73. Bogle, *Toms, Coons, Mulattoes, Mammies, and Bucks*, 8.

74. Vera and Gordon, *Screen Saviors*.

75. MacDonald, *Blacks and White TV*, 259.

76. Dates and Barlow, "Commercial Television," 260.

77. MacDonald, *Blacks and White TV*, 259.

78. Bogle, *Toms, Coons, Mulattoes, Mammies, and Bucks*, 175–76.

79. Artz, "Hegemony in Black and White," 75.

80. MacDonald, *Blacks and White TV*.

81. Bogle, *Toms, Coons, Mulattoes, Mammies, and Bucks*, 180.

82. Gail Dines, "King Kong and the White Woman: *Hustler* Magazine and the Demonization of Black Masculinity," in *Gender, Race, and Class in Media: A Text-Reader*, ed. Gail Dines and Jean M. Humez, 2nd ed., 451–61 (Thousand Oaks, Calif.: Sage Publications, 2003).

83. Bogle, *Toms, Coons, Mulattoes, Mammies, and Bucks*, 10.

84. Bogle, *Toms, Coons, Mulattoes, Mammies, and Bucks*, 13.

85. Bogle, *Toms, Coons, Mulattoes, Mammies, and Bucks*. More recent examples are from Pilgrim, "The Tom Caricature."

86. MacDonald, *Blacks and White TV*, 134.

87. MacDonald, *Blacks and White TV*.

88. Paula Giddings, *Where and When I Enter: The Impact of Black Women on Race and*

Sex in America (New York: William Morrow, 1981); Patricia Morton, *Disfigured Images: The Historical Assault on Afro-American Women* (New York: Greenwood Press, 1991).

89. Bogle, *Toms, Coons, Mulattoes, Mammies, and Bucks.*

90. Jacquie Jones, "The New Ghetto Aesthetic," in *Mediated Messages and African-American Culture: Contemporary Issues,* ed. Venise T. Berry and Carmen L. Maning-Miller, 40–51 (Thousand Oaks, Calif.: Sage Publications, 1996).

91. MacDonald, *Blacks and White TV.*

92. Jane Rhodes, "Television's Realist Portrayal of African-American Women and the Case of *L.A. Law,*" in *Gender, Race, and Class in Media: A Text-Reader,* ed. Gail Dines and Jean M. Humez, 95–118 (Thousand Oaks, Calif.: Sage Publications, 1995).

93. Jones, "The New Ghetto Aesthetic."

94. Ruth Elizabeth Burks, "Intimations of Invisibility: Black Women and Contemporary Hollywood Cinema," in *Mediated Messages and African-American Culture: Contemporary Issues,* ed. Venise T. Berry and Carmen L. Maning-Miller, 24–39 (Thousand Oaks, Calif.: Sage Publications, 1996).

95. Patton, "Ally McBeal and Her Homes."

96. Rogin, "Democracy and Burnt Cork," 187.

97. Bogle, *Toms, Coons, Mulattoes, Mammies, and Bucks.*

98. Snead, *White Screens, Black Images,* 55.

99. MacDonald, *Blacks and White TV,* 56.

100. Bogle, *Toms, Coons, Mulattoes, Mammies, and Bucks;* Sharon Willis, *High Contrast: Race and Gender in Contemporary Hollywood Films* (Durham, N.C.: Duke University Press, 1997).

101. Krin Gabbard, *Black Magic: White Hollywood and African American Culture* (New Brunswick, N.J.: Rutgers University Press, 2004).

102. Morton, *Disfigured Images;* Reid, *Redefining Black Film.*

103. Larson, "Black Women on *All My Children*"; MacDonald, *Blacks and White TV;* Moore, "Blackface in Prime Time."

104. MacDonald, *Blacks and White TV,* 34.

105. Moore, "Blackface in Prime Time."

106. Miles, *Seeing Is Believing.*

107. MacDonald, *Blacks and White TV.*

108. Snead, *White Screens, Black Images,* 51.

109. George Lipsitz, "Genre Anxiety and Racial Representation in 1970s Cinema," in *Refiguring American Film Genres: History and Theory,* ed. Nick Browne, 208–32 (Berkeley: University of California Press, 1994).

110. Phillip Brian Harper, "Extra-Special Effects: Televisual Representation and the Claims of 'the Black Experience'" in *Living Color: Race and Television in the United States,* ed. Sasha Torres, 62–81 (Durham, N.C.: Duke University Press, 1998).

111. Bogle, *Toms, Coons, Mulattoes, Mammies, and Bucks;* Ed Guerrero, "The Black Image in Protective Custody: Hollywood's Biracial Buddy Films of the Eighties," in *Black American Cinema,* ed. Manthia Diawara, 237–46 (New York: Routledge, 1993).

112. Miles, *Seeing Is Believing,* 135.

113. MacDonald, *Blacks and White TV,* 259.

114. MacDonald, *Blacks and White TV.*

115. Neil Vidmar and Milton Rokeach, "Archie Bunker's Bigotry: A Study in Selective Perception and Exposure," *Journal of Communication* 24 (1974): 36–47.

116. Vera and Gordon, *Screen Saviors.*

117. Dates and Barlow, "Commercial Television," 273.

118. Dates and Barlow, "Commercial Television," 276.

119. MacDonald, *Blacks and White TV.*

120. Michael Ryan and Douglas Kellner, *Camera Politica: The Politics and Ideology of Contemporary Hollywood Film* (Bloomington: Indiana University Press, 1988), 126.

121. Miles, *Seeing Is Believing*, 125.

122. Bogle, *Toms, Coons, Mulattoes, Mammies, and Bucks*, 263.

123. Bogle, *Toms, Coons, Mulattoes, Mammies, and Bucks*; MacDonald, *Blacks and White TV*.

124. MacDonald, *Blacks and White TV*.

125. MacDonald, *Blacks and White TV*.

126. Moore, "Blackface in Prime Time."

127. Ryan and Kellner, *Camera Politica*.

128. Vera and Gordon, *Screen Saviors*.

129. Bogle, *Toms, Coons, Mulattoes, Mammies, and Bucks*.

130. Artz, "Hegemony in Black and White," 71.

131. Artz, "Hegemony in Black and White."

132. Artz, "Hegemony in Black and White," 76.

133. Chris Jordon, *Movies and the Reagan Presidency: Success and Ethics* (Westport, Conn.: Praeger, 2003).

134. MacDonald, *Blacks and White TV*, 124.

135. Wilson, "Confronting 'the Indian Problem,'" 80.

136. Nelson, "Black Situation Comedies and the Politics of Television Art."

137. Bodroghkozy, Aniko. "'Is this What You Mean by Color TV?' Race, Gender, and Contested Meanings in NBC's *Julia*," in *Gender, Race, and Class in Media: A Text-Reader*, ed. Gail Dines and Jean M. Humez, 413–23 (Thousand Oaks, Calif.: Sage Publications, 1995).

138. Michael Parenti, *Make-Believe Media: The Politics of Entertainment* (New York: St. Martin's Press, 1992).

139. Dates and Barlow, "Commercial Television."

140. Sut Jhally and Justin Lewis, *Enlightened Racism: The Cosby Show, Audiences, and the Myth of the American Dream* (Boulder, Colo.: Westview Press, 1992).

141. Jhally and Lewis, *Enlightened Racism*.

142. Parenti, *Make-Believe Media*.

143. MacDonald, *Blacks and White TV*.

144. Williams, *Playing the Race Card*.

145. Moore, "Blackface in Prime Time."

146. MacDonald, *Blacks and White TV*.

147. MacDonald, *Blacks and White TV*, 223.

148. Bogle, *Toms, Coons, Mulattoes, Mammies, and Bucks*.

149. Snead, *White Screens, Black Images*.

150. J. Ronald Green, "'Twoness' in the Style of Oscar Micheaux," in *Black American Cinema*, ed. Manthia Diawara, 26–48 (New York: Routledge, 1993).

151. Thomas Cripps, "Film," in *Split Image: African Americans in the Mass Media* (Washington, D.C.: Howard University Press, 1990).

152. MacDonald, *Blacks and White TV*.

153. MacDonald, *Blacks and White TV*.

154. Robin R. Means Coleman, "Prospects for Locating Racial Democracy in Media: The NAACP Network Television Boycott," *Qualitative Research Reports in Communication* 3(2) (2002): 25–31.

155. MacDonald, *Blacks and White TV*.

156. Bogle, *Toms, Coons, Mulattoes, Mammies, and Bucks*.

157. Cripps, "Film."

158. Cripps, "Film."

159. Kathryn C. Montgomery, *Target: Prime Time; Advocacy Groups and the Struggle over Entertainment Television* (New York: Oxford University Press, 1989).

160. MacDonald, *Blacks and White TV.*

161. MacDonald, *Blacks and White TV.*

162. Montgomery, *Target.*

163. MacDonald, *Blacks and White TV.*

164. Montgomery, *Target.*

165. Dates and Barlow, "Commercial Television."

166. MacDonald, *Blacks and White TV.*

167. Montgomery, *Target,* 129.

168. Reid, *Redefining Black Film.*

169. Manthia Diawara, "Black American Cinema: The New Realism," in *Black American Cinema,* ed. Manthia Diawara, 3–25 (New York: Routledge, 1993).

170. Snead, *White Screens, Black Images,* 111.

171. Snead, *White Screens, Black Images.*

172. Snead, *White Screens, Black Images.*

173. Green, "'Twoness' in the Style of Oscar Micheaux."

174. Reid, *Redefining Black Film.*

175. Snead, *White Screens, Black Images.*

176. Robert Skalar, *Movie-Made America: A Cultural History of American Movies* (New York: Vintage Books, 1994).

177. Tommy L. Lott, *The Invention of Race: Black Culture and Politics of Representation* (Malden, Mass.: Blackwell Publishers, 1999).

178. Toni Cade Bambara, "Reading the Signs, Empowering the Eye: *Daughters of the Dust* and the Black Independent Cinema Movement," in *Black American Cinema,* ed. Manthia Diawara, 118–44 (New York: Routledge, 1993); Reid, *Redefining Black Film.*

179. Bambara, "Reading the Signs, Empowering the Eye"; Ntongela Masilela, "The Los Angeles School of Black Filmmakers," in *Black American Cinema,* ed. Manthia Diawara, 107–17 (New York: Routledge, 1993.

180. Miles, *Seeing Is Believing,* 128.

181. Miles, *Seeing Is Believing,* 128.

182. Reid, *Redefining Black Film,* 131.

183. Reid, *Redefining Black Film*; Clyde Taylor, "New U.S. Black Cinema," in *Movies and Mass Culture,* ed. John Belton, 231–46 (New Brunswick, N.J.: Rutgers University Press, 1996).

184. Lott, *The Invention of Race.*

185. Opposing views are taken by William A. Harris, "Cultural Engineering and the Films of Spike Lee," in *Mediated Messages and African-American Culture: Contemporary Issues,* ed. Venise T. Berry and Carmen L. Manning-Miller, 3–23 (Thousand Oaks, Calif.: Sage Publications, 1996); Burks, "Intimations of Invisibility," and Reid, *Redefining Black Film.*

186. Cripps, "Film," 166.

187. Reid, *Redefining Black Film.*

188. Burks, "Intimations of Invisibility"; Jones, "The New Ghetto Aesthetic"; Reid, *Redefining Black Film.*

189. Bogle, *Toms, Coons, Mulattoes, Mammies, and Bucks.*

190. Darren W. Davis and Christian Davenport, "The Political and Social Relevancy of Malcolm X: The Stability of African American Political Attitudes," *Journal of Politics* 59(2) (1997): 550–64.

191. Rocchio, *Reel Racism.*

192. Bogle, *Toms, Coons, Mulattoes, Mammies, and Bucks.*

193. Jones, "The New Ghetto Aesthetic."

194. Bogle, *Toms, Coons, Mulattoes, Mammies, and Bucks.*

195. Diawara, "Black American Cinema."

196. Burks, "Intimations of Invisibility."

197. Reid, *Redefining Black Film.*

198. Bambara, "Reading the Signs, Empowering the Eye," 121.

199. Bogle, *Toms, Coons, Mulattoes, Mammies, and Bucks*.

CHAPTER 4

1. Clint C. Wilson and Félix Gutiérrez, *Race, Multiculturalism, and the Media: From Mass Communication to Class Communication* (Thousand Oaks, Calif.: Sage Publications, 1995).

2. Ward Churchill, "Fantasies of the Master Race: Categories of Stereotyping of American Indians in Film," in *Film and Theory: An Anthology*, ed. Robert Stam and Toby Miller, 697–703 (Malden, Mass.: Blackwell Publishers, 2000), 697.

3. Jeffrey Walker, "Deconstructing an American Myth: *The Last of the Mohicans* (1992)," in *Hollywood's Indian: The Portrayal of the Native American in Film*, ed. Peter C. Rollins and John E. O'Connor, 170–86 (Lexington: University of Kentucky Press, 1998), 174.

4. Ward Churchill, *Fantasies of the Master Race: Literature, Cinema and the Colonization of American Indians* (San Francisco: City Lights Books, 1998).

5. Martin Barker and Roger Sabin, *The Lasting of the Mohicans: History of an American Myth* (Jackson: University Press of Mississippi, 1995).

6. Haney Geiogamah (Kiowa) and D. Michael Pavel (Skokomish), "Developing Television for American Indian and Alaska Native Children in the Late 20th Century," in *Children and Television: Images in a Changing Sociocultural World*, ed. Gordon L. Berry and Joy Keiko Asamen, 191–204 (Newbury Park, Calif.: Sage Publications, 1993).

7. Screen Actor Guild Employment Statistics, press release, July 1, 2002, available at http://actorsnw.com/articles/sag070101.php (accessed July 7, 2004).

8. Annette M. Taylor, "Cultural Heritage in *Northern Exposure*," in *Dressing in Feathers: The Construction of the Indian in American Popular Culture*, ed. S. Elizabeth Bird, 229–44 (Boulder, Colo.: Westview Press, 1996).

9. S. Elizabeth Bird, "Gendered Construction of the American Indian in Popular Media," *Journal of Communication* 49(3) (1999): 61–83.

10. Taylor, "Cultural Heritage in *Northern Exposure*."

11. Lynn Elber, "Study: TV Diversity Still Lags," Associated Press report, June 4, 2002, available on the Children NOW website at www.childrennow.org/newsroom/news-02/cam-ra-6-4-02.htm (accessed July 7, 2004).

12. Geiogamah and Pavel, "Developing Television for American Indian and Alaska Native Children in the Late 20th Century."

13. Taylor, "Cultural Heritage in *Northern Exposure*," 239.

14. Taylor, "Cultural Heritage in *Northern Exposure*," 239.

15. Churchill, *Fantasies of the Master Race*; Churchill, "Fantasies of the Master Race."

16. Churchill, "Fantasies of the Master Race," 698.

17. Michael J. Riley, "Trapped in the History of Film: Racial Conflict and Allure in *The Vanishing American*," in *Hollywood's Indian: The Portrayal of the Native American in Film*, ed. Peter C. Rollins and John E. O'Connor, 58–72 (Lexington: University of Kentucky Press, 1998), 67.

18. Churchill, *Fantasies of the Master Race*.

19. S. M. Leuthold, "Native American Responses to the Western," *American Indian Culture and Research Journal* 19(1) (1995): 153–89; J. Tompkin, *West of Everything* (New York: Oxford University Press, 1992).

20. Churchill, *Fantasies of the Master Race*; Ken Nolley, "The Representation of Conquest: John Ford and the Hollywood Indian, 1939–1964," in *Hollywood's Indian: The Portrayal of the*

Native American in Film, ed. Peter C. Rollins and John E. O'Connor, 73–90 (Lexington: University of Kentucky Press, 1998).

21. Churchill, *Fantasies of the Master Race.*

22. Bird, "Gendered Construction of the American Indian in Popular Media."

23. Churchill, "Fantasies of the Master Race."

24. Churchill, *Fantasies of the Master Race*, 175.

25. Ted Jojola, "Absurd Reality II: Hollywood Goes to the Indians," in *Hollywood's Indian: The Portrayal of the Native American in Film*, ed. Peter C. Rollins and John E. O'Connor, 12–26 (Lexington: University of Kentucky Press, 1998), 12.

26. Nolley, "The Representation of Conquest."

27. Gretchen M. Bataille and Bob Hicks, "American Indians in Popular Films," in *Beyond the Stars: Stock Characters in American Popular Film*, ed. Paul Loukides and Linda K. Fuller, 9–22 (Bowling Green, Ohio: Bowling Green State University Press, 1990).

28. Bird, "Gendered Construction of the American Indian in Popular Media."

29. Jojola, "Absurd Reality II."

30. Churchill, *Fantasies of the Master Race*, 174.

31. Sherman Alexie, *Smoke Signals* (New York: Hyperion, 1998), 158.

32. Nolley, "The Representation of Conquest."

33. Eric Gary Anderson, "Driving the Red Road: *Powwow Highway* (1989)," in *Hollywood's Indian: The Portrayal of the Native American in Film*, ed. Peter C. Rollins and John E. O'Connor, 137–52 (Lexington: University of Kentucky Press, 1998).

34. Bird, "Gendered Construction of the American Indian in Popular Media."

35. Wilson and Gutiérrez, *Race, Multiculturalism, and the Media*, 95.

36. Nolley, "The Representation of Conquest."

37. Anderson, "Driving the Red Road"; Churchill, *Fantasies of the Master Race*; Margo Kasdan and Susan Tavernetti, "Native Americans in a Revisionist Western: *Little Big Man* (1970)," in *Hollywood's Indian: The Portrayal of the Native American in Film*, ed. Peter C. Rollins and John E. O'Connor, 121–36 (Lexington: University of Kentucky Press, 1998); Hernán Vera and Andrew M. Gordon, *Screen Saviors: Hollywood Fictions of Whiteness* (Lanham, Md.: Rowman & Littlefield, 2003).

38. Anderson, "Driving the Red Road"; Vera and Gordon, *Screen Saviors.*

39. Robert F. Berkhofer Jr., *The White Man's Indian: Images of the American Indian from Columbus to the Present* (New York: Alfred A. Knopf, 1978), xv.

40. Berkhofer, *The White Man's Indian*, 27–28.

41. Berkhofer, *The White Man's Indian.*

42. Berkhofer, *The White Man's Indian.*

43. Wilson and Gutiérrez, *Race, Multiculturalism, and the Media.*

44. Barker and Sabin, *The Lasting of the Mohicans.*

45. James A. Sandos and Larry E. Burgess, "The Hollywood Indian versus Native Americans: *Tell Them Willie Boy Is Here*," in *Hollywood's Indian: The Portrayal of the Native American in Film*, ed. Peter C. Rollins and John E. O'Connor, 107–20 (Lexington: University of Kentucky Press, 1998).

46. Bird, "Gendered Construction of the American Indian in Popular Media."

47. Frank Manchel, "Cultural Confusion: *Broken Arrow* (1950)," in *Hollywood's Indian: The Portrayal of the Native American in Film*, ed. Peter C. Rollins and John E. O'Connor (Lexington: University of Kentucky Press, 1998).

48. Barker and Sabin, *The Lasting of the Mohicans.*

49. Sandos and Burgess, "The Hollywood Indian," 113.

50. Raymond F. Stedman, *Shadows of the Indian: Stereotypes in American Culture* (Norman: University of Oklahoma Press, 1982).

51. Bird, "Gendered Construction of the American Indian in Popular Media."

52. Wilson and Gutiérrez, *Race, Multiculturalism, and the Media*, 95.

53. Manchel, "Cultural Confusion."

54. Sandos and Burgess, "The Hollywood Indian," 113.

55. Bird, "Gendered Construction of the American Indian in Popular Media."

56. Bird, "Gendered Construction of the American Indian in Popular Media."

57. Pauline Turner Strong, "Playing Indian in the 1990s: Pocahontas and the Indian in the Cupboard," in *Hollywood's Indian: The Portrayal of the Native American in Film*, ed. Peter C. Rollins and John E. O'Connor, 187–205 (Lexington: University of Kentucky Press, 1998).

58. Bird, "Gendered Construction of the American Indian in Popular Media."

59. S. Elizabeth Bird, "Introduction: Constructing the Indian, 1830–1990s," in *Dressing in Feathers: The Construction of the Indian in American Popular Culture*, ed. S. Elizabeth Bird, 1–12 (Boulder, Colo.: Westview Press, 1996), 2.

60. Joseph Natoli, *Hauntings: Popular Film and American Culture 1990–1992* (Albany: State University of New York Press, 1994).

61. Kasdan and Tavernetti, "Native Americans in a Revisionist Western," 122.

62. Barker and Sabin, *The Lasting of the Mohicans*, 14.

63. Barker and Sabin, *The Lasting of the Mohicans*.

64. Bird, "Gendered Construction of the American Indian in Popular Media."

65. Jojola, "Absurd Reality II."

66. Jojola, "Absurd Reality II," 21.

67. Taylor, "Cultural Heritage in *Northern Exposure*," 237.

68. Kasdan and Tavernetti, "Native Americans in a Revisionist Western," 124.

69. Kasdan and Tavernetti, "Native Americans in a Revisionist Western," 1998.

70. Bird, "Gendered Construction of the American Indian in Popular Media."

71. Kasdan and Tavernetti, "Native Americans in a Revisionist Western."

72. Barker and Sabin, *The Lasting of the Mohicans*, 12.

73. Churchill, *Fantasies of the Master Race*.

74. John E. O'Connor, "The White Man's Indian: An Institutional Approach," in *Hollywood's Indian: The Portrayal of the Native American in Film*, ed. Peter C. Rollins and John E. O'Connor, 27–38 (Lexington: University of Kentucky Press, 1998), 33.

75. Churchill, *Fantasies of the Master Race*.

76. Nolley, "The Representation of Conquest."

77. Nolley, "The Representation of Conquest."

78. O'Connor, "The White Man's Indian."

79. Churchill, *Fantasies of the Master Race*.

80. Nolley, "The Representation of Conquest."

81. Churchill, *Fantasies of the Master Race*.

82. Churchill, *Fantasies of the Master Race*.

83. Barker and Sabin, *The Lasting of the Mohicans*.

84. Churchill, *Fantasies of the Master Race*.

85. Riley, "Trapped in the History of Film," 70.

86. Barker and Sabin, *The Lasting of the Mohicans*, 13.

87. Anderson, "Driving the Red Road."

88. Churchill, *Fantasies of the Master Race*.

89. Nolley, "The Representation of Conquest."

90. Churchill, *Fantasies of the Master Race*.

91. Sandos and Burgess, "The Hollywood Indian."

92. Churchill, *Fantasies of the Master Race*.

93. Bataille and Hicks, "American Indians in Popular Films"; O'Connor, "The White Man's Indian."

94. Bataille and Hicks, "American Indians in Popular Films."

95. Churchill, *Fantasies of the Master Race*.

96. Anderson, "Driving the Red Road."

97. Robert Kolker, *Film, Form, and Culture* (Boston: McGraw-Hill College, 1999).

98. Kasdan and Tavernetti, "Native Americans in a Revisionist Western."

99. Robert Baird, "Going Indian: Discovery, Adoption, and Renaming toward a 'True America,' from *Deerslayer* to *Dances with Wolves*," in *Dressing in Feathers: The Construction of the Indian in American Popular Culture*, ed. S. Elizabeth Bird, 195–209 (Boulder, Colo.: Westview Press, 1996).

100. Interview with Steven Rockwell, University of Michigan at Flint, August 6, 2004.

101. Roberta E. Pearson, "The Revenge of Rain-in-the-Face? Or, Custers and Indians on the Silent Screen," in *The Birth of Whiteness: Race and the Emergence of U.S. Cinema*, ed. Daniel Bernardi, 273–99 (New Brunswick, N.J.: Rutgers University Press, 1996), 275.

102. Berkhofer, *The White Man's Indian*, 31.

103. Barker and Sabin, *The Lasting of the Mohicans*.

104. Kolker, *Film, Form, and Culture*.

105. Wilson and Gutiérrez, *Race, Multiculturalism, and the Media*, 63.

106. Churchill, *Fantasies of the Master Race*.

107. Manchel, "Cultural Confusion," 97.

108. Nolley, "The Representation of Conquest," 80.

109. Bird, "Gendered Construction of the American Indian in Popular Media."

110. Manchel, "Cultural Confusion," 97.

111. Manchel, "Cultural Confusion," 101.

112. Nolley, "The Representation of Conquest."

113. Sandos and Burgess, "The Hollywood Indian," 114.

114. Kasdan and Tavernetti, "Native Americans in a Revisionist Western," 125, 127.

115. Kasdan and Tavernetti, "Native Americans in a Revisionist Western," 130.

116. Kasdan and Tavernetti, "Native Americans in a Revisionist Western," 128.

117. Robert Skalar, *Movie-Made America: A Cultural History of American Movies* (New York: Vintage Books, 1994).

118. Kasdan and Tavernetti, "Native Americans in a Revisionist Western."

119. Churchill, *Fantasies of the Master Race*.

120. Strong, "Playing Indian."

121. Baird, "Going Indian."

122. Bird, "Gendered Construction of the American Indian in Popular Media."

123. Bird, "Introduction," 2.

124. S. Elizabeth Bird, "Not My Fantasy: The Persistence of Indian Imagery in Dr. Quinn, Medicine Woman," in *Dressing in Feathers: The Construction of the Indian in American Popular Culture*, ed. S. Elizabeth Bird, 245–62 (Boulder, Colo.: Westview Press, 1996), 258.

125. Churchill, *Fantasies of the Master Race*.

126. Jose E. Limón, "Stereotyping and Chicano Resistance: An Historical Dimension (1973)," in *Chicanos and Film: Representation and Resistance*, ed. Chon A. Noriega, 3–17 (Minneapolis: University of Minnesota Press, 1992).

127. Robert Stam, "Permutations of Difference: Introduction," in *Film and Theory: An Anthology*, ed. Robert Stam and Toby Miller, 661–68 (Malden, Mass.: Blackwell Publishers, 2000).

128. Pamela Wilson, "Confronting 'the Indian Problem': Media Discourses of Race, Ethnicity, Nation, and Empire in 1950s America," in *Living Color: Race and Television in the United States*, ed. Sasha Torres, 35–61 (Durham, N.C.: Duke University Press, 1998).

129. O'Connor, "The White Man's Indian."

130. O'Connor, "The White Man's Indian," 34.

131. Jojola, "Absurd Reality II."

132. Neil A. Engelhart, "Logo or Libel? Chief Wahoo, Multiculturalism, and the Politics of Sports Mascots," in *Mass Politics: The Politics of Popular Culture*, ed. Daniel M. Shea, 63–74 (New York: St. Martin's Press, 1999).

133. Victoria Smith Holden, William Holden, and Gary Davis, "The Sports Team Nickname: Controversy: A Study in Community and Race Relations," in *Facing Difference: Race, Gender,*

and Mass Media, ed. Shirley Biagi and Marilyn Kern-Foxworth, 69–75 (Thousand Oaks, Calif.: Pine Forge Press, 1997).

134. Engelhart, "Logo or Libel?" 68.

135. Marilyn Kern-Foxworth, "Aunt Jemima, the Frito Bandito, and Crazy Horse: Selling Stereotypes American Style," in *Mass Politics: The Politics of Popular Culture*, ed. Daniel M. Shea, 81–90 (New York: St. Martin's Press, 1999).

136. Kern-Foxworth, "Aunt Jemima, the Frito Bandito, and Crazy Horse: Selling Stereotypes American Style."

137. Jojola, "Absurd Reality II," 21.

138. Jojola, "Absurd Reality II."

139. Geiogamah and Pavel, "Developing Television," 201.

140. Geiogamah and Pavel, "Developing Television."

141. Bataille and Hicks, "American Indians in Popular Films," 14.

142. Anderson, "Driving the Red Road."

143. Anderson, "Driving the Red Road"; Sandos and Burgess, "The Hollywood Indian."

144. Riley, "Trapped in the History of Film," 64.

145. Skalar, *Movie-Made America*.

146. Sandos and Burgess, "The Hollywood Indian."

147. Bird, "Gendered Construction of the American Indian in Popular Media."

148. Mara Donaldson, "Teaching Apocalyptic, Teaching Apocalyptically: A Metaphorical-Pedagogy for the End of the World," in *Teaching Apocalypse*, ed. Tina Pippin (Atlanta: Scholars Press, 1999).

149. Alexie, *Smoke Signals*, 160.

150. Bird, "Gendered Construction of the American Indian in Popular Media."

151. Churchill, "Fantasies of the Master Race," 703.

CHAPTER 5

1. Bradley S. Greenberg and Jeffrey E. Brand, "Minorities and the Mass Media: 1970s to 1990s," in *Media Effects: Advances in Theory and Research*, ed. Jennings Bryant and Dolf Zillmann, 273–314 (Hillsdale, N.J.: Lawrence Erlbaum Associates, 1994).

2. S. Robert Lichter and Daniel R. Amundson, *Distorted Reality* (Washington, D.C.: Center for Media and Public Affairs, 1994).

3. Joan L. Conners, "Color TV? Diversity in Prime-Time TV," in *Race/Gender/Media: Considering Diversity across Audiences, Content, and Producers*, ed. Rebecca Ann Lind, 206–12 (Boston: Pearson Education, 2004).

4. Screen Actor Guild Employment Statistics, press release, July 1, 2002, available at http://actorsnw.com/articles/sag070101.php (accessed July 7, 2004).

5. Federico A. Subervi-Vélez and Susan Colsant, "The Television Worlds of Latino Children," in *Children and Television: Images in a Changing Sociocultural World*, ed. Gordon L. Berry and Joy Keiko Asamen, 215–28 (Newbury Park, Calif.: Sage Publications, 1993).

6. Chon Noriega, "Citizen Chicano: The Trials and Titillations of Ethnicity in the American Cinema, 1935–1962," in *Latin Looks: Images of Latinas and Latinos in the U.S. Media*, ed. Clara E. Rodríguez, 81–103 (Boulder, Colo.: Westview Press, 1997).

7. Richie Pérez, "From Assimilation to Annihilation: Puerto Rican Images in U.S. Films," in *Latin Looks: Images of Latinas and Latinos in the U.S. Media*, ed. Clara E. Rodríguez, 142–63 (Boulder, Colo.: Westview Press, 1997).

8. Conners, "Color TV?"

9. Marco Portales, *Crowding Out Latinos: Mexican Americans in the Public Consciousness* (Philadelphia: Temple University Press, 2000).

10. Carlos E. Cortés, "Chicanos in Film: History of the Image," in *Latin Looks: Images of Latinas and Latinos in the U.S. Media*, ed. Clara E. Rodríguez, 121–41 (Boulder, Colo.: Westview Press, 1997).

11. Cortés, "Chicanos in Film," 134.

12. Linda Williams, "Type and Stereotype: Chicano Images in Film," in *Latin Looks: Images of Latinas and Latinos in the U.S. Media*, ed. Clara E. Rodríguez, 214–20 (Boulder, Colo.: Westview Press, 1997), 216.

13. Conners, "Color TV?" The percentage of characters identified as "negative" during the fall 1999 season were 27.3 percent for Hispanics, 22.8 percent for whites, 8.1 percent for African Americans, and 9.15 for Asian Americans.

14. Clint C. Wilson and Félix Gutiérrez, *Race, Multiculturalism, and the Media: From Mass Communication to Class Communication* (Thousand Oaks, Calif.: Sage Publications, 1995).

15. Chon Noriega, "Introduction," in *Chicanos and Film: Representation and Resistance*, ed. Chon A. Noriega, xi–xxvi (Minneapolis: University of Minnesota Press, 1992).

16. Charles Ramírez Berg, "Stereotyping in Films in General and of the Hispanic in Particular," in *Latin Looks: Images of Latinas and Latinos in the U.S. Media*, ed. Clara E. Rodríguez, 104–20 (Boulder, Colo.: Westview Press, 1997), 113.

17. Pérez, "From Assimilation to Annihilation," 148.

18. Cortés, "Chicanos in Film"; Berg, "Stereotyping in Films in General and of the Hispanic in Particular"; Clara E. Rodríguez, "Keeping It Reel? Films of the 1980s and 1990s," in *Latin Looks: Images of Latinas and Latinos in the U.S. Media*, ed. Clara E. Rodríguez, 180–84 (Boulder, Colo.: Westview Press, 1997).

19. Berg, "Stereotyping in Films in General and of the Hispanic in Particular."

20. Rodríguez, "Keeping It Reel?"

21. Cortés, "Chicanos in Film," 138.

22. Pérez, "From Assimilation to Annihilation."

23. Charles Ramírez Berg, *Latino Images in Film: Stereotypes, Subversion, and Resistance* (Austin: University of Texas Press, 2002).

24. Pérez, "From Assimilation to Annihilation."

25. Noriega, "Citizen Chicano," 90.

26. Alberto Sandoval Sánchez, "*West Side Story*: A Puerto Rican Reading of 'America,'" in *Latin Looks: Images of Latinas and Latinos in the U.S. Media*, ed. Clara E. Rodríguez 164–79 (Boulder, Colo.: Westview Press, 1997), 167.

27. Sánchez, "*West Side Story*."

28. Portales, *Crowding Out Latinos*.

29. Berg, "Stereotyping in Films in General and of the Hispanic in Particular," 114.

30. Pérez, "From Assimilation to Annihilation," 154.

31. Lillian Jiménez, "From the Margin to the Center: Puerto Rican Cinema in New York," in *Latin Looks: Images of Latinas and Latinos in the U.S. Media*, ed. Clara E. Rodríguez, 188–99 (Boulder, Colo.: Westview Press, 1997), 188.

32. Pérez, "From Assimilation to Annihilation."

33. Berg, "Stereotyping in Films in General and of the Hispanic in Particular," 115.

34. Cortés, "Chicanos in Film"; Clara E. Rodríguez, "Visual Retrospective: Latino Film Stars," in *Latin Looks: Images of Latinas and Latinos in the U.S. Media*, ed. Clara E. Rodríguez, 80–84 (Boulder, Colo.: Westview Press, 1997).

35. Jiménez, "From the Margin to the Center."

36. Antonio Rios-Bustamante, "Latino Participation in the Hollywood Film Industry, 1911–1945," in *Chicanos and Film: Representation and Resistance*, ed. Chon A. Noriega, 18–28 (Minneapolis: University of Minnesota Press, 1997).

37. Berg, *Latino Images in Film*.

38. Berg, *Latino Images in Film*.

39. Cortés, "Chicanos in Film," 83.

40. Pérez, "From Assimilation to Annihilation"; Rodriguez, "Keeping It Reel?"; Rosa Linda Fregoso, *The Bronze Screen: Chicana and Chicano Film Culture* (Minneapolis: University of Minnesota Press, 1993).

41. Cortés, "Chicanos in Film."

42. Cortés, "Chicanos in Film," 129–30.

43. Berg, "Stereotyping in Films in General and of the Hispanic in Particular."

44. Cortés, "Chicanos in Film."

45. Dolores Del Rio, at www.infoplease.com/ipea/A0759900.html (accessed July 9, 2004).

46. Berg, "Stereotyping in Films in General and of the Hispanic in Particular."

47. Berg, "Stereotyping in Films in General and of the Hispanic in Particular," 115.

48. Berg, "Stereotyping in Films in General and of the Hispanic in Particular"; Cortés, "Chicanos in Film."

49. Cortés, "Chicanos in Film."

50. Berg, "Stereotyping in Films in General and of the Hispanic in Particular," 113.

51. Rodríguez, "Keeping It Reel?" 80–81.

52. Cortés, "Chicanos in Film."

53. Pérez, "From Assimilation to Annihilation."

54. Berg, *Latino Images in Film*.

55. Cortés, "Chicanos in Film."

56. Cortés, "Chicanos in Film."

57. Berg, "Stereotyping in Films in General and of the Hispanic in Particular."

58. Charles Ramírez Berg, "Bordertown, the Assimilation Narrative and the Chicano Social Problem Film," in *Chicanos and Film: Representation and Resistance*, ed. Chon A. Noriega (Minneapolis: University of Minnesota Press, 1992), 33.

59. Pérez, "From Assimilation to Annihilation," 152.

60. Pérez, "From Assimilation to Annihilation."

61. Fregoso, *The Bronze Screen*.

62. Berg, "Bordertown, the Assimilation Narrative and the Chicano Social Problem Film."

63. Pérez, "From Assimilation to Annihilation," 152.

64. Berg, "Bordertown, the Assimilation Narrative and the Chicano Social Problem Film."

65. Berg, "Bordertown, the Assimilation Narrative and the Chicano Social Problem Film," 32.

66. Berg, "Stereotyping in Films in General and of the Hispanic in Particular."

67. Berg, "Bordertown, the Assimilation Narrative and the Chicano Social Problem Film"; Noriega, "Citizen Chicano."

68. Berg, "Bordertown, the Assimilation Narrative and the Chicano Social Problem Film," 33.

69. Pérez, "From Assimilation to Annihilation."

70. Sánchez, "*West Side Story.*"

71. Sánchez, "*West Side Story.*"

72. Pérez, "From Assimilation to Annihilation," 157.

73. Pérez, "From Assimilation to Annihilation," 157.

74. Limón, "Stereotyping and Chicano Resistance."

75. Rios-Bustamante, "Latino Participation in the Hollywood Film Industry, 1911–1945."

76. Jiménez, "From the Margin to the Center," 189.

77. Pérez, "From Assimilation to Annihilation," 156.

78. Pérez, "From Assimilation to Annihilation," 157.

79. Pérez, "From Assimilation to Annihilation."

80. Fregoso, *The Bronze Screen*.

81. Pérez, "From Assimilation to Annihilation," 162.

82. Santiago Nieves and Frank Algarin, "Two Film Reviews: *My Family/Mi Familia* and

The Perez Family," in *Latin Looks: Images of Latinas and Latinos in the U.S. Media*, ed. Clara E. Rodríguez, 221–24 (Boulder, Colo.: Westview Press, 1997), 223.

83. Fregoso, *The Bronze Screen.*

84. Fregoso, *The Bronze Screen*, xiv–xv.

85. Noriega, "Introduction."

86. Fregoso, *The Bronze Screen.*

87. Fregoso, *The Bronze Screen*, 8.

88. Fregoso, *The Bronze Screen.*

89. Noriega, "Citizen Chicano."

90. Fregoso, *The Bronze Screen.*

91. Jiménez, "From the Margin to the Center," 188.

92. Jiménez, "From the Margin to the Center," 198.

93. Fregoso, *The Bronze Screen.*

94. Fernando Delgado, "Moving beyond the Screen: Hollywood and Mexican American Stereotypes," in *Cultural Diversity and the U.S. Media*, ed. Yahya R. Kamalipour and Theresa Carilli, 169–79 (Albany: State University of New York Press, 1998).

95. Berg, "Stereotyping in Films in General and of the Hispanic in Particular."

96. Subervi-Vélez and Colsant, "The Television Worlds of Latino Children."

97. Fregoso, *The Bronze Screen.*

CHAPTER 6

1. Mark P. Orbe, Ruth Seymour, and Mee-Eun Kang, "Ethnic Humor and Ingroup/Outgroup Positioning: Explicating Viewer Perceptions of *All-American Girl*," in *Cultural Diversity and the U.S. Media*, ed. Yahya R. Kamalipour and Theresa Carilli, 125–36 (Albany: State University of New York Press, 1998); Darrell Y. Hamamoto, *Monitoring Peril: Asian Americans and the Politics of TV Representation* (Minneapolis: University of Minnesota Press, 1994); Media Action Network for Asian Americans (MANAA), "A Memo from MANAA to Hollywood: Asian Stereotypes, Restrictive Portrayals of Asians in the Media and How to Balance Them," 1998, available at www.manaa.org (accessed February 20, 2005).

2. Hamamoto, *Monitoring Peril.*

3. Hamamoto, *Monitoring Peril*; Clint C. Wilson and Félix Gutiérrez, *Race, Multiculturalism, and the Media: From Mass Communication to Class Communication* (Thousand Oaks, Calif.: Sage Publications, 1995).

4. Wilson and Gutiérrez, *Race, Multiculturalism, and the Media.*

5. Orbe, Seymour, and Kang, "Ethnic Humor and Ingroup/Outgroup Positioning."

6. Jessica Hagedorn, "Asian Women in Film: No Joy, No Luck," in *Facing Difference: Race, Gender, and Mass Media*, ed. Shirley Biagi and Marilyn Kern-Foxworth, 32–37 (Thousand Oaks, Calif.: Pine Forge Press, 1997); MANAA, "A Memo from MANAA to Hollywood"; Wilson and Gutiérrez, *Race, Multiculturalism, and the Media.*

7. Orbe, Seymour, and Kang, "Ethnic Humor and Ingroup/Outgroup Positioning," 125.

8. Robert Kolker, *Film, Form, and Culture* (Boston: McGraw-Hill College, 1999).

9. Hagedorn, "Asian Women in Film."

10. Wilson and Gutiérrez, *Race, Multiculturalism, and the Media.*

11. Yoko Yoshikawa, "The Heat Is on *Miss Saigon* Coalition: Organizing across Race and Sexuality," in *The State of Asian America: Activism and Resistance in the 1990s*, ed. Karin Auguilar–San Juan, 275–94 (Boston: South End Press, 1994).

12. Esther Ghymn, "Asians in Film and Other Media," in *Asian American Studies: Identity, Images, Issues Past and Present*, ed. Esther Mikyung Ghymn, 135–50 (New York: Peter Lang Publishing, 2000).

13. Hamamoto, *Monitoring Peril*, 60.

14. Ghymn, "Asians in Film and Other Media."

15. Hamamoto, *Monitoring Peril*, 60.

16. Hamamoto, *Monitoring Peril*.

17. Chyng Feng Sun, "Ling Woo in Historical Context: The New Face of Asian American Stereotypes on Television," in *Gender, Race, and Class in Media: A Text-Reader*, ed. Gail Dines and Jean M. Humez, 2nd ed., 656–64 (Thousand Oaks, Calif.: Sage Publications, 2003).

18. Screen Actor Guild Employment Statistics, press release, July 1, 2002, available at http://actorsnw.com/articles/sag070101.php (accessed July 7, 2004).

19. Joan L. Conners, "Color TV? Diversity in Prime-Time TV," in *Race/Gender/Media: Considering Diversity across Audiences, Content, and Producers*, ed. Rebecca Ann Lind, 206–12 (Boston: Pearson Education, 2004).

20. Orbe, Seymour, and Kang, "Ethnic Humor and Ingroup/Outgroup Positioning."

21. Hamamoto, *Monitoring Peril*.

22. Wilson and Gutiérrez, *Race, Multiculturalism, and the Media*, 94.

23. Hamamoto, *Monitoring Peril*.

24. Dick Stromgren, "The Chinese Syndrome: The Evolving Image of Chinese and Chinese-Americans in Hollywood Films," in *Beyond the Stars: Stock Characters in American Popular Film*, ed. Paul Loukides and Linda K. Fuller, 61–77 (Bowling Green, Ohio: Bowling Green State University Press, 1990), 66.

25. Hamamoto, *Monitoring Peril*; Wilson and Gutiérrez, *Race, Multiculturalism, and the Media*.

26. Wilson and Gutiérrez, *Race, Multiculturalism, and the Media*.

27. Stromgren, "The Chinese Syndrome."

28. Ghymn, "Asians in Film and Other Media."

29. Wilson and Gutiérrez, *Race, Multiculturalism, and the Media*, 91.

30. Ralph R. Donald, "Savages, Swine, and Buffoons: Hollywood Stereotypes of the Japanese, Germans, and Italians during World War II," in *Race/Gender/Media: Considering Diversity across Audiences, Content, and Producers*, ed. Rebecca Ann Lind, 191–98 (Boston: Pearson Education, 2004).

31. Donald, "Savages, Swine, and Buffoons."

32. Hamamoto, *Monitoring Peril*.

33. Hamamoto, *Monitoring Peril*, 50.

34. Peter X. Feng, *Identities in Motion: Asian American Film and Video* (Durham, N.C.: Duke University Press, 2002).

35. Richard Fung, "Seeing Yellow: Asian Identities in Film and Video," in *The State of Asian America: Activism and Resistance in the 1990s*, ed. Karin Auguilar–San Juan, 161–71 (Boston: South End Press, 1994).

36. Patti Iiyama and Harry H. L. Kitano, "Asian Americans and the Media," in *Television and the Socialization of the Minority Child*, ed. Gordon L. Berry and Claudia Mitchell-Kernan, 151–86 (New York: Academic Press, 1982).

37. Laura Hyun-Yi Kang, "The Desiring of Asian Female Bodies: Interracial Romance and Cinematic Subjection," in *Screening Asian Americans*, ed. Peter X. Feng, 71–100 (New Brunswick, N.J.: Rutgers University Press, 2002), 77.

38. Hagedorn, "Asian Women in Film," 33.

39. Hagedorn, "Asian Women in Film."

40. Hamamoto, *Monitoring Peril*, 42–47.

41. Mark Williams, "Entertaining 'Difference': Strains of Orientalism in Early Los Angeles Television," in *Living Color: Race and Television in the United States*, ed. Sasha Torres, 12–34 (Durham, N.C.: Duke University Press, 1998).

42. MANAA, "A Memo from MANAA to Hollywood," 3.

43. Hamamoto, *Monitoring Peril*.

44. Hamamoto, *Monitoring Peril*.

45. Hamamoto, *Monitoring Peril*, 25.

46. MANAA, "A Memo from MANAA to Hollywood," 4.

47. Tracey Owens Patton, "Ally McBeal and Her Homes: The Reification of White Stereotypes of the Other," *Journal of Black Studies* 32(2) (2001): 229–60.

48. Stromgren, "The Chinese Syndrome."

49. Hamamoto, *Monitoring Peril*, 192, 193.

50. Stephanie Greco Larson, "Black Women on *All My Children*," *Journal of Popular Film and Television* 22 (1994): 44–48.

51. Yuan Shu, "Reading the Kung Fu Film in an American Context: From Bruce Lee to Jackie Chan," *Journal of Popular Film and Television* 31(2) (2003): 50–55.

52. Shasha Torres, "Introduction," in *Living Color: Race and Television in the United States*, ed. Sasha Torres, 1–11 (Durham, N.C.: Duke University Press, 1998), 3.

53. Fung, "Seeing Yellow," 169.

54. Hamamoto, *Monitoring Peril*.

55. MANAA, "A Memo from MANAA to Hollywood."

56. Larson, "Black Women on *All My Children*."

57. Hamamoto, *Monitoring Peril*; Rita Chaudhny Sethi, "Smells Like Racism: A Plan for Mobilizing against Asian-American Bias," in *The State of Asian America: Activism and Resistance in the 1990s*, ed. Karin Auguilar–San Juan, 235–50 (Boston: South End Press, 1994); Sharon Willis, *High Contrast: Race and Gender in Contemporary Hollywood Films* (Durham, N.C.: Duke University Press, 1997).

58. Hamamoto, *Monitoring Peril*.

59. Wilson and Gutiérrez, *Race, Multiculturalism, and the Media*.

60. Hamamoto, *Monitoring Peril*.

61. Kang, "The Desiring of Asian Female Bodies."

62. Iiyama and Kitano, "Asian Americans and the Media," 162.

63. Hamamoto, *Monitoring Peril*, 36 37.

64. Hamamoto, *Monitoring Peril*, 52.

65. Williams, "Entertaining 'Difference,'" 18, 20.

66. Kang, "The Desiring of Asian Female Bodies," 94.

67. Stromgren, "The Chinese Syndrome," 74.

68. Kang, "The Desiring of Asian Female Bodies."

69. Leon Hunt, *Kung Fu Cult Masters: From Bruce Lee to Crouching Tiger* (London: Wallflower Press, 2003), 158.

70. Hamamoto, *Monitoring Peril*, 46.

71. Hamamoto, *Monitoring Peril*, 45.

72. MANAA, "A Memo from MANAA to Hollywood," 1.

73. Hamamoto, *Monitoring Peril*, 71.

74. Hamamoto, *Monitoring Peril*, 160.

75. Wilson and Gutiérrez, *Race, Multiculturalism, and the Media*.

76. MANAA, "A Memo from MANAA to Hollywood."

77. Wilson and Gutiérrez, *Race, Multiculturalism, and the Media*.

78. Stromgren, "The Chinese Syndrome."

79. Yoshikawa, "The Heat Is on *Miss Saigon* Coalition."

80. Yoshikawa, "The Heat Is on *Miss Saigon* Coalition," 280.

81. Yoshikawa, "The Heat Is on *Miss Saigon* Coalition," 280.

82. Yoshikawa, "The Heat Is on *Miss Saigon* Coalition," 277.

83. Stephen Gong, "A History of Progress: Asian American Media Arts Centers, 1970–1990," in *Screening Asian Americans*, ed. Peter X. Feng, 101–10 (New Brunswick, N.J.: Rutgers University Press, 2002).

84. Fung, "Seeing Yellow," 165.

85. Stromgren, "The Chinese Syndrome."

86. George Lipsitz, "Genre Anxiety and Racial Representation in 1970s Cinema," in *Refiguring American Film Genres: History and Theory*, ed. Nick Browne, 208–32 (Berkeley: University of California Press, 1994), 229.

87. Feng, *Identities in Motion*.

88. Fung, "Seeing Yellow," 169.

89. Feng, *Identities in Motion*.

90. Hagedorn, "Asian Women in Film."

91. Ghymn, "Asians in Film and Other Media."

92. Hagedorn, "Asian Women in Film."

93. Chisun Lee, "The Ling Thing," *Village Voice* 44(48) (1999): 65.

94. Ghymn, "Asians in Film and Other Media."

95. Shu, "Reading the Kung Fu Film in an American Context," 51.

96. Gina Marchetti, "Jackie Chan and the Black Connection," in *Keyframes: Popular Cinema and Cultural Studies*, ed. Matthew Tinkcom and Amy Villarejo, 137–58 (New York: Routledge, 2001).

CHAPTER 7

1. Benjamin Page, *Who Deliberates? Mass Media in Modern Democracy* (Chicago: University of Chicago Press, 1996), 112–15.

2. Robert M. Entman, *Democracy without Citizens* (New York: Oxford University Press, 1989); Page, *Who Deliberates?*

3. Clint C. Wilson and Félix Gutiérrez, *Race, Multiculturalism, and the Media: From Mass Communication to Class Communication* (Thousand Oaks, Calif.: Sage Publications, 1995), 153.

4. Christopher P. Campbell, *Race, Myth and the News* (Thousand Oaks, Calif.: Sage Publications, 1995).

5. Wilson and Gutiérrez, *Race, Multiculturalism, and the Media*, 155.

6. Robert M. Entman and Andrew Rojecki, *The Black Image in the White Mind: Media and Race in America* (Chicago: University of Chicago Press, 2000), 63.

7. Don Heider, *White News: Why Local News Programs Don't Cover People of Color* (Mahwah, N.J.: Lawrence Erlbaum Associates, 2000); Wilson and Gutiérrez, *Race, Multiculturalism, and the Media*.

8. Wilson and Gutiérrez, *Race, Multiculturalism, and the Media*.

9. Campbell, *Race, Myth and the News*, 42.

10. Jannette L. Dates and William Barlow, "Introduction: The War of Images," in *Split Image: African Americans in the Mass Media*, ed. Jannette L. Dates and William Barlow, 1–21 (Washington, D.C.: Howard University Press, 1990).

11. Mary Ann Weston, *Native Americans in the News: Images of Indians in the Twentieth Century Press* (Westport, Conn.: Greenwood Press, 1996), 163.

12. Wilson and Gutiérrez, *Race, Multiculturalism, and the Media*, 158.

13. Weston, *Native Americans in the News*, 2.

14. Doris Graber, *Mass Media and American Politics*, 6th ed. (Washington, D.C.: Congressional Quarterly Press, 2001).

15. It is probably more accurate to say "like us" and "than us" since news is primarily conveyed to white audiences by white reporters.

16. Herbert J. Gans, *Deciding What's News: A Study of CBS Evening News, NBC Nightly News, Newsweek, and Time* (New York: Pantheon Books, 1979).

17. Stephanie Greco Larson and Martha Bailey, "ABC's 'Person of the Week': American

Values on Television News," *Journalism and Mass Communication Quarterly* 75 (1998): 487–99.

18. Wilson and Gutiérrez, *Race, Multiculturalism, and the Media*, 157.

19. Gans, *Deciding What's News*, 23.

20. Wilson and Gutiérrez, *Race, Multiculturalism, and the Media*.

21. Travis L. Dixon and Daniel Linz, "Overrepresentation and Underrepresentation of African Americans and Latinos as Lawbreakers on Television News," *Journal of Communication* 50 (2000): 131–54; Mary Beth Oliver, "Portrayals of Crime, Race, and Aggression in 'Reality-Based' Police Shows: A Content Analysis," *Journal of Broadcasting and Electronic Media* 38 (1994): 179–92.

22. Wilson and Gutiérrez, *Race, Multiculturalism, and the Media*, 157.

23. Carol Bradley Shirley, "Where Have You Been?" *Columbia Journalism Review* 31(2) (July 8, 1992): 25–26.

24. Bartholomew H. Sparrow, *Uncertain Guardians: The News Media and a Political Institution* (Baltimore: Johns Hopkins University Press, 1999), 123–24, 76.

25. Sparrow, *Uncertain Guardians*.

26. Peter Golding, "The Missing Dimension: News Media and the Management of Change," *Mass Media and Social Change*, ed. E. Katz and T. Szecsko, 63–82 (London: Sage Publications, 1981), 79.

27. Entman and Rojecki, *The Black Image in the White Mind*.

28. Jorge Quiroga, "Hispanic Voices: Is the Press Listening?" in *Latin Looks: Images of Latinas and Latinos in the U.S. Media*, ed. Clara E. Rodríguez, 36–57 (Boulder, Colo.: Westview Press, 1997); Weston, *Native Americans in the News*.

29. W. Lance Bennett, *News: The Politics of Illusion*, 2nd ed. (New York: Longman Press, 1988), 117.

30. Bennett, *News: The Politics of Illusion*.

31. Entman and Rojecki, *The Black Image in the White Mind*.

32. Gans, *Deciding What's News*, 284.

33. Gans, *Deciding What's News*.

34. Bennett, *News: The Politics of Illusion*, 14.

35. Wilson and Gutiérrez, *Race, Multiculturalism, and the Media*.

36. Entman and Rojecki, *The Black Image in the White Mind*.

37. Pamela Newkirk, *Within the Veil: Black Journalists, White Media* (New York: New York University Press, 2000).

38. Drummond, "About Face, from Alliance to Alienation"; Entman and Rojecki, *The Black Image in the White Mind*; Wilson and Gutiérrez, *Race, Multiculturalism, and the Media*.

39. Debra Gersh Hernandez, "Two Steps Forward, One Step Back," in *Facing Difference: Race, Gender, and Mass Media*, ed. Shirley Biagi and Marilyn Kern-Foxworth, 193–95 (Thousand Oaks, Calif.: Pine Forge Press, 1997); David K. Shipler, "Blacks in the Newsroom," *Columbia Journalism Review* 30 (May 6, 1998).

40. Timothy P. Fong, *The Contemporary Asian American Experience: Beyond the Model Minority* (Upper Saddle River, N.J.: Prentice Hall, 1998).

41. Virginia D. Mansfield-Richardson, *Asian Americans and the Mass Media: A Content Analysis of Twenty U.S. Newspapers and a Survey of Asian American Journalists* (unpublished Ph.D. diss., Ohio State University, 1996).

42. Peter Skerry, *Mexican Americans: The Ambivalent Minority* (Cambridge, Mass.: Harvard University Press, 1993).

43. Entman and Rojecki, *The Black Image in the White Mind*, 87.

44. Newkirk, *Within the Veil*; Shipler, "Blacks in the Newsroom."

45. Baird, "That Special Perspective They Say They Want"; Don Heider, *White News: Why*

Local News Programs Don't Cover People of Color (Mahwah, N.J.: Lawrence Erlbaum Associates, 2000).

46. Drummond, "About Face, from Alliance to Alienation."

47. Shipler, "Blacks in the Newsroom."

48. Newkirk, *Within the Veil*, 138.

49. Newkirk, *Within the Veil*.

50. Hemant Shah and Michael C. Thornton, "Racial Ideology in U.S. Mainstream News Magazine Coverage of Black-Latino Interaction, 1980–1992," *Critical Studies in Mass Communication* 11(2) (1994): 141–61.

51. Susan Herbst, *Reading Public Opinion: How Political Actors View the Democratic Process* (Chicago: University of Chicago Press, 1998).

52. David Domke, "Strategic Elites, the Press, and Race Relations," *Journal of Communication* 50 (2000): 115–40.

53. George Gerbner, Larry Gross, M. Morgan, and Nancy Signorielli, "The 'Mainstreaming' of America: Violence Profile No. 11," *Journal of Communication* 30(3) (1980): 10–29.

54. Nancy Signorielli and Michael Morgan, "Cultivation Analysis: Conceptualization and Methodology," in *Cultivation Analysis: New Directions in the Media Effects Research*, ed. Nancy Signorielli and Michael Morgan, 13–34 (Newbury Park, Calif.: Sage Publications, 1990).

55. Entman and Rojecki, *The Black Image in the White Mind*.

56. Oscar H. Gandy Jr., *Communication and Race: A Structural Perspective* (London: Arnold, 1998), 84.

57. Skerry, *Mexican Americans*, 321.

58. Franklin D. Gilliam Jr. and Shanto Iyengar, "Prime Suspects: The Influence of Local Television News on the Viewing Public," *American Journal of Political Science* 44(3) (2000): 560–73; Darnell M. Hunt, *Screening the Los Angeles "Riots": Race, Seeing and Resistance* (New York: Cambridge University Press, 1997); Darnell M. Hunt, "O. J. Live: Raced Ways of Seeing Innocence and Guilt," in *Cultural Diversity and the U.S. Media*, ed. Yahya R. Kamalipour and Theresa Carilli, 183–203 (Albany: State University of New York Press, 1998).

59. D. Weaver, D. Graber, M. McCombs, and C. Eyal, *Media Agenda Setting in a Presidential Election: Issues, Images, and Interest* (New York: Prager, 1981).

60. Shanto Iyengar, *Is Anyone Responsible? How Television Frames Political Issues* (Chicago: University of Chicago Press, 1991).

61. Iyengar, *Is Anyone Responsible?*

62. Sheila T. Murphy, "The Impact of Factual versus Fictional Media Portrayals on Cultural Stereotypes," *Annals of the American Academy of Political and Social Science* 560 (1998): 165–78.

63. Thomas E. Nelson and Elaine A. Willey, "Issue Frames That Strike a Value Balance: A Political Psychology Perspective," in *Framing Public Life: Perspectives on Media and Our Understanding of the Social World*, ed. Stephen D. Reese, Oscar H. Gandy Jr., and August E. Grant, 245–66 (Mahwah, N.J.: Lawrence Erlbaum Associates, 2001).

64. Martin Gilens, *Why Americans Hate Welfare* (Chicago: University of Chicago Press, 1999); Franklin D. Gilliam, Shanto Iyengar, Adam Simon, and Oliver Wright, "Crime in Black and White: The Violent, Scary World of Local News," *The Harvard International Journal of Press/Politics* 1 (1996): 6–23; Gilliam and Iyengar, "Prime Suspects"; Paul M. Kellstedt, "Media Framing and the Dynamics of Racial Policy Preferences," *American Journal of Political Science* 44(2) (2000): 239–55.

65. Sparrow, *Uncertain Guardians*.

66. Thomas E. Nelson, Rosalee A. Clawson, and Zoe M. Oxley, "Media Framing of Civil Liberties Conflict and Its Effects on Tolerance," *American Political Science Review* 91(3) (1997): 567–83.

67. Thomas E. Nelson and Donald R. Kinder, "Issue Frames and Group-Centrism in American Public Opinion," *Journal of Politics* 58 (1996): 1055–78.

68. Paul M. Kellstedt, *The Mass Media and the Dynamics of American Racial Attitudes* (New York: Cambridge University Press, 2003).

69. Kellstedt, "Media Framing and the Dynamics of Racial Policy Preferences."

70. Thomas E. Nelson and Elaine A. Willey, "Issue Frames That Strike a Value Balance: A Political Psychology Perspective," in *Framing Public Life: Perspectives on Media and Our Understanding of the Social World*, ed. Stephen D. Reese, Oscar H. Gandy Jr., and August E. Grant, 245–66 (Mahwah, N.J.: Lawrence Erlbaum Associates, 2001).

71. John Fiske and S. Taylor, *Social Cognition* (New York: McGraw-Hill, 1991).

72. David Domke, Kelley McCoy, and Marcos Torres, "News Media, Racial Perceptions, and Political Cognition," *Communication Research* 26(5) (1999): 570–607.

73. Gilens, *Why Americans Hate Welfare.*

74. Kellstedt, *The Mass Media and the Dynamics of American Racial Attitudes*, 123.

75. James M. Avery, Mark Peffley, and Jason Glass, "Race Matters: The Impact of News Coverage of Welfare Reform on Public Opinion" (presented at the American Political Science Association Meetings, Washington, D.C., 2000).

76. Gilliam, Iyengar, Simon, and Wright, "Crime in Black and White," 19.

77. Gilliam and Iyengar, "Prime Suspects."

78. Newkirk, *Within the Veil*, 18.

79. Gilliam and Iyengar, "Prime Suspects."

80. Gilliam and Iyengar, "Prime Suspects."

81. Newkirk, *Within the Veil.*

82. Gilliam and Iyengar, "Prime Suspects," 570.

83. Hunt, *Screening the Los Angeles "Riots."*

84. John Lie and Nancy Abelmann, "The 1992 Los Angeles Riots and the 'Black-Korean Conflict'," in *Koreans in the Hood: Conflict with African Americans*, ed. Kwang Chung Kim, 75–87 (Baltimore: Johns Hopkins University Press, 1999).

85. Jung Sun Park, "Identity Politics: Chicago Korean-Americans and the Los Angeles 'Riots'," in *Koreans in the Hood: Conflict with African Americans*, ed. Kwang Chung Kim, 202–31 (Baltimore: Johns Hopkins University Press, 1999).

86. Kyeyoung Park, "Use and Abuse of Race and Culture: Black-Korean Tension in American," in *Koreans in the Hood: Conflict with African Americans*, ed. Kwang Chung Kim, 60–74 (Baltimore: Johns Hopkins University Press, 1999).

87. Lie and Abelmann, "The 1992 Los Angeles Riots and the 'Black-Korean Conflict,'" 85.

88. Park, "Use and Abuse of Race and Culture."

89. Felipe Korzenny, Betty Ann Griffis, Bradley S. Greenberg, Judee K. Burgoon, and Michael Burgoon, "How Community Leaders, Newspaper Executives, and Reporters Perceive Mexican Americans and the Mass Media," in *Mexican Americans and the Mass Media*, ed. Bradley S. Greenberg, Michael Burgoon, Judee K. Burgoon, and Felipe Korzenny, 55–75 (Norwood, N.J.: Ablex Publishing Co., 1983), 67.

90. Federico A. Subervi-Vélez and Susan Colsant, "The Television Worlds of Latino Children," in *Children and Television: Images in a Changing Sociocultural World*, ed. Gordon L. Berry and Joy Keiko Asamen, 47–72 (Newbury Park, Calif.: Sage Publications, 1993).

91. Susan Herbst, *Politics at the Margins: Historical Studies of Public Expression outside the Mainstream* (New York: Cambridge University Press, 1994).

92. Herbst, *Politics at the Margins*, 28.

93. Herbst, *Politics at the Margins*, 166.

94. Wilson and Gutiérrez, *Race, Multiculturalism, and the Media.*

95. Jae Chul Shim, "The Importance of Ethnic Newspapers to U.S. Newcomers," in *Facing Difference: Race, Gender, and Mass Media*, ed. Shirley Biagi and Marilyn Kern-Foxworth, 250–55 (Thousand Oaks, Calif.: Pine Forge Press, 1997), 252.

96. Pamela Paul, "News, Noticias, Nouvelles," *American Demographics* 23(11) (2001): 26–32.

CHAPTER 8

1. Lauren Kessler, *The Dissident Press: Alternative Journalism in American History* (Beverly Hills, Calif.: Sage Publications, 1984).

2. Paul M. Kellstedt, *The Mass Media and the Dynamics of American Racial Attitudes* (New York: Cambridge University Press, 2003).

3. Bradley S. Greenberg, Carrie Heeter, Judee K. Burgoon, Michael Burgoon, and Felipe Korzenny, "A Content Analysis of Newspaper Coverage of Mexican Americans," in *Mexican Americans and the Mass Media*, ed. Bradley S. Greenberg, Michael Burgoon, Judee K. Burgoon, and Felipe Korzenny, 201–23 (Norwood, N.J.: Ablex Publishing Co., 1983).

4. Brigitte L. Nacos and Natasha Hritzuk, "The Portrayal of Black Americans in the Mass Media: Perceptions and Reality, in *Black and Multiracial Politics in America*, ed. Yvette M. Alex-Assenoh and Lawrence J. Hanks, 165–95 (New York: New York University Press, 2000).

5. Nacos and Hritzuk, "The Portrayal of Black Americans in the Mass Media."

6. Nacos and Hritzuk, "The Portrayal of Black Americans in the Mass Media."

7. Joann Byrd, "Blacks, Whites in News Pictures," in *Facing Difference: Race, Gender, and Mass Media*, ed. Shirley Biagi and Marilyn Kern-Foxworth, 95–97 (Thousand Oaks, Calif.: Pine Forge Press, 1997).

8. Robert M. Entman and Andrew Rojecki, *The Black Image in the White Mind: Media and Race in America* (Chicago: University of Chicago Press, 2000).

9. Pamela Newkirk, *Within the Veil: Black Journalists, White Media* (New York: New York University Press, 2000).

10. Christopher P. Campbell, *Race, Myth and the News* (Thousand Oaks, Calif.: Sage Publications, 1995); William J. Drummond, "About Face, from Alliance to Alienation: Blacks and the News Media," *The American Enterprise* (July 8, 1990): 23–29; Entman and Rojecki, *The Black Image in the White Mind*; Carolyn Martindale, *The White Press and Black America* (New York: Greenwood Press, 1986); Nacos and Hritzuk, "The Portrayal of Black Americans in the Mass Media."

11. Eddith A. Dashiell, "Broadcast TV News Coverage of the O. J. Simpson Murder Case," in *Mediated Messages and African-American Culture: Contemporary Issues*, ed. Venise T. Berry and Carmen Manning-Miller, 159–71 (Thousand Oaks, Calif.: Sage Publications, 1996).

12. Entman and Rojecki, *The Black Image in the White Mind*.

13. Byrd, "Blacks, Whites in News Pictures"; Newkirk, *Within the Veil*.

14. Entman and Rojecki, *The Black Image in the White Mind*.

15. Michael R. Winston, "Racial Consciousness and the Evolution of Mass Communications in the United States," *Daedalus* 11(4) (1982): 171–82.

16. Marvin Dunn and Alex Stepick III, "Blacks in Miami," in *Miami Now! Immigration, Ethnicity, and Social Change*, ed. Guillermo J. Grenier and Alex Stepick III, 41–56 (Gainsville: University Press of Florida, 1992).

17. Paul Messaris and Linus Abraham, "The Role of Images in Framing News Stories," in *Framing Public Life: Perspectives on Media and Our Understanding of the Social World*, ed. Stephen D. Reese, Oscar H. Gandy Jr., and August I. Grant, 215–26 (Mahwah, N.J.: Lawrence Erlbaum Associates, 2001).

18. David A. Copeland, "The Proceedings of the Rebellious Negroes: News of Slave Insurrections and Crimes in Colonial Newspapers," *American Journalism: A Journal of Media History* 12(2) (1995): 83–106.

19. Jerry W. Knudson, *In the News: American Journalists View Their Craft* (Wilmington: Scholarly Resources, 2000).

20. Ian Law, *Race in the News* (New York: Palgrave, 2002).

21. Jack Lule, "The Rape of Mike Tyson: Race, the Press, and Symbolic Types," *Critical Studies in Mass Communication* 12(2) (1995): 176–95; Newkirk, *Within the Veil*.

22. Christopher P. Campbell, "Beyond Employment Diversity: Rethinking Contemporary Racist News Representations," in *Cultural Diversity and the U.S. Media*, ed. Yahya R. Kamalipour and Theresa Carilli, 51–64 (Albany: State University of New York Press, 1998), 55.

23. Campbell, "Beyond Employment Diversity."

24. Entman and Rojecki, *The Black Image in the White Mind*; Kathleen Hall Jamieson, *Dirty Politics: Deception, Distraction and Democracy* (New York: Oxford University Press, 1992).

25. Campbell, "Beyond Employment Diversity."

26. Franklin D. Gilliam, Shanto Iyengar, Adam Simon, and Oliver Wright, "Crime in Black and White: The Violent, Scary World of Local News," *The Harvard International Journal of Press/Politics* 1 (1996): 6–23.

27. Newkirk, *Within the Veil*.

28. Dennis M. Rome, "Stereotyping by the Media: Murderers, Rapists, and Drug Addicts," in *Images of Color, Images of Crime*, ed. Coramae Richey Mann and Marjorie S. Zatz, 85–96 (Los Angeles: Roxbury Publishing Co., 1998).

29. Entman and Rojecki, *The Black Image in the White Mind*.

30. Gilliam, Iyengar, Simon, and Wright, "Crime in Black and White"; Travis L. Dixon and Daniel Linz, "Overrepresentation and Underrepresentation of African Americans and Latinos as Lawbreakers on Television News," *Journal of Communication* 50 (2000): 131–54.

31. Dixon and Linz, "Overrepresentation and Underrepresentation of African Americans and Latinos as Lawbreakers on Television News."

32. Entman and Rojecki, *The Black Image in the White Mind*.

33. Martindale, *The White Press and Black America*; Carolyn Martindale, "Only in Glimpses: Portrayal of America's Largest Minority Groups by the *New York Times*, 1934–1994," in *Facing Difference: Race, Gender, and Mass Media*, ed. Shirley Biagi and Marilyn Kern-Foxworth, 89–95 (Thousand Oaks, Calif.: Pine Forge Press, 1997).

34. Byrd, "Blacks, Whites in News Pictures."

35. Mary Beth Oliver, "Portrayals of Crime, Race, and Aggression in 'Reality-Based' Police Shows: A Content Analysis," *Journal of Broadcasting and Electronic Media* 38 (1994): 179–92.

36. David T. Z. Mindich, *Just the Facts: How "Objectivity" Came to Define American Journalism* (New York: New York University Press, 1998).

37. Carl Rivers, *Slick Spins and Fractured Facts: How Cultural Myths Distort the News* (New York: Columbia University Press, 1996).

38. Rivers, *Slick Spins and Fractured Facts*, 159.

39. Jimmie L. Reeves and Richard Campbell, "Coloring the Crack Crisis," in *The Media in Black and White*, ed. Everette E. Dennis and Edward C. Pease, 61–67 (New Brunswick, N.J.: Transaction Publishers, 1997).

40. Drummond, "About Face, from Alliance to Alienation."

41. Entman and Rojecki, *The Black Image in the White Mind*, 78.

42. John Fiske, *Media Matters: Race and Gender in U.S. Politics* (Minneapolis: University of Minnesota Press, 1996); Darnell M. Hunt, *Screening the Los Angeles "Riots": Race, Seeing and Resistance* (New York: Cambridge University Press, 1997).

43. John Caldwell, "Televisual Politics: Negotiating Race in the L.A. Rebellion," in *Living Color: Race and Television in the United States*, ed. Sasha Torres, 161–94 (Durham, N.C.: Duke University Press, 1998); Jyotika Ramaprasad, "How Four Newspapers Covered the 1992 Los Angeles 'Riots'," in *Mediated Messages and African-American Culture: Contemporary Issues*, ed. Venise T. Berry and Carmen L. Manning-Miller, 76–95 (Thousand Oaks, Calif.: Sage Publications, 1996).

44. Caldwell, "Televisual Politics," 163.

45. Caldwell, "Televisual Politics."

46. Newkirk, *Within the Veil*.

47. Andre F. Shashaty, "The Missing Beat," *Columbia Journalism Review* 31(2) (July 8, 1992): 26.

48. Lisa G. Baird, "That Special Perspective They Say They Want," *Columbia Journalism Review* 31(2) (July 8, 1992): 27.

49. Carol Bradley Shirley, "Where Have You Been?" *Columbia Journalism Review* 31(2) (July 8, 1992): 25–26.

50. Stephanie O'Neill, "'Get the Hell out of Here!' A City Ablaze Casts a Glaring Light on the Press," *Columbia Journalism Review* 31(2) (July 8, 1992): 23–24.

51. Kellstedt, *The Mass Media and the Dynamics of American Racial Attitudes*.

52. Entman and Rojecki, *The Black Image in the White Mind*; Martin Gilens, *Why Americans Hate Welfare* (Chicago: University of Chicago Press, 1999).

53. Entman and Rojecki, *The Black Image in the White Mind*.

54. Entman and Rojecki, *The Black Image in the White Mind*.

55. Gilens, *Why Americans Hate Welfare*.

56. Rosalee A. Clawson and Rakuya Trice, "Poverty as We Know It: Media Portrayals of the Poor," *Public Opinion Quarterly* 64 (2000): 53–64.

57. Clawson and Trice, "Poverty as We Know It"; Gilens, *Why Americans Hate Welfare*.

58. Clawson and Trice, "Poverty as We Know It."

59. Herman Gray, "Television, Black Americans, and the American Dream," in *Mediated Messages and African-American Culture: Contemporary Issues*, ed. Venise T. Berry and Carmen L. Manning-Miller, 131–45 (Thousand Oaks, Calif.: Sage Publications, 1996), 136–37; Sut Jhally and Justin Lewis, *Enlightened Racism: The Cosby Show, Audiences, and the Myth of the American Dream* (Boulder, Colo.: Westview Press, 1992).

60. Robert M. Entman, "Manufacturing Discord: Media in the Affirmative Action Debate," *The Harvard International Journal of Press/Politics* 2 (1997): 32–51; Herbert J. Gans, *Deciding What's News: A Study of CBS Evening News, NBC Nightly News, Newsweek, and Time* (New York: Vintage Press, 1979).

61. Jhally and Lewis, *Enlightened Racism*.

62. Jhally and Lewis, *Enlightened Racism*.

63. Newkirk, *Within the Veil*.

64. Kellstedt, *The Mass Media and the Dynamics of American Racial Attitudes*.

65. Campbell, *Race, Myth and the News*.

66. Campbell, *Race, Myth and the News*, 111.

67. Entman and Rojecki, *The Black Image in the White Mind*.

68. Entman and Rojecki, *The Black Image in the White Mind*, 87.

69. Stephanie Greco Larson and Martha Bailey, "ABC's 'Person of the Week': American Values on Television News," *Journalism and Mass Communication Quarterly* 75 (1998): 487–99.

70. Dana Cloud, "Hegemony or Concordance? The Rhetoric of Tokenism in Oprah Winfrey's Rags-to-Riches Biography," *Critical Studies in Mass Communication* 13(2) (1996): 115–37.

71. Tom Grochowski, "Gender, Race, and the O. J. Simpson Case: How the Media 'Framed' O.J.," in *Race/Gender/Media: Considering Diversity across Audiences, Content, and Producers*, ed. Rebecca Ann Lind, 154–60 (Boston: Pearson Education, 2004), 155.

72. Grochowski, "Gender, Race, and the O. J. Simpson Case."

73. Gray, "Television, Black Americans, and the American Dream."

74. Gray, "Television, Black Americans, and the American Dream," 144.

75. Messaris and Abraham, "The Role of Images in Framing News Stories."

76. JoNina A. Abron, "The Image of African Americans in the U.S. Press," *The Black Scholar* 21(2) (1990): 49–52.

77. Entman and Rojecki, *The Black Image in the White Mind*, 105.

78. Entman, "Manufacturing Discord."

79. William A. Gamson, *Talking Politics* (New York: Cambridge University Press, 1992).

80. Entman, "Manufacturing Discord."

81. Thomas E. Nelson and Donald R. Kinder, "Issue Frames and Group-Centrism in American Public Opinion," *Journal of Politics* 58 (1996): 1055–78.

82. Gamson, *Talking Politics*.

83. Caldwell, "Televisual Politics."

84. John Lie and Nancy Abelmann, "The 1992 Los Angeles Riots and the 'Black-Korean Conflict,'" in *Koreans in the Hood: Conflict with African Americans*, ed. Kwang Chung Kim, 75–87 (Baltimore: Johns Hopkins University Press, 1999).

85. Elaine H. Kim, "Home Is Where the Han Is: A Korean American Perspective on the Los Angeles Upheavals," in *Reading Rodney King, Reading Urban Rebellion*, ed. Robert Gooding-Williams, 215–35 (New York: Routledge, 1993).

86. Sumi K. Cho, "Korean Americans vs. African Americans: Conflict and Construction," in *Reading Rodney King, Reading Urban Uprising*, ed. Robert Gooding-Williams, 196–214 (New York: Routledge, 1993).

87. Cho, "Korean Americans vs. African Americans," 206.

88. David Shaw, "The Simpson Legacy: The Race Card," in *Facing Difference: Race, Gender, and Mass Media*, ed. Shirley Biagi and Marilyn Kern-Foxworth, 239–44 (Thousand Oaks, Calif.: Pine Forge Press, 1997), 240.

89. Shaw, "The Simpson Legacy."

90. Reginald Owens, "Entering the Twenty-First Century: Oppression and the African American Press," in *Mediated Messages and African-American Culture: Contemporary Issues*, ed. Venise T. Berry and Carmen L. Manning-Miller, 96–116 (Thousand Oaks, Calif.: Sage Publications, 1996), 113.

91. Kessler, *The Dissident Press*, 28.

92. Graham Russell Hodges, "David Ruggles," *Media Studies Journal* 14 (2000): 8–15.

93. Kessler, *The Dissident Press*; Knudson, *In the News*.

94. Owens, "Entering the Twenty-First Century."

95. Felecia G. Jones Ross, "The Brownville Affair and the Political Values of Cleveland Black Newspapers," *American Journalism: A Journal of Media History* 12(2) (1995): 107–22.

96. Mindich, *Just the Facts*, 118.

97. Mindich, *Just the Facts*.

98. Mindich, *Just the Facts*; Pamela Newkirk, "Ida B. Wells-Barnett," *Media Studies Journal* 14 (2000): 26–31.

99. Knudson, *In the News*; Mindich, *Just the Facts*; Newkirk, "Ida B. Wells-Barnett."

100. Mindich, *Just the Facts*, 128.

101. Mindich, *Just the Facts*, 132.

102. Leonard Ray Teel, "The African American Press and the Campaign for a Federal Anti-Lynching Law, 1933–4: Putting Civil Rights on the National Agenda," *American Journalism: A Journal of Media History* 8(2/3) (1991): 84–107.

103. Susan Herbst, *Politics at the Margins: Historical Studies of Public Expression outside the Mainstream* (New York: Cambridge University Press, 1994), 69.

104. Knudson, *In the News*, 165.

105. Armistad Pride and Clint C. Wilson II, *A History of the Black Press* (Washington, D.C.: Howard University Press, 1997).

106. Theodore Kornweibel Jr., "'The Most Dangerous of All Negro Journals': Federal Efforts to Suppress the Chicago Defender during World War I," *American Journalism: A Journal of Media History* 11(2) (1994): 154–68.

107. Frederick G. Detweiler, *The Negro Press in the United States* (College Park, Md.: McGrath Publishing Co., 1968).

108. Albert Kreiling, "The Commercialization of the Black Press and the Rise of Race News in Chicago," in *Ruthless Criticism: New Perspectives in U.S. Communication History*, ed.

William S. Solomon and Robert W. McChesney, 176–203 (Minneapolis: University of Minnesota Press, 1993), 191.

109. Owens, "Entering the Twenty-First Century."

110. Herbst, *Politics at the Margins*.

111. Kessler, *The Dissident Press*; Knudson, *In the News*.

112. Earnest L. Perry, "A Common Purpose: The Negro Newspaper Publishers Association's Fight for Equality during World War II," *American Journalism: A Journal of Media History* 19(2) (2002): 31–43.

113. Kessler, *The Dissident Press*; Owens, "Entering the Twenty-First Century."

114. Kessler, *The Dissident Press*.

115. Owens, "Entering the Twenty-First Century."

116. Kessler, *The Dissident Press*; Pride and Wilson, *A History of the Black Press*.

117. E. R. Shipp, "O. J. and the Black Media: Neither a Typical Hero nor a Typical Victim, He Challenges Typical Coverage," *Columbia Journalism Review* 33(4) (November 12, 1994): 39–41.

118. Newkirk, *Within the Veil*, 213.

119. Ronald N. Jacobs, *Race, Media, and the Crisis of Civil Society: From Watts to Rodney King* (Cambridge: Cambridge University Press, 2000).

120. Kimberly Ann Gross, "Rioting in Black and White: The Portrayal of Racial Unrest in Black and Mainstream Newspapers" (presented at the American Political Science Association Meetings, Washington, D.C., 1997).

121. Jacobs, *Race, Media, and the Crisis*; Gross, "Rioting in Black and White."

122. Rosalee A. Clawson and Eric N. Wattenburg, "Support for a Supreme Court Affirmative Action Decision: A Story in Black and White," *American Politics Research* 31(3) (2003): 251–79.

123. Pride and Wilson, *A History of the Black Press*, 257.

124. Catherine A. Squires, "Black Talk Radio: Defining Community Needs and Identity," *The Harvard International Journal of Press/Politics* 5(2) (2000): 73–95.

125. Sharon Albert-Honore, "Empowering Voices: KUCB and Black Liberation Radio," in *Mediated Messages and African-American Culture: Contemporary Issues*, ed. Venise T. Berry and Carmen L. Manning-Miller, 201–17 (Thousand Oaks, Calif.: Sage Publications, 1996); Squires, "Black Talk Radio."

126. Albert-Honore, "Empowering Voices," 202.

127. Squires, "Black Talk Radio."

128. Squires, "Black Talk Radio," 82.

129. Albert-Honore, "Empowering Voices"; Fiske, *Media Matters*.

130. Albert-Honore, "Empowering Voices," 215.

131. Fiske, *Media Matters*, 192.

132. Fiske, *Media Matters*.

133. George L. Daniels and Dwight E. Brooks, "The Tom Joyner Morning Show: Activist Urban Radio in the Age of Consolidation," in *Race/Gender/Media: Considering Diversity across Audiences, Content, and Producers*, ed. Rebecca Ann Lind, 307–14 (Boston: Pearson Education, 2004).

134. Tommy Lee Lott, "Documenting Social Issues: Black Journal, 1968–1970," in *Struggles for Representation: African American Documentary Film and Video*, ed. Phyllis R. Klotman and Janet K. Cutler, 71–98 (Bloomington: Indiana University Press, 1999).

135. Felecia G. Jones, "The Black Audience and the BET Channel," *Journal of Broadcasting and Electronic Media* 34(4) (1990): 477–86.

136. Yemi Toure, "The End of Black Entertainment Television," 2004, available on the Media Alliance website at www.media-alliance.org/article.php?story=20031109003422874 (accessed July 20, 2004).

137. Robin R. Means Coleman, "Prospects for Locating Racial Democracy in Media: The

NAACP Network Television Boycott," *Qualitative Research Reports in Communication* 3(2) (2002): 25–31.

CHAPTER 9

1. Mary Ann Weston, *Native Americans in the News: Images of Indians in the Twentieth Century Press* (Westport, Conn.: Greenwood Press, 1996).

2. Weston, *Native Americans in the News*, 8.

3. Weston, *Native Americans in the News*.

4. Tara McCoy, *The Mascot Controversy: A Comparative Study on How Native Americans Are Portrayed in the Media* (unpublished manuscript, 2003).

5. Don Heider, *White News: Why Local News Programs Don't Cover People of Color* (Mahwah, N.J.: Lawrence Erlbaum Associates, 2000).

6. John M. Coward, *The Newspaper Indian: Native American Identity in the Press 1820–90* (Urbana: University of Illinois, 1999); Weston, *Native Americans in the News*.

7. Weston, *Native Americans in the News*.

8. Carolyn Martindale, "Only in Glimpses: Portrayal of America's Largest Minority Groups by the *New York Times*, 1934–1994," in *Facing Difference: Race, Gender, and Mass Media*, ed. Shirley Biagi and Marilyn Kern-Foxworth (Thousand Oaks, Calif.: Pine Forge Press, 1997).

9. Weston, *Native Americans in the News*.

10. Martindale, "Only in Glimpses."

11. John Merton Marrs, "Project Chariot, Nuclear Zeal, Easy Journalism and the Fate of Eskimos," *American Journalism: A Journal of Media History* 16(3) (1999): 71–98.

12. Marrs, "Project Chariot, Nuclear Zeal, Easy Journalism and the Fate of Eskimos."

13. James E. Murphy and Sharon M. Murphy, *Let My People Know: American Indian Journalism, 1828–1978* (Norman: University of Oklahoma Press, 1981), 3.

14. Weston, *Native Americans in the News*.

15. Weston, *Native Americans in the News*.

16. Weston, *Native Americans in the News*, 13.

17. Coward, *The Newspaper Indian*, 39.

18. John M. Coward, "Creating the Ideal Indian: The Case of the Poncas," *Journalism History* 21(3) (1995): 112–21.

19. Coward, "Creating the Ideal Indian," 114.

20. Coward, "Creating the Ideal Indian."

21. Coward, "Creating the Ideal Indian," 116.

22. Coward, "Creating the Ideal Indian."

23. Coward, "Creating the Ideal Indian."

24. Weston, *Native Americans in the News*.

25. Weston, *Native Americans in the News*.

26. Coward, *The Newspaper Indian*, 91.

27. Weston, *Native Americans in the News*.

28. Weston, *Native Americans in the News*.

29. Weston, *Native Americans in the News*, 79.

30. Weston, *Native Americans in the News*.

31. John M. Coward, "Selling the Southwestern Indian: Ideology and Image in Arizona Highways, 1925–1940," *American Journalism: A Journal of Media History* 20(2) (2003): 12–31.

32. Coward, "Selling the Southwestern Indian," 27.

33. Coward, "Selling the Southwestern Indian."

34. Weston, *Native Americans in the News*, 94.

35. Weston, *Native Americans in the News.*

36. M. L. Stein, "Racial Stereotyping and the Media," *Editor & Publisher* 127(32) (August 6, 1994): 12–13.

37. McCoy, *The Mascot Controversy.*

38. Cynthia-Lou Coleman, "A War of Words: How News Frames Define Legitimacy in a Native Conflict," in *Dressing in Feathers: The Construction of the Indian in American Popular Culture,* ed. S. Elizabeth Bird, 181–93 (Boulder, Colo.: Westview Press, 1996), 181.

39. Coleman, "A War of Words," 185.

40. Coleman, "A War of Words."

41. Patricia A. Curtin, "From Pity to Necessity: How National Events Shaped Coverage of the Plains Indian War," *American Journalism: A Journal of Media History* 12(1) (1995): 3–21.

42. Curtin, *Redeeming the Wasteland,* 18.

43. Curtin, *Redeeming the Wasteland,* 20.

44. Curtin, *Redeeming the Wasteland,* 3.

45. Coward, *The Newspaper Indian.*

46. Coward, *The Newspaper Indian,* 233.

47. Joel D. Weisman, "About the Ambush at Wounded Knee," *Columbia Journalism Review* 14 (September 10, 1975): 28–31, 30.

48. Martindale, "Only in Glimpses."

49. JoAnn M. Valenti, "Reporting Hantavirus: The Impact of Cultural Diversity in Environmental and Health News," in *Cultural Diversity and the U.S. Media,* ed. Yahya R. Kamalipour and Theresa Carilli, 231–44 (Albany: State University of New York Press, 1998).

50. Weston, *Native Americans in the News.*

51. Valenti, "Reporting Hantavirus."

52. Michael Haederle, "When Worlds Collide: Navajos and the News Media," in *Facing Difference: Race, Gender, and Mass Media,* ed. Shirley Biagi and Marilyn Kern-Foxworth, 128–31 (Thousand Oaks, Calif.: Pine Forge Press, 1997).

53. Valenti, "Reporting Hantavirus."

54. Heider, *White News,* 46.

55. Christopher P. Campbell, *Race, Myth and the News* (Thousand Oaks, Calif.: Sage Publications, 1995).

56. Campbell, *Race, Myth and the News,* 52–53.

57. Coleman, "A War of Words," 184.

58. Murphy and Murphy, *Let My People Know,* 27.

59. Murphy and Murphy, *Let My People Know,* 30.

60. Murphy and Murphy, *Let My People Know.*

61. John M. Coward, "Promoting the Progressive Indian: Lee Harkins and the *American Indian Magazine,*" *American Journalism: A Journal of Media History* 14(1) (1997): 3–18.

62. Valenti, "Reporting Hantavirus."

63. Karen Lincoln Michel, "Repression on the Reservation," *Columbia Journalism Review* 37(4) (November 12, 1998): 48–50.

64. M. L. Stein, "Indian Newspapers and Tribal Censorship," *Editor & Publisher* 125 (20) (May 16, 1992): 14, 47.

65. Mark N. Trahant, "Native American Newspapers," *Media Studies Journal* 14 (2000): 106–13.

66. Jeannette Henry, "Forward," in *Let My People Know: American Indian Journalism, 1828–1978,* ed. James E. Murphy and Susan M. Murphy, v–xvi (Norman: University of Oklahoma Press, 1982).

67. Richard LaCourse, "A Native Press Primer," *Columbia Journalism Review* 37(4) (November 12, 1998): 51; Stein, "Indian Newspapers and Tribal Censorship"; Trahant, "Native American Newspapers."

68. Michel, "Repression on the Reservation."

69. Stein, "Indian Newspapers and Tribal Censorship."

70. Paul Chaat Smith and Robert Allen Warrior, *Like a Hurricane: The Indian Movement from Alcatraz to Wounded Knee* (New York: New Press, 1996).

71. Trahant, "Native American Newspapers."

72. Henry, "Forward," vii–viii.

73. Interview with Stephen Rockwell, University of Michigan at Flint, August 6, 2004.

74. Trahant, "Native American Newspapers."

75. Shiela Reaves, "Native American Journalists: Finding a Pipeline into Journalism," *Newspaper Research Journal* 16(4) (1995): 57–73.

76. Henry, "Forward."

77. Oscar Patterson III, "The Press Held Hostage: Terrorism in a Small North Carolina Town," *American Journalism: A Journal of Media History* 15(4) (1998): 125–39.

78. Philip J. Deloria, *Playing Indian* (New Haven, Conn.: Yale University Press, 1968).

79. "About Indian Country Today," 2004, available on the Indian Country Today website, at www.indiancountry.com/aboutus (accessed July 23, 2004).

80. McCoy, *The Mascot Controversy.*

81. Deloria, *Playing Indian.* The articles referred to by Deloria were published in July and August of 1992.

82. Marrs, "Project Chariot, Nuclear Zeal, Easy Journalism and the Fate of Eskimos."

83. John Creed, "The Value of Cultural Journalism to Diversity in the Mainline Press: Cae of Alaska's Chukchi News Service," *The Journalism Educator* 49(3) (1994): 64–71.

84. Murphy and Murphy, *Let My People Know,* 131.

85. Bruce Smith and Jerry Brigham, "Native Radio in the United States: The Beginning of a New Oral Tradition," in *Facing Difference: Race, Gender, and Mass Media,* ed. Shirley Biagi and Marilyn Kern-Foxworth, 160–66 (Thousand Oaks, Calif.: Pine Forge Press, 1997).

86. Smith and Brigham, "Native Radio in the United States," 161.

87. John Christian Hopkins, "Tribes Key into Computer Highway," in *Facing Difference: Race, Gender, and Mass Media,* ed. Shirley Biagi and Marilyn Kern-Foxworth, 260–61 (Thousand Oaks, Calif.: Pine Forge Press, 1997).

88. Hopkins, "Tribes Key into Computer Highway."

89. Ellen L. Arnold and Darcy C. Plymire, "The Cherokee Indians and the Internet," in *Gender, Race, and Class in Media: A Text-Reader,* ed. Gail Dines and Jean M. Humez, 2nd ed., 715–22 (Thousand Oaks, Calif.: Sage Publications, 2003).

CHAPTER 10

1. National Council of La Raza, "Out of the Picture: Hispanics in the Media," in *Latin Looks: Images of Latinas and Latinos in the U.S. Media,* ed. Clara E. Rodríguez, 21–36 (Boulder, Colo.: Westview Press, 1997).

2. Robert M. Entman and Andrew Rojecki, *The Black Image in the White Mind: Media and Race in America* (Chicago: University of Chicago Press, 2000).

3. Melita Marie Garza, "Hola, América! Newsstand 2000," in *The Media in Black and White,* ed. Everette E. Dennis and Edward C. Pease, 129–36 (New Brunswick, N.J.: Transaction 1997).

4. Entman and Rojecki, *The Black Image in the White Mind;* Rod Carbeth and Diane Alverio, *Network Brownout: The Portrayal of Latinos in Network Television News* (Washington, D.C.: National Association of Hispanic Journalists, 1996). Rod Carbeth and Diane Alverio, *Network Brownout: The Portrayal of Latinos in Network Television News* (Washington, D.C.: National Association of Hispanic Journalists and the National Council of La Raza, 1997); Mark Fitzgerald, "TV Network News Tunes Out Hispanics," *Editor & Publisher* 131(27) (July 4, 1998): 36.

5. Carolyn Martindale, "Only in Glimpses: Portrayal of America's Largest Minority Groups by the *New York Times*, 1934–1994," in *Facing Difference: Race, Gender, and Mass Media*, ed. Shirley Biagi and Marilyn Kern-Foxworth, 89–95 (Thousand Oaks, Calif.: Pine Forge Press, 1997).

6. Bradley S. Greenberg, Carrie Heeter, Judee K. Burgoon, Michael Burgoon, and Felipe Korzenny, "A Content Analysis of Newspaper Coverage of Mexican Americans," in *Mexican Americans and the Mass Media*, ed. Bradley S. Greenberg, Michael Burgoon, Judee K. Burgoon, and Felipe Korzenny, 201–23 (Norwood, N.J.: Ablex Publishing Co., 1983).

7. Louis DeSipio and James Richard Henson, "Cuban Americans, Latinos, and the Print Media: Shaping Ethnic Identities," *The Harvard International Journal of Press/Politics* 2(3) (1997): 52–70.

8. Cecilia Alvear, "No Chicanos on TV," *Nieman Reports* 52(3) (1998): 49–50.

9. Carrie Heeter, Bradley S. Greenberg, Bradley M. Mendelson, Judee K. Burgoon, Michael Burgoon, and Filipe Korzenny, "Cross Media Coverage of Local Hispanic American News," *Journal of Broadcasting* 27(4) (1983): 395–402.

10. J. V. Turk, J. Richard, R. L. Bryson, and S. M. Johnson, "Hispanic Americans in the News in Two Southwestern Cities," *Journalism Quarterly* 66 (1989): 107–13.

11. Heeter, Greenberg, Mendelson, Burgoon, Burgoon, and Korzenny, "Cross Media Coverage of Local Hispanic American News"; Jorge Quiroga, "Hispanic Voices: Is the Press Listening?" in *Latin Looks: Images of Latinas and Latinos in the U.S. Media*, ed. Clara E. Rodríguez (Boulder, Colo.: Westview Press, 1997).

12. Melita Marie Garza, "The Wisdom of the Past in Exploring the Current Status of Chicanos"; Hemant Shah and Michael C. Thornton, "Racial Ideology in U.S. Mainstream News Magazine Coverage of Black-Latino Interaction, 1980–1992," *Critical Studies in Mass Communication* 11(2) (1994): 141–61.

13. Octavio Emilio Nuiry, "Press Pass," *Hispanic* 10(5) (May 1997): 30–38.

14. Fitzgerald, "TV Network News Tunes out Hispanics."

15. Nuiry, "Press Pass."

16. Heeter, Greenberg, Mendelson, Burgoon, Burgoon, and Korzenny, "Cross Media Coverage of Local Hispanic American News."

17. Lucila Vargas, "Genderizing Latino News: An Analysis of a Local Newspaper's Coverage of Latino Current Affairs," *Critical Studies in Media Communication* 17(3) (2000): 261–93.

18. Quiroga, "Hispanic Voices."

19. Robert M. Entman, "Manufacturing Discord: Media in the Affirmative Action Debate," *The Harvard International Journal of Press/Politics* 2 (1997): 32–51.

20. John Caldwell, "Televisual Politics: Negotiating Race in the L.A. Rebellion," in *Living Color: Race and Television in the United States*, ed. Sasha Torres, 161–94 (Durham, N.C.: Duke University Press, 1998).

21. Darnell M. Hunt, *Screening the Los Angeles "Riots": Race, Seeing and Resistance* (New York: Cambridge University Press, 1997); Quiroga, "Hispanic Voices."

22. Mike Davis, "Uprising and Repression in L.A.," in *Reading Rodney King, Reading Urban Uprising*, ed. Robert Gooding-Williams, 142–56 (New York: Routledge, 1993).

23. Peter Skerry, *Mexican Americans: The Ambivalent Minority* (Cambridge, Mass.: Harvard University Press, 1993).

24. Shah and Thornton, "Racial Ideology in U.S."

25. National Council of La Raza, "Out of the Picture."

26. Entman and Rojecki, *The Black Image in the White Mind*.

27. Carbeth and Alverio, *Network Brownout*.

28. Quiroga, "Hispanic Voices," 37.

29. Vargas, "Genderizing Latino News."

30. Quiroga, "Hispanic Voices," 39.

31. Skerry, *Mexican Americans*.

32. DeSipio and Henson, "Cuban Americans, Latinos, and the Print Media."

33. Megan Larson, "News Hues," *Brandweek* 40(43) (November 15, 1999): S40–S43.

34. DeSipio and Henson, "Cuban Americans, Latinos, and the Print Media."

35. DeSipio and Henson, "Cuban Americans, Latinos, and the Print Media."

36. Gonzalo Soruco, *Cubans and the Mass Media in South Florida* (Gainesville: University Press of Florida, 1996).

37. DeSipio and Henson, "Cuban Americans, Latinos, and the Print Media."

38. Soruco, *Cubans and the Mass Media in South Florida*.

39. M. L. Stein, "Racial Stereotyping and the Media," *Editor & Publisher* 127 (32) (August 6, 1994): 12–13.

40. Turk, Richard, Bryson, and Johnson, "Hispanic Americans in the News in Two Southwestern Cities."

41. Vargas, "Genderizing Latino News," 285.

42. Joe Rodriguez, "Welfare Reform and Latinos = Immigration and Cultural Politics," *Nieman Reports* 53(2) (1999): 45–47.

43. Lucila Vargas and Bruce DePyssler, "Using Media Literacy to Explore Stereotypes of Mexican Immigrants," *Social Education* 62(7) (1998): 407–12.

44. Leo R. Chavez, *Covering Immigration: Popular Images and the Politics of Nation* (Berkeley: University of California Press, 2001), 260.

45. Kent A. Ono and John M. Sloop, *Shifting Borders: Rhetoric, Immigration, and California's Proposition 187* (Philadelphia: Temple University Press, 2002).

46. Otto Santa Ana, *Brown Tide Rising: Metaphors of Latinos in Contemporary American Public Discourse* (Austin: University of Texas Press, 2002).

47. Clint C. Wilson and Félix Gutiérrez, *Race, Multiculturalism, and the Media: From Mass Communication to Class Communication* (Thousand Oaks, Calif.: Sage Publications, 1995), 49.

48. Christopher P. Campbell, *Race, Myth and the News* (Thousand Oaks, Calif.: Sage Publications, 1995).

49. National Council of La Raza, "Out of the Picture."

50. Shah and Thornton, "Racial Ideology in U.S. Mainstream News Magazine Coverage of Black-Latino Interaction, 1980–1992."

51. Martindale, "Only in Glimpses."

52. Katrin Pomper, "Reinforcing Stereotypes: Press Coverage about Immigrants by the *New York Times*, *Los Angeles Times* and *Chicago Tribune*, 1984–1994" (presented at the Annual Meeting of the Association for Education and Mass Communication, Anaheim, Calif., 1996). Referred to in Vargas, "Genderizing Latino News."

53. Travis L. Dixon and Daniel Linz, "Overrepresentation and Underrepresentation of African Americans and Latinos as Lawbreakers on Television News," *Journal of Communication* 50 (2000): 131–54.

54. Maria Christina Santana and Ron F. Smith, "News Coverage of Hispanics Surpasses Expectations," *Newspaper Research Journal* 22(2) (2001): 94–105.

55. Vargas, "Genderizing Latino News."

56. Santana and Smith, "News Coverage of Hispanics Surpasses Expectations."

57. Vargas, "Genderizing Latino News."

58. Franklin D. Gilliam, Shanto Iyengar, Adam Simon, and Oliver Wright, "Crime in Black and White: The Violent, Scary World of Local News," *The Harvard International Journal of Press/Politics* 1(3) (1996): 6–23.

59. Dixon and Linz, "Overrepresentation and Underrepresentation of African Americans and Latinos as Lawbreakers on Television News."

60. David Domke, Kelley McCoy, and Marcos Torres, "News Media, Racial Perceptions, and Political Cognition," *Communication Research* 26(5) (1999): 570–607.

61. Rita J. Simon and Susan H. Alexander, *The Ambivalent Welcome: Print Media, Public Opinion, and Immigration* (Westport, Conn.: Praeger, 1993).

62. Simon and Alexander, *The Ambivalent Welcome.*

63. Vargas, "Genderizing Latino News."

64. John J. Miller, "Immigration, the Press and the New Racism," *Media Studies Journal* 8 (1994): 19–28, 23.

65. Ana, *Brown Tide Rising.*

66. Miller, "Immigration, the Press and the New Racism," 23.

67. Chavez, *Covering Immigration,* 216.

68. Chavez, *Covering Immigration,* 300 or 301.

69. Brent Cunningham, "The Latino Puzzle Challenges the Heartland," *Columbia Journalism Review* 40(6) (2002): 36–40. Vargas, "Genderizing Latino News."

70. Cunningham, "The Latino Puzzle Challenges the Heartland."

71. Campbell, *Race, Myth and the News,* 71.

72. Campbell, *Race, Myth and the News.*

73. Campbell, *Race, Myth and the News,* 71, 72.

74. Shah and Thornton, "Racial Ideology in U.S. Mainstream News Magazine Coverage of Black-Latino Interaction, 1980–1992."

75. Shah and Thornton, "Racial Ideology in U.S. Mainstream News Magazine Coverage of Black-Latino Interaction, 1980–1992," 148.

76. Shah and Thornton, "Racial Ideology in U.S. Mainstream News Magazine Coverage of Black-Latino Interaction, 1980–1992," 152.

77. Juan Gonzales, "Forgotten Pages: Spanish-Language Newspapers in the Southwest," *Journalism History* 4(2) (1977): 50–51.

78. Joseph Torres, "Invisible Ink?" *Hispanic* 12(10) (October 1999): 22–31.

79. Cynthia Corzo, "Talk Radio En Espanol Is a Hit," *Hispanic* 12(6) (June 1999): 17.

80. América Rodriguez, *Making Latino News: Race, Language, Class* (Thousand Oaks, Calif.: Sage Publications, 1999).

81. Marcia Mogelonsky, "First Language Comes First," *American Demographics* 17(10) (October 1995): 21.

82. Federico A. Subervi-Vélez, "Hispanic-Oriented Media," in *Latin Looks: Images of Latinas and Latinos in the U.S. Media,* ed. Clara E. Rodríguez, 225–38 (Boulder, Colo.: Westview Press, 1997), 225.

83. Garza, "The Wisdom of the Past in Exploring the Current Status of Chicanos," 129.

84. Charlie Ericksen, "The Road Not Taken," *Editor & Publisher* 133(20) (May 15, 2000): 46.

85. América Rodriguez, "Cultural Agendas: The Case of Latino-Oriented U.S. Media," in *Communication and Democracy: Exploring the Intellectual Frontiers in Agenda Setting Theory,* ed. Maxwell McCombs and Donald L. Shaw, 183–94 (Mahwah, N.J.: Lawrence Erlbaum Associates, 1997).

86. Gonzales, "Forgotten Pages."

87. Gonzales, "Forgotten Pages," 51.

88. Félix Gutiérrez, "Francisco P. Ramírez," *Media Studies Journal* 14 (2000): 16–23, 19.

89. Gutiérrez, "Francisco P. Ramírez," 23.

90. Rodriguez, *Making Latino News.*

91. Gene Fowler and Bill Crawford, *Border Radio: Pitchmen, Psychics, and Other Amazing Broadcasters of the American Airwaves,* 2nd ed. (Austin: University of Texas Press, 2002).

92. Fowler and Crawford, *Border Radio,* 279.

93. Rodriguez, *Making Latino News.*

94. Subervi-Vélez, "Hispanic-Oriented Media," 232.

95. Joseph Contreras, "Covering Elian in Print: How Did the *Miami Herald* Do?" *The Harvard International Journal of Press/Politics* 5(4) (2000): 123–27.

96. Sheila L. Croucher, *Imagining Miami: Ethnic Politics in a Postmodern World* (Charlottesville: University Press of Virginia, 1997).

97. Lisandro Pérez, "Cuban Miami," in *Miami Now! Immigration, Ethnicity, and Social Change*, ed. Guillermo J. Grenier and Alex Stepick III, 83–108 (Gainsville: University Press of Florida, 1992), 96.

98. Soruco, *Cubans and the Mass Media in South Florida*.

99. Mike Clary, "Would You Create Another Newspaper to Compete with Your Own? In Miami, the *Herald* Did," *Columbia Journalism Review* 39(1) (May 6, 2000): 56–58.

100. Clary, "Would You Create Another Newspaper to Compete with Your Own."

101. Mike McQueen, "In the Cauldron," *American Journalism Review* 22(5) (June 2000): 28–33.

102. Soruco, *Cubans and the Mass Media in South Florida*, 38.

103. Pérez, "Cuban Miami," 99.

104. Garza, "The Wisdom of the Past in Exploring the Current Status of Chicanos."

105. Garza, "The Wisdom of the Past in Exploring the Current Status of Chicanos"; Subervi-Véliz, "Hispanic-Oriented Media."

106. Skerry, *Mexican Americans*.

107. Louis Aguilar, "Times' Latino Section Opposed," *Hispanic* 10(12) (December 1997): 10–12.

108. Joel Simon, "Puerto Rico: Publishing News, Losing Ads," *Columbia Journalism Review* 36(3) (September 10, 1997): 20–21.

109. Aguilar, "Times' Latino Section Opposed."

110. Leslie Jackson Turner and Chris W. Allan, "Mexican and Latino Media Behavior in Los Angeles," *The American Behavioral Scientist* 40(7) (1997): 884–901.

111. Subervi-Vélez, "Hispanic-Oriented Media."

112. Rodriguez, "Cultural Agendas."

113. Rodriguez, "Cultural Agendas."

114. Rodriguez, "Cultural Agendas," 97, 98.

115. Rodriguez, "Cultural Agendas."

116. Rodriguez, "Cultural Agendas."

117. Kenton T. Wilkinson, "Collective Situational Ethnicity and Latino Subgroups' Struggle for Influence in U.S. Spanish-Language Television," *Communication Quarterly* 50(3) (2002): 422–43.

118. Federico A. Subervi-Vélez, "Spanish-Language Daily Newspapers and the 1984 Elections," *Journalism Quarterly* 65 (1988): 678–85.

119. Rodriguez, "Cultural Agendas."

CHAPTER 11

1. Joann Lee, "A Look at Asians as Portrayed in the News," *Editor & Publisher* 127(18) (April 30, 1994): 56–57.

2. Carolyn Martindale, "Only in Glimpses: Portrayal of America's Largest Minority Groups by the *New York Times*, 1934–1994," in *Facing Difference: Race, Gender, and Mass Media*, ed. Shirley Biagi and Marilyn Kern-Foxworth, 89–95 (Thousand Oaks, Calif.: Pine Forge Press, 1997).

3. Virginia D. Mansfield-Richardson, "Asian Americans and the Mass Media: A Content Analysis of Twenty U.S. Newspapers and a Survey of Asian American Journalists" (unpublished Ph.D. diss., Ohio State University, 1996).

4. Setsuko Matsunaga Nishi, "Asian Americans at the Intersection of International and Domestic Tensions: An Analysis of Newspaper Coverage," in *Across the Pacific: Asian Americans and Globalization*, ed. Evelyn Hu-DeHart, 152–90 (Philadelphia: Temple University Press, 1999).

5. Martindale, "Only in Glimpses."

6. Martindale, "Only in Glimpses."

7. Nishi, "Asian Americans at the Intersection of International and Domestic Tensions."

8. Mansfield-Richardson, "Asian Americans and the Mass Media."

9. Tacku Lee and Albert Hahn, "Campaign Finance, the Mass Media, and the Racial Formation of Asian American" (unpublished manuscript, Kennedy Center of Government, Harvard University, 1998).

10. Don Heider, *White News: Why Local News Programs Don't Cover People of Color* (Mahwah, N.J.: Lawrence Erlbaum Associates, 2000).

11. Herman B. Chiu, "Power of the Press: How Newspapers in Four Communities Erased Thousands of Chinese from Oregon History," *American Journalism: A Journal of Media History* 16(1) (1999): 59–77.

12. Chiu, "Power of the Press."

13. Chiu, "Power of the Press."

14. Mansfield-Richardson, "Asian Americans and the Mass Media."

15. William Wong, "Covering the Invisible 'Model Minority,'" in *The Media in Black and White*, ed. Everette E. Dennis and Edward C. Pease, 45–52 (New Brunswick, N.J.: Transaction Publishers, 1997).

16. Lee, "A Look at Asians as Portrayed in the News."

17. Jung Sun Park, "Identity Politics: Chicago Korean-Americans and the Los Angeles 'Riots,'" in *Koreans in the Hood: Conflict with African Americans*, ed. Kwang Chung Kim, 202–31 (Baltimore: Johns Hopkins University Press, 1999), 214.

18. Sumi K. Cho, "Korean Americans vs. African Americans: Conflict and Construction," in *Reading Rodney King, Reading Urban Uprising*, ed. Robert Gooding-Williams, 196–214 (New York: Routledge, 1993); Elaine H. Kim, "Home Is Where the Han Is: A Korean American Perspective on the Los Angeles Upheavals," in *Reading Rodney King, Reading Urban Rebellion*, ed. Robert Gooding-Williams, 215–35 (New York: Routledge, 1993); John Lie and Nancy Abelmann, "The 1992 Los Angeles Riots and the 'Black-Korean Conflict,'" in *Koreans in the Hood: Conflict with African Americans*, ed. Kwang Chung Kim, 75–87 (Baltimore: Johns Hopkins University Press, 1999); Park, J. S., "Identity Politics."

19. Nishi, "Asian Americans at the Intersection of International and Domestic Tensions."

20. Lee, "A Look at Asians as Portrayed in the News."

21. Wong, "Covering the Invisible 'Model Minority.'"

22. Darrell Y. Hamamoto, *Monitored Peril: Asian Americans and the Politics of TV Representation* (Minneapolis: University of Minnesota Press, 1994), 183.

23. Mansfield-Richardson, "Asian Americans and the Mass Media."

24. Martindale, "Only in Glimpses."

25. Lee, "A Look at Asians as Portrayed in the News."

26. Darrell Y. Hamamoto, "They're So Cute When They're Young," in *Children and Television: Images in a Changing Sociocultural World*, ed. Gordon L. Berry and Jon Keiko Asamen (Newbury Park, Calif.: Sage, 1993), 200.

27. Brian Locke, "Here Comes the Judge: The Dancing Itos and the Televisual Construction of the Enemy Asian Male," in *Living Color: Race and Television in the United States*, ed. Sasha Torres, 239–54 (Durham, N.C.: Duke University Press, 1998); Mansfield-Richardson, "Asian Americans and the Mass Media"; Wong, "Covering the Invisible 'Model Minority.'"

28. Hamamoto, *Monitored Peril.*

29. Cho, "Korean Americans vs. African Americans"; Park, "Identity Politics"; Kyeyoung Park, "Use and Abuse of Race and Culture: Black-Korean Tension in American," in *Koreans in the Hood: Conflict with African Americans*, ed. Kwang Chung Kim, 60–74 (Baltimore: Johns Hopkins University Press, 1999).

30. Cho, "Korean Americans vs. African Americans," 204.

31. Park, "Identity Politics."

32. Quoted in Chiu, "Power of the Press," 66.

33. John Fiske, *Media Matters: Race and Gender in U.S. Politics* (Minneapolis: University of Minnesota Press, 1996), 162.

34. Nishi, "Asian Americans at the Intersection of International and Domestic Tensions," 183.

35. Spencer K. Turnbull, "Wen Ho Lee and the Consequences of Enduring Asian American Stereotypes," *UCLA Asian American Law Journal* 72 (spring 2001): 74–75, 72.

36. Lee, "A Look at Asians as Portrayed in the News."

37. M. L. Stein, "Indian Newspapers and Tribal Censorship," *Editor & Publisher* 125(20) (May 16, 1992): 14–46.

38. Bradley J. Hamm, "Redefining Racism: Newspaper Justification for the 1924 Exclusion of Japanese Immigrants," *American Journalism: A Journal of Media History* 16(3) (1999): 53–69.

39. Thomas C. Nakayama, "Model Minority' and the Media: Discourse on Asian Americans," *Journal of Communication Inquiry* 12 (1988): 65–73.

40. Park, "Identity Politics."

41. Joann Lee, "Mistaken Heading Underscores Racial Presumptions," *Editor & Publisher* 131(17) (April 25, 1998): 64.

42. Hamm, "Redefining Racism," 65.

43. Stacy Jones, "From Obscurity to Scapegoat," *Editor & Publisher* 130(35) (August 30, 1997): 7; Joann Lee, "DNC Fund Raising and the 'Yellow Peril,'" *Editor & Publisher* 130(22) (May 31, 1997): 48, 36.

44. Taeku Lee, "The Backdoor and the Backlash: Campaign Finance and the Polarization of Chinese Americans," *Asian American Policy Review* 9 (1999): 30–55.

45. Unpublished paper by Taeku Lee and Albert Hahn referenced in Taeku Lee, "The Backdoor and the Backlash: Campaign Finance and the Politicization of Chinese Americans," in *Asian American Politics: Law, Participation, and Policy*, ed. Don T. Nakanishi and James S. Lai, 261–80 (Lanham, Md.: Rowman & Littlefield, 2003).

46. Frank Wu and May Nicholson, "Have You No Decency? Racial Aspects of Media Coverage on the John Huang Matter," *Asian American Policy Review* 7 (1997): 1–38.

47. L. Ling-chi Wang, "Race, Class, Citizenship, and Extraterritoriality: Asian Americans and the 1996 Campaign Finance Scandal," *Amerasia Journal* 24(1) (1998): 1–21.

48. Wong, "Covering the Invisible 'Model Minority.'"

49. Locke, "Here Comes the Judge."

50. Tom Verducci, "Orient Express: A Pair of Young Asian Pitchers, the Dodgers' Chan Ho Park and the Mariners' Makoto Suzuki, Have Thrown Baseball for a Loop," *Sports Illustrated* (March 28, 1994): 24–27.

51. Jones, "From Obscurity to Scapegoat."

52. Quoted in Chiu, "Power of the Press," 66.

53. Chiu, "Power of the Press."

54. Lee, "A Look at Asians as Portrayed in the News"; Nakayama, "'Model Minority' and the Media."

55. Chiung Hwang Chen, "'Outwhiting the Whites': An Examination of the Persistence of Asian American Model Minority Discourse," in *Race/Gender/Media: Considering Diversity across Audiences, Content, and Producers*, ed. Rebecca Ann Lind, 146–53 (Boston: Pearson Education, 2004).

56. Timothy P. Fong, *The Contemporary Asian American Experience: Beyond the Model Minority* (Upper Saddle River, N.J.: Prentice Hall, 1998); Hamamoto, *Monitoring Peril*.

57. Nakayama, "'Model Minority' and the Media," 68.

58. Mansfield-Richardson, "Asian Americans and the Mass Media."

59. Nishi, "Asian Americans at the Intersection of International and Domestic Tensions."

60. Chen, "'Outwhiting the Whites,'" 152.

61. Chen, "'Outwhiting the Whites.'"

62. Nakayama, "Model Minority' and the Media."

63. David Tokiharu Mayeda, "Media Portrayals of Major League Baseball Pitchers Hideo Nomo and Hideki Irabu," *Journal of Sport and Social Issues* 23(2) (1999): 203–71.

64. Hamm, "Redefining Racism."

65. Hamm, "Redefining Racism."

66. Nakayama, "'Model Minority' and the Media," 70.

67. Cho, "Korean Americans vs. African Americans."

68. Thomas K. Nakayama, "Stereotyping by the Media: Framing Asian Americans," in *Images of Color, Images of Crime*, ed. Coramae Richey Mann and Marjorie S. Zatz, 179–87 (Los Angeles: Roxbury Publishing Co., 1998).

69. Patricia A. Curtin, "Press Coverage of the 442nd Regimental Combat Team (Separate-Nisei): A Case Study in Agenda Building," *American Journalism: A Journal of Media History* 12(3) (1995): 225–41.

70. Michael Curtin, *Redeeming the Wasteland: Television Documentary and Cold War Politics* (New Brunswick, N.J.: Rutgers University Press, 1995).

71. Curtin, *Redeeming the Wasteland*.

72. Chen, "'Outwhiting the Whites,'" 152.

73. Cho, "Korean Americans vs. African Americans," 204.

74. Hyun Ban and R. C. Adams, "*Los Angeles Times* Coverage of Korean Americans before, after 1992 Riots," *Newspaper Research Journal* 18(3/4) (1997): 64–78.

75. Park, "Identity Politics," 212.

76. Park, "Identity Politics."

77. Park, "Use and Abuse of Race and Culture."

78. Austin Ranney, *Channels of Power: The Impact of Television on American Politics* (New York: Basic Books, 1983).

79. Nishi, "Asian Americans at the Intersection of International and Domestic Tensions."

80. Hamamoto, *Monitored Peril*.

81. Nishi, "Asian Americans at the Intersection of International and Domestic Tensions."

82. Sonni Efron, "Japanese Roots Still Ignite Bias," *Los Angeles Times*, Orange County Edition, December 5, 1991, A1, A36, A38.

83. Wong, "Covering the Invisible 'Model Minority,'" 46.

84. Lloyd Chiasson, "The Japanese American Enigma," in *The Press in Times of Crisis*, ed. Lloyd Chiasson Jr., 137–52 (Westport, Conn.: Praeger, 1995); Morton Grodzin, *Americans Betrayed* (Chicago: University of Chicago Press, 1949); Walt Stromer, "Why I Went Along: 1942 and the Invisible Evacuees," *Columbia Journalism Review* 31(5) (January 2, 1993): 15–17.

85. Catherine A. Luther, "Reflections of Cultural Identities in Conflict: Japanese American Internment Camp Newspapers during World War II," *Journalism History* 29(2) (2003): 69–81.

86. Grodzin, *Americans Betrayed*.

87. Chiasson, "The Japanese American Enigma," 148.

88. Brian Thornton, "Heroic Editors in Short Supply during Japanese Internment," *Newspaper Research Journal* 23(2/3) (2002): 99–113.

89. Chiasson, "The Japanese American Enigma."

90. Stromer, "Why I Went Along," 16.

91. Stromer, "Why I Went Along," 17.

92. Thornton, "Heroic Editors in Short Supply during Japanese Internment."

93. Curtin, *Redeeming the Wasteland*.

94. Thornton, "Heroic Editors in Short Supply during Japanese Internment."

95. Clint C. Wilson and Félix Gutiérrez, *Race, Multiculturalism, and the Media: From Mass Communication to Class Communication* (Thousand Oaks, Calif.: Sage Publications, 1995).

96. Takeya Mizuno, "Self-Censorship by Coercion: The Federal Government and the California Japanese-Language Newspapers from Pearl Harbor to Internment," *American Journalism: A Journal of Media History* 17(3) (2000): 31–57.

97. Jere Takahashi, *Nisei/Sansei: Shifting Japanese American Identities and Politics* (Philadelphia: Temple University Press, 1997).

98. Mizuno, "Self-Censorship by Coercion," 37.

99. Mizuno, "Self-Censorship by Coercion," 35.

100. Mizuno, "Self-Censorship by Coercion," 41.

101. Mizuno, "Self-Censorship by Coercion," 43.

102. Luther, "Reflections of Cultural Identities in Conflict."

103. Mansfield-Richardson, "Asian Americans and the Mass Media."

104. Mark Trumbull, "Demographics, Computers Multiply Asian-Language Media in the U.S.," *Christian Science Monitor*, July 24, 1995, 13.

105. Christopher Chow, "Casting Our Voices: Part 2 of 2," *Chinese American Forum* 16(1) (2000): 30–33.

106. Jae Chul Shim, "The Importance of Ethnic Newspapers to U.S. Newcomers," in *Facing Difference: Race, Gender, and Mass Media*, ed. Shirley Biagi and Marilyn Kern-Foxworth (Thousand Oaks, Calif.: Pine Forge Press, 1997), 253.

107. Cho, "Korean Americans vs. African Americans."

108. Rick Bonus, "Homeland Memories and Media: Filipino Images and Imaginations in America," in *Filipino Americans: Transformation and Identity*, ed. Maria P. P. Root, 208–18 (Thousand Oaks, Calif.: Sage Publications, 1997).

109. Bonus, "Homeland Memories and Media," 212.

110. Bonus, "Homeland Memories and Media," 217.

111. Hamamoto, *Monitored Peril*.

112. Bill Nichols, "Historical Consciousness and the Viewer: *Who Killed Vincent Chin?*" in *The Persistence of History: Cinema, Television, and the Modern Event*, ed. Vivian Sobchack, 55–68 (New York: Routledge Press, 1996), 62.

CHAPTER 12

1. Harvey Molotch, "Media and Movements," in *The Dynamics of Social Movements*, ed. Mayer N. Zald and John D. McCarthy, 71–93 (Cambridge, Mass.: Winthrop Publishers, 1979), 71.

2. William A. Gamson and Gadi Wolfsfeld, "Movement and Media as Interacting Systems," *The Annals*, 528 (1993): 114–25.

3. Jackie Smith, John D. McCarthy, Clark McPhail, and Boguslaw Augustyn, "From Protest to Agenda Building: Description Bias in Media Coverage of Protest Events in Washington, D.C.," *Social Forces* 79(4) (2001): 1397–1423.

4. Molotch, "Media and Movements," 71.

5. Thomas R. Dye and Harmon Ziegler, *The Irony of Democracy*, 12th ed. (Belmont, Calif.: Wadsworth Publishing, 2002).

6. Smith, McCarthy, McPhail, and Augustyn, "From Protest to Agenda Building."

7. Smith, McCarthy, McPhail, and Augustyn, "From Protest to Agenda Building."

8. Gamson and Wolfsfeld, "Movement and Media as Interacting Systems"; Todd Gitlin, *The Whole World Is Watching: Mass Media in the Making and Unmaking of the New Left* (Berkeley: University of California Press, 1980).

9. Melvin Small, *Covering Dissent: The Media and the Anti-Vietnam War Movement* (New Brunswick, N.J.: Rutgers University Press, 1994), 2.

10. Gamson and Wolfsfeld, "Movement and Media as Interacting Systems."

11. Smith, McCarthy, McPhail, and Augustyn, "From Protest to Agenda Building."

12. Shanto Iyengar, *Is Anyone Responsible? How Television Frames Political Issues* (Chicago: University of Chicago Press, 1991).

13. Gitlin, *The Whole World Is Watching*, 122–23.

14. James H. Wittebols, "News from the Noninstitutional World: U.S. and Canadian Television News Coverage of Social Protest," *Political Communication* 13 (1996): 345–61, 358.

15. Molotch, "Media and Movements"; Michael Parenti, *Inventing Reality: The Politics of the Mass Media* (New York: St. Martin's Press, 1986).

16. Gitlin, *The Whole World Is Watching*; John D. McCarthy, Jackie Smith, and Mayer N. Zald, "Accessing Public, Media, Electoral, and Governmental Agendas," in *Comparative Perspectives on Social Movements: Political Opportunities, Mobilizing Structures, and Cultural Framing*, ed. Doug McAdams, John D. McCarthy, and Mayer N. Zald, 291–311 (New York: Cambridge University Press, 1996).

17. Stephen E. Rada, "Manipulating the Media: A Case Study of a Chicano Strike in Texas," *Journalism Quarterly* 54 (1977): 109–113, 113.

18. Andrew Rojecki, *Silencing the Opposition: Antinuclear Movements and the Media in the Cold War* (Urbana: University of Illinois Press, 1999).

19. Smith, McCarthy, McPhail, and Augustyn, "From Protest to Agenda Building."

20. Douglas M. McLeod and James K. Hertog, "Social Control, Social Change and the Mass Media's Role in the Regulation of Protest Groups," *Mass Media, Social Control, and Social Change: A Macrosocial Perspective*, ed. David Demers and K. Viswanath, 305–30 (Ames: Iowa State University Press, 1999), 312–13.

21. McLeod and Hertog, "Social Control, Social Change and the Mass Media's Role in the Regulation of Protest Groups."

22. Wittebols, "News from the Noninstitutional World," 358.

23. Wittebols, "News from the Noninstitutional World," 354.

24. Wittebols, "News from the Noninstitutional World," 358.

25. Molotch, "Media and Movements."

26. Gamson and Wolfsfeld, "Movement and Media as Interacting Systems," 122.

27. McLeod and Hertog, "Social Control, Social Change and the Mass Media's Role in the Regulation of Protest Groups," 312–13.

28. Rojecki, *Silencing the Opposition*.

29. W. Lance Bennett, *News: The Politics of Illusion*, 5th ed. (New York: Longman Press, 2003).

30. Clarice N. Olien, Phillip J. Tichenor, and George A. Donohue, "Media Coverage and Social Movements," in *Information Campaigns: Balancing Social Values and Social Change*, ed. Charles T. Salmon, 139–63 (Newbury Park, Calif.: Sage Publications, 1990), 160.

31. Molotch, "Media and Movements," 91.

32. Gamson and Wolfsfeld, "Movement and Media as Interacting Systems"; David J. Garrow, *Protest at Selma: Martin Luther King, Jr. and the Voting Rights Act of 1965* (New Haven, Conn.: Yale University Press, 1978).

33. Gitlin, *The Whole World Is Watching*.

34. Gamson and Wolfsfeld, "Movement and Media as Interacting Systems."

35. John D. McCarthy, C. McPhail, and Jackie Smith, "Images of Protest: Dimensions of Selection Bias in Media Coverage of Washington Demonstrations, 1982 and 1991," *American Sociological Review* 61 (1996): 478–99.

36. Richard B. Kielbowitz and Clifford Scherer, "The Role of the Press in the Dynamics of Social Movements," in *Research in Social Movements: Conflict and Change*, ed. Louis Kriesberg, 71–96 (Greenwich, Conn.: JAI Press, 1986).

37. Gitlin, *The Whole World Is Watching*.

38. Gitlin, *The Whole World Is Watching*; Molotch, "Media and Movements."

39. Gamson and Wolfsfeld, "Movement and Media as Interacting Systems."

40. Molotch, "Media and Movements."

41. Gitlin, *The Whole World Is Watching*.

42. Gamson and Wolfsfeld, "Movement and Media as Interacting Systems"; Gitlin, *The Whole World Is Watching*.

43. Gitlin, *The Whole World Is Watching*.

44. Gamson and Wolfsfeld, "Movement and Media as Interacting Systems"; Gitlin, *The Whole World Is Watching*; Douglas M. McLeod and James K. Hertog, "The Manufacture of Public Opinion by Reporters: Informal Cues for Public Perceptions of Protest Groups," *Discourse and Society* 3 (1992): 259–75.

45. Anthony Downs, "Up and Down with Ecology: The Issue Attention Cycle," *Public Interest* 28 (1972): 38–50.

46. Smith, McCarthy, McPhail, and Augustyn, "From Protest to Agenda Building."

47. Rojecki, *Silencing the Opposition*.

48. Olien, Tichenor, and Donohue, "Media Coverage and Social Movements," 148.

49. Downs, "Up and Down with Ecology"; Olien, Tichenor, and Donohue, "Media Coverage and Social Movements."

50. Molotch, "Media and Movements."

51. Lawrence Alfred Powell, John B. Williamson, and Kenneth J. Branco, *The Senior Rights Movement: Framing the Policy Debate in America* (New York: Twayne Publishers, 1996).

52. Gitlin, *The Whole World Is Watching*.

53. Gamson and Wolfsfeld, "Movement and Media as Interacting Systems," 119.

54. Downs, "Up and Down with Ecology."

55. Downs, "Up and Down with Ecology"; Smith, McCarthy, McPhail, and Augustyn, "From Protest to Agenda Building."

56. Antonio Gramsci, *Selections from the Prison Notebooks of Antonio Gramsci*, ed. Quintin Hoare and Geoffrey Nowell Smith (London: Lawrence and Wishart, 1971).

57. Powell, Williamson, and Branco, *The Senior Rights Movement*.

58. Frances Fox Piven and Richard A. Cloward, *Poor People's Movements: Why They Succeed, How They Fail* (New York: Vintage Books, 1977); Gitlin, *The Whole World Is Watching*.

59. Doug McAdams, "The Framing Function of Movement Tactics: Strategic Dramaturgy in the American Civil Rights Movement," in *Comparative Perspectives on Social Movements: Political Opportunities, Mobilizing Structures, and Cultural Framing*, ed. Doug McAdams, John D. McCarthy, and Mayer N. Zald, 338–56 (New York: Cambridge University Press, 1996).

60. McLeod and Hertog, "Social Control, Social Change and the Mass Media's Role in the Regulation of Protest Groups"; Gitlin, *The Whole World Is Watching*.

61. Edward Herman and Noam Chomsky, *Manufacturing Consent* (New York, NY: Pantheon, 1988).

62. Smith, McCarthy, McPhail, and Augustyn, "From Protest to Agenda Building."

63. Molotch, "Media and Movements."

64. Daniel C. Hallin, *The Uncensored War: The Media and Vietnam* (Berkeley: University of California Press, 1986).

65. Rojecki, *Silencing the Opposition*.

66. Pablo Mora, "Conflict a Constant in PBS Series," *Denver Post*, April 7, 1996, E1.

67. Ward Churchill, "The Bloody Wake of Alcatraz: Political Repression of the American Indian Movement during the 1970s," in *American Indian Activism: Alcatraz to the Longest Walk*, ed. Troy Johnson, Joanne Nagel, and Duane Champagne, 242–84 (Urbana: University of Illinois Press, 1997); Carlos Muñoz Jr., *Youth, Identity, Power: The Chicano Movement* (New York: Verso, 1989); Glenn Omatsu, "The 'Four Prisons' and the Movements of Liberation: Asian American Activism from the 1960s to the 1990s," in *The State of Asian America: Activism*

and Resistance in the 1990s, ed. Karin Aguilar–San Juan, 19–69 (Boston: South End Press, 1994); Jere Takahashi, *Nisei/Sansei: Shifting Japanese American Identities and Politics* (Philadelphia: Temple University Press, 1997); William Wei, *The Asian American Movement* (Philadelphia: Temple University Press, 1993).

68. Omatsu, "The 'Four Prisons' and the Movements of Liberation"; Muñoz, *Youth, Identity, Power*; Takahashi, *Nisei/Sansei*.

CHAPTER 13

1. Rodger Streitmatter, *Mightier Than the Sword: How the News Media Have Shaped American History* (Boulder, Colo.: Westview Press, 1997), 170–71.

2. Streitmatter, *Mightier Than the Sword*, 186.

3. William J. Drummond, "About Face, from Alliance to Alienation: Blacks and the News Media," *The American Enterprise* (July 8, 1990): 23–29. David J. Garrow, *Protest at Selma: Martin Luther King, Jr. and the Voting Rights Act of 1965* (New Haven, Conn.: Yale University Press, 1978). J. Fred MacDonald, *Blacks and White TV: African Americans in Television since 1948*, 2nd ed. (Chicago: Nelson-Hall Publishers, 1992). Carolyn Martindale, *The White Press and Black America* (New York: Greenwood Press, 1986). Benjamin I. Page and Robert Y. Shapiro, *The Rational Public: Fifty Years of Trends in Americans' Policy Preferences* (Chicago: University of Chicago Press, 1992). Mary Ann Watson, *The Expanding Vista: American Television in the Kennedy Years* (New York: Oxford University Press, 1990).

4. Garrow, *Protest at Selma*.

5. Michael O'Neill, *The Roar of the Crowd: How Television and People Power Are Changing the World* (New York: Times Books, 1993), 44.

6. Streitmatter, *Mightier Than the Sword*, 171.

7. Drummond, "About Face, from Alliance to Alienation"; MacDonald, *Blacks and White TV*; Watson, *The Expanding Vista*.

8. Drummond, "About Face, from Alliance to Alienation," 24.

9. MacDonald, *Blacks and White TV*, 117.

10. Julian Bond, "The Media and the Movement: Looking Back from the Southern Front," in *Media, Culture, and the Modern African American Freedom Struggle*, ed. Brian Ward, 16–40 (Gainsville: University Press of Florida, 2001), 25.

11. Michael J. Robinson, "Television and American Politics: 1956–1976," *The Public Interest* 48 (1977): 3–39, 12.

12. Watson, *The Expanding Vista*, 98.

13. Garrow, *Protest at Selma*; Streitmatter, *Mightier Than the Sword*; Watson, *The Expanding Vista*.

14. James Dickerson, *Dixie's Dirty Secret: The True Story of How the Government, the Media, and the Mob Conspired to Combat Integration and the Vietnam Antiwar Movement* (Armonk, N.Y.: M. E. Sharpe, 1998); Garrow, *Protest at Selma*; Peter B. Levy, *The Civil Rights Movement* (Westport, Conn.: Greenwood Press, 1998); Streitmatter, *Mightier Than the Sword*; Watson, *The Expanding Vista*.

15. Bond, "The Media and the Movement."

16. Herbert J. Gans, *Deciding What's News: A Study of CBS Evening News, NBC Nightly News, Newsweek, and Time* (New York: Vintage Press, 1979), 297.

17. Garrow, *Protest at Selma*; Richard Lentz, *Symbols, the News Magazines, and Martin Luther King* (Baton Rouge: Louisiana State University Press, 1990).

18. Todd Gitlin, *The Whole World Is Watching: Mass Media in the Making and Unmaking of the New Left* (Berkeley: University of California Press, 1980); Garrow, *Protest at Selma*; Lentz, *Symbols, the News Magazines, and Martin Luther King*.

19. Drummond, "About Face, from Alliance to Alienation."

20. Henry Hampton, *Eyes on the Prize: American's Civil Rights Years* (Boston: Blackside, 1987).

21. Tom W. Smith, "America's Most Important Problem—A Trend Analysis, 1946–1976," *Public Opinion Quarterly* 44(2) (1980): 164–80, 170.

22. Smith, "America's Most Important Problem," 171.

23. Garrow, *Protest at Selma*; Donald R. Kinder and Lynn M. Sanders, *Divided by Color: Racial Politics and Democratic Ideals* (Chicago: University of Chicago Press, 1996); Robinson, "Television and American Politics"; James P. Winter and Chaim H. Eyal, "Agenda-Setting for the Civil Rights Issue," in *Agenda Setting: Reading on Media, Public Opinion, and Policymaking*, ed. David Protess and Maxwell McCombs, 101–7 (Hillsdale, N.J.: Lawrence Erlbaum Associates, 1991).

24. Page and Shapiro, *The Rational Public*, 77.

25. Kinder and Sanders, *Divided by Color*, 102.

26. Richard Reeves, *President Kennedy: Profile in Power* (New York: Simon and Schuster, 1993); Streitmatter, *Mightier Than the Sword*, 179.

27. Mary L. Dudziak, "Birmingham, Addis Ababa and the Image of America: International Influence on U.S. Civil Rights Politics in the Kennedy Administration" (presented at the Annual Meeting of the American Political Science Association, Washington, D.C., 2000).

28. Richard Lentz, "Snarls Echoing Round the World: The 1963 Birmingham Civil Rights Campaign on the World Stage," *American Journalism: A Journal of Media History* 17(2) (2000): 69–96.

29. Robert Dallek, *Flawed Giant: Lyndon Johnson and His Times, 1961–1973* (New York: Oxford University Press, 1998).

30. Garrow, *Protest at Selma*.

31. Edward Jay Epstein, *News from Nowhere* (New York: Vintage, 1973), 219–20.

32. G. Ray Funkhouser, "The Issues of the Sixties: An Exploratory Study in the Dynamics of Public Opinion," *Public Opinion Quarterly* 37 (1973): 62–75.

33. Paul M. Kellstedt, *The Mass Media and the Dynamics of American Racial Attitudes* (New York: Cambridge University Press, 2003).

34. Jenny Walker, "A Media Made Movement? Black Violence and Nonviolence in the Historiography of the Civil Rights Movement," in *Media, Culture, and the Modern African American Freedom Struggle*, ed. Brian Ward, 41–66 (Gainsville: University Press of Florida, 2001); Pamela Newkirk, *Within the Veil: Black Journalists, White Media* (New York: New York University Press, 2000).

35. Walter Gieber, "Two Communicators of the News: A Study of the Roles of Sources and Reporters," *Social Forces* 39(1) (1960–1961): 76–83.

36. Martindale, *The White Press and Black America*.

37. James Forman, *The Making of Black Revolutionaries: A Personal Account* (New York: MacMillan, 1972), 242.

38. Paula B. Johnson, David O. Sears, and John B. McConahay, "Black Invisibility, the Press, and the Los Angeles Riot," *American Journal of Sociology* 76(4) (1971): 698–721.

39. Johnson, Sears, and McConahay, "Black Invisibility, the Press, and the Los Angeles Riot," 710.

40. Bernard Roshco, "What the Black Press Said Last Summer," *Columbia Journalism Review* 4 (1967): 6–10; Jerry W. Knudson, *In the News: American Journalists View Their Craft* (Wilmington: Scholarly Resources, 2000); Newkirk, *Within the Veil*.

41. Lauren Kessler, *The Dissident Press: Alternative Journalism in American History* (Beverly Hills, Calif.: Sage Publications, 1984); Arthur Kaul, "The Unraveling of America," in *The Press in Times of Crisis*, ed. Lloyd Chiasson Jr., 169–87 (Westport, Conn.: Praeger, 1995); Newkirk, *Within the Veil*.

42. Martindale, *The White Press and Black America*.

43. Martindale, *The White Press and Black America*, 96.

44. Martindale, *The White Press and Black America*.

45. Michael R. Winston, "Racial Consciousness and the Evolution of Mass Communications in the United States," *Daedalus* 11(4) (1982): 171–82, 180.

46. Gans, *Deciding What's News*.

47. Roy E. Carter Jr., "Segregation and the News: A Regional Content Study," *Journalism Quarterly* 34(1) (1957): 3–18.

48. Ann K. Johnson, *Urban Ghetto Riots, 1965–1968: A Comparison of Soviet and American Press Coverage* (New York: Columbia University Press, 1996).

49. Martindale, *The White Press and Black America*, 122.

50. Martindale, *The White Press and Black America*, 122.

51. Martindale, *The White Press and Black America*.

52. Martindale, *The White Press and Black America*, 97.

53. Michael Weniger, *One Step Forward, Two Steps Back: The Student Nonviolent Coordinating Committee and Mass Media* (unpublished manuscript, 2002).

54. Kinder and Sanders, *Divided by Color*.

55. Bond, "The Media and the Movement."

56. Martindale, *The White Press and Black America*, 63.

57. Joseph Klapper, *The Effects of Mass Communication* (New York: Free Press, 1960).

58. For an example of this in the context of media coverage of the civil rights movement, see Allison Graham, "Remapping Dogpatch: Northern Media on the Southern Circuit," *The Arkansas Historical Quarterly* 56(3) (1997): 334–40.

59. Lentz, *Symbols, the News Magazines, and Martin Luther King*, 78.

60. Page and Shapiro, *The Rational Public*; Paul Burstein, *Discrimination, Jobs, and Politics: Employment Opportunity in the United States since the New Deal* (Chicago: University of Chicago Press, 1985).

61. Page and Shapiro, *The Rational Public*, 79.

62. Page and Shapiro, *The Rational Public*, 77–78.

63. Kellstedt, *The Mass Media and the Dynamics of American Racial Attitudes*.

64. Burstein, *Discrimination, Jobs, and Politics*.

65. Burstein, *Discrimination, Jobs, and Politics*, 85.

66. Alex Leidhold, "Virginius Dabney and Lenoir Chambers: Two Southern Liberal Newspaper Editors Face Virginia's Massive Resistance to Public School Integration," *American Journalism: A Journal of Media History* 15(4) (1998).

67. MacDonald, *Blacks and White TV*, 77.

68. Martindale, *The White Press and Black America*.

69. Edwin D. Williams, "Dimout in Jackson," *Columbia Journalism Review* 9(2) (1970): 56–58.

70. Kinder and Sanders, *Divided by Color*.

71. Garrow, *Protest at Selma*; Kinder and Sanders, *Divided by Color*.

72. Kinder and Sanders, *Divided by Color*, 102.

73. Lentz, *Symbols, the News Magazines, and Martin Luther King*.

74. Richard Lentz, "The Resurrection of the Prophet: Dr. Martin Luther King, Jr., and the News Weeklies," *American Journalism: A Journal of Media History* 4(2) (1987): 59–81.

75. David Halberstam, *The Fifties* (New York: Villard Books, 1993), 684.

76. Alfred Hero, *The Southerner and World Affairs* (Baton Rouge: Louisiana State University Press, 1965); Leidhold, "Virginius Dabney and Lenoir Chambers," 35–68; Ann Waldron, *Hodding Carter: The Reconstruction of a Racist* (Chapel Hill, N.C.: Algonquin Books of Chapel Hill, 1993); Susan Weill, "Conserving Racial Segregation in 1954: *Brown v. Board of Education* and the Mississippi Daily Press," *American Journalism: A Journal of Media History* 16(4) (1999): 77–99.

77. Richard A. Pride, *The Political Use of Racial Narratives: School Desegregation in Mobile, Alabama, 1954–1997* (Urbana: University of Illinois Press, 2002).

78. Gerald N. Rosenberg, *The Hollow Hope: Can Courts Bring About Social Change?* (Chicago: University of Chicago Press, 1991).

79. Dickerson, *Dixie's Dirty Secret*, 30.

80. Weill, "Conserving Racial Segregation in 1954."

81. Weill, "Conserving Racial Segregation in 1954."

82. Weill, "Conserving Racial Segregation in 1954."

83. Weill, "Conserving Racial Segregation in 1954."

84. Dickerson, *Dixie's Dirty Secret*.

85. Newkirk, *Within the Veil*.

86. Weill, "Conserving Racial Segregation in 1954," 93.

87. Weill, "Conserving Racial Segregation in 1954."

88. Carter, "Segregation and the News."

89. Waldron, *Hodding Carter*.

90. Hugh Davis Graham, *Crisis in Print: Desegregation and the Press in Tennessee* (Nashville, Tenn.: Vanderbilt University Press, 1967), 58.

91. Carter, "Segregation and the News."

92. Leidhold, "Virginius Dabney and Lenoir Chambers," 37.

93. Leidhold, "Virginius Dabney and Lenoir Chambers."

94. Halberstam, *The Fifties*, 678.

95. Streitmatter, *Mightier Than the Sword*.

96. Bond, "The Media and the Movement," 28.

97. Halberstam, *The Fifties*.

98. Melissa Hickman Barlow, "Race and the Problem of Crime in Time and Newsweek Cover Stories, 1946 to 1995," *Social Justice* 25(2) (1998): 149–83.

99. Graham, "Ramapping Dogpatch," 338. The article referred to in the essay is from *Time*, September 24, 1957, 12–13.

100. Hank Klibanoff, "L. Alex Wilson," *Media Studies Quarterly* 14(2) (2000): 60–68.

101. Halberstam, *The Fifties*.

102. Graham, *Crisis in Print*, 169.

103. Graham, *Crisis in Print*.

104. Waldron, *Hodding Carter*.

105. Watson, *The Expanding Vista*.

106. MacDonald, *Blacks and White TV*.

107. Dickerson, *Dixie's Dirty Secret*, 67.

108. Watson, *The Expanding Vista*, 95; Charles A. Simmons, *The African American Press: A History of News Coverage during National Crises, with Special Reference to Four Black Newspapers, 1827–1965* (Jefferson, N.C.: McFarland and Co., 1998).

109. Watson, *The Expanding Vista*, 96.

110. Dickerson, *Dixie's Dirty Secret*.

111. Williams, "Dimout in Jackson," 56.

112. Waldron, *Hodding Carter*.

113. Graham, *Crisis in Print*.

114. Graham, *Crisis in Print*, 215.

115. Graham, *Crisis in Print*, 219.

116. Hampton, *Eyes on the Prize*; Juan Williams, *Eyes on the Prize: America's Civil Rights Years, 1954–1965* (New York: Viking Penguin, 1988).

117. Levy, *The Civil Rights Movement*, 52.

118. Bond, "The Media and the Movement."

119. Charles M. Payne, *I've Got the Light of Freedom: The Organizing Tradition and the Mississippi Freedom Struggle* (Berkeley: University of California Press, 1996).

120. Klibanoff, "L. Alex Wilson"; Waldron, *Hodding Carter.*

121. Klibanoff, "L. Alex Wilson."

122. Wendy Kozol, *Life's America: Family and Nation in Postwar Photojournalism* (Philadelphia: Temple University Press, 1994).

123. Dickerson, *Dixie's Dirty Secret*; Kozol, *Life's America.*

124. Kozol, *Life's America.*

125. Dickerson, *Dixie's Dirty Secret.*

126. Lentz, *Symbols, the News Magazines, and Martin Luther King*, 44.

127. Sharon Bramlett-Solomon, "Southern vs. Northern Newspaper Coverage of the Dime Store Demonstration Movement: A Study of News Play and News Source Diversity," *Mass Media Review* 15 (1988): 24–30.

128. Graham, *Crisis in Print*, 207.

129. Lentz, *Symbols, the News Magazines, and Martin Luther King*, 44.

130. Lentz, *Symbols, the News Magazines, and Martin Luther King.*

131. Lentz, *Symbols, the News Magazines, and Martin Luther King*, 47.

132. Bond, "The Media and the Movement."

133. Dickerson, *Dixie's Dirty Secret*; Levy, *The Civil Rights Movement*; Streitmatter, *Mightier Than the Sword.*

134. Dickerson, *Dixie's Dirty Secret.*

135. Rhoda Lois Blumberg, *Civil Rights: The 1960s Freedom Struggle* (Boston: Twayne Publishers, 1984).

136. George Gallup, *The Gallup Poll: Public Opinion 1935–1971*, Vol. 3 (New York: Random House, 1972), 1723, 1724.

137. Lentz, *Symbols, the News Magazines, and Martin Luther King*, 52.

138. Lentz, *Symbols, the News Magazines, and Martin Luther King*, 57.

139. Dickerson, *Dixie's Dirty Secret.*

140. Graham, *Crisis in Print*, 211.

141. Graham, *Crisis in Print.*

142. Simmons, *The African American Press.*

143. Simmons, *The African American Press.*

144. Bond, "The Media and the Movement."

145. Hampton, *Eyes on the Prize.*

146. Jinx C. Broussard, "Saviors or Scalawags: The Mississippi Black Press's Contrasting Coverage of Civil Rights Workers and Freedom Summer, June–August 1964," *American Journalism: A Journal of Media History* 19(3) (2002): 63–85.

147. Broussard, "Saviors or Scalawags," 69.

148. Broussard, "Saviors or Scalawags."

149. Broussard, "Saviors or Scalawags," 79.

150. Vanessa Murphree, "The *Student Voice* 'Purging the Rabies of Racism' 1960–1965," *American Journalism: A Journal of Media History* 2(1) (2003): 73–91, 74.

151. Murphree, "The *Student Voice* 'Purging the Rabies of Racism' 1960–1965."

152. Murphree, "The *Student Voice* 'Purging the Rabies of Racism' 1960–1965."

153. Blumberg, *Civil Rights.*

154. Lentz, "Snarls Echoing Round the World"; Lentz, *Symbols, the News Magazines, and Martin Luther King.*

155. Garrow, *Protest at Selma.*

156. Garrow, *Protest at Selma*, 148.

157. Lentz, *Symbols, the News Magazines, and Martin Luther King*, 82.

158. Lentz, *Symbols, the News Magazines, and Martin Luther King*, 88.

159. Lentz, *Symbols, the News Magazines, and Martin Luther King*, 87.

160. Watson, *The Expanding Vista.*

161. MacDonald, *Blacks and White TV*, 109.

162. Watson, *The Expanding Vista*.

163. Streitmatter, *Mightier Than the Sword*.

164. Watson, *The Expanding Vista*.

165. Watson, *The Expanding Vista*, 109.

166. Streitmatter, *Mightier Than the Sword*.

167. Simmons, *The African American Press*.

168. Murphree, "The *Student Voice* 'Purging the Rabies of Racism' 1960–1965."

169. Lentz, *Symbols, the News Magazines, and Martin Luther King*, 104.

170. Lentz, *Symbols, the News Magazines, and Martin Luther King*, 104.

171. Lentz, *Symbols, the News Magazines, and Martin Luther King*, 106.

172. Lentz, *Symbols, the News Magazines, and Martin Luther King*, 107.

173. Blumberg, *Civil Rights*.

174. Garrow, *Protest at Selma*; Streitmatter, *Mightier Than the Sword*.

175. Garrow, *Protest at Selma*.

176. Gitlin, *The Whole World Is Watching*, 59.

177. Garrow, *Protest at Selma*.

178. Lentz, *Symbols, the News Magazines, and Martin Luther King*, 147.

179. Lentz, *Symbols, the News Magazines, and Martin Luther King*, 148.

180. Lentz, *Symbols, the News Magazines, and Martin Luther King*, 156.

181. Lentz, *Symbols, the News Magazines, and Martin Luther King*, 157.

182. Lentz, *Symbols, the News Magazines, and Martin Luther King*, 158.

183. Garrow, *Protest at Selma*.

184. Ronald N. Jacobs, *Race, Media, and the Crisis of Civil Society: From Watts to Rodney King* (Cambridge: Cambridge University Press, 2000).

185. Kaul, "The Unraveling of America."

186. Johnson, *Urban Ghetto Riots, 1965–1968*; David L. Paletz and Robert Dunn, "Press Coverage of Civil Disorders: A Case Study of Winston-Salem, 1967," *Public Opinion Quarterly* 33(3) (1969): 328–45.

187. Fred Fedler, "The Media and Minority Groups: A Study of Adequacy of Access," *Journalism Quarterly* 50(1) (1973): 109–17; Gans, *Deciding What's News*.

188. Barlow, "Race and the Problem of Crime in Time and Newsweek Cover Stories."

189. Johnson, Sears, and McConahay, "Black Invisibility, the Press, and the Los Angeles Riot"; Jacobs, *Race, Media, and the Crisis*.

190. Barlow, "Race and the Problem of Crime in Time and Newsweek Cover Stories."

191. Jacobs, *Race, Media, and the Crisis*.

192. Martindale, *The White Press and Black America*.

193. William Rasberry, "Politics, Blacks, and the Press," in *Politics and the Press* (Washington, D.C.: Acropolis Books, 1970).

194. Newkirk, *Within the Veil*, 67.

195. Johnson, *Urban Ghetto Riots, 1965–1968*, 84.

196. Kinder and Sanders, *Divided by Color*, 103.

197. Kinder and Sanders, *Divided by Color*, 321.

198. Gans, *Deciding What's News*, 54.

199. Johnson, *Urban Ghetto Riots, 1965–1968*.

200. Jacobs, *Race, Media, and the Crisis*, 58.

201. Kaul, "The Unraveling of America."

202. Jacobs, *Race, Media, and the Crisis*, 58.

203. Johnson, Sears, and McConahay, "Black Invisibility, the Press, and the Los Angeles Riot," 717.

204. Paletz and Dunn, "Press Coverage of Civil Disorders."

205. Richard A. Pride and Daniel H. Clarke, "Race Relations in Television News: A Content Analysis of the Networks," *Journalism Quarterly* 50(2) (1973): 319–28, 326.

206. Jacobs, *Race, Media, and the Crisis*, 58.

207. Johnson, *Urban Ghetto Riots, 1965–1968*, 46.

208. Paletz and Dunn, "Press Coverage of Civil Disorders," 355.

209. Paletz and Dunn, "Press Coverage of Civil Disorders."

210. Johnson, Sears, and McConahay, "Black Invisibility, the Press, and the Los Angeles Riot."

211. Paletz and Dunn, "Press Coverage of Civil Disorders," 345.

212. Jacobs, *Race, Media, and the Crisis*, 60.

213. Jacobs, *Race, Media, and the Crisis*, 72.

214. Kaul, "The Unraveling of America."

215. Jacobs, *Race, Media, and the Crisis*, 57.

216. Jacobs, *Race, Media, and the Crisis*, 80.

217. Dickerson, *Dixie's Dirty Secret*; Newkirk, *Within the Veil*; Simmons, *The African American Press*.

218. Jane Rhodes, "Fanning the Flames of Racial Discord: The National Press and the Black Panthers Party," *The Harvard International Journal of Press/Politics* 4(4) (1999): 95–118.

219. Levy, *The Civil Rights Movement*.

220. Rhodes, "Fanning the Flames of Racial Discord," 101.

221. Johnson, *Urban Ghetto Riots, 1965–1968*.

222. Clayborne Carson, *In Struggle: SNCC and the Black Awakening of the 1960s* (Cambridge, Mass.: Harvard University Press, 1981).

223. Epstein, *News from Nowhere*.

224. Gans, *Deciding What's News*.

225. Rhodes, "Fanning the Flames of Racial Discord."

226. Pride and Clarke, "Race Relations in Television News."

227. Rhodes, "Fanning the Flames of Racial Discord."

228. Rhodes, "Fanning the Flames of Racial Discord."

229. Michael E. Staub, "Black Panthers, New Journalism, and the Rewriting of the Sixties," *Representations* 57 (1997): 53–72.

230. Quoted in Rhodes, "Fanning the Flames of Racial Discord," 110.

231. Rhodes, "Fanning the Flames of Racial Discord."

232. Rhodes, "Fanning the Flames of Racial Discord."

233. Jack Lule, "News Strategies and the Death of Huey Newton," *Journalism Quarterly* 70(2) (1993): 287–99.

234. Kessler, *The Dissident Press*.

235. Rhodes, "Fanning the Flames of Racial Discord."

236. Michael R. Smith, *Violent Beginnings: The Story of the Black Panther Party, 1968–1973* (unpublished manuscript, 2002).

237. Roshco, "What the Black Press Said Last Summer."

CHAPTER 14

1. Mary Ann Weston, *Native Americans in the News: Images of Indians in the Twentieth Century Press* (Westport, Conn.: Greenwood Press, 1996), 129.

2. Tim Baylor, "Media Framing of Movement Protest: The Case of American Indian Protest," *The Social Science Journal* 33(3) (1996): 241–55.

3. Deborah LeVeen, "Organization or Disruption? Strategy Options for Marginal Groups: The Case of the Chicago Indian Village," in *Social Movements of the Sixties and Seventies*, ed. Jo Freeman, 211–34 (New York: Longman Press, 1983).

4. William Hewitt, "The Camera's Red Lens: Television Coverage of Wounded Knee II,"

in *Facing Difference: Race, Gender, and Mass Media*, ed. Shirley Biagi and Marilyn Kern-Foxworth, 15–23 (Thousand Oaks, Calif.: Pine Forge Press, 1997).

5. Troy Johnson, *The Occupation of Alcatraz Island: Indian Self-Determination and the Rise of Indian Activism* (Urbana: University of Illinois Press, 1996), 220.

6. Johnson, *The Occupation of Alcatraz Island.*

7. Baylor, "Media Framing of Movement Protest"; Hewitt, "The Camera's Red Lens."

8. Paul Chaat Smith and Robert Allen Warrior, *Like a Hurricane: The Indian Movement from Alcatraz to Wounded Knee* (New York: New Press, 1996); Weston, *Native Americans in the News.*

9. Smith and Warrior, *Like a Hurricane.*

10. Baylor, "Media Framing of Movement Protest."

11. Weston, *Native Americans in the News*, 145.

12. Baylor, "Media Framing of Movement Protest."

13. Baylor, "Media Framing of Movement Protest," 244.

14. Baylor, "Media Framing of Movement Protest."

15. Ann K. Johnson, *Urban Ghetto Riots, 1965–1968: A Comparison of Soviet and American Press Coverage* (New York: Columbia University Press, 1996).

16. Weston, *Native Americans in the News.*

17. Johnson, *The Occupation of Alcatraz Island.*

18. Smith and Warrior, *Like a Hurricane*, 111.

19. Johnson, *The Occupation of Alcatraz Island.*

20. Weston, *Native Americans in the News.*

21. Smith and Warrior, *Like a Hurricane*; Weston, *Native Americans in the News.*

22. Robert Allen Warrior, "Past and Present at Wounded Knee," *Media Studies Journal* 11(2) (1997): 68–75.

23. Johnson, *The Occupation of Alcatraz Island.*

24. Smith and Warrior, *Like a Hurricane*; Weston, *Native Americans in the News.*

25. Tim Findley, "Alcatraz Recollections," in *American Indian Activism: Alcatraz to the Longest Walk*, ed. Troy Johnson, Joanne Nagel, and Duane Champagne, 74–87 (Urbana: University of Illinois Press, 1997).

26. Findley, "Alcatraz Recollections"; Smith and Warrior, *Like a Hurricane.*

27. Johnson, *The Occupation of Alcatraz Island.*

28. LaNada Boyer, "Reflections of Alcatraz," in *American Indian Activism: Alcatraz to the Longest Walk*, ed. Troy Johnson, Joanne Nagel, and Duane Champagne, 88–103 (Urbana: University of Illinois Press, 1997).

29. Weston, *Native Americans in the News*, 138.

30. Smith and Warrior, *Like a Hurricane*, 20.

31. Weston, *Native Americans in the News.*

32. Smith and Warrior, *Like a Hurricane*, 38.

33. Smith and Warrior, *Like a Hurricane*, 11.

34. Smith and Warrior, *Like a Hurricane.*

35. Weston, *Native Americans in the News*, 139.

36. Johnson, *The Occupation of Alcatraz Island.*

37. Findley, "Alcatraz Recollections"; Johnson, *The Occupation of Alcatraz Island*; Smith and Warrior, *Like a Hurricane.*

38. Findley, "Alcatraz Recollections," 84.

39. Johnson, *Urban Ghetto Riots, 1965–1968*; Smith and Warrior, *Like a Hurricane.*

40. Steve Talbot, "Free Alcatraz: The Culture of Native American Liberation," *Journal of Ethnic Studies* 6(3) (1978): 90.

41. Johnson, *The Occupation of Alcatraz Island.*

42. Smith and Warrior, *Like a Hurricane*, 155.

43. Smith and Warrior, *Like a Hurricane.*

44. Smith and Warrior, *Like a Hurricane.*

45. Warrior, "Past and Present at Wounded Knee."

46. Smith and Warrior, *Like a Hurricane*, 168.

47. Smith and Warrior, *Like a Hurricane*, 181.

48. Smith and Warrior, *Like a Hurricane*.

49. Smith and Warrior, *Like a Hurricane*, 177.

50. Hewitt, "The Camera's Red Lens"; Warrior, "Past and Present at Wounded Knee."

51. Weston, *Native Americans in the News*.

52. Warrior, "Past and Present at Wounded Knee," 72.

53. Smith and Warrior, *Like a Hurricane*.

54. Smith and Warrior, *Like a Hurricane*, 250.

55. Hewitt, "The Camera's Red Lens."

56. Warrior, "Past and Present at Wounded Knee."

57. Hewitt, "The Camera's Red Lens," 17.

58. Weston, *Native Americans in the News*, 142.

59. Weston, *Native Americans in the News*.

60. Warrior, "Past and Present at Wounded Knee."

61. Weston, *Native Americans in the News*.

62. Smith and Warrior, *Like a Hurricane*.

63. Hewitt, "The Camera's Red Lens."

64. Hewitt, "The Camera's Red Lens."

65. Weston, *Native Americans in the News*.

66. Warrior, "Past and Present at Wounded Knee."

67. Hewitt, "The Camera's Red Lens."

68. Baylor, "Media Framing of Movement Protest"; Hewitt, "The Camera's Red Lens."

69. Smith and Warrior, *Like a Hurricane*.

70. Smith and Warrior, *Like a Hurricane*, 210.

71. Hewitt, "The Camera's Red Lens."

72. Smith and Warrior, *Like a Hurricane*, 264.

73. Hewitt, "The Camera's Red Lens," 17.

74. Warrior, "Past and Present at Wounded Knee," 69.

75. Smith and Warrior, *Like a Hurricane*, 212.

76. Weston, *Native Americans in the News*, 147.

77. James E. Murphy and Sharon M. Murphy, *Let My People Know: American Indian Journalism, 1828–1978* (Norman: University of Oklahoma Press, 1981).

78. Baylor, "Media Framing of Movement Protest."

79. Juan Gómez-Quinones, *Chicano Politics: Reality and Promise, 1940–1990* (Albuquerque: University of New Mexico Press, 1990), 103.

80. Carlos Muñoz Jr., *Youth, Identity, Power: The Chicano Movement* (New York: Verso, 1989).

81. David E. Hayes-Bautista and Gregory Rodriguez, "The Chicano Movement: More Nostalgia Than a Reality," *Los Angeles Times*, September 17, 1995, 6.

82. Francisco J. Lewels, *The Uses of the Media by the Chicano Movement: A Study in Minority Access* (New York: Praeger, 1974).

83. Muñoz, *Youth, Identity, Power*.

84. Rodolfo Acuña, *Occupied America: A History of Chicanos*, 3rd ed. (New York: Harper and Row, 1988).

85. Federico A. Subervi-Véliz (unpublished manuscript).

86. Ken Parish Perkins, "Television: The Man Who Dignified Farm Workers," *Fort Worth Star-Telegram*, April 16, 1997, 1; Lewels, *The Uses of the Media by the Chicano Movement*; J. Craig Jenkins, "The Transformation of a Constituency into a Movement: Farmworker Organizing in California," in *Social Movements of the Sixties and Seventies*, ed. Jo Freeman, 52–70 (New York: Longman Press, 1983).

87. Jenkins, "The Transformation of a Constituency into a Movement."

88. Richard J. Jensen and John C. Hammerback, "Chicano Utopianism in the Southwest," in *Postmodern Political Communication: The Fringe Challenges the Center*, ed. Andrew King, 85–98 (Westport, Conn.: Praeger, 1992), 93.

89. Lewels, *The Uses of the Media by the Chicano Movement*.

90. Jenkins, "The Transformation of a Constituency into a Movement."

91. Gómez-Quiñones, *Chicano Politics*.

92. Jensen and Hammerback, "Chicano Utopianism in the Southwest."

93. Lewels, *The Uses of the Media by the Chicano Movement*.

94. Lewels, *The Uses of the Media by the Chicano Movement*, 17.

95. Richard Lentz, *Symbols, the News Magazines, and Martin Luther King* (Baton Rouge: Louisiana State University Press, 1990); Muñoz, *Youth, Identity, Power*.

96. Muñoz, *Youth, Identity, Power*.

97. Stephen E. Rada, "Manipulating the Media: A Case Study of a Chicano Strike in Texas," *Journalism Quarterly* 54 (1977): 109–13.

98. Lewels, *The Uses of the Media by the Chicano Movement*, 17.

99. Jenkins, "The Transformation of a Constituency into a Movement"; Rada, "Manipulating the Media."

100. Lewels, *The Uses of the Media by the Chicano Movement*.

101. Lewels, *The Uses of the Media by the Chicano Movement*.

102. Lewels, *The Uses of the Media by the Chicano Movement*, 22.

103. Lewels, *The Uses of the Media by the Chicano Movement*.

104. Lewels, *The Uses of the Media by the Chicano Movement*; Sharon Murphy, *Other Voices: Black, Chicano, and American Indian Press* (Dayton, Ohio: Pflaum/Standard, 1974).

105. Carlos Larralde, *Mexican American Movements and Leaders* (Los Alamitos, Calif.: Hwong Publishing Co., 1976); Perkins, "Television."

106. Armando Navarro, *La Raza Unida Party: A Chicano Challenge to the U.S. Two-Party Dictatorship* (Philadelphia: Temple University Press, 2000).

107. Richard J. Jensen and John C. Hammerback, "No Revolutions without Poets: The Rhetoric of Rodlofo 'Corky' Gonzáles," *The Western Journal of Speech Communication* 46 (1982): 72–91, 73; Muñoz, *Youth, Identity, Power*; Ruben Salazar, *Border Correspondent, Selected Writings, 1955–1970*, ed. Mario T. García (Berkeley: University of California Press, 1995).

108. Jensen and Hammerback, "No Revolutions without Poets."

109. Larralde, *Mexican American Movements and Leaders*, 198.

110. Jensen and Hammerback, "No Revolutions without Poets," 91.

111. John C. Ensslin, "Crusade Leaves Many Legacies," *Denver Rocky Mountain News*, September 21, 1999, 28A.

112. Gómez-Quinones, *Chicano Politics*, 112.

113. Ensslin, "Crusade Leaves Many Legacies."

114. Navarro, *La Raza Unida Party*.

115. Gómez-Quiñones, *Chicano Politics*; Navarro, *La Raza Unida Party*.

116. Navarro, *La Raza Unida Party*.

117. Lentz, *Symbols, the News Magazines, and Martin Luther King*; Navarro, *La Raza Unida Party*.

118. Navarro, *La Raza Unida Party*.

119. Gómez-Quiñones, *Chicano Politics*.

120. Lentz, *Symbols, the News Magazines, and Martin Luther King*.

121. Lentz, *Symbols, the News Magazines, and Martin Luther King*, 324.

122. Salazar, *Border Correspondent*, 207.

123. Eric D. Blanchard, "The Poor People and the 'White Press,'" *Columbia Journalism Review* 7(3) (fall 1968): 61–65.

124. Blanchard, "The Poor People and the 'White Press,'" 62.

125. Gómez-Quinones, *Chicano Politics*.

126. Muñoz, *Youth, Identity, Power*.

127. Gómez-Quinones, *Chicano Politics*.

128. Mark Fiorill, *What Chicano Movement? The Media and the Chicano Movement, 1963–1973* (unpublished manuscript, 2002).

129. Mario T. García, "Introduction," in *Border Correspondent, Selected Writings, 1955–1970*, Ruben Salazar (author), ed. Mario T. García (Berkeley: University of California Press, 1995).

130. García, "Introduction."

131. Frank Del Olmo, "Ruben Salazar—Misunderstood Martyr," *Media Studies Journal* 11 (1997): 58–67.

132. García, "Introduction," 33.

133. García, "Introduction," 28.

134. Del Olmo, "Ruben Salazar."

135. García, "Introduction"; América Rodriguez, *Making Latino News: Race, Language, Class* (Thousand Oaks: Calif.: Sage Publications, 1999).

136. García, "Introduction"; Rodriguez, *Making Latino News*.

137. García, "Introduction."

138. Fiorill, *What Chicano Movement?* 16.

139. García, "Introduction."

140. Gerald Garza, "The Wisdom of the Past in Exploring the Current Status of Chicanos," *Los Angeles Times*, August 26, 1990, 6; Rodriguez, 2000.

141. Del Olmo, "Ruben Salazar."

142. Mary Anne Perez, "East Los Angeles: Brown Berets Return to Stem Violence," *Los Angeles Times*, August 15, 1993, 7.

143. Peter Skerry, *Mexican Americans: The Ambivalent Minority* (Cambridge, Mass.: Harvard University Press, 1993).

144. Frank Del Olmo, "Who Remembers the Invasion of Catalina?" *Los Angeles Times*, June 29, 1997, 5.

145. Lewels, *The Uses of the Media by the Chicano Movement*.

146. Lewels, *The Uses of the Media by the Chicano Movement*, 112–13.

147. Gómez-Quinones, *Chicano Politics*.

148. Murphy, *Other Voices*.

149. Lewels, *The Uses of the Media by the Chicano Movement*.

150. Rodriguez, *Making Latino News*.

151. Subervi-Vélez, unpublished manuscript.

152. Kim Geron, "An Exploration of the Asian American Movement through the Prism of Social Movement Theory" (presented at the American Political Science Association Meetings, Washington, D.C., August 2000); Glenn Omatsu, "The 'Four Prisons' and the Movements of Liberation: Asian American Activism from the 1960s to the 1990s," in *The State of Asian America: Activism and Resistance in the 1990s*, ed. Karin Aguilar–San Juan, 19–69 (Boston: South End Press, 1994); William Wei, *The Asian American Movement* (Philadelphia: Temple University Press, 1993).

153. Omatsu, "The 'Four Prisons' and the Movements of Liberation."

154. Geron, "An Exploration of the Asian American Movement through the Prism of Social Movement Theory," 2.

155. Omatsu, "The 'Four Prisons' and the Movements of Liberation."

156. Jere Takahashi, *Nisei/Sansei: Shifting Japanese American Identities and Politics* (Philadelphia: Temple University Press, 1997).

157. Omatsu, "The 'Four Prisons' and the Movements of Liberation."

158. John J. Miller, "Paragons or Pariahs? Arguing with Asian-American Success," *Reason* (1993): 48–50.

159. Wei, *The Asian American Movement*.

160. Geron, "An Exploration of the Asian American Movement through the Prism of Social Movement Theory."

161. Omatsu, "The 'Four Prisons' and the Movements of Liberation," 26.

162. Wei, *The Asian American Movement*.

163. Karen Umemoto, "On Strike! San Francisco State College Strike, 1968–69," *Amerasia Journal* 15 (1991): 3–41, 24.

164. Wei, *The Asian American Movement*.

165. Wei, *The Asian American Movement*, 27.

166. Wei, *The Asian American Movement*, 208.

167. Virginia D. Mansfield-Richardson, "Asian Americans and the Mass Media: A Content Analysis of Twenty U.S. Newspapers and a Survey of Asian American Journalists" (unpublished Ph.D. diss., Ohio State University, 1996); Umemoto, "On Strike!"; Wei, *The Asian American Movement*.

168. Wei, *The Asian American Movement*, 130.

169. Umemoto, "On Strike!"

170. Mansfield-Richardson, "Asian Americans and the Mass Media."

171. Wei, *The Asian American Movement*, 102.

172. Wei, *The Asian American Movement*.

173. Wei, *The Asian American Movement*.

174. Wei, *The Asian American Movement*.

175. Wei, *The Asian American Movement*, 100.

CHAPTER 15

1. W. Lance Bennett, *News: The Politics of Illusion*, 5th ed. (New York: Longman Press, 2003).

2. W. Lance Bennett, *The Governing Crisis: Media, Money, and Marketing in American Elections* (New York: St. Martin's Press, 1992).

3. Michael Jay Robinson, "A Statesman Is a Dead Politician: Candidate Images on Network News," in *What's News: The Media in American Society*, ed. Elie Abel, 159–86 (San Francisco: Institute for Contemporary Studies, 1981).

4. Thomas E. Patterson and Robert D. McClure, *The Unseeing Eye: The Myth of Television Power in National Elections* (New York: Putnam, 1976); Thomas E. Patterson, *Out of Order* (New York: Alfred A. Knopf, 1993).

5. Stephanie Greco Larson, "Misunderstanding Margin of Error: Network News Coverage of Polls during the 2000 General Election," *The Harvard International Journal of Press/Politics* 8(1) (2003): 66–80.

6. Donald R. Matthews, "'Winnowing': The News Media and the 1976 Presidential Nominations," in *Race for the Presidency: The Media and the Nominating Process*, ed. James David Barber, 55–78 (Englewood Cliffs, N.J.: Prentice Hall, 1978).

7. Michael J. Robinson and Margaret A. Sheehan, *Over the Wire and on TV* (New York: Russell Sage Foundation, 1983).

8. Michael J. Robinson and Maura Clancey, "The Media in Campaign '84: General Election Coverage: Part I," in *The Mass Media in Campaign '84*, ed. Michael J. Robinson and Austin Ranney, 27–33 (Washington, D.C.: American Enterprise Institute, 1985); Maura Clancey and Michael J. Robinson, "General Election Campaign: Part I," in *The Mass Media in Campaign '84*, ed. Michael J. Robinson and Austin Ranney, 27–33 (Washington, D.C.: American Enterprise Institute, 1985).

9. Patterson, *Out of Order*.

10. Patterson, *Out of Order*.

11. James Ceaser and Andrew Busch, *Upside Down and Inside Out: The 1992 Elections and American Politics* (Lanham, Md.: Rowman & Littlefield, 1993); Robinson and Sheehan, *Over the Wire and on TV.*

12. Peter Clarke and Susan H. Evans, *Covering Campaigns: Journalism in Congressional Elections* (Palo Alto, Calif.: Stanford University Press, 1983).

13. Anita Dunn, "The Best Campaign Wins: Local Press Coverage of Nonpresidential Races," in *Campaigns and Elections: American Style,* ed. James A. Thurber and Candice J. Nelson, 112–25 (Boulder, Colo.: Westview Press, 1995).

14. Kim Fridkin Kahn, *The Political Consequences of Being a Woman: Stereotypes Influence the Conduct and Consequences of Political Campaigns* (New York: Columbia University Press, 1996).

15. Kahn, *The Political Consequences of Being a Woman;* Kim Fridkin Kahn and Edie Goldenberg, "Women Candidates in the News: An Examination of Gender Differences in U.S. Senate Campaign Coverage," *Public Opinion Quarterly* 55 (1991): 180–99.

16. Maria Braden, *Women Politicians and the Media* (Lexington: University of Kentucky Press, 1996). Mary Vavrus, "Working the Senate from the Outside In: The Mediated Construction of a Feminist Political Campaign," *Critical Studies in Media Communication* 15 (1998): 213–35; Linda Witt, Karen M. Paget, and Glenna Matthews, *Running as a Woman: Gender and Power in American Politics* (New York: Free Press, 1994).

17. Michael John Burton and Daniel M. Shea, *Campaign Mode: Strategic Vision in Congressional Elections* (Lanham, Md.: Rowman & Littlefield, 2003).

18. Jane Bryant, "Paid Media Advertising," in *Campaigns and Elections: American Style,* ed. James A. Thurber and Candice J. Nelson, 84–100 (Boulder, Colo.: Westview Press, 1995).

19. According to a national opinion poll from 2000 (the National Election Study), 40 percent called themselves independents compared to Democrats (35%) and Republicans (25%).

20. Charles E. Jones and Michael L. Clemons, "A Model of Racial Crossover Voting: An Assessment of the Wilder Victory," in *Dilemmas of Black Politics: Issues of Leadership and Strategy,* ed. Georgia A. Persons, 128–46 (New York: HarperCollins, 1993). Robinson and Sheehan, *Over the Wire and on TV.*

21. Larry Bartels, "Candidate Choice and the Dynamics of the Presidential Nominating Process," *American Journal of Political Science* 25 (1987): 112–18.

22. Bennett, *The Governing Crisis.* Burton and Shea, *Campaign Mode.*

23. Doris Graber, *Mass Media and American Politics,* 5th ed. (Washington, D.C.: Congressional Quarterly Press, 1997).

24. Shanto Iyengar, *Is Anyone Responsible? How Television Frames National Issues* (Chicago: University of Chicago Press, 1991).

25. Iyengar, *Is Anyone Responsible?*

26. Sidney Blumenthal, *The Permanent Campaign,* rev. ed. (Boston: Beacon Press, 1982); Samuel Kernell, *Going Public: New Strategies of Presidential Leadership,* 3rd ed. (Washington, D.C.: Congressional Quarterly Press, 1997).

27. Gary Lee Malecha and Daniel J. Reagan, "Congressional Leaders on Television: Patterns of House and Senate Leadership Coverage" (presented at the Southwestern Political Science Association Meetings, Fort Worth, Tex., 2001); Donald B. Harris, "The Rise of the Public Speakership," *Political Science Quarterly* 113(2) (1998): 193–212; Barbara Sinclair, "Leadership Strategies in the Modern Congress," in *Congressional Politics* ed. Christopher J. Deering, 135–54 (Chicago: Dorsey Press, 1989).

28. Timothy E. Cook, *Making Laws and Making News: Media Strategies in the U.S. House of Representatives* (Washington, D.C.: Brookings Institution, 1989).

29. Cook, *Making Laws and Making News;* Timothy E. Cook, "House Members as National Newsmakers: The Effects of Televising Congress," *Legislative Studies Quarterly* 11 (1986): 203–26.

30. Cook, *Making Laws and Making News;* Karen M. Kedrowski, *Media Entrepreneurs and*

the Media Enterprise in the U.S. Congress (Cresskill, N.J.: Hampton Press, 1996); Stephanie Greco Larson, *Creating Consent of the Governed: A Member of Congress and the Local Media* (Carbondale: Southern Illinois University Press, 1992).

31. Cook, *Making Laws and Making News*, 68.

32. James E. Campbell, John R. Alford, and Keith Henry, "Television Markets and Congressional Elections," *Legislative Studies Quarterly* 9(4) (1984): 665–78.

33. Larson, *Creating Consent of the Governed*; Michael J. Robinson, "Three Faces of Congressional Media," in *The New Congress*, eds. Thomas E. Mann and Norman J. Ornstein, 55–98 (Washington, D.C.: American Enterprise Institute, 1981).

34. Cook, *Making Laws and Making News*; Larson, *Creating Consent of the Governed*; Robinson, "Three Faces of Congressional Media."

35. Austin Ranney, *Channels of Power: The Impact of Television on American Politics* (New York: Basic Books, 1983).

36. Cook, "House Members as National Newsmakers"; S. Robert Lichter and Daniel R. Amundson, "Less News Is Worse News: Television News Coverage of Congress, 1972–1992," in *Congress, the Press, and the Public*, ed. Thomas E. Mann and Norman J. Ornstein, 131–40 (Washington, D.C.: American Enterprise Institute and Brookings Institution, 1994).

37. Larry J. Sabato, *Feeding Frenzy: Attack Journalism and American Politics, A New Lanahan Edition* (Baltimore: Lanahan Publishers, 2000).

38. This is why political advertisements are sometimes made to look like news and airtime during news shows is preferred. See Kathleen Hall Jamieson and Karlyn Kohrs Campbell, *The Interplay of Influence: News, Advertising, Politics, and the Mass Media* (Belmont, Calif.: Wadsworth, 1992).

39. Paul M. Sniderman and Thomas Piazza, *The Scar of Race* (Cambridge, Mass.: Harvard University Press, 1993).

40. Michael Omi and Howard Winant, *Racial Formation in the United States: From the 1960s to the 1990s* (New York: Routledge, 1994).

CHAPTER 16

1. Anju G. Chaudhary, "Press Portrayal of Black Officials," *Journalism Quarterly* 57(4) (1980): 636–41.

2. Nayda Terkildsen and David F. Damore, "The Dynamics of Racialized Media Coverage in Congressional Elections," *The Journal of Politics* 61(3) (1999): 680–99.

3. George Sylvie, "Black Mayoral Candidates and the Press: Running for Coverage," *The Howard Journal of Communication* 6 (1995): 89–101.

4. Sylvie, "Black Mayoral Candidates and the Press."

5. Lucius J. Barker, Mack H. Jones, and Katherine Tate, *African Americans and the American Political System*, 4th ed. (Upper Saddle River, N.J.: Prentice Hall, 1999).

6. Doris Graber, "Media Magic: Fashioning Characters for the 1983 Mayoral Race," in *The Making of the Mayor, Chicago 1983*, ed. Melvin G. Holli and Paul M. Green, 53–84 (Grand Rapids, Mich.: William B. Eerdmans Publishing Co., 1984); Timothy F. Grainey, Lori A. Kusmierek, and Dennis R. Pollack, "How Three Chicago Newspapers Covered the Washington-Epton Campaign," *Journalism Quarterly* 61 (1984): 352–63.

7. Graber, "Media Magic," 65.

8. Graber, "Media Magic."

9. Grainey, Kusmierek, and Pollack, "How Three Chicago Newspapers Covered the Washington-Epton Campaign."

10. Chaudhary, "Press Portrayal of Black Officials," and Terkildsen and Damore, "The Dynamics of Racialized Media Coverage in Congressional Elections."

11. S. Robert Lichter, Daniel Amundson, and Richard Noyes, *The Video Campaign: Network Coverage of the 1988 Primaries* (Washington, D.C.: American Enterprise Institute for Public Policy Research Center for Media and Public Affairs, 1988).

12. Lichter, Amundson, and Noyes, *The Video Campaign.*

13. Lichter, Amundson, and Noyes, *The Video Campaign.*

14. Cragg Hines, "Blame Abe Lincoln and Steve Forbes," *Nieman Reports* (2000): 37–38.

15. Clarence Lusane, *African Americans at the Crossroads: The Restructuring of Black Leadership and the 1992 Elections* (Boston: South End Press, 1994).

16. Jeremy Zilber and David Niven, *Racialized Coverage of Congress: The News in Black and White* (Westport, Conn.: Praeger, 2000).

17. John T. Barber and Oscar H. Gandy Jr., "Press Portrayal of African-American and white United States Representatives," *Howard Journal of Communication* 2(2) (1990): 213–25; Brian Schaffner and Mark Gadson "Reinforcing Stereotypes? Race and Local Television News Coverage of Congress," *Social Science Quarterly* 85(3) (2004): 604–21; Zilber and Niven, *Racialized Coverage of Congress.*

18. Barber and Gandy, "Press Portrayal of African-American and White United States Representatives."

19. Brigitte L. Nacos and Natasha Hritzuk, "The Portrayal of Black America in the Mass Media: Perception and Reality," in *Black and Multiracial Politics in America*, ed. Yvette M. Alex-Assensoh and Lawrence J. Hanks, 165–95 (New York: New York University Press, 2000).

20. Schaffner and Gadson, "Reinforcing Stereotypes?"

21. Lichter, Amundson, and Noyes, *The Video Campaign.*

22. Jon C. Teaford, "King Richard Hatcher: Mayor of Gary," *Journal of Negro History* 77(3) (1992): 126–40.

23. Howard Gillette, "Protest and Power in Washington, D.C.: The Troubled Legacy of Marion Berry," in *African-American Mayors: Race, Politics, and the American City*, ed. David R. Colburn and Jeffrey S. Adler (Urbana: University of Illinois Press, 2001), 201.

24. Chaudhary, "Press Portrayal of Black Officials"; Sylvie, "Black Mayoral Candidates and the Press."

25. Chaudhary, "Press Portrayal of Black Officials."

26. Sylvie, "Black Mayoral Candidates and the Press."

27. Grainey, Kusmierek, and Pollack, "How Three Chicago Newspapers Covered the Washington-Epton Campaign."

28. Graber, "Media Magic," 62.

29. Jan E. Leighley, *Mass Media and Politics: A Social Science Perspective* (Boston: Houghton Mifflin, 2004), 92.

30. Paul Kleppner, *Chicago Divided: The Making of a Black Mayor* (Dekalb: North Illinois University Press, 1985).

31. Charles E. Jones and Michael L. Clemons, "A Model of Racial Crossover Voting: An Assessment of the Wilder Victory," in *Dilemmas of Black Politics: Issues of Leadership and Strategy*, ed. Georgia A. Persons, 128–46 (New York: HarperCollins, 1993); Lichter, Amundson, and Noyes, *The Video Campaign.*

32. Laurence Zuckerman, "Has He Got a Free Ride?" *Time* (April 18, 1988): 24.

33. Zuckerman, "Has He Got a Free Ride?"; Lichter, Amundson, and Noyes, *The Video Campaign.*

34. Lichter, Amundson, and Noyes, *The Video Campaign.*

35. Robert M. Entman and Andrew Rojecki, *The Black Image in the White Mind: Media and Race in America* (Chicago: University of Chicago Press, 2000).

36. Lichter, Amundson, and Noyes, *The Video Campaign.*

37. D. Riffe, D. Sneed, and R. Van Ommeren, "Black Elected Officials Find Press Coverage Insensitive, Incomplete, and Inaccurate," *The Howard Journal of Communication* 2 (1990): 397–406.

38. Riffe, Sneed, and Van Ommeren, "Black Elected Officials Find Press Coverage Insensitive, Incomplete, and Inaccurate," 397.

39. Barber and Gandy, "Press Portrayal of African-American and White United States Representatives."

40. Zilber and Niven, *Racialized Coverage of Congress.*

41. Donald Bogle, *Toms, Coons, Mulattoes, Mammies, and Bucks: An Interpretive History of Blacks in American Films,* 3rd ed. (New York: Continuum, 1999).

42. Robert M. Entman and Andrew Rojecki, *The Black Image in the White Mind: Media and Race in America* (Chicago: University of Chicago Press, 2000).

43. Sylvie, "Black Mayoral Candidates and the Press."

44. James M. Glaser, *Race, Campaign Politics, and the Realignment in the South* (New Haven, Conn.: Yale University Press, 1996).

45. Glaser, *Race, Campaign Politics, and the Realignment in the South.*

46. Sheila D. Collins, *The Rainbow Challenge: The Jackson Campaign and the Future of U.S. Politics* (New York: Monthly Review Press, 1984), 277.

47. C. Anthony Broh, *A Horse by a Different Color: Television's Treatment of Jesse Jackson's 1984 Presidential Campaign* (Washington, D.C.: Joint Center for Political Studies, 1987).

48. Broh, *A Horse by a Different Color,* 68.

49. Pamela Newkirk, *Within the Veil: Black Journalists, White Media* (New York: New York University Press, 2000), 26.

50. Newkirk, *Within the Veil.*

51. Entman and Rojecki, *The Black Image in the White Mind.*

52. Jim A. Kuypers, *Press Bias and Politics: How the Media Frame Controversial Issues* (Westport, Conn.: Praeger, 2002).

53. Entman and Rojecki, *The Black Image in the White Mind,* 134.

54. Thomas F. Pettigrew and Denise A. Alston, *Tom Bradley's Campaigns for Governor: The Dilemma of Race and Political Strategies* (Washington, D.C.: Joint Center for Political Studies, 1988).

55. Laurence Barrett, "Race-Baiting Wins Again," *Time* 136(22) (November 19, 1990): 43.

56. Robert M. Entman, "Modern Racism and the Images of Blacks in Local Television News," *Critical Studies in Mass Communication* 7 (1990): 332–45.

57. Entman, "Modern Racism and the Images of Blacks in Local Television News," 341.

58. Teun A. Van Dijk, "New(s) Racism: A Discourse Analytical Approach," in *Ethnic Minorities and the Media,* ed. Simon Cottle, 33–49 (Buckingham, U.K.: Open University Press, 2000).

59. Arnold Gibbons, *Race, Politics, and the White Media: The Jesse Jackson Campaigns* (Lanham, Md.: University Press of America, 1993), 94.

60. Broh, *A Horse by a Different Color.*

61. Broh, *A Horse by a Different Color,* 77.

62. Zilber and Niven, *Racialized Coverage of Congress.*

63. Linda Witt, Karen M. Paget, and Glenna Matthews, *Running as a Woman: Gender and Power in American Politics* (New York: Free Press, 1994).

64. Maria Braden, *Women Politicians and the Media* (Lexington: University of Kentucky Press, 1996).

65. Todd Gitlin, *The Whole World Is Watching: Mass Media in the Making and Unmaking of the New Left* (Berkeley: University of California Press, 1980).

66. Ted G. Jelen, "Carol Moseley-Braun: The Insider as Insurgent," in *The Year of the Woman: Myths and Realities,* ed. Elizabeth Adell Cook, Sue Thomas, and Clyde Wilcox, 71–86 (Boulder, Colo.: Westview Press, 1993).

67. Braden, *Women Politicians and the Media.*

68. Carmen L. Manning-Miller, "Carol Moseley-Braun: Black Women's Political Images in the Media," in *Mediated Messages and African-American Culture: Contemporary Issues,* ed.

Venise T. Berry and Carmen L. Manning-Miller, 117–28 (Thousand Oaks, Calif.: Sage Publications, 1996).

69. Braden, *Women Politicians and the Media*.

70. J. Gregory Payne, "Shaping the Race Issue: A Special Kind of Journalism," *Political Communication and Persuasion* 5 (1998): 145–60, 146.

71. Grainey, Kusmierek, and Pollack, "How Three Chicago Newspapers Covered the Washington-Epton Campaign."

72. Keith Reeves, *Voting Hopes or Fears? White Voters, Black Candidates, and Racial Politics in America* (New York: Oxford University Press, 1997).

73. Sylvie, "Black Mayoral Candidates and the Press."

74. Reeves, *Voting Hopes or Fears?*

75. Terkildsen and Damore, "The Dynamics of Racialized Media Coverage in Congressional Elections."

76. Terkildsen and Damore, "The Dynamics of Racialized Media Coverage in Congressional Elections."

77. Rikeesha Cannon, Brian R. Sala, and Britt Wilms, "Divided by Color? Contrasting Self- and Media Framing of Black Candidates in Biracial, Statewide Campaigns" (presented at the Annual Meetings of the American Political Science Association, Atlanta, 1999).

78. Cannon, Sala, and Wilms, "Divided by Color?"

79. Terkildsen and Damore, "The Dynamics of Racialized Media Coverage in Congressional Elections."

80. Terkildsen and Damore, "The Dynamics of Racialized Media Coverage in Congressional Elections."

81. Barber and Gandy, "Press Portrayal of African-American and White United States Representatives."

82. Zilber and Niven, *Racialized Coverage of Congress*, 101.

83. Zilber and Niven, *Racialized Coverage of Congress*, 61.

84. Schaffner and Gadson, "Reinforcing Stereotypes?" 619.

85. Paul Luebke, *Tar Heel Politics* (Chapel Hill: University of North Carolina Press, 1998), 171.

86. Kathleen Hall Jamieson, *Dirty Politics: Deception, Distraction and Democracy* (New York: Oxford University Press, 1992), 97.

87. Jamieson, *Dirty Politics*; Luebke, *Tar Heel Politics*, 183.

88. Glaser, *Race, Campaign Politics, and the Realignment in the South* (emphasis added).

89. Thomas E. Cavanagh and Lorn S. Foster, *Jesse Jackson's Campaign: The Primaries and Caucuses* (Washington, D.C.: Joint Center for Political Studies, 1984).

90. Gibbons, *Race, Politics, and the White Media*, 141.

91. Robert K. Tiemens, Malcolm O. Sillars, Dennis C. Alexander, and David Werling, "Television Coverage of Jesse Jackson's Speech to the 1984 Democratic National Convention," *Journal of Broadcasting and Electronic Media* 32(1) (1988): 1–22.

92. Collins, *The Rainbow Challenge*.

93. Payne, "Shaping the Race Issue," 149.

94. Payne, "Shaping the Race Issue."

95. Payne, "Shaping the Race Issue."

96. Pettigrew and Alston, *Tom Bradley's Campaigns for Governor*, 33.

97. Pettigrew and Alston, *Tom Bradley's Campaigns for Governor*.

98. Payne, "Shaping the Race Issue."

99. Marilyn Davis and Alex Willingham, "Andrew Young and the Georgia State Elections of 1990," in *Dilemmas of Black Politics: Issues of Leadership and Strategy*, ed. Georgia A. Persons, 147–75 (New York: Harper Collins, 1993).

100. Davis and Willingham, "Andrew Young and the Georgia State Elections of 1990," 157, 163.

101. Davis and Willingham, "Andrew Young and the Georgia State Elections of 1990," 163.

102. Quoted in Cavanagh and Foster, *Jesse Jackson's Campaign*, 12.

103. Graber, "Media Magic"; Kleppner, *Chicago Divided*.

104. Graber, "Media Magic," 71.

105. Kleppner, *Chicago Divided*.

106. Jones and Clemons, "A Model of Racial Crossover Voting."

107. Kleppner, *Chicago Divided*.

108. Graber, "Media Magic," 71.

109. Reeves, *Voting Hopes or Fears?*

110. Zilber and Niven, *Racialized Coverage of Congress*.

111. Davis and Willingham, "Andrew Young and the Georgia State Elections of 1990."

112. Sharon D. Wright, "Electoral and Biracial Coalition: Possible Election Strategy for African American Candidates in Louisville, Kentucky," *Journal of Black Studies* 25(6) (1995): 749–58, 752.

113. Huey L. Perry, "Introduction: An Analysis of Major Themes in the Concept of Deracialization," in *Race, Politics, and the Governance in the United States*, ed. Huey L. Perry (Gainsville: University Press of Florida, 1996), 1.

114. Jones and Clemons, "A Model of Racial Crossover Voting."

115. Jones and Clemons, "A Model of Racial Crossover Voting," 132.

116. Saundra C. Ardrey, "Cleveland and the Politics of Resurgence: The Search for Effective Political Control," in *Dilemmas of Black Politics: Issues of Leadership and Strategy*, ed. Georgia A. Persons, 109–27 (New York: Harper Collins, 1993); Jones and Clemons, "A Model of Racial Crossover Voting."

117. Charles S. Bullock, "Racial Crossover Voting and the Election of Black Officials," *The Journal of Politics* 46(1) (1984): 238–51; Jones and Clemons, "A Model of Racial Crossover Voting."

118. Bullock, "Racial Crossover Voting and the Election of Black Officials."

119. Ardrey, "Cleveland and the Politics of Resurgence," 117.

120. Jones and Clemons, "A Model of Racial Crossover Voting."

121. James L. Lloren, Sharon K. Parsons, and Huey L. Perry, "The Election of Troy Carter to the Louisiana House of Representatives," in *Race, Politics, and the Governance in the United States*, ed. Huey L. Perry, 107–23 (Gainesville: University Press of Florida, 1996).

122. Davis and Willingham, "Andrew Young and the Georgia State Elections of 1990"; Payne, "Shaping the Race Issue"; Terkildsen and Damore, "The Dynamics of Racialized Media Coverage in Congressional Elections."

123. Cherie Maestas, "Racing in the Shadows: The 2002 Texas Senate Race," in *Running on Empty? Political Discourse in Congressional Elections*, ed. L. Sandy Maisel and Darrell M. West, 185–99 (Lanham, Md.: Rowman & Littlefield, 2004).

124. Manning-Miller, "Carol Moseley-Braun: Black Women's Political Images in the Media."

125. Braden, *Women Politicians and the Media*, 188.

126. Terkildsen and Damore, "The Dynamics of Racialized Media Coverage in Congressional Elections."

127. Perry, "Introduction."

128. Carol A. Pierannunzi and John D. Hutchenson Jr., "The Rise and Fall of Deracialization: Andrew Young as Mayor and Gubernatorial Candidate," in *Race, Politics, and the Governance in the United States*, ed. Huey L. Perry, 96–106 (Gainesville: University Press of Florida, 1996).

129. Stephanie Greco Larson and Lydia Marie Andrade, "National Television News Coverage of Women in the House of Representatives, 1988–1998" (presented at the Southern Political Science Association Meeting, Savannah, Ga., 1999).

130. Laverne McCain Gill, *African American Women in Congress: Forming and Transforming History* (New Brunswick, N.J.: Rutgers University Press, 1997).

131. Gill, *African American Women in Congress*.

132. Gill, *African American Women in Congress*, 159; Myra Marx Ferree, "A Woman for President? Changing Responses: 1958–1972," *Public Opinion Quarterly* 38(3) (1974): 390–99.

133. Graber, "Media Magic"; Grainey, Kusmierek, and Pollack, "How Three Chicago Newspapers Covered the Washington-Epton Campaign."

134. Glaser, *Race, Campaign Politics, and the Realignment in the South*.

135. Heather R. Parker, "Tom Bradley and the Politics of Race," in *African-American Mayors: Race, Politics, and the American City*, ed. David R. Colburn and Jeffrey S. Adler, 153–77 (Urbana: University of Illinois Press, 2001).

136. Gill, *African American Women in Congress*.

137. Gill, *African American Women in Congress*, 109.

138. Roland E. Wolseley, *The Black Press, U.S.A.* (Ames: Iowa State University, 1971).

CHAPTER 17

1. *Denver Post*, October 31, 1992, A18.

2. *Denver Post*, September 29, 1992, B5.

3. *Denver Post*, November 2, 1992, A4.

4. *Denver Post*, September 7, 1992, B5.

5. *Denver Post*, October 10, 1992, A1; *Denver Post*, October 11, 1992, A1.

6. *Denver Post*, October 25, 1992, A12.

7. *Denver Post*, October 11, 1992, C1.

8. *Denver Post*, September 23, 1992, B1.

9. *Denver Post*, October 8, 1992, A1; *Denver Post*, October 25, 1992, A12.

10. *Denver Post*, October 4, 1992, A21.

11. *Denver Post*, September 23, 1992, B1; *Denver Post*, October 25, 1992, A12.

12. *Denver Post*, September 23, 1992, B1.

13. *Denver Post*, October 25, 1992, A12.

14. *Denver Post*, October 25, 1992, A12.

15. *Denver Post*, September 7, 1992, B5.

16. *Denver Post*, October 10, 1992, A1.

17. *Denver Post*, October 11, 1992, A1.

18. *Denver Post*, September 23, 1992, 1B.

19. *Denver Post*, September 23, 1992, 1B.

20. *Denver Post*, November 1, 1992, A23.

21. *Denver Post*, October 8, 1992, A1.

22. AP, February 6, 2002.

23. AP, March 12, 2002.

24. AP, May 30, 2002.

25. AP, May 16, 2002.

26. AP, April 15, 2002.

27. AP, March 12, 2002.

28. AP, April 18, 2002.

29. AP, April 13, 2002.

30. AP, April 18, 2002; AP, April 19, 2002.

31. AP, April 13, 2002.

32. AP, May 23, 2002.

33. AP, May 29, 2002.

34. AP, May 3, 2002.

35. Michael J. Robinson and Margaret A. Sheehan, *Over the Wire and on TV: CBS and UPI in Campaign '80* (New York: Russell Sage Foundation, 1983).

36. AP, March 25, 2002.

37. AP, April 5, 2002.

38. AP, May 3, 2002.

39. AP, March 13, 2002; AP, March 23, 2002; AP, April 4, 2002.

40. AP, March 25, 2002.

41. Paula D. McClain and Joseph Stewart Jr., *Can We All Get Along? Racial and Ethnic Minorities in American Politics*, 3rd ed. (Boulder, Colo.: Westview Press, 2001).

42. The four articles from *Indian Country Today* that came up in the search were not included here because they are not in a mainstream newspaper. Instead, they can be looked at as examples from the parallel press.

43. There were a few stories in which more than one Native American legislator's name appeared. They were counted only once.

44. *Anchorage Daily News*, July 8, 2001, F4.

45. *Anchorage Daily News*, December 28, 2001, B8.

46. *Arkansas Democrat-Gazette*, March 10, 2001, B8.

47. *Santa Fe New Mexican*, April 29, 2001, F6.

48. *Las Vegas Review-Journal*, June 13, 2001, B9.

49. AP, January 26, 2001.

50. AP, September 12, 2001; *Albuquerque Tribune*, September 12, 2001.

51. AP, July 19, 2001.

52. *Denver Post*, March 3, 2001, B7.

53. *Wilmington (Del.) Star-News*, April 29, 2001, E4.

54. AP, May 22, 2001.

55. *Durham Herald-Sun*, April 26, 2001, A1.

56. *Santa Fe New Mexican*, February 20, 2001, A6.

57. AP, April 26, 2001.

58. AP, March 22, 2001.

59. AP, February 21, 2001.

60. *Las Vegas Review-Journal*, June 4, 2001, B1.

61. AP, February 1, 2001.

62. *Albuquerque Journal*, April 25, 2001, D3.

63. There were a few other stories that do not fit into these categories. In a letter to company stockholders that was quoted in a newspaper, Albert Kookesh wrote, "Our elders would say, the water is rough, but we have a big canoe" (*Anchorage Daily News*, February 21, 2001). In another, the district's poor native population is used to explain why a legislator claimed more optional pay (AP, February 1, 2001). Another dealt with the change in leadership in the Senate and speculates that one member's vote was due to "Indian needs" (*Santa Fe New Mexican*, January 18, 2001, A1).

64. These included references to racial discrimination generally.

65. *Santa Fe New Mexican*, January 18, 2001, A1.

66. *Las Vegas Review-Journal*, June 4, 2001, B1.

67. *Albuquerque Journal*, April 25, 2001, D3; *Albuquerque Journal*, April 26, 2001, A14.

68. AP, January 24, 2001.

69. AP, February 22, 2001.

70. AP, January 17, 2001.

71. AP, September 12, 2001; *Albuquerque Tribune*, September 12, 2001, A12.

72. *Santa Fe New Mexican*, March 16, 2001, A5.

73. Eric Gary Anderson, "Driving the Red Road: *Powwow Highway* (1989)," in *Hollywood's Indian: The Portrayal of the Native American in Film*, ed. Peter C. Rollins and John E. O'Connor, 137–52 (Lexington: University of Kentucky Press, 1998).

74. Clint C. Wilson and Félix Gutiérrez, *Race, Multiculturalism, and the Media: From Mass Communication to Class Communication* (Thousand Oaks, Calif.: Sage Publications, 1995).

75. Ward Churchill, *Fantasies of the Master Race: Literature, Cinema and the Colonization of American Indians* (San Francisco: City Lights Books, 1998).

76. AP, March 10, 2001.

77. *Las Vegas Review-Journal*, June 4, 2001.

78. AP, January 22, 2001.

79. AP, February 1, 2001.

80. *Albuquerque Tribune*, March 2, 2001.

81. AP, January 15, 2001; AP, January 19, 2001.

82. AP, October 5, 2001.

83. *Indian Country Today*, July 23, 2001.

84. *Indian Country Today*, October 12, 2001.

85. *Indian Country Today*, June 26, 2001; *Indian Country Today*, July 2, 2001; *Indian Country Today*, October 12, 2001.

86. *Indian Country Today*, July 2, 2001.

87. *Indian Country Today*, October 12, 2001.

88. *Indian Country Today*, June 26, 2001.

CHAPTER 18

1. Rodolfo O. de la Garza and Louis DeSipio, "Latinos and the 1992 Elections: A National Perspective," in *Ethnic Ironies: Latino Politics in the 1992 Election*, ed. Rodolfo O. de la Garza and Louis DeSipio, 3–50 (Boulder, Colo.: Westview Press, 1996).

2. Federico Subervi-Véliz and Stacey L. Connaughton, "Targeting the Latino Vote: The Democratic Party's 1996 Mass-Communication Strategy," in *Awash in the Mainstream: Latino Politics in the 1996 Elections*, ed. Rodolfo O. de la Garza and Louis DeSipio, 47–72 (Boulder, Colo.: Westview Press, 1997).

3. Armando Navarro, *La Raza Unida Party: A Chicano Challenge to the U.S. Two-Party Dictatorship* (Philadelphia: Temple University Press, 2000).

4. Mario T. Garcia, *Mexican Americans: Leadership, Ideology, and Identity 1930–1960* (New Haven, Conn.: Yale University Press, 1989).

5. James I. Bowie and Frederic I. Solop, "'The Virginian' vs. 'The Little Mexican': The 2002 Race in Arizona 1," in *Running on Empty? Political Discourse in Congressional Elections*, ed. L. Sandy Maisel and Darrell M. West, 85–98 (Lanham, Md.: Rowman & Littlefield, 2004).

6. Rodney E. Hero, *Latinos and the U.S. Political System: Two-Tiered Pluralism* (Philadelphia: Temple University Press, 1992).

7. Hero, *Latinos and the U.S. Political System*; Leland T. Saito, *Race and Politics: Asian Americans, Latinos, and Whites in a Los Angeles Suburb* (Urbana: University of Illinois Press, 1998).

8. Guillermo J. Grenier with Fabiana Invernizzi, Linda Salup, and Jorge Schmidt, "Los Bravos de la Política: Politics and Cubans in Miami," in *Barrio Ballots: Latino Politics in the 1990 Elections*, ed. Rodolfo O. de la Garza, Martha Menchaca, and Louis DeSipio, 161–96 (Boulder, Colo.: Westview Press, 1994).

9. Michael John Burton and Daniel M. Shea, *Campaign Mode: Strategic Vision in Congressional Elections* (Lanham, Md.: Rowman & Littlefield, 2003).

10. "Our Turn," *San Antonio Express-News*, October 17, 1996, Part A, editorial page.

11. Only one story was coded as bad news for Jones, also due to his not answering questions.

12. "Morales Says Bonilla Forgot His Heritage, Call Him 'Coconut,'" *San Antonio Express-News*, September 26, 1996, A16.

13. "Clinton Challenges Dole, GOP by Stumping in Lone Star State," *San Antonio Express-News*, September 28, 1996, A13; "Morales Pressing on Despite Hitting Bumps on along the Trail," *San Antonio Express-News*, October 6, 1996, A23; "Republican Texas Sen. Phil Gramm ran over the Common Man Campaign," *San Antonio Express-News*, November 6, 1996, A6.

14. "Sacred Cows Run Scared at Gridiron," *San Antonio Express-News*, October 2, 1996, G1.

15. "'Coconut' Remark a Low Blow," *San Antonio Express-News*, September 28, 1996, B6.

16. "Morales Apologizes Day after Calling Bonilla a 'Coconut,'" *San Antonio Express-News*, September 27, 1996, A18.

17. Regarding these issues, on one, Bonilla supported the community, on another, he opposed it, and on the third, he had no comment.

18. "Jones Long Shot against Bonilla," *San Antonio Express-News*, October 3, 1996, B5.

19. "State Demos Join Effort to Separate Scandal, Elections," *San Antonio Express-News*, September 18, 1998, A13.

20. "Walker Refusing to Give Up," *San Antonio Express-News*, October 26, 1998, A9.

21. "Redistricting Goals Reached, in One Race," *Newsday*, September 16, 1992, 28.

22. "Can Latinos Win a Second Seat?" *Newsday*, July 20, 1992, 32.

23. "Mayor Takes Latino Plunge, Backs a Key Solar Rival," *Newsday*, August 11, 1992, 4.

24. "The New York Interview with Nydia Velazquez: We Have Been Disenfranchised Too Long," *Newsday*, September 21, 1992, 37.

25. "POLS and POLITICS GOP: In NY, It's Anybody's Vote," *Newsday*, August 14, 1992, 18.

26. "Primary '92: Velazquez Wins, Solarz Out in 12th," *Newsday*, September 16, 1992, 7.

27. Maria Braden, *Women Politicians and the Media* (Lexington: University of Kentucky Press, 1996).

28. "A Touch One: The Case for Stephen Solarz," *Newsday*, September 10, 1992, 50.

29. "Debate Free-for-All Punches, Charges Traded," *Newsday*, August 27, 1992, 23.

30. "Primary '92: Velazquez Wins, Solarz Out in 12th," *Newsday*, September 16, 1992, 7.

31. "Primary '92: Velazquez Wins, Solarz Out in 12th," *Newsday*, September 16, 1992, 7.

32. "Latino Cry: 'People Won,'" *Newsday*, September 17, 1992, 3.

33. "The New York Interview with Nydia Velazquez: We Have Been Disenfranchised Too Long," *Newsday*, September 21, 1992.

34. "Velazquez: A Boon for Puerto Rico," *Newsday*, September 27, 1992, 18.

35. "Along for the Ride, Puerto Rico Trip Wins the Mayor Points," *Newsday*, September 25, 1992, 38.

36. "Hometown Celebrates Local Who Made Good: Red Carpet for Velazquez in Puerto Rico," *Newsday*, September 26, 1992, 10.

37. "Politics after Pepper," *St. Petersburg Times*, June 11, 1989, B1.

38. "Bush Lends Clout to Campaign," *St. Petersburg Times*, August 17, 1989, B1.

39. "Martinez Reassuring Republicans on Key Issues," *St. Petersburg Times*, August 20, 1989, B4.

40. "Cuban-American Is Elected to Fill Pepper's Seat in Congress," *St. Petersburg Times*, August 30, 1989, A1.

41. "Bush Lends Clout to Campaign," *St. Petersburg Times*, August 17, 1989, B1.

42. "Cuban-American Is Elected to Fill Pepper's Seat in Congress," *St. Petersburg Times*, August 30, 1989, A1.

43. Mike Clary, "Would You Create Another Newspaper to Compete with Your Own? In Miami, the *Herald* Did," *Columbia Journalism Review* 39(1) (May 6, 2000): 56–58; Sheila L.

Croucher, *Imagining Miami: Ethnic Politics in a Postmodern World* (Charlottesville: University Press of Virginia, 1997).

44. "Politicians Wrangle over Hialeah, Fla., Horse-Racing Track," *Miami Herald*, May 13, 2001, B1.

45. "Florida Democrat Running for U.S. House Wants to Alter Cuba Policy," *Miami Herald*, October 4, 2002, B1.

46. "Distracted Voters Pose Challenge for Miami Mayoral Candidate," *Miami Herald*, November 4, 2001.

47. "Two Cuban-Americans Vying for New Miami-Dade Congressional Seat," *Miami Herald*, October 18, 2002, AP.

48. "Florida Democrat Running for U.S. House Wants to Alter Cuba Policy," *Miami Herald*, October 4, 2002, B1.

49. "How to Campaign in the New House District 25? There's Always Cuba," *Miami New Times*, October 31, 2002.

50. "How to Campaign in the New House District 25? There's Always Cuba," *Miami New Times*, October 31, 2002.

51. "How to Campaign in the New House District 25? There's Always Cuba," *Miami New Times*, October 31, 2002.

CHAPTER 19

1. James S. Lai and Don T. Nakanishi, *National Asian Pacific American Political Almanac, Special Election Edition* (Los Angeles: UCLA Asian American Studies Center, 2001).

2. James S. Lai, Wendy K. Tam-Cho, Thomas P. Kim, and Okiyoshi Takeda, "Campaigns, Elections, and Elected Officials," *PS: Political Science and Politics* 34(3) (2001): 631–37.

3. Lai, Tam-Cho, Kim, and Takeda, "Campaigns, Elections, and Elected Officials."

4. James S. Lai, "Asian Pacific Americans and the Pan-Ethnic Question," in *Minority Politics in the New Millennium*, ed. Richard A Keiser and Katherine Underwood, 203–6 (New York: Garland Publishing, 2000).

5. Lai, Tam-Cho, Kim, and Takeda, "Campaigns, Elections, and Elected Officials."

6. Paul M. Ong and Don T. Nakanishi, "Becoming Citizens, Becoming Voters: The Naturalization and Political Participation of Asian Pacific Immigrants," in *Reframing the Immigration Debate*, ed. Bill Ong Hing and Ronald Lee, 275–305 (Los Angeles: LEAP, Asian Pacific American Public Policy Institute and UCLA Asian American Studies Center, 1996).

7. Lai, Tam-Cho, Kim, and Takeda, "Campaigns, Elections, and Elected Officials."

8. *Seattle Times*, September 18, 1996, A1.

9. *Seattle Times*, October 7, 1996, A6.

10. *Seattle Times*, October 25, 1996, A6.

11. *Seattle Times*, October 20, 1996, B8.

12. *Seattle Times*, October 17, 1996, B1.

13. *Seattle Times*, September 18, 1996, B4.

14. *Seattle Times*, October 24, 1996, B5.

15. *Seattle Times*, September 19, 1996, C1.

16. *Seattle Times*, September 19, 1996, B1; *Seattle Times*, September 20, 1996, A1; *Seattle Times*, October 17, 1996, B7; *Seattle Times*, November 3, 1996, B7.

17. *Seattle Times*, October 7, 1996, B1.

18. *Seattle Times*, September 19, 1996, B1.

19. *Seattle Times*, September 27, 1996, B1.

20. *Seattle Times*, September 28, 1996, A1.

21. *Seattle Times*, October 4, 1996, B1.

22. *Seattle Times*, September 19, 1996, C1.

23. *Seattle Times*, September 18, 1996, B4.

24. *Seattle Times*, October 23, 1996, B5.

25. *Seattle Times*, September 29, 1996, B4; *Seattle Times*, October 16, 1996, B3; *Seattle Times*, October 21, 1996, F1; *Seattle Times*, October 24, 1996, G8.

26. *Seattle Times*, October 13, 1996, B10; *Seattle Times*, October 27, 1996, B6.

27. *Seattle Times*, September 19, 1996, A1; *Seattle Times*, September 20, 1996, A1; *Seattle Times*, October 19, 1996, A13.

28. *Seattle Times*, September 20, 1996, B4; *Seattle Times*, September 29, 1996, B6; *Seattle Times*, September 10, 1996, A1; *Seattle Times*, October 10, 1996, B7; *Seattle Times*, October 10, 1996, B1; *Seattle Times*, October 11, 1996, B4; *Seattle Times*, October 14, 1996, B5; *Seattle Times*, October 15, 1996, B5; *Seattle Times*, October 17, 1996, B1; *Seattle Times*, October 23, 1996, B4.

29. *Seattle Times*, October 17, 1996, B1.

30. *Seattle Times*, October 10, 1996, B1.

31. *Seattle Times*, October 27, 1996, B7.

32. *Seattle Times*, October 24, 1996, B5.

33. *Seattle Times*, October 14, 1996, B5.

34. *Seattle Times*, October 6, 1996, B7; *Seattle Times*, October 15, 1996, B5; *Seattle Times*, October 21, 1996, B5; *Seattle Times*, October 24, 2006, B5; *Seattle Times*, November 3, 1996, B7.

35. *Seattle Times*, October 21, 1996, B5.

36. *Seattle Times*, October 25, 1996, B5.

37. *Seattle Times*, October 20, 1996, B1.

38. *Seattle Times*, September 19, 1996, C1.

39. *Seattle Times*, September 27, 1996, B5.

40. *Seattle Times*, October 20, 1996, L4.

41. Linda Witt, Karen M. Paget, and Glenna Matthews, *Running as a Woman: Gender and Power in American Politics* (New York: Free Press, 1994).

42. *Seattle Times*, September 19, 1996, B1.

43. *Seattle Times*, October 2, 1996, A1.

44. *Seattle Times*, September 29, 1996, B4.

45. *Seattle Times*, November 1, 1996, H8.

46. *Seattle Times*, October 2, 1996, A1.

47. *Seattle Times*, November 1, 1996, H8.

48. *Seattle Times*, October 20, 1996, B2; *Seattle Times*, October 22, 1996, B3.

49. *Seattle Times*, October 28, 1996, B1.

50. *Seattle Times*, October 13, 1996, B10.

51. *Seattle Times*, September 18, 1996, C1.

52. *Seattle Times*, October 2, 1996, A1.

53. *Los Angeles Times*, May 23, 1998, A1.

54. *Los Angeles Times*, May 7, 1998, A1.

55. *Los Angeles Times*, May 7, 1998, A1.

56. *Los Angeles Times*, February 7, 1998, B1.

57. *Los Angeles Times*, March 11, 1998, A3.

58. *Los Angeles Times*, March 25, 1998, A24.

59. *Los Angeles Times*, March 27, 1998, B1.

60. *Los Angeles Times*, May 7, 1998, A1.

61. *Los Angeles Times*, March 27, 1998, B1.

62. *Los Angeles Times*, March 25, 1998, A24.

63. *Los Angeles Times*, March 11, 1998, A3.

64. *Los Angeles Times*, March 11, 1998, A3.

65. *Los Angeles Times*, March 15, 1998, M4.
66. *Los Angeles Times*, May 14, 1998, B8.
67. *Los Angeles Times*, May 14, 1998, B8.
68. *Los Angeles Times*, May 7, 1998, A1.
69. *Los Angeles Times*, February 7, 1998, B1.
70. *Los Angeles Times*, March 27, 1998, B1.
71. *Los Angeles Times*, May 16, 1998, B2.
72. *Los Angeles Times*, May 18, 1998, B2.
73. *Los Angeles Times*, May 7, 1998, A1.
74. *Los Angeles Times*, March 11, 1998, B3.
75. *Los Angeles Times*, March 15, 1998, M4.
76. *San Francisco Chronicle*, May 20, 1994, A10.
77. *San Francisco Chronicle*, October 13, 1992, A18.
78. *San Francisco Chronicle*, June 10, 1992, A2.
79. *Los Angeles Times*, April 11, 2000, A3.
80. *Los Angeles Times*, February 14, 2000, B4.
81. *Los Angeles Times*, July 20, 1996, B7.
82. *San Francisco Chronicle*, September 11, 1998, A17.
83. *San Francisco Chronicle*, October 13, 1992, A18.
84. *San Francisco Chronicle*, October 13, 1992, A18.
85. *San Francisco Chronicle*, June 24, 1993, A4.
86. *San Francisco Chronicle*, June 10, 1994, A2.
87. *San Francisco Chronicle*, July 24, 1992, A24.
88. *San Francisco Chronicle*, February 9, 1994, A12.
89. Copley News Service, September 25, 1998.
90. *San Francisco Chronicle*, June 11, 1993, A10.
91. *San Francisco Chronicle*, June 24, 1993, A4.
92. *Fresno Bee*, November 11, 1999, A19.
93. Two stories that could not be categorized in this way were excluded from analysis.
94. *San Francisco Chronicle*, October 31, 1992, A1.
95. *Los Angeles Times*, April 11, 2000, A3.
96. *San Francisco Chronicle*, October 30, 1993, A7.
97. *Los Angeles Times*, May 2, 1997, A3.
98. *Los Angeles Times*, May 2, 1997, A3.
99. *Los Angeles Times*, May 2, 1997, A3.
100. Leland T. Saito, *Race and Politics: Asian Americans, Latinos, and Whites in a Los Angeles Suburb* (Urbana: University of Illinois Press, 1998).

CHAPTER 20

1. Hernán Vera and Andrew M. Gordon, *Screen Saviors: Hollywood Fictions of Whiteness* (Lanham, Md.: Rowman & Littlefield, 2003).
2. George Lipsitz, "Genre Anxiety and Racial Representation in 1970s Cinema," in *Refiguring American Film Genres: History and Theory*, ed. Nick Browne, 208–32 (Berkeley: University of California Press, 1994).
3. Robert Skalar, *Movie-Made America: A Cultural History of American Movies* (New York: Vintage Books, 1994), 316.
4. Marilyn Kern-Foxworth, "Aunt Jemima, the Frito Bandito, and Crazy Horse: Selling Stereotypes American Style," in *Mass Politics: The Politics of Popular Culture*, ed. Daniel M. Shea, 81–90 (New York: St. Martin's Press, 1999), 82.

5. Cortés, "Chicanos in Film"; Clint C. Wilson and Félix Gutiérrez, *Race, Multiculturalism, and the Media: From Mass Communication to Class Communication* (Thousand Oaks, Calif.: Sage Publications, 1995).

6. Vera and Gordon, *Screen Saviors*, x.

7. Brian J. Woodman, "Represented in the Margins: Images of African American Soldiers in Vietnam War Combat Films," *Journal of Film and Video* 53(2/3) (2001): 38–60.

8. Woodman, "Represented in the Margins."

9. Woodman, "Represented in the Margins," 44.

10. Woodman, "Represented in the Margins," 54.

11. Herman Gray, *Watching Race: Television and the Struggle for "Blackness" Minnesota* (Minneapolis: University of Minnesota Press, 1995).

12. Kristal Brent Zook, "The Fox Network and the Revolution in Black Television," in *Gender, Race, and Class in Media: A Text-Reader*, ed. Gail Dines and Jean M. Humez, 2nd ed., 586–96 (Thousand Oaks, Calif.: Sage Publications, 2003).

13. Gray, *Watching Race*.

14. Zook, "The Fox Network."

15. Thomas A. Mascaro, "Shades of Black on Homicide: Life on the Street: Progress in Portrayals of African American Men," *Journal of Popular Film and Television* 32(1) (2004): 10–19.

16. Mascaro, "Shades of Black on Homicide," 10.

17. Linda Williams, *Playing the Race Card: Melodramas of Black and White from Uncle Tom to O. J. Simpson* (Princeton, N.J.: Princeton University Press, 2001).

18. Williams, *Playing the Race Card*, 308.

19. Williams, *Playing the Race Card*, 300.

20. Joan L. Conners, "Color TV? Diversity in Prime-Time TV," in *Race/Gender/Media: Considering Diversity across Audiences, Content, and Producers*, ed. Rebecca Ann Lind, 206–12 (Boston: Pearson Education, 2004).

21. Roberta E. Pearson, "The Revenge of Rain-in-the-Face? Or, Custers and Indians on the Silent Screen," in *The Birth of Whiteness: Race and the Emergence of U.S. Cinema*, ed. Daniel Bernardi, 273–99 (New Brunswick, N.J.: Rutgers University Press, 1996).

22. Esther Ghymn, "Asians in Film and Other Media," in *Asian American Studies: Identity, Images, Issues Past and Present*, ed. Esther Mikyung Ghymn, 135–50 (New York: Peter Lang Publishing, 2000).

23. William McGowan, *Coloring the News: How Crusading for Diversity Has Corrupted American Journalism* (San Francisco: Encounter Books, 2001).

24. Leonard Downie Jr. and Robert G. Kaiser, *The News about the News: American Journalism in Peril* (New York: Vintage Books, 2002); Beth Sanders, *Fear and Favor in the Newsroom* (San Francisco: California Newsreel, 1996).

25. Ann K. Johnson, *Urban Ghetto Riots, 1965–1968: A Comparison of Soviet and American Press Coverage* (New York: Columbia University Press, 1996); Carolyn Martindale, *The White Press and Black America* (New York: Greenwood Press, 1986).

26. Herman B. Chiu, "Power of the Press: How Newspapers in Four Communities Erased Thousands of Chinese from Oregon History," *American Journalism: A Journal of Media History* 16(1) (1999): 59–77.

27. Jim A. Kuypers, *Press Bias and Politics: How the Media Frame Controversial Issues* (Westport, Conn.: Praeger, 2002).

28. W. Lance Bennett, *News: The Politics of Illusion*, 5th ed. (New York: Longman Press, 2003), 206.

29. Joann Lee, "A Look at Asians as Portrayed in the News," *Editor & Publisher* 127(18) (April 30, 1994): 56–57.

30. Chiung Hwang Chen uses this quote from a story in *Newsweek* (June 21, 1971, 77–78) as emblematic of model minority in "'Outwhiting the Whites': An Examination of the Persis-

tence of Asian American Model Minority Discourse," in *Race/Gender/Media: Considering Diversity across Audiences, Content, and Producers*, ed. Rebecca Ann Lind, 146–53 (Boston: Pearson Education, 2004).

31. Richard A. Pride, *The Political Use of Racial Narratives: School Desegregation in Mobile, Alabama, 1954–1997* (Urbana: University of Illinois Press, 2002).

32. For a review of these, see Bennett, *News: The Politics of Illusion*, 2003.

33. McGowan, *Coloring the News*; Kuypers, *Press Bias and Politics*.

34. McGowan, *Coloring the News*, 30.

35. McGowan, *Coloring the News*.

36. Eric Alterman, *What Liberal Media? The Truth about Bias and the News* (New York: Basic Books, 2003).

37. McGowan, *Coloring the News*.

38. Kuypers, *Press Bias and Politics*.

39. Kuypers, *Press Bias and Politics*, 113.

40. Robert M. Entman and Andrew Rojecki, *The Black Image in the White Mind: Media and Race in America* (Chicago: University of Chicago Press, 2000).

41. Entman and Rojecki, *The Black Image in the White Mind*.

42. Kuypers, *Press Bias and Politics*.

43. Daniel C. Hallin, *The Uncensored War: The Media and Vietnam* (Berkeley: University of California Press, 1986).

44. Kuypers, *Press Bias and Politics*.

45. Stuart Hall, "Encoding/Decoding," in *Culture, Media, Language: Working Papers in Cultural Studies 1972–1979*, ed. S. Hall, D. Hobson, A. Lowe, and P. Willis, 128–34 (London: Unwin Hyman, 1980).

46. Darrell M. Hunt, *Screening the Los Angeles "Riots": Race, Seeing, and Resistance* (New York: Cambridge University Press, 1997), 162.

47. Media Action Network for Asian Americans (MANAA), "A Memo from MANAA to Hollywood: Asian Stereotypes, Restrictive Portrayals of Asians in the Media and How to Balance Them," 1998, available at www.manaa.org (accessed February 20, 2005).

48. Jessica Hagedorn, "Asian Women in Film: No Joy, No Luck," in *Facing Difference: Race, Gender, and Mass Media*, ed. Shirley Biagi and Marilyn Kern-Foxworth, 32–37 (Thousand Oaks, Calif.: Pine Forge Press, 1997).

49. Chisun Lee, "The Ling Thing," *Village Voice* 44(48) (1999): 65; Chyng Feng Sun, "Ling Woo in Historical Context: The New Face of Asian American Stereotypes on Television," in *Gender, Race, and Class in Media: A Text-Reader*, ed. Gail Dines and Jean M. Humez, 2nd ed., 656–64 (Thousand Oaks, Calif.: Sage Publications, 2003).

50. Robin R. Means Coleman, "Black Sitcom Portrayals," in *Gender, Race, and Class in Media: A Text-Reader*, ed. Gail Dines and Jean M. Humez, 2nd ed., 79–88 (Thousand Oaks, Calif.: Sage Publications, 1995).

51. Kristal Brent Zook, "*Living Single* and the 'Fight for Mr. Right,' Latifah Don't Play," in *Gender, Race, and Class in Media: A Text-Reader*, ed. Gail Dines and Jean M. Humez, 2nd ed., 129–35 (Thousand Oaks, Calif.: Sage Publications, 2003).

52. Michael O'Shaughnessy and Jane Sandler, *Media and Society: An Introduction*, 2nd ed. (South Melbourne, Australia: Oxford University Press, 2002).

53. N. Klein, "Culture Jamming: Ads under Attack," in *No Logo*, ed. N. Klein, 279–309 (London: Harper Collins, 2000).

54. Hall Foster, *Recodings: Art, Spectacle, Cultural Politics* (Port Townsend, Wash.: Bay Press, 1985).

55. Lisa Taylor and Andrew Willis, *Media Studies: Texts, Institutions, and Audiences* (Oxford: Blackwell Publishers, 1999).

56. John Fiske, *Understanding the Popular* (Boston: Unwin Hyman, 1989).

57. Antonio Gramsci, *Selections from the Prison Notebooks of Antonio Gramsci*, ed. Quintin Hoare and Geoffrey Nowell Smith (New York: International Publishers, 1971).

58. John Fiske, *Media Matters: Race and Gender in U.S. Politics* (Minneapolis: University of Minnesota Press, 1996).

Index

ABOUT THE AUTHOR

~~~~~~

Stephanie Greco Larson (Ph.D., Florida State University, 1987) is professor and chair of political science at Dickinson College in Carlisle, Pennsylvania. Her research on the content and consequences of media coverage of politics and mass publics has appeared in the *American Journal of Political Science, Political Communication, Journalism & Mass Communication Quarterly, Journal of Broadcasting & Electronic Media, Media Studies Journal, Journal of Popular Film & Television, Press/Politics*, and various edited books. She is author of *Creating Consent of the Governed: A Member of Congress and the Local Media* (1992) and *Public Opinion: Using MicroCase ExplorIt* (2003)